THE
MUSIC MAN

T H E
MUSIC MAN

THE LIFE AND GOOD TIMES OF A SONGWRITER

LESLIE BRICUSSE

metro

Published by Metro Publishing Ltd,
3 Bramber Court, 2 Bramber Road,
London W14 9PB, England

www.blake.co.uk

First published in hardback in 2006

ISBN-13: 978 1 84358 167 3
ISBN-10: 1 84358 167 1

British Library Cataloguing-in-Publication Data:

A catalogue record for this book is available from the British Library.

Design by www.envydesign.co.uk

Printed in Great Britain by William Clowes Ltd, Beccles, Suffolk

1 3 5 7 9 10 8 6 4 2

Papers used by John Blake Publishing are natural, recyclable products made from wood grown in sustainable forests. The manufacturing processes conform to the environmental regulations of the country of origin.

For Evie –
the one unchanging key of my life...

Double Oscar and Grammy winner Leslie Bricusse is a writer-composer-lyricist who has contributed to many musical films and plays during his career. He was born in London, and educated at University College School and Gonville and Caius College, Cambridge. At Cambridge, he was President of the Footlights Revue Club and founded the Musical Comedy Club. There, he co-authored, directed and performed in his first two musical shows, *Out of the Blue* and *Lady at the Wheel*, both of which made their way to London's West End. He also found time in the gaps to acquire a Master of Arts degree.

The late, great Beatrice Lillie plucked him out of the Footlights Revue at the Phoenix Theatre, and made him her leading man in *An Evening with Beatrice Lillie* at the Globe Theatre, where he spent the first year of his professional life writing another musical, *The Boy on the Corner*, and the screenplay and score of his first motion picture, *Charley Moon*, which won his first Ivor Novello Award. That year, he decided to drop the possibilities of directing and performing, and concentrate his career on becoming a full-time writer-composer-lyricist.

His subsequent stage musicals include *Stop the World — I Want to Get Off*; *The Roar Of the Greasepaint — The Smell of the Crowd*; *Pickwick*; *Harvey*; *The Good Old Bad Old Days*; *Goodbye, Mr Chips*; *Henry's Wives*; *Scrooge*; *One Shining Moment*; *Sherlock Holmes*; *Jekyll and Hyde*; and *Victor/Victoria*. He has written songs and/or screenplays for such films as *Doctor Dolittle*; *Scrooge*; *Willy Wonka and the Chocolate Factory*; *Goodbye, Mr Chips*; *Superman*; *Victor/Victoria*; *Santa Claus — The Movie*; *Home Alone* and *Home Alone II*; *Hook*; *Tom and Jerry — The Movie* and various *Pink Panthers*.

Bricusse has written more than 40 musical shows and films, and over the years has had the good fortune to enjoy fruitful collaborations with a wonderful array of musical talents, including Anthony Newley, Henry Mancini, John Williams, John Barry, Jerry Goldsmith, Jule Styne, Quincy Jones, Andre Previn, Frank Wildhorn and Peter Illyich Tchaikovsky (whose *Nutcracker Suite* he adapted into a song score).

His better-known songs include 'What Kind of Fool Am I?'; 'Once In a Lifetime'; 'Gonna Build a Mountain'; 'Who Can I Turn To?'; 'The Joker'; 'If I Ruled the World'; 'My Kind of Girl'; 'Talk to the Animals'; 'You and I'; 'Feeling Good'; 'When I Look in Your Eyes'; 'Goldfinger'; 'Can You Read My Mind?' (the love theme from *Superman*); 'You Only Live Twice'; 'Le Jazz Hot'; 'On a Wonderful Day Like Today'; 'Two for the Road'; 'The Candy Man'; 'This Is the Moment'; 'Crazy World'; 'Pure Imagination' and 'Oompa-Loompa-Doompa-Dee-Doo'.

He has been nominated for ten Academy Awards, nine Grammys and four Tonys, and has won two Oscars, a Grammy and eight Ivor Novello Awards, the premier British music award.

Hundreds of Bricusse's songs have been recorded by major artists, including Frank Sinatra, Nat King Cole, Judy Garland, Aretha Franklin, Barbra Streisand, Sammy Davis Jr (who recorded 60 Bricusse songs), Tony Bennett, Shirley Bassey, Tom Jones, Petula Clark, Julie Andrews, Liza Minnelli, Andy Williams, Rex Harrison, Kate Smith, Elaine Paige, Anthony Newley, Michael Feinstein, Bette Midler, The Moody Blues, Nancy Sinatra, Lena

Horne, Sergio Mendes, Nina Simone, Dionne Warwick, Robert Goulet, Matt Monro, Ray Charles, Ethel Merman, Placido Domingo, Jennifer Holliday, Danny Kaye, Robbie Williams, Mariah Carey, Linda Eder, Diana Krall, Maroon 5, Michael Bublé and The Black Eyed Peas.

In 1989, he received the Kennedy Award for consistent excellence in British songwriting, bestowed by the British Academy of Songwriters, Composers and Authors, and was inducted into the American Songwriters' Hall of Fame – only the fourth Englishman to be so honoured – after Noël Coward, John Lennon and Paul McCartney.

Jekyll and Hyde, written with Frank Wildhorn, ran for four years at the Plymouth Theater in New York, and has had a dozen international productions around the world, the most recent in Tokyo, Prague, Madrid and Paris. *Victor/Victoria*, written with Blake Edwards and Henry Mancini, which successively starred Julie Andrews, Liza Minnelli and Raquel Welch on Broadway, can now be seen across America and elsewhere around the world, having been produced in Madrid in 2005 and Mexico City and Moscow in 2006.

Bricusse's children's stage musical version of Roald Dahl's *Willy Wonka* opened at the Kennedy Center for the Performing Arts in Washington DC in November 2004, before embarking on a three-year national tour of the United States.

Another Bricusse perennial, his musical version of *Scrooge*, in which Anthony Newley starred at the Dominion Theatre in London's West End, is also seen annually in many productions around the world. Currently, the title role is being played by Richard Chamberlain in the USA and Tommy Steele at the London Palladium in the UK.

For *Doctor Dolittle*, another current stage musical, which played four years in the UK, starring Phillip Schofield and almost one hundred assorted animatronic animals created by Jim Henson's Creature Shop, Bricusse serves as librettist, composer, lyricist and co-producer. Further productions are planned in Europe,

Australia, South Korea and Japan. A major US production opened in the summer of 2005, currently starring Tommy Tune.

His next project is a remarkable musical biography of the world's greatest entertainer, the late Sammy Davis Jr, entitled *Sammy*. Bricusse has also completed the book and lyrics of his musical adaptation of *Cyrano de Bergerac*, his new collaboration with Frank Wildhorn, which will open in the UK in 2007, as will Bricusse's compilation songbook show, *Brick by Brick by Bricusse*.

Preface

I would like to thank eight lovely people for their invaluable help in the realisation of this work – Evie, Ginger, Jon, John the Second, John the Third, Lucian, Phil and Barbara. They know why.

Leslie Bricusse
06/06/06
Saint-Paul de Vence

Contents

THE KEY CHANGES

Author's note

Dear Reader

Never having written a book before, let alone a memoir, I recently sent the draft manuscript of *The Music Man* to half a dozen of my oldest and closest friends who feature heavily in the story, together with the following letter, inviting their comments.

The few pages that follow − their responses − are without doubt by far my favourite in the entire book and will probably be yours, too!

LB

ALBION RIVERSIDE
LONDON

06.06.06

My dear ——— :

I recently decided to jot down, before my brain relinquishes the facility to recall them, a few anecdotes about some of the more remarkable people and extraordinary incidents that have plotted and populated, entertained and blessed, and crowded and influenced the course of my life.

I am presuming to send you the results of these ramblings, in the hope that they will at best amuse you, or at worst lull you into a deep and peaceful sleep, either of which will be beneficial to you and thus justify the presumption.

If you have the first of these reactions, do please find a moment to let me know. If the second, I will send you a generous supply of Melatonin, which taken at bedtime should work equally effectively in the future

Somerset Maugham pointed out that there are three rules to observe when writing your memoirs. Unfortunately no-one knows what they are.

All love —

Brickman

FOREWORD BY ELTON JOHN

Leslie Bricusse and I both grew up in Pinner and will demand a blue plaque when we're gone! We were infatuated with cinema and music, and both became songwriters.

His friendship and encouragement have meant so much to me, and his career is one that I will always aspire to. What people he has worked with – such incredible tales of games, brilliance and fun. He has worked and written for the best, and in this brilliant book has chronicled it all for us to share. (Not Cher.)

His recall of events is crystal clear, and his irresistible take on people is fabulous.

Rule 1: *Never* turn down an invitation to lunch or dinner with Leslie and Evie. You listen and laugh and wish you had been there.

His catalogue of songs is enormous – his achievements endless. Anyone who has written 'What Kind of Fool am I?' and 'My Old Man's a Dustman' should be revered forever.

Bricusse is an amazing man full of life, love and, like me, is still searching for the perfect song. I love him dearly. After reading this book I love him even more. (And you too, Evie!)

Elton John with Evie Bricusse.

FOREWORD BY MICHAEL CAINE

Leslie and I have been close friends for 45 years and together have had fun and laughter in many wonderful places with some of the most interesting people, but it wasn't until I read this book that I realised that Leslie has been doing this with everybody for years and years. One of the great features of our friendship has been that every time we have dinner I always come away knowing what my social life is going to be for the next six months.

When you read this book, I suggest you make notes of where Leslie travelled, holidayed, sunbathed, ate, slept and worked and your life will be sorted out for the next 45 years. His story is not only one of a great and talented life but a journey by a man of great taste, not only in places and restaurants but in the people he chooses to work with and the ones who were lucky enough to be his friends. It is a glamorous and fulfilling life and a unique journey by a man who is himself unique by any standard.

Oh! And, by the way, he happens to be one of the world's great songwriters.

He continues to work and play with the same intensity and style that you will experience in this extraordinary book.

Shakira Caine, Leslie Bricusse, Evie, Joan Collins, Michael Caine,
and Roger and Kristina Moore

FOREWORD BY JULIE ANDREWS

Darling Leslie,

Your *Music Man* is wonderful! Thank you so much for sending it. The book made me laugh aloud so many times. I'm in awe that you have pulled off such a monumental feat.

Your stories about the war were so evocative – and some of your young war experiences so like my own. I delighted in reading *all* the hilarious things (about Rex Harrison especially), loved your passages about Lerner and Loewe, and, though I knew a lot of the characters, I now feel I know *all* the others as well.

I think the Department of Fate will prove your *terrific* tome to be a huge, resounding success. I'm so happy that you finally wrote it, Leslie. It's a book that I, along with a thousand others, I'm sure, have been longing for you to write – and you've pulled it off.

Much, much love to you and Evie. I long to see you soon. Meanwhile, my congratulations once again.

As always – Jools

Leslie Bricusse and Julie Andrews.

FOREWORD BY ROGER MOORE

When one of one's oldest and dearest friends sends you 400 and some pages chronicling his life and asks you to write a foreword, a feeling of absolute inadequacy, in penmanship terms, is apt to raise its ugly head, especially when you discover that your part in his life has been so accurately documented.

I have had the privilege of knowing Leslie and Evie for well over 40 years, a couple loved and admired by their myriad of friends; it was therefore fascinating discovering a thousand new things about them, and I am sure that you, dear reader, if you have never met them, will feel as you draw to the end of *The Music Man* that you too are a part of their family.

Leslie's recall is extraordinary, his description of his childhood from the streets of south-west London to the suburban pleasantness (sic) of Pinner, the war years, his first theatrical moment in his parents' garage and the birth of his love for words and music make fascinating reading. This is truly a love story, a man's love, not only for his darling Evie, but also for life, for friends and for theatre.

In Leslie's covering letter to me that came with *The Music Man* he suggested that Somerset Maugham pointed out that there were three rules to observe when writing your memoirs, unfortunately no one knows what they are. I beg to differ, Leslie does and they are: be entertaining, be truthful and leave the reader wanting more. I cannot wait for more changes, from major to minor and back again.

FOREWORD BY JOAN COLLINS

Candid and hilarious, you'll devour Leslie Bricusse's autobiography in one delicious sitting. He has met, and worked with, practically everybody who is anybody in the movie and theatre world, and his book is full of wonderfully witty anecdotes about Frank and Sammy and Liza and Liz and Richard and Rex and Mia and – oh well, you name 'em, he knows 'em!

His recall is amazing, and having spent literally thousands of memorably great good times with Evie and Leslie over many years – practically most of my adult life – I can vouch for the authenticity of all the classic and comical tales Leslie tells. I was there – or not far away – for a lot of them!

FOREWORD BY BRYAN FORBES

Evie and Leslie Bricusse have been our very close friends for five decades and, reading this book, Nanette and I were reminded of so many good times we have shared.

Suddenly, when you see his life put down in print, you realise how much Leslie has achieved in a variety of fields, the number of people he has worked with – most of them stars in the true meaning of the word, not so-called celebrities whose only claim to fame is being known for something that hasn't anything to do with talent.

'Brickman', as he is called in the trade, has worked with most of the giants of show business and his telling of those times, the nightmares, the successes and failures makes for compelling reading.

Someone once said you need a little madness to survive in our business and that madness is encapsulated here in page-turning pleasure for the reader. His life has been a rollercoaster ride, the life of a special man and a special friend I am happy to salute.

Evie Bricusse and Bryan and
Nanette Forbes at 'Seven Pines'.

Opening Key: A Minor

It was my first first night. My heart was in my mouth. The atmosphere was electric. A hush of expectation fell over the capacity audience as the emerald velvet curtains slowly parted to reveal the dimly lit empty stage of the bijou theatre.

This memorable theatrical moment occurred in the garage of my parents' house in Pinner, Middlesex, a dozen or so miles outside London, in the late autumn of 1942. The 'stage' was the converted casing of a discarded Singer sewing machine, and the emerald curtains had been created by my mother from a tired old green velvet cushion that very afternoon.

We were at the height of World War Two, and the urgent needs of Mrs Churchill's Aid-To-Russia Fund had prompted me at age 11 to write, produce, direct and perform my first theatrical venture, with an all-star cast featuring my collection of four glove puppets – a frog, a monkey, a parrot and an owl. The capacity audience of 12 consisted of reluctant but good-natured neighbouring parents, dragged from their cosy homes and warm firesides on this cold November night by my loyal and persistent school friends, to sit huddled and shivering, wrapped in scarves and overcoats, on a random selection of ill-matched kitchen and dining chairs, in a chilly garage illuminated by a solitary naked 60-watt light bulb, around the outer edges of a silent and sinister pool of congealed sump oil that had dripped from my father's temporarily absent Morris Oxford, and forced to watch my 45 minutes of killer entertainment.

For this dubious privilege, each adult generously donated a half-crown to the cause, enabling me the next morning to send Mrs Churchill at Number Ten Downing Street the princely sum of 30 shillings. Along with Dunkirk, El Alamein and the Normandy landings, I naturally regarded this as one of the major turning points of the war, and, while Mrs Churchill didn't necessarily agree with me, she did nonetheless send me a very charming letter of gratitude, signed 'Clementine Churchill' in her generous hand. Within weeks, Hitler retreated from Stalingrad, and the rest you know.

My father Cedric and my mother Ann had decided to move out of London to the suburban pleasantness of Pinner when I was a tender two-year-old and my sister Patricia a sophisticated nine. We had previously lived in south-west London at Number 99, Brookwood Road, Southfields, where I was born just around the corner from Southfields Metropolitan Railway Station, a mundane spot which acquired a Mecca-like aura for 13 days every summer, from the last week of June into the first days of July, as the place where countless thousands of avid tennis fans disembarked daily to converge on the hallowed green grass courts of the All-England Lawn Tennis and Croquet Club at Wimbledon.

Wimbledon − the very name smells of strawberries and sunshine. The snob in me sometimes likes to pretend that I was born in Wimbledon, but the conscientious Jiminy Cricket deep within me knows perfectly well that it was actually Wandsworth. Thus my nose stays small. For although the borders of Wimbledon are only a Boris Becker backhand away from Number 99,

Brookwood Road, it is a very long way, believe me, from SW18 to SW19. Worse than that, Number 99, Brookwood Road has long since disappeared, so a blue plaque is out of the question.

It baffled me throughout my childhood, and does to this day, that my parents, having been blessed with such elegant and mellifluous monikers as Cedric and Ann, should have been prepared to go through life, as they did, uncomplainingly allowing themselves to be known to their friends as Sid and Nance. Why? A rose by any other name may smell as sweet, but it certainly doesn't *sound* as good.

So Pinner it was, and Pinner it remained until I was 18. In 1933, number 103, Cannon Lane cost the staggering sum of £695 for two reception rooms, three bedrooms and all mod cons, plus about a quarter-acre of garden. Sounds reasonable, but, if you were earning £12 a week and had two kids to raise, you needed a 20-year mortgage to get you through it.

My dad's father, Joseph Bricusse, whom I only ever met once in my young life before booze took him out, was a spectacular and charming Belgian rogue and drunkard who abandoned his sweet and pretty young English wife, née Edith Pratt, of Gloucestershire, and their four children – Cedric, Gordon, Eric and Eileen, aged four, three, two and one – in their early infancy. His most spectacular non-claim to fame came at the age of 20 when a young fellow-waiter in the dining room proposed that, if they each raised £50, they could rent space and open a café together. Needless to say, Grandpa Joseph drank his 50 quid's worth. So young Joe Lyons went on without him to create England's most successful chain of teashops, restaurants and catering services, and tea at Lyons' Corner House in Coventry Street in London's West End became one of the first and most memorable treats of my early childhood.

My father paid the highest price, being called upon as the eldest child to become a breadwinner long before his time. He had virtually no childhood, and an early scholarship to a school of quality, the first step towards a better life, went unused in the name of survival. Instead, he spent his early teens selling newspapers on Waterloo Station, which led in time to a minor post on a WH Smith bookstall, still at Waterloo, and then eventual promotion to bookstall manager. Connections within the newspaper business finally landed him a job in the circulation department of Kemsley Newspapers, which was what Cedric-called-Sid was doing when I appeared on the scene some 15–20 years later.

My father was a quiet, kind, gentle, introspective soul, who slowly became a victim of the wretched childhood he had inherited. Too much responsibility too soon, complicated by long hours, an irregular diet and, though to a lesser extent than his own father, drinking, born I suspect of frustration, combined to damage his health by his early thirties, and he never really recovered from those early insurmountable setbacks. On a level playing field, I have always believed he would have scored. Unfortunately, life doesn't wish to know about level playing fields. You have to create your own. While it is all spectacularly unfair, that's the way it is. You play the game you're given. So it was left to my father and my mother to try to create the level playing field for my sister and myself, and that, God bless them both, they did. The education they never had, we had. The stable family life they never knew, we knew. And the good and fortunate life we have each enjoyed owes all its birth-pang beginnings to them, to Cedric and Ann, to Sid and Nance.

To match the 25 per cent of Belgian blood that I inherited from my father came the 25 per cent Irish provided by my mother, whose father hailed from Belfast, so we won't get into that. Those grandparents were sadly long departed before I arrived, but I am reliably informed that alcohol plays a featured role in that side of the story, too. So I have little or no trouble figuring out the historical background for my lifelong love of fine wine. Suffice to say I was probably born 50 per cent English and 50 proof.

One thing I know for sure is that I inherited my distinguished theatrical background from my mother's side of the family. Her mother scrubbed the front steps of the Apollo Theatre for an unspecified number of years. And while that doesn't exactly put me on a par with the Barrymores or the Redgraves, it still counts, because *someone* has to scrub the front steps before the public can contemplate entering the theatre to watch the Barrymores and the Redgraves.

My mother loved to sing. She had a beautifully toned soprano voice but an alarmingly limited repertoire. She reprised 'Roses of Picardy' on a regular monthly basis throughout all the years of my childhood, and I remember now with sadness that that was the song she told me she had auditioned as a young girl when some benevolent lady offered to sponsor her further musical education. Like my father, the opportunity was denied her by circumstance, and her concert appearances for the rest of her life were restricted to the kitchen of 103, Cannon Lane, Pinner.

Ann Mary Mills was the youngest of three sisters, who all got married in their teens and lost their husbands in the Western Front trenches of World War One, like countless thousands of others in that worst of all wars. The three sisters – my mother and my two aunts – were given a delightful trio of Brontë-esque and Dickensian literary names – Nell, Jane and Ann – which were promptly corrupted into Nellie, Jin and Nance, by which they were everlastingly known thereafter, probably the root cause of my lasting distaste for diminutives.

In 1923, my mother Ann-called-Nance was hesitant to remarry when my father, who was four years younger than her, proposed to her, but happily for me she relented, and 18 months later, happily for her, my sister Patricia was born. I was to be kept waiting a further six years, one month, two weeks and two days.

My first officially authenticated vivid memory, when I was two, is of daily trips in my pram along the straight terraced street that was Brookwood Road to a grocer's shop on the far right-hand corner of the street. The bald, benign, bespectacled proprietor – Richard Attenborough would play him in the film – would beam down upon me from behind the counter, while I sat eye-to-eye with a long, low row of big, square, glass-topped biscuit tins, set at an angle of 45 degrees, containing the cookies that I would later come to know and love as Pat-a-Cakes, Lincoln Creams and Chocolate Ruffles. My sister Pat assures me that this recollection is accurate in every detail. We moved from Southfields to Pinner shortly after my second birthday, so I ask you to accept this story unchallenged.

A 1930s childhood in Pinner, Middlesex, was a beautiful thing – certainly until Sunday, 3 September 1939. For my fifth birthday, I received a bright-red tin pedal car in which I broke every known world land speed record several times each week. I modestly refrained from telling even my parents of these amazing early achievements in such a dangerous field of endeavour.

My father's first car arrived on the scene around the same time, courtesy of Kemsley Newspapers, for whom he was promoted from sales representative to Circulation Manager for the *Sunday Chronicle*. The car was a Morris 8, and for years to come the family would be subjected to 'the Sunday drive', which for reasons I have never quite understood was always exactly the same drive, identical to within a yard. Hatfield, an innocuous Hertfordshire village whose magic has always eluded me, was the Mecca of these boringly repetitive pilgrimages and nobody knew why, not even my father. It was as though it was the car's decision, rather than his. I lost any sense of affection I might have had for Hatfield on the very first Sunday, when the little car became wedged in a huge pothole in the driving rain for four hours, until we were finally towed to safety. The incident severely dented my mother's confidence in Dad's driving ability and the Irish half of her was always quite explicit on such occasions. I have hated Hatfield from that day to this. I apologise to the citizens of Hatfield for this injustice.

I ran my life out of the third and smallest bedroom of the house – a 7ft-long by 5ft-wide domain that was to be my mini-kingdom from the ages of two to eighteen. My entire childhood was centred on these 35 square feet, the supreme headquarters of my young life, where all my early dreams were engendered. I used every inch of cubic space in that room as my imagination and I grew year by year. The small single bed to which I graduated from my baby-crib created my first life crisis by more than halving what was already a minimal play space. I slowly learned to overcome that problem, and one of the major accomplishments of my infancy was the ever-increasing ingenuity with which I used that space – building into and out of every inch of every corner of the room – a talent I have expanded and refined in every room of every home I have ever lived in, driving several people insane in the process.

By the time I was nine, my tiny room had become home to me, my bed, my dog, a wardrobe, two bookcases, a desk, a gramophone and, best of all, around three sides of the room, above my bed, halfway up the wall, neatly tucked in below the sill of the one small window, my pride, my joy... my electric train set, perched upon bracketed shelves of my own design but not execution, with a loop at either end which enabled my train to run all night, which occasionally it did when I fell asleep to the sound of its friendly buzz. It became known as 'The Night Train to Munich' when the film came out. I had enough stuff in that room to fill a mid-size warehouse, and my squirrelly habits drove my beloved mum to the limits of patience and sometimes, when her Irish half was in the ascendant, beyond.

Cannon Lane Elementary School, which took care of the first half-dozen years of my education, from the ages of five to eleven, was reached by a pleasant 15-minute walk through fields that separated, though not for long, the ever-increasing number of new housing developments that proliferated during that era, as the between-the-wars suburbs continued to explode.

Miss Smith, the po-faced, grey-hair-straight-back-in-a-bun headmistress of that establishment, who seemingly had no first name, would have walked over Lotte Lenya for the role of Rosa Klebb in *From Russia with Love*. Miss Smith made Elsa Lanchester look like Shirley Temple. She ran our lives from a small detached house in the school grounds, watching our world from a distance, like the evil forces on the planet Krypton. She could vaporise any one of us with her laser-like gaze at anything less than 40 feet. She was probably a perfectly nice woman, but she was also a great non-communicator. She never addressed one single word to me during the entire six years I was at the school. Her remoteness from our everyday lives, a small detached woman in a small detached house, lent her an aura of near-mythical other-worldliness; to our infant perceptions, she was the equivalent of Countess Dracula in her Transylvanian castle.

Happily, our everyday lives were in the hands of the jolly and rotund Mrs Tomlinson, a North Country mothering type whose main interests in life were geography and the currant buns served at mid-morning break. She took great comfort from both, and I can still see her, pointer in her left hand and the last currant bun in her right, like a happy circus elephant, smugly indicating The Map of the World that hung in permanent splendour next to the blackboard in her classroom, proudly reminding us that 'all the red bits are the British Empire, which together make up one-quarter of the world's land surface'. My, how things change.

Speaking of Shirley Temple, it was the happy weekly habit of my parents to take my sister and myself to the Langham Cinema in Pinner Village to see whatever film was playing – from Dorothy Lamour and her sarong in *Her Jungle Love* to Orson Welles's mind-blowing triple-threat début in *Citizen Kane*. And it was there in the dark that I first clapped eyes on the divinely dimpled and outrageously talented Miss T, singing and dancing her pretty little brains out in *Bright Eyes*, to which we are indebted for the immortal 'On the Good Ship Lollipop'. For me, at that tender age, the most amazing thing among the many amazing things about Miss T was that she was only a couple of years older than I was. There she was, a fully fledged, number-one-at-the-box-office major Hollywood star at the age of seven – *six* when she made the film! – and here was I, five pushing six,

living in a London suburb, having barely started school. I have
never forgotten the profound impact of that realisation, that life
was passing me by.

From early childhood, I have always been a collector – stamps,
rare books, photographs, art, wine, theatre and film memorabilia,
all manner of junk and treasures. Thanks to a cunning ploy at the
age of eight, my first collection was of movie posters. When we
went to the Langham Cinema every Monday evening, the kindly
young assistant manager would have saved me one of the
previous week's front-of-house movie posters, glad to be rid of
it. The rest were binned. Movie posters were not thought of as
collectibles at that time. I kept the posters rolled together in an
ever-fattening tube in my bedroom. After a year, it was
substantial. After two years, it was heavy. After three, a major
hazard. I had *Tarzan* posters, and Shirley Temple, Fred and
Ginger, *Citizen Kane, Casablanca, The Great Dictator, Robin Hood*
that I wish I had today. The big, cumbersome, ever-growing roll
of movie posters drove my mother crazy. It was always in the way
when she went in to make my bed, and inevitably came the dire
day when she heaved the whole thing out of my 5-by-7 domain
on the to-her reasonable and to-me indefensible grounds that
you could not turn around in the tiny room without falling over
the damn thing. So the dustman grumpily hauled away with him
the offending tube that today would be worth well in excess of
a hundred thousand pounds, on a zero investment. I have never
collected movie posters again.

Music had played little or no part in my life up to that point,
apart from Mummy's occasional 'Roses of Picardy' wafting
through from the kitchen when she was in a cheerful mood, but
it was about to. My obligatory schoolboy piano lessons had just
started, made palatable only by the weekly appearance of the
delectable Miss Morrison – another lady with no apparent first
name, whom I regarded with some reverence as a cross between
Hedy Lamarr and Joan Bennett – but, in my case, piano practice
made considerably less than perfect. I abhorred playing the same

scales over and over again each day after school, so I invented elaborate excuses not to do so. Then, consumed with guilt, I tried to overcompensate in the last desperate 20 minutes before Hedy Lamarr reappeared the following Tuesday. I never fooled her for a moment.

Sister Pat was another case altogether. Diligent and persevering, in my eyes an insufferable goody-goody, she would practise interminably every afternoon, locked in the living room. Her speciality was any song by Deanna Durbin, and branded in my brain to this day are the first eight bars of 'When April Sings', which I think came from *A Hundred Men and a Girl*. Pat sang it very prettily, but always screwed up on the piano in the eighth bar before the return to the second 'A' section. The words – could I ever forget? – went:

> *The countryside is green again.*
> *The world is seventeen again.*
> *My heart awakes when April sings...*

Then the wrong chord, and back to the top again. I heard those eight bars a thousand times. I could perform them from my grave. Between 'When April Sings' coming from the living room and 'Roses of Picardy' from the kitchen, it is a miracle I ever went into the music business.

Tap-dancing lessons were even worse. That was sister Pat's idea, too. You must remember that, when I was five, she was eleven, and a great fan of Fred and Ginger. As was I, but with no desire to emulate them. How I allowed Pat to talk me into it, I'll never know. But suddenly one day, there I was, donning a pair of button-down black patent-leather tap shoes in the dancing school next to Pinner Church, about to endure the most embarrassing hour of my young existence. While Pat was hoofing merrily away on the far side of the big rehearsal room with a posse of cumbersome contemporaries, I found myself one of only two boys surrounded by seven or eight less than lovely, i.e. really ugly little girls, trying to tap-dance to guess what? 'On the Good Ship Lollipop.'

Unlike General MacArthur, I did not return. The humiliation of that hour stayed with me down the years. When I returned to Pinner recently, I found myself glaring at that rehearsal room with undisguised loathing I realised I had harboured since the summer of 1936!

I doubt that anyone truly knows at what point in their life music starts to have any recognisable influence. We hear music long before we are aware that it *is* music. It seeps slowly through our subconscious to become an irremovable part of our existence. It has always been there, thank God, and it always will be.

The first names I ever consciously associated with music were George and Ira Gershwin. They were at the peak of their powers during my infant years and the young genius George died, unforgivably, at the age of 38, when I was six. I remember hearing the news of his death on BBC radio that day in the summer of 1937. I had a real sense of loss, because I knew he had written 'Rhapsody in Blue' and 'An American in Paris', and with Ira 'I Got Rhythm', 'Summertime' and 'Embraceable You', all of which were wildly popular and constantly played at that time. I was particularly attracted by Ira's clever words in those songs, the crafty and crafted rhymes that were so pleasing to my young ears – lines like:

...Just one look at you,
My heart grew tipsy in me.
You and you alone
Bring out the gypsy in me...

and the slyness of following the unexpected 'embraceable' with the deliciously satisfying 'irreplaceable'.

I loved them then and I love them still. I had read in a leading London newspaper about 'George Gershwin and his lovely wife Ira'. It was some years before I realised that one of the most dazzling collaborations in words and music ever achieved should have been between two brothers, and that the lyric of "Love Is Here to Stay" — their last and for me their *best* collaboration — was Ira writing about the loss of George, which elevates this great love song above all others. How about *this* for a world-class lyric?

In time the Rockies may crumble —
Gibraltar may tumble —
They're only made of clay —
But our love is here to stay.

As the 1930s hurtled towards their fateful conclusion, the gathering clouds of war had no noticeable effect on Pinner, Middlesex, and certainly not on the extremely busy schedule of a seven-year-old. While Hitler was planning to conquer the world, I joined the Wolf Cubs, I learned to play tennis and I read the great children's magazines of the day — *Dandy* and *Beano*, graduating later to *Adventure, Hotspur, Champion* and *The Wizard*.

Above all, I discovered the *Just William* books by the immortal Richmal Crompton. I also co-founded with my best friend Raymond Harding a super-secret society of seven-year-old daredevil adventurers known as The Avenging Tawny Lancers, which was unanimously regarded — by us — as altogether superior to William's famous gang, The Outlaws, which consisted of William and his three great pals, Ginger, Henry and Douglas.

For one thing, The Avenging Tawny Lancers were far more exclusive, with a total membership of two — Ray and myself. Sometimes, when my mother allowed, we slept fearlessly outside in the garden in my Wolf Cub tent, dreaming up deeds of derring-do that would have made Indiana Jones's head spin. We even had our own Fantasy Island, which really *was* an island, maybe 30 yards long by 10 wide, in a pretty field dissected by what we saw as the raging waters of the mighty River Pinn, but was in fact a placid little stream that meandered through and around Pinner Village.

My only sad image of those halcyon years, when summer days were endlessly long and smelled of fresh-cut grass and carnations, was the big white ambulance that came to the house to take my father to the hospital. And it happened more than once, as the duodenal ulcers that had developed during his early years of striving to support first his own generation of family, and now ours, returned with painful vengeance. He suffered greatly, but he never complained, and he minimised his periods of convalescence to hurry back to work. I used to sit beside him at the dining table as he wrote his weekly business reports in the most beautiful handwriting I have ever seen.

Sister Pat achieved the first upward mobility of the new generation by securing a place at Harrow College for Girls, a prestigious school with posh uniforms in purple and green. Stung into sibling competitiveness, I promptly acquired a job helping our Irish milkman Larry on Saturday mornings. His bright-orange United Dairies milk-cart was drawn by a big white horse called Snowball, and Larry let me drive – an appropriately dashing activity for an undercover Secret Agent of the Avenging Tawny Lancers.

We always underestimate small children. Even now, when I think of a seven-year-old, my mind conjures up zoos and circuses and birthday cakes and tricycles, which is a serious insult to them. Today's seven-year-olds, let's face it, are a new super breed, computer-literate to a terrifying degree.

Even in the comparatively innocent age of my own infancy, kids were likewise underestimated and, of course, knew everything that was going on in the world. I vividly recall, in October 1938, on a routine Monday-evening family outing to see Johnny Weissmuller in the latest *Tarzan* movie, watching the Pathe Newsreel showing Neville Chamberlain cheerfully waving his 'Peace in Our Time' piece of paper, the accord of appeasement he had just signed in Munich with Herr Hitler. Hitler was smiling, too, and not without reason. He was about to march all over Czechoslovakia.

The next afternoon, walking home from school around four o'clock, I suddenly *knew* there was going to be a war. I *knew* it, and I was *seven*! Why, if it was that obvious to a seven-year-old, hadn't it also occurred to Mr Chamberlain? Or perhaps it had, poor man, and he was just hoping to buy some precious time. Two years later, he was dead, the war was on, and Churchill had stepped forward for his rendezvous with destiny.

The day of Sunday, 3 September 1939 was bright and sunny in the hub of my universe, Pinner. Hitler had invaded Poland two days before, and Chamberlain had given him two days to clear out. Fat chance. Dad's pretty younger sister, my aunt Eileen, had arranged to take sister Pat and myself swimming at the Harrow-on-the-Hill public baths that morning, and it was there in our swimsuits that we ushered in World War Two and the next six years of our lives. There, too, 30 minutes later, I first heard the agonising sound of an air-raid siren. For my childhood, that was the sound of war, that stomach-churning roller-coaster rise and fall of terrifying, ear-splitting harmony that we would hear a thousand times before it was all over. I often wondered how the air-raid siren would sound played against Gustav Holst's 'Mars – The God of War'. Pretty good, I suspect.

Gas-masks, ration-books and air-raid shelters were the first visible signs of change during the next six months of the 'phoney war'. At first, hilariously, we tried wearing the claustrophobic masks during a school history lesson, but the elephantine fart noises and gales of laughter that ensued caused this experiment to be swiftly abandoned. Air-raid shelters proliferated everywhere, in every street and back garden. In London's underground Tube stations, when the Blitz began in 1940, thousands of people would huddle together sleeping on the railway platforms, giving Henry Moore one of the major artistic inspirations of his life. And I loved ration books, with their hopelessly complicated multi-coloured cut-out coupons and surreal bureaucratic double-speak instructions. My favourite section was the one at the back of the book headed: 'DO NOTHING WITH THIS SECTION UNTIL TOLD WHAT TO DO WITH IT'.

Apart from these minor intrusions and inconveniences, daily life in Pinner changed little for the next six months as Hitler's vast forces bulldozed their way across a hopelessly unprepared Europe. But, through newspapers and radio, every daily development of the war consumed our lives. We read and we listened to every word as the situation worsened. My geography studies for the next five years would owe far more to war maps than the classroom.

By the spring of 1940, the only good thing that had happened in Britain was that Churchill had replaced Chamberlain. France was about to fall and, when it did, Hitler would be glaring at us across the English Channel from Calais, only 22 miles from Dover. No one who didn't hear them live on BBC radio can ever fully appreciate the truly inspirational impact that Churchill's great war speeches had on the British people. He was a formidable writer, but, more than that, he was a fantastic actor. Combining those awesome talents, he took the nation by the scruff of the neck, and held it together 'til the war was won, making everyone believe through his remarkable oratory that somehow, God alone knows how, we would endure. He was, and he remains, the greatest man who lived in my lifetime.

Traditionally, before the war, Mum and Dad would take sister Pat and myself to Broadstairs, a seaside resort in Kent, for two weeks' holiday every summer. In 1940, Dad decided we should take our fortnight by the sea earlier than usual – in June instead of August, and in Bournemouth, in Hampshire, rather than Broadstairs. Kent, at 22 miles, was considered too close for comfort to France, whereas Bournemouth was over a hundred miles from the French coast at Cherbourg and Le Havre. Dad's admirable reasoning, given what was happening in France, was that this might be the last family holiday we would get for some time... if ever.

And it was in Bournemouth, in the middle of June, that I finally met the war, or the results of war, face to face for the first time. Walking happily down the hill to the sea-front with its broad sandy beach on that first bright sunny morning, bucket and spade at the ready, we were met by an unimaginable sight.

As far as the eye could see, the beach was filled with thousands of exhausted soldiers, some in bedraggled khaki, and as many again in the vivid blue suits, white shirts and red ties of the wounded. These, we quickly realised, were the men of Dunkirk, a small fraction of the 350,000 survivors of the British Expeditionary Force who had been miraculously plucked from the jaws of death by every conceivable vessel, large and small, naval and civilian, that could be rallied to bring them back to safety across the Channel in one of the great rescue operations of history.

We spent the morning chatting and laughing with the soldiers. Weary and spent as they were, they were so overjoyed to be home, on that beach, in England, that *they* were trying to cheer *us* up, having lived through God knows what horrors in the hours and days and weeks before. They were the embodiment of what Churchill was calling for, and what the mighty Winston immortally labelled 'Their Finest Hour'. It was the first of many wartime experiences I was to have that would teach me the limitless power of the human spirit.

Most of the memories that stayed with me from that extraordinary time were visual images. On another Saturday in that same glorious and fateful summer of 1940, my father took me for my one and only meeting with his father, my ne'er-do-well Belgian grandfather, Joseph, who now lived in a tiny terraced house near Waterloo Station, the irony of which did not escape either of us. His abandonment of his family had caused his son to sell newspapers there as a young boy, and now he, the father, was ending his days a mere hundred yards away.

The tiny patio at the back of the house was filled to bursting with dozens of thriving tomato plants cascading their voluptuous red fruit down to the ground. Half-a-dozen hens paraded in front of them, carefully avoiding the sprinkling of fresh eggs they had laid on the bed of straw that covered the area.

Joseph Bricusse was then in his early sixties, but his worn, craggy face placed him in at least his late seventies. His lifestyle had clearly earned that extra decade-plus look. He had an air of faded elegance, of a man who had known how to live but had somehow overdone it. He was dressed like a musical comedy version of a roué, still clinging to the wreckage of the long-gone Edwardian era of his youth – stiff white collar, grey silk cravat, striped trousers, black morning jacket and a gold watch-chain, but no watch, all of which gave him a jaunty but hauntingly decadent appearance, the ghost of the long-dead maître d' of the Metropole Hotel restaurant that he had once aspired to be. He was charm itself, with a wicked smile and chuckle and, after half-a-century of living in London, still spoke atrocious English with a near-impenetrable Belgian accent. The small living room in which we stood was in total Dickensian disarray, obnoxiously mellowed by the pervasive odour of stale whisky that hung heavily in the air.

As we were leaving after an awkward half-hour – as awkward, I noticed, for my father as it was for myself – my grandfather suddenly plucked from a yellowing stack of old newspapers a huge leather-and-brass bound book and thrust it into my arms, knowing that, just as we had never met before, we would never meet again. The gift was an attempt to bridge two generations in an unspoken language all three of us might eventually understand. The book was a big surprise – a beautiful early edition of Milton's *Paradise Lost* in a contemporary (i.e. 17th-century) binding which, at nine, I was not yet ready to appreciate.

On the drive back home to Pinner, less than an hour later, as my father drove up the big hill that rises up from Spurling's Corner to Kingsbury above the Edgware Road, we looked across to our left at the stunning panoramic view of the entire City of London across the stretch of water known as the Welsh Harp. The sky was blood-red, crimson as a bad artist's fantasy sunset, yet it was still only three o'clock in the afternoon. Dad stopped the car. We got out and, together, we stood in silence and watched as the East End docks of the Port of London burned in an ocean of orange and scarlet fire after a massive German air attack. Perversely, it was one of the most beautiful sights I have ever seen.

Weather-wise, the summer of 1940 was the most magnificent I ever spent in England. At this blackest moment of the war, the sky was at its most brilliant azure blue, as though God were setting the stage for the glorious event that was about to lift British spirits to the very heavens – the Battle of Britain. It was truly the stuff of legend, when *Boys' Own* magazine heroism would become a daily reality. Forget your famous film stars and sporting heroes. This was authentic, the real thing, a new golden generation of young RAF pilots playing on the field of history. These men, flying two and three sorties a day in their not-enough Spitfires and Hurricanes, so hopelessly outnumbered they were called 'The Few', took on the might of the largest airforce ever assembled, the German Luftwaffe, for the most decisive battle of that phase of the war – air superiority – and wiped them out of the skies above our green and pleasant land. It was heart-stopping stuff.

I remember being taken on a picnic, and lying in a field watching as a flotilla of tiny planes, both British and German, dipped and weaved around one another, engaged in what looked like an aerial tarantella, but was in fact a deadly dogfight, Spitfires versus Messerschmitts. The scream of their faraway engines sounded like the squeaks of a thousand mosquitoes. They were there for about 30 seconds that seemed liked an eternity before they streaked away to the south, possibly because the German pilots were watching their fuel gauges. That fierce but romantic image stayed with me. These were the 20th-century knights of Camelot, jousting to the death in the sky for the honour of the King.

The London Blitz began immediately afterwards, as the autumn evenings shortened. My family shared a garden air-raid shelter with two other neighbouring families. Our ten-berth shelter was a substantially constructed, semi-subterranean edifice, with the visible top half attractively disguised as a garden rockery. Sister Pat and I joined the younger generation of all three families down there each evening when the air-raid sirens sounded punctually at 6.30pm. The parents came down later, after the nine o'clock BBC news depressed them all with the latest update on the war. It was going badly. Apart from the temporary respite from invasion provided by the victory in the Battle of Britain, and Churchill's uplifting speeches, there was no good news. Invasion may have been averted, but it had not been avoided. It still loomed large as a possibility for the following spring.

I have no idea how many nights we slept in that shelter during the subsequent couple of years, but it must have been hundreds. It was certainly a far less attractive version of camping out in the garden than that so recently enjoyed by the elite Avenging Tawny Lancers. I developed two abiding pet hates – spiders and the smell of hurricane lamps – and the yearning for my little 5-by-7 domain in the house upstairs became like a distant dream of Shangri-La.

But every cloud has a silver lining. Good things were starting to happen in the air-raid shelter, in the blossoming form of our next-door-but-one neighbour's daughter, Brenda. Throughout these next two war-torn years, aged 13–15, Brenda was developing an ever more spectacular bosom, which put an ever-increasing strain on her soft pink Viyella pyjamas, to say nothing of my dear self, who was now ten heading for eleven. My interest grew month by month, in direct proportion to Brenda's burgeoning breasts. Brenda slept on the top-level bunk directly across from mine. We were often the only two down there, and used to talk for hours. I was aware that she was conscious of my growing fascination with her soft pink pyjamas. Finally, I could bear it no more, and so I entered into serious negotiations with her to let me see the untold treasures contained within them. She steadfastly refused, blushing a far deeper shade of pink than her Viyella.

But the game was on and, thereafter, I regularly upped the stakes, 'til I finally reached my limit, offering her the greater part of my then kingdom, namely a chocolate Crunchie bar and a bag of Maltesers, priceless luxuries in that era of savage sweet rationing, and an offer no girl in her right mind would refuse. But Brenda did, and, when the Blitz finally eased off many months later, she departed with the purity of her by-now outrageous bosom still intact, safe from the lascivious advances of her thwarted young Lothario. On the plus side, the air-raid shelter was no longer the only new erection in the garden.

For daytime air-raids, we had the labyrinthine school shelters built on the playing fields. These raids were a welcome break from school lessons, and a mighty cheer went up every time the air-raid alert siren sounded and we all trooped out to the shelters. The jolly and rotund Mrs Tomlinson somehow knew about my by-now encyclopaedic knowledge of the *Just William* books. I knew every story by heart, and when called upon would happily retell them to an enraptured audience of contemporaries. It raised my status mightily and, in time, became a daily, sometimes twice-daily occurrence, like Vaudeville. When I ran out of Richmal Crompton stories, I would make up my own, and these improvisations were met with such gales of mirth that I was able to keep going through the longest air-raid until the 'All Clear' sounded. And it slowly dawned on me that I had the power to entertain people. From there, it was but a short step to my glove-puppet show in the garage, the 30 shillings raised for Mrs Churchill's Aid-To-Russia Fund, which, as I pointed out earlier, led directly to the successful conclusion of the war.

At the end of 1941, three more major world events caused things to change dramatically: the Japanese bombed Pearl Harbor; America entered the war; and I became a Senior Sixer in the Pinner Wolf Cubs, the leader of my pack. This sudden heady rise to power gave me three golden bands on the arm of my green sweater, to go with the nine proficiency badges that already adorned it, awarded for everything from Elementary First Aid to

Tying Untieable Knots. I had so many stripes and badges I looked like a small, green, logo-strewn racing-car.

Interestingly, this new technicolour mantle of responsibility affected me profoundly. My schoolwork improved dramatically. I was able to concentrate better on subjects that previously held little or no interest for me beyond positioning my desk-chair at an angle which gave me the optimum left-profile view of by far the prettiest girl in the class, Jill Chapman, on whom the gods had lavished far more gifts than anyone deserved, except possibly her. She had light golden hair, wide-set blue eyes, Gene Tierney's smile and better dimples than Shirley Temple. Sweet-natured, unspoiled and friendly, she was also the brainiest girl in the school. Not bad for ten... and she really was a ten. She knew she was good, but never showed off. Nonetheless, all those dazzling qualities combined to give her a slight aura of superiority and detachment.

My knowledge of geography continued to improve in leaps and bounds, thanks to the manic appetite with which I devoured every detail of every war map in every combat zone at breakfast each morning, to the extent of taking a magnifying-glass to my father's *Daily Express*. (He worked for Lord Kemsley, but treacherously read Kemsley's rival Lord Beaverbrook's newspapers.)

Newspapers. More even than radio in those pre-television days, they were my prime source of information, and I found myself increasingly fascinated by them. I persuaded my dad to take me to Kemsley House in Gray's Inn Road in central London some Saturday nights to watch the Sunday newspapers being printed. As Circulation Manager of the *Sunday Chronicle*, Saturday night was his busiest time of the week, and I was allowed to roam free through the building, watching the typesetters hand-racking up each page line by line and letter by letter, the papers speed-rolling off the presses, just like in Hollywood movies, and finally, around 5.00 or 6.00am, driving home through the early dawn back to Pinner with still-wet, shiny copies of every London paper on the back seat of the car. These privileged Saturday-night trips soon seduced me into the belief that journalism, to write for a newspaper, to play with words and spin them into fine fabric sentences, was to be my future. For the next few years, that dazzling possibility became the driving force of my existence.

At the end of that school year, in the summer of 1942, the glorious Jill Chapman and I were each awarded a scholarship to an English public school, regrettably not the same one. I never saw Jill again from the age of 11, but the enchanting memory of her childhood beauty and serenity is as clear in my mind today as it was in that long-ago Pinner primary school.

University College School Junior School is set in a spot as pretty as it sounds – Holly Hill, in the heart of Hampstead Village. It was boys only, which smacked of a satisfying elitism, and the curriculum involved a head-spinning collection of new studies – French, Latin, Ancient Greek, algebra and geometry – to go with all the usual stuff: history, geography, English, arithmetic, art and music. Sports changed, too. Soccer became rugger, and cricket, in my case, became tennis.

The days of Wolf Cubs and Avenging Tawny Lancers were suddenly and irrevocably over. There were no regrets. At that age, one just outgrew those things, like clothes. One moved on, again like clothes, to bigger things. Infant school jumpers became black-and-maroon striped blazers. Short trousers became long. Short stories became long. The *William* books became PG Wodehouse, Charles Dickens and Mark Twain by choice and Racine, Corneille, Molière, Shakespeare and Sophocles by academic demand.

To augment my meagre weekly allowance in the sophisticated new circle of eleven-year-olds in which I was now mingling, I found myself an absolute nightmare of a job with the local newsagent. Not for me the traditional early morning paper round. Oh, no, Leslie Cleverpants worked each morning, seven days a week, with the owner of the shop, Tom Wallis, a gruff but affable old bear of a man, marking the house numbers on all the newspapers that were to be delivered. These had to be ready for the delivery boys by 7am, so Old Tom and I would begin work before 6am, which in turn meant that I had to be up and stumbling around half-asleep getting ready for my school day in my five-by-seven kingdom by 5am every morning!

One cold, wet day I arrived and set to work, facing Old Tom across the counter stacked high with newspapers. He was unusually quiet. After he greeted me, he didn't speak a word. Fifteen minutes later, he spoke three I shall never forget.

'Young Tom's gone,' he said in a matter-of-fact way, and one large tear ran down his nose and landed on a photograph of Churchill on the front page of the *Daily Telegraph.* Young Tom, his only son, had been killed in action on some remote battlefield. I never learned quite where, it didn't matter quite where. Young Tom was dead was what mattered. And Old Tom went on working, as he did and had for over 40 years, dealing with his grief by keeping going.

School life on Holly Hill, by Hampstead Heath, continued as uninterrupted as the war allowed. Our aged headmaster, a wispy septuagenarian Classicist, Dr Bernard Lake, universally and affectionately known as Bunny, used to march around the school carrying, for reasons never clarified, a wooden Banta spear called an *assegai*, which was taller than he was, and gave him the appearance of being an elderly white relative of Mahatma Gandhi.

There had been rumours for months that Hitler was preparing a new Blitz on London, using pilotless planes and long-range guided missile rockets. These finally began to arrive in June 1944, exactly one week after the D-Day landings in Normandy. The pilotless planes, the V-1 flying bombs that were instantly nicknamed Doodlebugs, would fly across southern England at low altitude 'til their throaty, pre-programmed engines would cut out, Hitler hoped somewhere over central London, plunge to earth in about ten seconds and explode in death and destruction.

Bunny Lake's ideas on appropriate air-raid precautions for the school against these new attacks were as primitive as his Banta *assegai*. We did not go to air-raid shelters, because the school had none. Instead, all pupils were instructed to crouch down under their wooden desks whenever they heard a Doodlebug engine cut out, which we did, several times each day. While this might not afford maximum protection, it would certainly minimise lost lesson time. Flimsy at best as this arrangement was, since our little desks were positioned close to large windows, it worked for a while, until the day we heard a particularly noisy Doodlebug close overhead. The engine cut out. We dived under our desks and counted to ten. A huge explosion not too far away rattled the big windows. We got back up again and, as we did so, a second almighty explosion occurred less than a hundred yards away, severely damaging the block of flats next to the school. No one had realised that the loudness of the engine noise we had heard was due to two Doodlebugs cutting out simultaneously. Happily for us, the flats acted as a protective barrier for the school. But it was too close for comfort. We learned one thing for sure that day, that wooden desks do not an air-raid shelter make.

The total trust and the feeling of togetherness that existed among the British people at that time was something I was blessed to grow up with. The unquestioning faith I have always placed in people, sometimes mistakenly, I inherited from that remarkable period of my childhood. Every evening, as it grew dark and the night bombing was due to begin, cars coming out of London would stop at every bus-stop and pick up as many passengers as they had empty seats, to help a bunch of complete strangers get safely and quickly home.

The prevailing schoolboy craze of that era, when the war severely limited our choices of entertainment, was collecting train numbers, or 'train-spotting'. Squads of us would stand for hours, sometimes all day, at busy railway terminals all over London, pursuing this most bizarre of pastimes. And more than bizarre, it was obsessive. My mother used to look at me as though I was demented as she handed me sandwiches and I disappeared into the pouring rain on a bone-chilling January morning, with a maniacal glint in my eye.

And it was train-spotting that provided me with my most indelible memory of the war. On my way home from school one afternoon in mid-September 1944, I walked as usual down the hill from Hampstead to Finchley Road, where I would catch my train home to Pinner. On the way, as I occasionally did, I stopped at the spot where one could see steam trains leaving London on two neighbouring tracks, one above and one below the spot where I always stood. There was one other boy there, whom I did not know. Nothing of note beyond a couple of dismal-looking goods trains happened for about 15 minutes and, as one more equally uninteresting locomotive came into view, I picked up my school satchel, ready to leave. Suddenly, I felt something strike me sharply on the head. It was a bar of chocolate. In 1944, it might as well have been a bar of gold. I looked up at the train. It was a troop-train, crammed to overflowing with hundreds of soldiers. The passing blur of smiling faces and uniforms appeared to be an unusual mix of red-bereted British and American paratroopers.

For the next 30 or 40 seconds, time stood still as the unknown boy and I stood there in a trance as the waving, laughing men on the train tossed down an unending cascade of chocolate bars, dozen upon dozen of them, more chocolate than we had ever seen in our lives. And, just as suddenly, the train was gone, leaving two schoolboys staring at one another in disbelief, ankle-deep in chocolate, totally stunned by this surreal incident. We recovered, divided up the treasure and went our separate ways.

Two days later, I read in my father's *Daily Express* about the daring airborne attack on Arnhem in Holland and the brave but doomed attempt to seize the key bridges on the Rhine, particularly the one at Nijmegen, the infamous 'Bridge Too Far'. And I wondered just who these laughing, waving soldiers were, and where that troop-train was taking them. Were they part of the Arnhem attack? And, if so, how many of them had died in the 48 hours since they showered two schoolboys with the chocolate deluge of their dreams? The image of that passing train transporting so many young men from life to death haunts me still whenever I think of it.

By now, we all knew for sure that we were going to win the war, and that it was only a matter of time. The new aerial bombardment of London developed beyond the 30,000 V-1 'buzz-bombs', to the more lethal and sinister V-2 rockets, which came silently out of the sky and killed and destroyed with no warning and such murderous efficiency that even Blitz-hardened Londoners couldn't be bothered to find their usual derisive nickname for them.

Having spent more than five years of my life hurrying to get home from school each day as quickly as my legs and public transport could carry me, before Hitler tried yet again to get me, I now began to look with greater curiosity at the world around me. London's West End was only three or four miles down the hill from Hampstead, and, although it was out of bounds after dark and blacked out every night, I realised how comparatively little I knew The Greatest City in the World.

One evening after school, on an impulse, I took the forbidden trip to the West End. I wandered along Coventry Street, past Lyons' Corner House, with its memories of pre-war high teas and my grandfather's early business naivety, into Leicester Square, where five flagship movie theatres took up three of its four sides. My discovery that day of the north side of the square would prove to be as meaningful to me as discovering the North Pole had been to Peary almost half-a-century before.

The Empire Theatre, Leicester Square, was the London home of the fabled era of MGM musical movies that was just beginning. The mastermind behind this golden age was a famous songwriter, Arthur Freed, who had now graduated to the glorious double role of film producer and generalissimo in charge of all MGM musicals, in rather the same way that the President of the United States is also Head of the Armed Forces.

Anybody who combines, as Mr Freed did, the dazzling talents of Vincente Minnelli, Stanley Donen, Gene Kelly, Judy Garland,

Fred Astaire, Frank Sinatra, George and Ira Gershwin, Lerner and Loewe, Jerome Kern, Oscar Hammerstein, Rodgers and Hart, Cole Porter, Harold Arlen and Yip Harburg, Betty Comden and Adolph Green – the list is overwhelming – is certainly dealing with an art form. And it was into that magical new world of technicolour make-believe that I stepped for the first time one cold November afternoon when I wandered into the Empire, Leicester Square, to see my first-ever MGM musical.

Thus began my 'other' education, hearing, admiring and adoring the wondrous words and music of that genius-touched generation of between-the-war songwriters, who had taken the old Tin Pan Alley by the scruff of the neck and raised its lowly 32-bar sights to a new and glorious level of quality, wit, sophistication and polished elegance. The music junk dealers of the early 20th century had been replaced by purveyors of genuine jewellery, words and music that glittered and shone. The realisation that all this magic was being created on a daily basis in faraway Hollywood, to a large extent by people not much older than myself, brought back that frustrated and envious feeling I had first encountered several years before, watching the millionaire tot Shirley Temple belting out 'On the Good Ship Lollipop'.

The bottom rung of the lowest ladder in journalism was still at eye level with the height of my ambition, and the *Harrow Observer*, published every Thursday at 3 pence and serving Harrow, Kenton, Sudbury, Rayners Lane, Ruislip and Pinner, was the target of my literary lust and my intended passport to fame. But, at age 12, I realised that all that stuff was still as far off as a moonshot.

University College Senior School is a pleasant place set in the prime residential area of Hampstead. Like almost all public schools of that era, UCS was boys only, alas, though that majority opinion was not, I'm sure, shared by at least one senior master, nor the two or three of my now-celebrated gay contemporaries who were at that time graduating for the first time from short trousers to long trousers, and in some cases no trousers.

It was around this time that my dear discerning dad delivered into my life the greatest gift that any schoolboy could ever dream of – a gift of such unquantifiable magnificence that even today, looking back more than half-a-century, the accumulative joy it brought me still takes my breath away. It was a gift that became a thousand gifts. Through one of his press connections, Dad had struck up a strong friendship with a jocular, rotund man called Harold Hastings. And who was Harold Hastings? None other than the Chief Press Officer for Wembley Stadium and Sports Arena. And what did that mean to me? Simply that, for close to a decade, I had prime press seats for every major sporting event that occurred at this mighty Mecca of sport. Every international football match, every Cup Final, every ice-hockey game, every sporting occasion was mine for the asking, and I asked.

I had been, and have remained throughout my life, a sports fanatic from the age of five and, throughout the 1940s, because of this gift from the gods and Harold Hastings, I became an expert on several sports I might otherwise never have seen. I used to sit next to the famous moustachioed BBC radio sports commentator Raymond Glendenning in the front row of the huge, glass-fronted Press Box, while he described every kick of every Cup Final to the vast soccer-mad British public.

I became so knowledgeable about the current form of Britain's top racing greyhounds that, on one famous occasion, when I was 13, after having dinner with my parents and some friends in that same elegant Press Box, and having the gall to complete my homework up there, I correctly predicted the winners of all eight dog races, much to the wonderment of one of Dad's guests, who on a friendly and condescending whim indulged me by allowing me to be his tipster and backing all eight of them! I remember vividly that a wonderful dog called Bah's Choice broke the world 525-yard track record that evening in 29.03 seconds.

I watched ice hockey twice a week at the Sports Arena, and ice shows when they came there, and speedway racing at the Stadium. The Everest of my years at Wembley came in 1948, when

I was 17, when Harold Hastings made me, for the two most glorious weeks of my up-'til-then life, his press assistant at the 1948 Olympic Games in London. I saw everything, met everyone, and was *paid* to do it! Greater luck hath no 12-year-old than that his dad makes the Chief Press Officer at Wembley Stadium and Sports Arena his best friend! There is no question that this staggering slice of good fortune contributed vastly to my already optimistic outlook on life. As far as my morale was concerned, it won the war for me, two full years before the reality.

Like some giant pendulum of history, the war swung inevitably away from the enemy towards the Allies until the final great victories and surrenders of 1945 were achieved. My age group was just about the luckiest – eight years old when the war started, 14 when it ended – old enough to have experienced the outer edges of it and understood what it was all about, while young enough not to have witnessed most of its true horrors, as so many children in Europe and elsewhere had. We were also old enough to be aware how many tens of thousands of young men only four or five years older than we were now lay beneath the white headstones of war cemeteries scattered like confetti across the globe; and, above all, young enough *and* old enough to know how blessed we were by Fate to have in store for us the golden, peaceful future that had been bought for us at such a terrible price.

The war ended, but rationing didn't. Indeed, it was to continue far into the 1950s for some commodities. I kept my eye on my favourite section at the back of my ration book, headed 'DO NOTHING WITH THIS SECTION UNTIL TOLD WHAT TO DO WITH IT', waiting for The Great Moment that would justify the Government's far-seeing, long-range planning, but, alas, it never came.

Slowly, the peacetime freedoms returned. Wimbledon tennis resumed in 1946, as did international competition in all major sports. Foreign travel was allowed for the first time since 1939, almost half my life ago. The foreign travel allowance was minuscule, an arrangement admirably suited to our family's finances. Through my young French master at school, who actually was French, I arranged a student exchange trip with a student from the Lycée Henri Quatre in Paris. His name was Claude Coudurier, a tall, solemn and studious young man resembling the young Christopher Lee. He came to England first, and I spent three weeks showing him my London. The museums were a hit. The MGM musicals were not. Simple as that.

My return–match three weeks in Paris were somewhere between a revelation and a revolution. In swift succession, I discovered (a) Paris, (b) French cooking, and (c) *Cyrano de Bergerac*, with all of which I became instantly and totally enraptured, a condition from which I am happy to say I have never recovered to this day. Until Madame Coudurier, Claude's mother, placed her *gigot d'agneau* on the lunch table on my first-ever Paris Sunday and my taste buds exploded in rabid anticipation, I had never tasted garlic.

So there I was, after three days in France, hooked on Paris and garlic, like a cheap gastronomic junkie. The Couduriers completed the triple play by taking me to the Châtelet Theatre to see the only two plays by Edmond Rostand that survived his lifetime. One was *L'Aiglon*, a ponderous piece about the young Napoleon. When asked back at school what it was about, I said, 'It's about four hours.' The other was *Cyrano de Bergerac*. When asked what *that* one was about, I said, 'It's about the best and funniest and most romantic and most heart-breaking play I've ever seen in my life.' And I would say the same today.

Sister Pat got married. That was the next thing. Harcourt Eldon Greening Bull was Canadian, as anyone with a name like that deserves to be. He was a Captain at Canadian Military HQ in London, where Pat worked as a hotshot stenographer. And marriage to a Canadian more often than not entails living in Canada, as it did in this case. They were married at Pinner's picturesque 13th-century church at the top end of the picture-perfect Village High Street, which looks like the set that Pinewood Studios would build for yet another remake of *Pride and Prejudice*.

A short while thereafter, the war over and the threat of peace hanging heavily in the English air, they sailed into the sunset to live a happy-ever-after life in Hamilton, Ontario. Pat returned to England for part of the following summer, and − wonder of wonders − I sailed back from Southampton to New York with her on the great Cunard liner *Queen Elizabeth*, which afforded me my first intoxicating glimpse of Manhattan at the tender age of 16. But only a glimpse, because within hours Pat and I had to catch the overnight sleeper train to Hamilton, Ontario, just over the Canadian border.

At the end of the summer, I cunningly pre-planned my return schedule to give myself three magical days on my own in New York, where I promptly threw myself at the mercy and the feet of the twin arch-bitch-goddesses of Temptation and Tourism. From my supreme headquarters in the smallest single room (nothing new for me) of the less-than-so-so Franklin Hotel on West 47th Street, I went to the top of the Empire State Building, ate my first (and second and tenth) hamburgers, walked along Broadway and around Times Square, where the yellow cabs and the giant billboards and the movie houses and theatres with their bright lights and dazzling posters exuded a glamour beyond anything I had ever imagined.

On my last evening, before I sailed back on the *Queen Elizabeth* to the real world of post-war austerity England, came The Great Highlight − my first-ever visit to Radio City Music Hall, a 6,500-seat palace of solid gold, where for less than $2 I saw a mind-blowing stage show featuring the 36 world-famous Rockettes, high-kicking their beautiful brains out, followed by my first-ever Hollywood movie in America, an elegant romantic comedy entitled *The Bachelor and the Bobby-Soxer*, starring Cary Grant and a now grown-up and glamorous but still only two years older than me Shirley Temple. The film later went on to win an Academy Award for Best Original Screenplay for a young writer called Sidney Sheldon. As the *Queen Elizabeth* steamed slowly out of New York Harbor at sunset the next evening, I looked back at that remarkable skyline of skyscrapers, missing it already, and vowing, as Arnold Schwarzenegger would a few decades later, that I'd be back.

Peacetime in post-war London was in many ways worse than the war. The heroes all came home to a resounding welcome, but the delicious taste of victory soon faded. And, in no time at all, The Mighty were fallen. England's best friend President Roosevelt died in the last days of the war, and the doom-defying rhetoric and high heroics of Churchill were swiftly cast aside a few weeks later as he was swept from power by a tired nation that felt he had served his purpose as our greatest wartime leader, and that the rebuilding of the country could now be safely left in the hands of the next available Neville Chamberlain-like incompetent, who chanced to be an effective but colourless political figure called Clement Attlee, a man who was born to be a bank manager, but failed and ended up instead as Prime Minister of Great Britain in a vast and unexpected electoral landslide to the left.

But life went on, and produced new peacetime heroes. I spent much of the glorious summers of 1947 and 1948 at Lord's Cricket Ground in St John's Wood, handily located a couple of miles from the school, watching England's dashing cricket hero Denis Compton score more centuries in one season than anyone ever in the history of the game. I also witnessed the final Test Match innings at The Oval of the legendary Australian batsman Don Bradman, where all he needed to score was four runs to achieve a lifetime Test Cricket batting average of 100, and he was out for a duck. That gave him a lifetime average of 99.94. The second-best Test average in cricket history is somewhere in the low sixties, which will tell you precisely how good Don Bradman was.

And then there was Wimbledon. The captain of both the school and the school tennis team, John Barrett, and I returned each summer to the smooth green courts of my almost-birthplace whenever we could scrape into the sacred grounds during the near-religious 13 days of the tournament. Kramer, Gonzales,

Sedgman, Hoad, Rosewall and 'Little Mo' Connolly... we were privileged to watch all those great players whose names now grace the pages of Wimbledon's definitive history, written a few years ago by the same John Barrett.

We duly passed our Sixth Form Higher Certificate exams. Our school days were drawing to a close and, as our eighteenth birthdays and National Service loomed, there loomed with them the agonising decision about whether or not to sit for the university entrance exam. To be or not to be? One part of me argued, 'Enough studying... get on with your life,' while another voice warned, 'You will never pass this way again.'

The Cambridge University entrance exams are held each year in the first week of December, immediately after the end of the university Michaelmas Term. For four glorious days, we lived in Corpus Christi College as residents, taking our meals in the refectory and being treated in all respects as undergraduates. Corpus Christi, like Pinner Church, is 13th century, one of Cambridge's oldest, and there exists in every courtyard of every college in Cambridge a serene mood of unhurried calm that seems to pervade everyone and everything around it. It was like living in a friendly dream, and, if there are ghosts, I suspect the nicest of them went to Cambridge and hoped that we would follow. By the end of the four days, so did I.

Apart from the exams, there was an interview. Mine took place on the last day, at Gonville and Caius College, with a benign and revered old don, EK Bennett, affectionately known as Francis, who, were he not such a celebrated academic, could easily have beaten out Edmond Gwenn for the role of Kris Kringle in *Miracle on 34th Street*. And time truly stood still. I seemed to be there for hours. I felt focused as never before. He drew out of me things I had never expressed. I knew where I was going and what I wanted. I wanted to go to Cambridge, and Francis Bennett, I am sure, was the reason I got there.

There are no results given for the Cambridge University

entrance exams. You're not quite sure what it is you're waiting for. All I remember is opening an envelope several weeks later. The letter within offered me a place at Gonville and Caius College, and I accepted with shameless alacrity. Thus, I took the decision to devote the next five years, the first of my adulthood, to combining the obligatory agony of two years of military service with the voluntary ecstasy of three years at Cambridge, and to getting the agony part of it out of the way first. What other choice did I have? To go from the Army to Cambridge would be like ascending to Heaven from the depths of Hell. The reverse option was too dire even to contemplate, so I bit the bullet.

And so it came to pass that, on 10 May 1949, I made my way to Buller Barracks in Aldershot, to defend the realm and guarantee Britain's safety and security for the next couple of years, at least to the extent that a private soldier in the Royal Army Service Corps was capable of so doing.

I would prefer to draw a khaki veil over the next two years of my life. Filled with incident as they were, they did little to contribute to The March of Man in the larger sense of the term. The RASC is not one of those glamorous and romantic old British Army regiments with seventeen VCs and a history of derring-do spread across 200 years of great battles for the Empire. It is not even a regiment at all; it is a corps. And a very good corps, too, servicing many of the Army's needs, without which, etc. And it has a thumping good military march all its own, a sort of signature tune, called 'Wait for the Wagon', which I probably heard 18,000 times during my two-year military tenure. Either it was the only song the RASC band knew, or somebody stole the rest of their music.

Simply put, those two years were a total waste of my time and the Government's money, putting me through the Mons Officer Cadet Training School, then stationing me for a year-and-a-half in such strategic British military strongholds as Netheravon, near Middle Wallop, in Wiltshire, and North Luffenham, near Waltham-in-the-Wolds in Rutland. I am proud to record that at no time during my critical tour of duty in these key installations were they ever for a moment in danger of being occupied by the enemy.

A rowdy group of South African Air Force pilots were stationed at North Luffenham airfield when I was there. My company was practising air supply drops by parachute. The South Africans were converting from flying Douglas DC3s, the great old Dakotas, to a newer post-war aircraft. Their ringleader was a wonderful, hard-drinking, 25-year-old madman called Johnny Grobler. To picture him, think of John Belushi rather than Alan Arkin playing Yossarian in *Catch-22*. They used to invite me and a fellow second lieutenant called David MacLagan Thomas to join them on night training flights, as they had to accumulate a certain number of flying hours as part of their conversion course. On any given night, Johnny and his crew would fly us and a lifetime supply of alcohol north to Scotland or Scandinavia, or south to Spain or the Cote d'Azur, with a carefree abandon that seemed to defy all known rules of air traffic control. They had a maniacal flight plan all their own. They increased my chances of survival in any future air travel by treating me to *two* air crashes on *consecutive* days, the first by hitting the perimeter fence on our final approach, the second by contriving to collapse the undercarriage on landing, in the mistaken belief that we were taking off. Dear Johnny, I often wonder whether he lived to be 30. He didn't need a war for everyone around him to be facing death at every turn.

The aforesaid David MacLagan Thomas was a pleasant young playboy-cum-career officer in the Regular Army, and he had one admirable quality that cemented our friendship. He loved MGM musicals. More than that, he could play the songs, since he was a more-than-handy piano player, and a would-be composer. The lyricist I admired first and foremost from the MGM films was Lorenz Hart. I had seen the film *Words and Music*, about the early collaboration of Rodgers and Hart, 25 times, drawn back to it time and again as much by the songs themselves as the performances of them by Lena Horne, Judy Garland, Mickey

Rooney, Gene Kelly et al, among the galaxy of 'more stars than there are in the heavens' to which MGM so modestly laid claim. I knew every word of every lyric, pardon the pun, by heart. I had never actually tried to *write* a lyric – after all, I was planning to be a journalist, wasn't I? – but I understood the basic mechanics and sense of internal balance that the process required.

Late one evening in the Officers' Mess, David MacLagan Thomas played a handful of the famous songs that maintained his popularity there, and then performed a couple of his own somewhat Richard Rodgers-like melodies. One in particular I liked, so on a wild, possibly wine-induced impulse, I volunteered – the only time in my entire army career I ever volunteered for anything – to try and put a lyric on it.

Over the ensuing months, marooned in the all-enveloping gloom of an endless, cold and foggy North Luffenham winter, David and I wrote a series of totally unmemorable songs that we thought were so absolutely sublime that Cole Porter's days of songwriting supremacy were unquestionably numbered. Air-dropping imaginary supplies to non-existent armies on Salisbury Plain or Exmoor, a desultory operation at the best of times, now took a very bad second place to songwriting, which was to prove not only the salvation of my sanity but also the first semester of an education that never ends. Every time a songwriter writes a song, he is learning – learning how to write that particular song.

Long weekend leaves, from Friday night to Monday morning, were treated as being one step ahead of a jail-break. David's high-powered MG saloon was our getaway car and we would roar down the Great North Road to London. In the village of Stilton, we would stop to buy the famed cheeses for my parents and David's angelic mother Marjorie, known as Midge.

Neither six years at an all-boys' English public school nor two more as a reluctant National Service conscript in the British Army can be regarded as the ideal education for one's romantic life, and, since my Hollywood-influenced idea of a pretty girl was

Hedy Lamarr or Gene Tierney, neither Pinner nor Aldershot, nor certainly North Luffenham, seemed likely to produce any hot candidates in that rather bleak area of my life. But lightning strikes when and where it will, and it struck me at a drinks party at Midge's cosy little house in South Kensington when a friend of a friend walked in with a devastating-looking 5-foot-10 brunette with black hair and blue eyes, a heart-shaped face and a figure so glorious she made Rita Hayworth look like Grandma Moses. The heavenly creature's name was Dianne, and she was, of course, a model with a top West End agency. She seemed a little mature and sophisticated for teenage me, but she was such an indisputable dish that I somehow found the courage, as great warriors do in the heat of battle, to emerge from the fray with her phone number.

David was as impressed by this achievement as I was, and promptly proclaimed himself my campaign manager. Using Midge shamelessly as both beard and go-between, a series of little lunches or dinners were set up in the ensuing weeks. Midge revelled in her role as undercover double-agent, and Dianne was slowly drawn into our little web of intrigue. She and I spoke on the telephone as frequently as modelling assignments and military manoeuvres allowed, and I was dumbfounded to realise that God had given her a complete set of toys, for she also had a delicious sense of humour. She was as funny as she was beautiful.

It was a punishing schedule. David and I had to belt 100 miles-plus each way up and down the Great North Road every available weekend that Dianne and I were free to see one another. '*Vaut le voyage*', as the Michelin Guide says of its three-star gourmet restaurants.

I nicknamed the delectable Dianne 'Dido'. Dido was Pygmalion's sister. Long story short, the climax came one Sunday evening when Dianne asked me whether I would like to spend the following weekend at her parents' home in London. I stammered that I would love to. Midge winked broadly. Dianne smiled provocatively. David nodded sagely, and, in the car scorching back up the Great North Road to North Luffenham a few hours later, he proudly assured me in his capacity as campaign manager that meeting Mum and Dad was a significant step in the right direction. I was still a little concerned about the age difference. Midge and David both agreed she had to be 24 or 25 if she was a day – but things were otherwise going very much according to plan, so don't rock the boat!

Encouraged, I nervously presented myself at Dianne's family home the following Friday night promptly at nine o'clock, after yet another record-breaking, and nearly neck-breaking, drive from North Luffenham. Not knowing what to expect, I was greeted at the door by the goddess Dido herself, seductively sheathed in a breathtaking floor-length emerald silk robe. She took my trembling teenage hand and led me through to the living room, where an open bottle of champagne and two glasses sat waiting. I said I was really looking forward to meeting her parents. Dianne smiled the divine smile. 'Oh, they're in Paris,' she said casually. 'We'll do that next time!' She had never mentioned *meeting* her parents. She had merely invited me to spend the weekend at their home.

Dido thereby pressed the fast-forward button on my hitherto neglected education, and the weekend that ensued was one with which neither Pinner, Aldershot, North Luffenham nor probably Heaven itself could compete. Dido's nickname for herself was, understandably, Vesuvius. I thought the weekend could not possibly hold any further surprises. I was relaxed to the point of stupor, and our relationship had taken several quantum leaps forward. But there was one question still lurking at the back of my mind, which I hadn't dared to ask. I was about to leave. David was honking the MG horn outside. I summoned up all my legendary courage. 'When's your birthday?' I asked.

'June 29th,' she replied. 'Why?'

As casually as I could, in a strangled throwaway, I said, 'You've never even told me how old you are.'

She took my face in her hands, lowered and raised the

unnecessarily long, dark eyelashes, so that I drowned just one last time in those huge twin pools of blue as she flashed her irresistible pearl-white smile. 'I'm 16,' she said, kissed me full on the lips and closed the front door behind her.

And she was. At 17, she married someone else also called Leslie.

2nd Key: B Natural

Thursday, 1 October 1951 – which, according to that morning's *Daily Express*, was Julie Andrews's sixteenth birthday – was the day my parents drove me up to Cambridge in Dad's smart new black-and-red Ford Zephyr car and deposited me at the Porter's Lodge of Gonville and Caius College in Trinity Street. Eighteen-and-a-half years after I had first taken up residence, aged two, in my 5-by-7 domain at 103, Cannon Lane, I left my little childhood kingdom for the last time.

An elderly college porter led me and my suitcase slowly across Tree Court, into Old Court, where the ancient 13th-century Gate of Honour leads across to the University Senate House, which separates Caius (pronounced 'keys') from King's College. We passed under the archway of the Master's Lodge, opposite the college chapel, and then up the corner staircase between the Junior Common Room and the refectory to a small and ancient set of rooms which looked out across the narrow medieval Trinity Lane to the Great Court of Trinity College, Caius College's enormous next-door neighbour.

Every step of the way was a magical journey across seven

centuries of history. That is the miracle of both Oxford and Cambridge, that they have stood unchanged for the better part of 1,000 years. That is what you feel when you walk through either university, that the youth of today is in direct contact with the youth of bygone ages, pursuing the same paths of living and learning, walking beside the same rivers and, the most direct link of all, inhabiting the same rooms in the same buildings that have played host and home to every generation from then 'til now. That feeling of awe never left me throughout my time at Cambridge, and 'inspired' is the word for all it makes you feel. The next word is 'privileged'.

That said, there would prove to be one element of this perfect scenario for which I would be less than grateful. The glory that is Trinity Great Court is dominated at one end by a gigantic four-faced gold-and-black clock, its face maybe 10 feet or more square. I always knew what the time was during my first year at Cambridge, because that clock was right outside my living-room window, no more than 15 feet away across Trinity Lane. I never needed to look to see the time, because the bloody thing would go off with a resounding clang loud enough to give anyone within 100 yards a heart-attack, every 15 minutes, 24 hours a day. No one in England knew the time at any hour of the day or night better than I did. Greenwich could have used me as a back-up. For over half a year, I could guess the correct time within ten seconds.

There were various first-day traditions to be observed, such as meeting one's tutor to arrange tutorial and lecture schedules. My tutor was a lugubrious fellow called Eric Blackall, a shoo-in for membership of the Addams Family, a cross between Christopher Lee and Darth Vader. He was also a brilliant man who served a good glass of sherry, the highlight of all weekly 'supervisions', as they were euphemistically labelled, and another good indication that one was no longer at school. But, whenever I watched him walking by in his sinister, flowing black academic gown, I couldn't help feeling that in his spare time he perched Dracula-like on the battlements at night.

The Freshmen's team photograph, with the new inductees grandly decked out in academic gowns, made us feel appropriately learned and important, and was followed, best of all, by the Freshmen's First-Night Dinner, at which the Master's speech of welcome replaced the darker dictum of schooldays, i.e. 'Do as you're told!', with the loftier and friendlier principle of academia – 'We are here to help you!' It was a pleasant way of informing us that we would be treated as adults, and could therefore be trusted to behave as adults. If you can die for your country at 18, it is not unreasonable to assume that you are also old enough to handle a glass of beer, and even fraternise with the fresh-faced daughters of the local farm families. This assumption was thrown into some doubt by the constant late-evening vigils of the University Proctors, more Dracula-like figures in flowing black robes and mortar-boards, who patrolled the streets to apprehend any wayward students who were out after the official curfew hour of 10.00pm. A 'late pass' gave you 'til midnight. Many were the dark shadows of students flitting unseen from doorway to doorway, like so many teenage Harry Limes in *The Third Man*'s streets of Vienna, trying to escape detection. They lacked only the zither music accompaniment. Each Proctor was escorted by two uniformed strong-armed assistants, known as Bulldogs, who in other areas of society would be variously termed bodyguards, bouncers or bruisers.

I wasted no time setting my game plan in motion. At three o'clock the next afternoon, I went over to Great Court, Trinity and, in rooms directly beneath that Bloody Clock, I presented myself to the Secretary of the grandly named Footlights Dramatic Society, Mr Christopher Pym, a charming and languid PG Wodehouse character, a Bertie Wooster lookalike, who would have been unanimously elected to the Drones Club on the first ballot. 'The Footlights' was the university's celebrated intimate revue group, whose members wrote and performed sophisticated and witty satirical sketches and songs on the topics of the day.

At four o'clock, I met the President of the Footlights, the Hon Andrew Davidson, and the Treasurer, Mr Kennedy Thom, over at Pembroke College, and by four-thirty I was officially welcomed as a member of the Footlights. On my way back along King's Parade from Pembroke to Caius, I stopped by Ryder and Amies, the university gentleman's clothing emporium, to treat myself to the broad-striped red, turquoise and purple Footlights tie. By the time the Bloody Clock struck five, I was back in my rooms wearing it.

There was also the small matter of the Modern and Medieval Languages Tripos to consider, which was the reason I was at Cambridge in the first place. Furthermore, all these activities had to be combined with the many other choices available in everyday Cambridge life, such as trying to master the art of navigating a punt down the River Cam with a pole without falling in, then drinking a couple of pints of highly intoxicating Merrydown cider at the pub down by the lock gates without falling down, and finally, having failed, then trying to master the art of standing up. Coffee at The Copper Kettle; lunch at Miller's when affordable; tea at the Dorothy Café; and, of course, the rip-roaring weekly debates at the Cambridge Union, where major political grandees and other national luminaries would sometimes seriously and sometimes hilariously propose or oppose such insane and thought-provoking motions as 'That this house would sell its soul at the right price' or 'That this house would rather be a fish'.

Towering head and shoulders above all other '*divertissements*' in Cambridge was the Rex Cinema, which, week after week and year after year, performed miracles of double-feature programming of every great movie you ever wished to see. From *Bicycle Thieves* to *Casablanca* to *Les Enfants du Paradis* to *Horse Feathers* to *Birth of a Nation* and back again to, yes, MGM's oldest and latest musicals, the Rex Cinema unfailingly whetted the undergraduate movie appetite with uncannily tasty menus. It was there that I saw both *An American in Paris* and *Singin' in the Rain* for the first time, as well as *On the Town* for the 26th and 27th, and the appeal of these three classic musicals, all heavily indebted to the genius and charisma of Gene Kelly, restoked anew my passion for the musical form as the academic year progressed.

It was a far cry from the great Gershwin songs in *An American in Paris* to the clever-pants material required by the Footlights, and I had no idea how to bridge the gap between the two. I quickly realised the bridge was unbuildable. The two shores were too far apart. It was one or the other, or end up in the river. What mattered right now was to write something, anything, to justify my acceptance into the glittery Footlights Group.

I started to dabble with the idea of putting my own melodies to the lyrics I was writing. It was a stumbling and laborious process at first, but interesting in that, whenever I attempted to write both words and music, I found them arriving together. The sound and feel of one led to the sound and feel of the other, progressing them simultaneously, a very different process from being given a melody and putting a lyric to it and, in many ways, a more perilous one creatively. I was flying blind in two different aircraft at once, not sure where I was going, nor of the final destination, and praying that each would land safely in the same place as the other. I have crashed several squadrons of such aircraft between then and now.

I am one of the luckiest people I know, second only perhaps to Ringo Starr. Whenever I have needed a stepping-stone to be placed in my path, to help me keep moving forward in my life, some kindly figure in the Department of Fate has always noted my need and promptly dealt with it. A few days after I first met Christopher Pym, the Secretary of the Footlights, he contacted me to suggest that I get in touch with the new Organ Scholar at Clare College, Robin Beaumont, who, apart from being a serious classical musician, also thought he might enjoy slumming in the lower reaches of musical theatre and popular song, and had consequently also asked to join the Footlights.

Robin and I met the following afternoon. A studious and

thoughtful fellow, quiet by nature, with an astute sense of humour, and better-looking in a long-blond-hair and blue-eyed way than one would have thought Organ Scholars at Clare ought to be, he won my immediate respect by playing me two 32-bar songs that took my breath away. Both were so beautifully structured and musically accomplished that I felt I had just met Richard Rodgers's favourite nephew. The question now became whether I could provide Robin with Lorenz Hart's favourite nephew.

I showed Robin two or three of my less awful lyrics which, having just written them, I probably considered to be on a par with the best of Irving Berlin. One usually thinks that the last lyric one has completed is among the most brilliant ever written. It isn't until about the following Monday, when you haven't looked at it for two or three days, that it appears mundane and cliché-ridden.

Since I was probably the only undergraduate in the entire university population of 7,000 who was writing lyrics anyway, Robin's choice of collaborators was probably limited to two at most, and finding the other one would have involved a house-to-house search. Songwriting was not high on the average student's list of priorities, and was never likely to become a subject that could earn you a major degree, except, frankly, in a lesser American university. (I shall resist the temptation of saying in a Frank Loesser American university.) By my reckoning, the last lyricist of any consequence to be at Cambridge had been Lord Byron in 1805, so I had Robin pretty well cornered. We agreed to collaborate, confidently expecting to raise the standard of Footlights songwriting to Broadway levels within a few weeks, thence mounting a direct challenge to *Kiss Me, Kate* and *Guys and Dolls*.

The university year is divided into three terms, each of eight weeks, an annual total of 24 weeks, allowing students the extreme luxury of 28 weeks' holiday a year, which to a man or woman they all fervently believe they fully deserve as a just reward for the minimal amount of effort they have put into their studies. The Footlights' annual programme of entertainment was usually divided into two or three members–only 'smoking concerts' per term, depending on the available amount of performable songs and sketches. From these six or seven 'smokers' was chosen the best two hours of killer material, which would become the famous annual Footlights Revue, performed for two glamorous sold-out weeks at the Arts Theatre at the end of the summer term, during May Week. It was Cambridge's hottest theatre ticket of the year, every year.

For your better understanding of the Cambridge mentality, May Week lasted two weeks, and it was in June. The Footlights Revue was rehearsed throughout the most intense period of the Tripos exams which immediately preceded this, and on which our future university lives depended. So it is little wonder that the fame of the Footlighters rarely extended to achievements in the higher reaches of academe.

Robin and I contributed heavily to the 'smokers', held every third Friday upstairs at the Dorothy Café, and swiftly found ourselves caught up not only in the writing but also the performing of the material. My theatre CV up to that point was restricted to my wartime activities presenting glove-puppet shows in the garage of 103, Cannon Lane and telling *Just William* stories to my schoolmates in air-raid shelters. However, based on the old adage that songwriters perform their own songs better than most singers, we ploughed on and became increasingly involved, literally and figuratively, on both sides of the Footlights.

The outside world continued to turn, but Cambridge was another planet, a haven, a heaven, a time capsule sealed off from the real world. Occasionally, outside events of greater or lesser moment would impact on our lives. Greater was the death of King George VI on 6 February 1952, with that last haunting photograph of his gaunt, haggard face seeing his daughter Elizabeth off from London Airport en route to a state visit to Australia and New Zealand. A week later, the 25-year-old Princess would return as Queen Elizabeth II of England, and Empress of all those other places.

A lesser moment, just as memorable, was the glorious gaffe by the most senior BBC radio announcer, John Snagge, informing the world of 'the death in Paris early today of André Gide, the eminent man of French letters'.

It was not surprising that the so-called 'academic year' flew by. After all, three times eight weeks don't add up to much. Multiply *that* by three, and what one blithely calls three years at university turns out to be a mere 17 months. Nineteen months of vacations make up the balance, but at that age it is a balance with which no bone-idle student wishes to take issue.

After our first Footlights Revue, *Tip and Run*, which one would flatter to call average, was nonetheless the usual runaway success at the Arts Theatre and elevated its dozen or so less-than-talented performers to rock-star celebrity status for two brief weeks, Robin Beaumont and I sat down and racked what was left of our brains to see whether we could write the sort of songs we wanted to write and make them fit into the Footlights format. And we knew as we sat there that we couldn't. Ever the master of the stupid and obvious remark, I said profoundly, 'Revue is revue and musicals are musicals. You'd need two separate societies.'

And there, of course, staring us in the face was the answer. The next day I got permission from the university authorities to form The Cambridge University Musical Comedy Club. The summer vacation had already started, 17 weeks of unearned rest, and I promised Robin that as soon as we returned in October I would assemble the creative and production personnel for the as yet unknown musical that we were going to write.

I thought about nothing else all summer. I was fully aware from the outset that I was lowering myself into pretty deep waters with regard to the time commitments I would have to make. I had also just been made Secretary of the Footlights for the coming year – the Christopher Pym of my generation, so to speak – and I knew that that alone was as major a time-consuming extra-curricular responsibility as I should take on, without the added lunacy of creating a completely new university society, forming a committee and then writing, producing, casting and financing a brand-new, full-length, original musical comedy.

So as not to make things too easy for myself, I also took on the additional chore of writing the weekly 'Cambridge Diary' column for *Varsity* newspaper, which was now edited by an arrogant young man called Michael Winner, who was studying Law at Downing College, the perfect training for a future film director and food critic. Michael had a bizarre habit of promenading brazenly up and down King's Parade dressed in a velvet jacket and brocade waistcoat, carrying a gold-topped ebony cane. He lacked only a banner proclaiming 'Oscar Wilde Lives'. The young Winner, then as now, constantly walked the narrow line between outrageousness and obnoxiousness and, then as now, somehow always managed to get away with it – a rather neat lifelong trick. We are still good friends today, 50 years on.

True to the Jabberwocky Cambridge mentality, the Tripos (three-part) exams take place in two parts in Years One and Three of one's time there, so mercifully I had the comparatively peaceful Year Two in which to prepare for and deal with some of our potential musical headaches. Sensing I needed urgent help, the ever-dependable Department of Fate promptly intervened by delivering into the Footlights Membership and my life a brilliant young Classics and Philosophy scholar from St John's College, one Frederic Raphael.

Freddie was a heaven-sent gift. He had a massive intellect, a swift and acid wit, and a Gale Force Ten sense of humour. He was an ardent admirer of W Somerset Maugham, whom he called Willy, and was himself planning to become a career novelist. Freddie was the first person I had met of my own generation who, like myself, was seriously intending to travel the perilous path of writing for a living, which made me admire him even more. We immediately became fast friends. Here was the third corner of the triangle that Robin Beaumont and I had been seeking. Beyond contributing superior material to the Footlights smokers, Freddie agreed to collaborate with us on the first offering of the newborn Musical Comedy Club a year hence. I had developed a story outline for the project, built around the popular and glamorous Monte Carlo car rally. It was agreed that we would write the show during next summer's long vacation, and rehearse and open it in October and November. Freddie would write the book, and Robin and I the score.

I then scoured the university to find a business manager-cum-fundraiser. Once again, the Department of Fate placed him right under my nose. The Footlights membership was divided into two categories, active and social. One of the latter, a Jesus College man called Derek Taylor, inexplicably studying History for a career in hotel management, eagerly offered to take on the thankless task of raising and managing our finances. Enthusiasm being the prime requirement in all areas of our amateur endeavour, I accepted gratefully, and on that promising four-cornered foundation we constructed our dream.

Life in the Footlights provided a certain amount of high adventure. Apart from the members-only smokers, a group of us would occasionally provide a cabaret at major dinner-dance celebrations. One cold Saturday night, I was returning to Caius after such a party at around 4.00am, keeping a sharp eye out for marauding Proctors and Bulldogs. It was pretty safe at this hour. They usually gave up between midnight and 1.00am. There was no known college 'late pass' to accommodate 4.00am, so, in the best traditions of Colditz, every college had its secret entrances for the when-needed high-risk sport of 'climbing in'. Caius currently had two, one a simple first-floor window tucked away down Trinity Lane, safe from all but the most prying Proctorial eyes; the other was a highly dangerous last resort and therefore seldom used *Where Eagles Dare* proposition on the dangerously exposed third floor of the college's Gothic Tower facing down King's Parade, popularly known as 'The North Face'.

I made my way to Trinity Lane, clambered up to the first-floor window and found to my horror that it was firmly locked. The tenant of the rooms, I later learned, was away on a long-weekend 'exeat'. I walked round to the Tower, and squinted up at what from that angle looked like the Empire State Building. There was an additional hazard. I was wearing a big duffle coat to protect me from the winter chill. In each of the duffle coat's two big pockets was a magnum of champagne, a gift from the grateful gathering we had entertained earlier in the evening.

I considered my bleak options – to abandon the champagne, to stay where I was and be arrested, or to climb The North Face and be killed. Only one of the three options gave me any chance of coming out ahead, so, with that rare surge of courage that only 4.00am carries with it, I started to clamber up the Tower.

I learned a lot on my way up the drainpipe to the first floor. One, magnums of champagne are heavy. Two, duffle coats are cumbersome garments in such circumstances. Three, frosted drainpipes should never be climbed in sub-zero January temperatures without the benefit of a pair of warm gloves. Four, trying to overcome the combined hazards presented by One, Two and Three above at four o'clock in the morning is a severe test of both character and sanity.

I hauled myself crosswise up on to the first-floor window ledge. I had already decided to go back down. But I couldn't. The ledge itself was in the way, and the weight and bulk of the two magnums swinging around in my duffle-coat pockets made descending even more hazardous than ascending. Like a bad vaudeville act, I had nowhere to go but up. Halfway up stage two of my kamikaze ascent of the drainpipe, acrophobia set in as I realised I had passed the point of no return. When I finally dragged myself up to the second-floor window ledge and considered leaving the champagne there in order to save my life, bloody-mindedness set in to an equal degree. How could I ever reclaim the two giant bottles? How could I explain how they got there? Who would believe me? Shivering with both cold and fear, I undertook the third and last lap of my insane journey.

Edmund Hillary and Sherpa Tensing at the summit of Mount
Everest a few months later were probably the first humans ever to
share the pulsating ecstasy of achievement that I experienced as I
finally arrived on that top window ledge, body and mind and
champagne magnums barely intact. Triumphantly, I raised my
hand to open the window. It was locked. I looked at my watch. It
was 4.30am. I tapped on the window. I hammered on the
window. Nothing. There was no one there. I later learned that by
a cruel coincidence the occupant of these rooms was also away on
an exeat. I considered breaking the window, launching one of my
magnums against it like the Queen launching a battleship. While
that would solve my immediate problem, I was concerned about
the repercussions. How would I, should I, could I, as Secretary of
the Footlights, a senior officer of a respected university society,
explain the bizarre circumstances leading up to this
monumentally embarrassing moment? I decided to wait.

During the following four hours, perched on the slippery edge
of a 9-inch ledge seemingly some 2,000 feet above the uninviting
concrete of King's Parade, a number of strange but important
questions crossed my near-frozen mind. For example, what
lunatics had ever proposed and endorsed this insane stratospheric
spot as convenient for climbing in in the first place? And, if
somebody didn't arrive soon, how would anyone explain what
my frozen-stiff corpse was doing when found up here? Or worse,
down there? What would the distinguished university authorities
tell my stunned and bereaved mother? As one of the few if any
Cambridge graduates ever to have witnessed a winter sunrise
from outside the top window ledge of the Caius College Tower
and survived, I can tell you that sitting out there for what seemed
like the greater part of January makes you look at a lot of things
with a new perspective.

At long, long, long, long last, at around 8.15am, the door to the
room behind me opened, and a lady entered and screamed. She
ran across the room and let me in. Her name was Mrs Johnson.
Ada. I have never forgotten it. She was the cleaning lady for these

rooms, known as a 'bedder'. Knowing the rooms, she knew the circumstances. I shiveringly stammered my frosted-breath thanks. She apologised profusely for something that wasn't in any way her fault. It was most unusual for a bedder to be in college on a Sunday morning. Mrs J, Ada, my new best friend in the entire world, just happened to be passing, and had dropped in to leave some laundry for her 'gentleman'. On such mundane matters does the fate of the world revolve. Ada went home that Sunday morning with a magnum of Moët et Chandon champagne, already well chilled.

The no-exams university year swiftly came and went. The Footlights Revue for the two weeks in June that were called May Week was this time entitled *Cabbages and Kings*, and was the usual sell-out smash, with the audiences as ecstatic as ever. My theory about this was that the university as a whole was so relieved that lectures and studying and exams were at an end for the next four months that they would have given a standing ovation to a baby's funeral.

Freddie, Robin and I all set off in different directions to complete our musical. Freddie and I had agreed the detailed storyline and the characters, and had already lined up such key figures as the set designer, the choreographer and the costume lady for our return at the start of October. I knew exactly where all the songs in the show should go, and who would sing what. This came easily to me. It was my inheritance from the several hundred hours I had devoted to gazing at MGM musical screens, as well as studying how the songs drove the plot forward in the handful of great stage musicals I had so far seen in the West End – *Oklahoma, Carousel, Kiss Me, Kate, The King and I, South Pacific* and *Guys and Dolls*. If you're gonna go to musical theatre college, those six shows are pretty damn good colleges to go to.

Cole Porter was famous for the legendary style in which he wrote his theatre scores. He would charter an ultra-glamorous yacht in the Mediterranean, line its walls with priceless Impressionist paintings from his own private collection, invite half-a-dozen glitteringly witty guests who would have put the Algonquin Round Table to shame (unless the half-dozen guests happened to *be* members of the Algonquin Round Table, which they sometimes were), set sail and return to port five weeks later with a hit show containing something like 11 all-time classic songs. Those were the days.

I decided to experiment with the low-budget version of the same principle. Not having Cole Porter's millions at my disposal, and no Impressionist paintings of any consequence lying about the place, I organised myself an unlikely summer job in Canada, working with a provincial theatre repertory group called The Straw Hat Players. Robin Beaumont came along for the ride, and was sufficiently affluent, though still lacking the requisite collection of Impressionists, to pay his own way. We flew from London to Toronto via Gander in Newfoundland on the cheapest airline known to man – Flying Tiger Airlines – in an old converted World War Two bomber called a Lockheed Hudson.

'Converted' is a euphemism. To me, the plane still looked as though we were on a bombing raid. We flew at an altitude of about 50 feet, Bleriot-style, and door-to-door it took about 23 hours.

I first spent three wonderful weeks of reunion with sister Pat and Harcourt Eldon Greening Bull, who was by now a well-to-do, golf-playing stockbroker in downtown Hamilton. This does not mean he was playing golf in downtown Hamilton. It means he was a downtown stockbroker who played golf. Pat and Harkie had two children, my five-year-old goddaughter Leslie-Anne and her three-year-old baby brother Richard. I was now known as 'Uncle Leslie'. I found this infinitely depressing, and suddenly I saw my life slipping away.

Then Harcourt Etcetera hit a home run. He introduced me to the editor of the local newspaper, the *Hamilton Spectator*, a delightful man called Tom Farmer who, out of the blue, offered me a second job writing freelance articles for the paper at a princely $10 a pop, which to me was big bucks! Suddenly, both my intended careers were on parallel tracks – I was about to be both a journalist *and* a songwriter. Across the summer, I wrote 15–20 movie and theatre reviews and humorous articles for Tom Farmer and, God love him, he published them all. Though not by Cole Porter standards, I was rich. More importantly, I was now a published and professional journalist.

The Straw Hat Players were headquartered in a small Ontario lakeside town called Port Carling, and performed their plays both there and in a nearby town called Gravenhurst. I had a nondescript dogsbody job dignified with some grand-sounding and meaningless title like 'Assistant Supervising Production Co-ordinator', which made me feel like an unemployed general in the Moravian Army.

The big surprise was that the work The Straw Hat Players produced was of such high quality. They put on an impressive, wide-ranging programme of superior modern plays, finely staged by two significant London Old Vic directors, Pierre Lefevre and John Blatchley, and cast with well-known actors from Toronto.

Superior modern plays... all except one. As a grandstand finale to the season, for reasons that no one would explain and certainly no one would claim responsibility, The Straw Hat Players' final offering was nothing less than a world première, puffed up for local publicity purposes as being 'in association with Laurence Olivier Productions', though no glimmer of the great thespian was forthcoming other than the use of his name. The prize piece turned out to be an excruciatingly depressing Irish play of interminable length, three hours plus of unremitting gloom, entitled *The Unhallowed*, a jolly little tale, the turgid tragedy of a defrocked Catholic priest accused and condemned for indulging in a little after-hours necrophilia with the corpse of his dead sister – 'something,' as I observed at the time, 'for all the family'. Certainly, it was a piece with little potential as a West End musical. After 200 minutes of remorseless misery, the woebegone priest has his best idea of the evening, which is to commit suicide, one of the lighter moments of the play, and the first to earn a ripple of applause from the stunned audience. The play ends on another high note, the priest's funeral, with a quartet of Irish villagers singing the 'Dies Irae' as they lift his coffin and carry him off to his grave.

On the first night, the assistant stage manager, the company manager, myself and some man I had never seen before, all duly attired as Irish villagers and singing 'Dies irae, dies illa', in appropriately mournful bass voices, trooped on as rehearsed to pick up the coffin and carry the poor bastard actor playing the priest away to his final resting place. As we lifted the coffin up on to our shoulders, the bottom fell out of it, and the dead priest crashed back down on to the stage floor.

What would you have done? Here's what happened. The curtain stayed up, the quartet of Irish village idiots, still singing 'Dies irae', trooped out with the empty coffin, as though nothing had happened, and our prone star actor started to shake with silent laughter as our size-18 lady stage manager, in full view of a capacity audience, ran on stage and said to the dead priest, 'Are you all right, George?' Slow curtain. Pandemonium.

I have seen many great show-stopping moments of theatre around the world in my lifetime, but I have never ever seen and heard a laugh as heartfelt and prolonged as the tidal wave of mirth that now engulfed that tiny auditorium. And I immediately realised why. Who in theatre history before or since has ever had the gall to spend three hours setting up one single slapstick sight-gag? They should have kept it in. It was the only worthwhile thing in the play.

Robin Beaumont and I composed our score amid this madness, and working together each day was a soothing contrast to the ongoing chaos surrounding *The Unhallowed*. My proposal to the doomed play's director that we retain the funny ending was rejected out-of-hand, even though it provided the only glimmer of light in the local newspaper review, which otherwise read, appropriately enough, like an obituary. The director's attempts to 'fix' the unfixable play were like trying to raise the

Titanic with a rowing boat and a Black & Decker toolkit. And how wonderfully appropriate that we opened, and closed, in a place called Gravenhurst.

By the end of our stay, Robin and I had comfortably completed the 14 songs of the score to our first musical. Excited as school kids with their first football, we couldn't wait to get back to Cambridge and start rehearsals. We even tried to take the terrifying Flying Tiger's homeward transatlantic flight in our stride, but Lindbergh's 1927 crossing was easier, and probably faster, too.

Back in London, typical of the top-flight professional that he would soon become, Freddie Raphael had completed a fast and funny libretto to the show, which we entitled *Lady at the Wheel*. Back in England, he and I welded the book and score together and agreed that he would direct the play and I the musical numbers. Neither of us had ever attempted anything remotely like this before – zero experience – but that's what it is to be young. It was shaping up to be a great adventure. It was also shaping up to be a destructive device of nuclear potential.

If you want to talk about the audacity of youth, or the blind leading the blind, let me tell you how we financed the show. Our financial wizard, Derek Taylor, had put together an impressive souvenir programme, selling many pages of advertising to local Cambridge businesses, thereby raising enough money to pay for our pre-production start-up costs. The actual budget of the production itself was structured in a unique fashion that would have had any established West End producer reaching for the old-fashioned open-blade cut-throat razor. We calculated the budget at exactly the absolute financial capacity of the Arts Theatre. In other words, if we sold every ticket for every performance for the eight performances of our one-week stay, we would break even, pay all our bills and owe no one a penny. Anything less than that didn't look good. The price of every unsold ticket would become part of our debt. How we would deal with that was never discussed, because we took on a blind-eye 'I do not see the signal' attitude of Nelsonian defiance and resolve. We even dug up an old wartime London Blitz favourite for the rehearsal room: 'There is no depression in this house; and we are not interested in the possibilities of defeat. They do not exist.'

The venerable manager of the Arts Theatre, Mr Norman Higgins, to my surprise and delight, indulged our radical avant-garde views on theatre economics with mingled resignation and alarm, although I did notice during the ensuing weeks that his famously ginger hair was fading rapidly to grey. But to his eternal credit, at the risk of his eternal debit, he let us get on with it, and ultimately get away with it.

I surveyed the academic year that lay ahead, my last at Cambridge. The Department of Fate had the heat turned up to full. In addition to the final casting and rehearsals of *Lady at the Wheel* and running the Musical Comedy Club, of which I was President, I had also been made President of the Footlights, which meant I would be assembling, co-writing, directing and performing in the May Week Revue, again at the Arts Theatre, in something less than six months from now. On top of all this was the small matter of the final Tripos exams, which would also be looming at the same time.

Right now, that would have to wait. Putting on two complete full-length original musical shows within six months doesn't leave time to think about a great deal else. I took refuge behind another great pompous William James quote to defend myself against critics, doubters and the feeble-hearted: 'It is only by risking our persons from one hour to another that we live at all!' ... Gulp! (The gulp is mine!)

Caius College generously allocated me a splendid set of rooms for my final year. Presidents of university societies are traditionally accorded privileged accommodation, but mine was particularly spacious and elegant, with a living room large enough to absorb the thoughtfully provided grand piano. Exactly 30 years before, these had been the rooms of the great British sprinter Harold

Abrahams, who won the 100 metres gold medal at the 1924 Paris Olympics, immortalised in the Oscar-winning film *Chariots of Fire*. Once again, I felt that overpoweringly strong sense of the continuity of the generations in this place, and it reinforced the desire to do great things. Winning an Olympic gold medal, I was reasonably certain, would not be one of them.

Lady at the Wheel opened triumphantly five weeks later, exceeding everyone's wildest expectations. The *Cambridge Daily News* review was ecstatic, calling the show 'the Everest of university theatre productions'. We proceeded to sell every single ticket at every single performance, removing the sword of Damocles from above all our heads and causing Derek Taylor, drunk with power, to announce triumphantly on the last night that, if his calculations were correct, we would actually show a profit of eight shillings and sixpence. We considered blowing the whole amount on a Chinese dinner, but decided against it, for fear of being accused of professionalism, and we gave it to the Red Cross instead.

It was a fabulous experience for many reasons. Newspaper columnists, magazine photographers, BBC and West End theatre producers descended on Cambridge in force, to feed on the little fishes like sharks in a David Attenborough documentary. Freddie, Robin and I realised for the first time that there was a real possibility of life after Cambridge. Julie Wilson, the glamorous American musical star of both *Kiss Me, Kate* and *South Pacific*, whom I had met and befriended in London, came up for the final performance. There was serious talk of transferring the show to the West End, where the British Musical had been considered far less fun than the British Museum for about a decade, until the recent arrival of Sandy Wilson's delicious 1920s pastiche *The Boy Friend*. But we all knew it was not a practical proposition to try to transfer a hotch-potch of decadent university students to the even more decadent bright lights of Shaftesbury Avenue, and so that alluring prospect was quietly allowed to die.

My own two-fold contribution to the all-important aspect of casting *Lady at the Wheel* was quite unplanned but ultimately fruitful, in more ways than one. I had first spotted the bountiful and sexy blonde who was to become our choreographer over a year before, be-bopping her admirably appointed chassis to a standstill at a dinner-dance at the Dorothy Café. I later learned that she was not only a good dancer but also a dancing teacher, so her qualifications, like everything else about her, were ample. She was extremely pretty, known in Cambridge as Marilyn Monroe, and indeed an impressive lookalike. The Cambridge Marilyn was called Hazel. She was the daughter of a wealthy local farmer. She drove around town in a convertible two-seater MG, the second car of that make destined to further my musical career. And, when rehearsals began, so did Hazel and I, a sweet and tender romance that would last the rest of my time at Cambridge.

My second contribution to the cast, other than the Wealthy Farmer's Daughter, was the Famous Politician's Daughter. But more of that later.

The success of *Lady at the Wheel* established beyond doubt the credibility of the Musical Comedy Club. The following year, others went on to create a worthy Cambridge musical version of Max Beerbohm's wondrous Oxford fantasy *Zuleika Dobson*, which was good enough to merit a subsequent West End production. After that, the usual paucity of would-be Rodgers and Harts sent the club into decline, and Cambridge is still waiting for its next Lord Byron.

It was shaping up to be a vintage Footlights year. We had good material, and we knew it. Good performers, too, with diversified musical and comedic abilities. As far as Norman Higgins, the Cerberus guarding the Arts Theatre, was concerned, we were walking on water. I noticed that the colour of Norman's hair was subtly reverting from its *Lady at the Wheel* grey to a vibrant new orange, and one day in his office I noticed on his bookshelf a large jar of an exotic ladies' hair-tint product labelled Sable Mink Flame. I said nothing, but I allowed my mind to boggle.

Freddie Raphael delivered the Footlights Revue's *coup de foudre* (which at the time was fractured French for 'lawnmower') on the second Monday of rehearsals. Two nights before, watching the annual St John's College Revue, he had seen a 19-year-old freshman perform a dazzling satire about a day in the life of the BBC. It had stopped the show. Freddie said it would fit into our show like a glove. The 19-year-old's name was Jonathan Miller.

Out of the Blue, I have to say, was a sensational show, full of smart, relevant, highly topical and downright funny material, interspersed with sharp satirical songs. And Jonathan Miller was the icing on the cake. An instant star in any company at any level. The show took off like a moon rocket. Thanks to *Lady at the Wheel*, London was already vaguely aware that there was something going on in Cambridge, but this really was *something!* Before the end of the first week, we had a firm offer to play the show in Oxford, and two offers to transfer to the West End. And this time it was possible. The academic year and, for most of us, our undergraduate careers were over. The timing was perfect. So we did it.

No one could remember when, if ever, any theatrical production from Cambridge had ever made the perilous journey to The Other Place, such was the all-pervading rivalry between the two universities. But there we were for one heavenly week at The Playhouse Theatre and, to the credit of the Dark Blues, *Out of the Blue* was received, albeit grudgingly, with the same acclaim as in Cambridge. Oxford were generous hosts, and the Footlighters were royally treated and lavishly feted.

On a visit to Brasenose College, I was reunited with an old friend from my Army Officer Training School days, a lovely Australian fellow called John Piper. We had a hilarious reminiscing dinner together, and he introduced me to a fellow Australian pupil and friend from Geelong Grammar School in Melbourne with these visionary words: 'Leslie, I want you to meet my friend Rupert Murdoch. He's going to take over the world.' Rupert, like us, was 22 years old.

The Phoenix Theatre in London, for three unforgettable weeks, was home to the first Footlights Revue ever to transfer to the West End. *Out of the Blue* was received there as ecstatically as it had been in Oxford and Cambridge, and was a bona fide hit, the theatre manager informed me, that could easily have run for a year. But three golden weeks were good enough for us; (a) because we were amateurs, and (b) because we were bursting to get started at long last on our lives and careers, even though, for the most part, we had no idea what they were destined to be. I most certainly didn't. I knew what I wanted, and I also knew that I would have to wait for the Department of Fate to show me how to get it.

Jonathan Miller was the talk of the town, being hailed as England's answer to the revered Danny Kaye, whom he strongly resembled. His picture was in every magazine in England. Amused by his instant stardom, he took it all in his 19-year-old stride, then coolly turned his back on it to return to Cambridge to study Philosophy and Medicine. He would re-emerge in the theatre five years later at the Edinburgh Festival in the *Gone with the Wind* of intimate revues, *Beyond the Fringe*, making up a rare quartet with Peter Cook, Alan Bennett and Dudley Moore, two each from Oxford and Cambridge.

The Department of Fate telephoned me exactly three days after the London opening of *Out of the Blue*. This, too, was out of the blue. The call came from the Shaftesbury Avenue office of HM Tennant, London's leading theatre producers, asking me whether I would like to work with Beatrice Lillie, who was about to bring her hit Broadway show *An Evening with Beatrice Lillie* to London. Though I had never seen her, I well knew the name Beatrice Lillie, which, for some reason, I associated with Noël Coward. She had been a star for as long as he had, and maybe longer. I told the Department of Fate 'Yes'.

At three o'clock the next afternoon, I squeezed into the minuscule elevator, comfortable for one, suggestive for two, which connected the box-office vestibule of the Globe Theatre in

Shaftesbury Avenue with HM Tennant's executive offices above. I was ushered into the beautiful lair of the super-suave supremo of the organisation, Hugh 'Binkie' Beaumont, a man of rare charm and smooth-beyond-smooth manner. I was hoping I was going to be asked to contribute a song or a sketch to Miss Lillie's show, possibly something from *Out of the Blue*. Not at all. Miss Lillie, it appeared, was already in London. She had seen *Out of the Blue* two nights before. She wanted to know whether I would be interested in being her leading man playing opposite her in *An Evening with...* If so, a meeting with her had been arranged at her apartment at 55, Park Lane at five o'clock that afternoon.

55, Park Lane is admirably situated next door to the Dorchester Hotel. The door to the apartment was opened by an enormously overweight young man who smilingly introduced himself as John Philip. 'I'm Bea's manager. Come on in.'

He led me through to the predominantly green living room. On the wall on the left as we entered was a stunning Modigliani portrait of a boy with bright-orange hair. I mentally named it *Norman Higgins as a Child*. Sitting facing it, in a huge green armchair, was a tiny, chic woman with one of the best smiles I have ever seen. On the back of her head, encasing her hair and accentuating her sharp profile, was a red silk pillbox hat, her trademark.

She greeted me warmly, sweetly. I felt instantly at home. Within minutes, I was enraptured by the magic spell she cast. And God, she was funny. Everything she said, and the way she said it, had an electric undercurrent of wit and style, as though she understood things in a way the rest of the world didn't... which I was soon to realise was exactly the case.

My whole world changed that day, at that meeting. Bea, which she instantly insisted I call her, explained why I was there. Her Broadway leading man, a well-known British stage and screen actor named Reginald Gardiner, could not come to London for the bizarre yet readily understandable reason that he owed an English ex-wife 28 years of back alimony. Bea had seen and liked

Out of the Blue, was aware that apart from writing for and performing in it I had also directed it, and would I therefore like to write, perform and direct myself in three new pieces of material, plus play in a couple of sketches with her and also compère *An Evening with Beatrice Lillie*? The Godfather Don Corleone wasn't the first to 'make him an offer he can't refuse'. It was Bea Lillie.

By the end of the next day, I had acquired an agent. Binkie Beaumont arranged for me to meet one of the senior directors of the mighty MCA Agency in Piccadilly, Robin Fox, the only man in London who was even smoother than Binkie. The two of them in a room together would have made the place an oil slick. Robin was a Force Ten charmer as well, a killer with the ladies, the epitome of the dashingly handsome English cad. He appointed as my agent the wondrously named Jock Jacobsen. Jock was a sweet little man, and a good agent, but even he didn't know how he arrived at that name. But it didn't stop him from making a healthy deal on my behalf, for considerably more money than I could have hoped for.

That summer, people started getting married. Freddie Raphael had already married his lovely long-term girlfriend Betty, who was known inexplicably as Beetle. That lasted. Lovely Hazel, the farmer's daughter, a few months after our departure from Cambridge, surprisingly married my Vice-President of the Footlights, David Conyers, who must have stepped smartly into my shoes when I left, for which I cannot blame him. David was a bluff, pleasant, pink-cheeked fellow, a dead ringer for the young Nigel Bruce, the actor who played Doctor Watson to Basil Rathbone's Sherlock Holmes in all those movies. Hazel and David were an odd pairing, and that one, sadly, *didn't* last.

I was distressed, not to say aghast, to see so many of my young contemporaries rushing headlong like lemmings over the matrimonial cliff. I had long since firmly made up my mind not to marry 'til I was 35, calculating that I would need a dozen years or so to establish myself in the career I wanted. I did not delude myself. I knew full well that the profession I had chosen was a particularly perilous one that definitely came without a parachute.

The previous summer, in London, I had met and become friends with an extremely attractive, humorous, scatty, upmarket girl called Julie Hamilton. She was 19. She was a blue-eyed blonde, and couldn't make up her mind whether she wanted to become an actress or a photographer. Her mother was a successful screenwriter and film director called Jill Craigie, who was married to the celebrated and extremely left-wing Labour MP Michael Foot. And Julie was the Famous Politician's Daughter who became my afore-mentioned second contribution to the cast of *Lady at the Wheel*. She was adorable and funny as the slightly crazy third leading girl in the show. Now, back in London, after my insane final year at Cambridge and the grandstand West End Footlights finale, Julie and I became closer, spending every day together.

Michael Foot was one of four brilliant sons of an equally brilliant father, Isaac Foot, a celebrated leading Liberal politician of the 1920s. What was unique about the four sons, Hugh, Dingle, Michael and John, known as The Four Feet, is that all four, in their university days, had been President of the Union, three at Oxford and one at Cambridge, a family achievement never equalled, and unlikely ever to be bettered.

Isaac Foot had a large, rambling country house in Truro, Cornwall, and Julie now suggested that it would be fun to drive down to Cornwall and spend a part of the summer there before I started rehearsals with Bea.

Cornwall was as seductive as always, but London was calling. I had new stuff to write, and more still to learn. Above all, I had to come to terms with the awesome thought of sharing a West End stage with a Broadway legend, a star for 40 years, known and loved throughout showbusiness as 'the funniest woman in the world'. And, having had some time to allow the enormity of my undertaking to sink in, I had landed a fabulous job I wasn't sure I wanted.

I never had any desire to be a performer. It wasn't part of my game plan. Almost any out-of-work actor you could name was better qualified for this job than I was. My total experience of performing had been the three amateur Footlights Revues and a few cabaret shows. And now here I was facing the daunting prospect of going toe-to-toe with the most lethally talented and brilliantly funny singer-comedienne of the 20th century! I suppose I can only thank my blind amateur naivety, my innate stupidity and my lucky stars that I wasn't scared to death by the mere thought of the massive presumption of accepting this amazing and unlikely opportunity that a crazed Department of Fate had placed in my path. But deep down I knew I had to go along with what could only be a fabulous ride. It turned out to be much more.

Who can explain how or why the truly great miracles of our lives happen? But in Bea Lillie, nearly 40 years my senior, I found a kindred spirit, the first of my life, a wondrous and loving friend, and the fairy godmother of my dreams. Bea's only son, Bobby, otherwise Sir Robert Peel, the last of many generations of that name, had been killed in the war at the age of 23, the age I now was, a decade before. Suffice to say that she adopted me, Auntie Mame style, and became the guardian angel of my young life. My debt to her is beyond calculating.

From the first day of rehearsals, I stepped into a new, sophisticated West End theatrical world in which everyone's name was 'Daaaahling'. Our director was a delightfully morose-looking camp choreographer called Billy Chappell, who looked like a cross between a swish basset-hound and a miniature Fernandel, the comedic French screen actor. Billy had a great sense of impending-doom humour, and was a fully paid-up member of the HM Tennant hierarchy.

Binkie Beaumont's partner at the top end of the organisation was the slightly sinister John Perry. In the first week, they invited me for a house-party weekend to their country house in Cambridgeshire called 'Pinkingtons'. I found out from our handsome and heterosexual young company manager, Andrew Broughton, that Pinkingtons was popularly known in the theatre community as 'Pinchingbums'. Though I couldn't know if this was true or not, I declined the invitation with thanks.

Bea was on my case from the beginning, making sure I was properly introduced to life in London. Well as I knew the city, I had never lived there. Bea was like The Good Fairy Glinda in *The Wizard of Oz*. Four or maybe five times a week, we lunched or dined at her favourite restaurant, Le Caprice in Arlington Street, a few yards down from The Ritz Hotel and, several weeks before I would need it when the show opened in London, she found me a great little apartment about 25 yards away at the quiet dead end of the street, beside Arlington House.

The Caprice lunches and dinners were invariably shared by the same quartet, essentially the cast of the show-to-be. There was Bea, myself, the vastly overweight John Philip, whose bulk was easily explained by the prodigious quantities of food he ordered and vacuumed up at every opportunity, and finally Bea's old friend, New York actress Constance Carpenter, a charming, kindly and extremely well-preserved, stiff-haired blonde of advanced years, whose good looks were embalmed in a mask of make-up so thick it gave her the appearance of a plaster-cast prototype of an extremely old children's doll.

Rehearsals were easy, and mainly for my benefit. Bea, Connie and John already knew the show inside out and backwards, having performed it hundreds of times on Broadway. I had to learn the two new solo pieces I had written for myself, plus the two Act openers that would bring Bea on. I also shared a couple of sketches with her and the others, including the famous old tongue-twister in which Bea came into a department store to order two-dozen double damask dinner napkins, and I played the well-meaning idiot shop assistant who verbally screwed it all up.

During the weeks before we went out on tour, I stayed with the Foot family at their lovely and massively book-laden house on Rosslyn Hill in Hampstead, only a few hundred yards away from my former school. Michael Foot, plainly well on track to emulate his father Isaac, was the leading light of the left of the left-wing Tribune Group, named after the weekly journal he edited. I was amazed by the constant stream of major Labour Party figures like Aneurin Bevan and Ian Mikardo to be seen regularly wandering through the house, faces so famous they were the subject of everyday newspaper cartoons. We all played snooker together.

Suddenly, out of nowhere, Bea and I were up in Liverpool and the show was on. I stood in the wings on the first night, as Bea's two great New York pianists, Eadie and Rack, played their masterly four-handed overture medley of her famous Noël Coward and Irving Berlin songs and I wondered what the hell I was doing there. I felt an absolute sham, doing this jammy job that would better belong to someone else. I was supposedly going to be a writer, wasn't I? Not a song-and-dance man. For a few moments, I hated both myself and the show, then the music stopped, I was on stage and promptly forgot all about it.

The show went well, the legions of Lillie fans turned out to see her, the press loved it and were even kind to me. Same thing in Glasgow and Edinburgh and, before you could blink, we were back in London, at the very same Globe Theatre, which was to be our home for the next year, where just a few weeks ago I had first ascended in the minuscule elevator to meet the great Binkie Beaumont, wunderkind of the West End and proprietor of Pinchingbums.

Having successfully negotiated the hazards of the first night and the press, the show settled down into a comfortable run that would carry through to the following spring, to be followed by a national tour. Year one looked good for me financially, but I already knew that I loathed and despised what I was doing. I adored Bea, the unbelievable opportunity she had given me, and everything about her. And it was good for the ego to see one's name prominently displayed on Shaftesbury Avenue. What was wrong was that I absolutely hated performing. I didn't enjoy physically being on stage in front of an audience. I couldn't stand doing the same thing over and over again, every night, week after week, like a performing seal. And I resented not being able to see my friends, who worked by day and were free at night, while I worked at night and was free by day. Above all, I knew that in the past few months, due to heady circumstances beyond my control, the career that I wanted had somehow been shunted into a siding, while the career that I *didn't* want was on the fast track. What to do?

The unlikely answer was provided by a cunning tactical move on the part of London's only Jew with a kilt, Jock Jacobsen, under the supervision, I'm sure, of the Department of Fate. Jock's prime golden client was an affable young singer-comedian named Max Bygraves, who had recently become one of the two or three biggest box-office attractions in British Music Hall. Through Jock, Max and I had met a few weeks before when we were both performing in Liverpool, and I had written and Max had recorded my first-ever published and recorded song, built around his trademark catchphrase 'It's a good idea, son!' This silly little song was about to prove that everything happens for a reason.

Aware of his growing broad-based popular appeal, British Lion Films offered Max his first starring role in a movie, to be based on the title character of a recently popular novel called *Charley Moon*, about a country lad who becomes a big stage star. Not exactly weighed down with originality, it was a natural film vehicle, and Max was the right age and the right type to play it. Jock quickly made the deal and then, bagpipes akimbo, to everyone's surprise, including mine, he boldly proposed to British Lion that I should write both the screenplay and the songs. British Lion, to their credit and my amazement, took the gamble, God love 'em, and made it a 'first-time' movie across the board by signing not only myself but a young first-time director called Guy Hamilton, who would go on to glory as a maker of some of the better James Bond movies.

Now I was in seventh heaven, writing my screenplay and songs by day and doing the show with Bea at night. Weekends, which meant late Saturday night 'til Monday afternoon for theatre folk, were spent at Bea's lovely old Queen Anne house, Peel Fold, on the river at Henley-on-Thames, a tradition that would continue in my life for more than a decade. In private life, Bea was Lady Peel, and Sunday lunch chez Bea was unlike any other on planet Earth. It was an all-star show in its own right, always featuring a sprinkling of Bea's old chums, legendary theatre names like Gladys Cooper, Edith Evans, Dorothy Dickson, Noël Coward, Clifton Webb and Robert Morley, not in the customary white tie and tiaras with which one associated them theatrically, but in civilian clothing, suitably be-tweeded for the setting and the occasion.

After six euphoric weeks, I had completed the first drafts of my first screenplay and my first film song score. The years of watching MGM musicals were paying their first dividend, because I understood the mechanics of musical film structure. I then, in a rare moment of common sense, decided to spread my bets. Rather than risk being thought a smart-ass by trying to do everything myself, I asked Freddie and Robin to collaborate with me on the final script and songs. We had agreed we would collaborate again when the opportunity presented itself, and here it was. I had an end-of-January deadline to deliver everything, in order for Guy Hamilton to be able to start shooting the movie at Shepperton Studios in the late spring. It ended up being a pleasant little film, like the book not overburdened with originality, but nobody got killed, and Robin and I received an Ivor Novello Award for the film's hit song 'Out of Town'.

This was the first of several collaborations with Freddie, but sadly the last with Robin. I always felt that Robin had the musical intelligence and the gift of melody to become an English Richard Rodgers. Unfortunately, he wasn't up for the fray, because some deep-seated intellectual snobbism made him feel that it was beneath him to be writing popular songs. He was particularly averse to Max Bygraves's 'Singalonga' style. I pointed out to him that every ladder had a bottom rung, whereby one reached the higher ones. But Robin was a classicist at heart, a collaborative problem I would face more than once in my life. He gradually faded out of our lives until we never heard from him again. The story could have been so different, and I wish it had been.

Life with Bea, on the other hand, was never dull. In December, we had a week off. We spent Christmas at Peel Fold, then she, John and I went to Paris for five days over New Year. There were many highlights, including New Year's Eve midnight mass at Sacré-Coeur. The next day, Bea and I had a quiet lunch with the goddess Ingrid Bergman, who was starring in the play *Tea and Sympathy* at the Théâtre de Paris. Like the entire male population of the world, I had been in love with Ingrid Bergman throughout the 1940s. After lunch, the three of us went shopping along the Rue de Rivoli, and Ingrid bought me a beautiful pair of soft beige suede gloves. I wore them for 30 years, 'til they disintegrated on my hands.

Daily lunches were at Fouquet's with a young newspaper columnist from the *Herald Tribune* called Art Buchwald, who went on to become ART BUCHWALD. It is remarkable that this dry-humoured, artful gent would continue to write those irreplaceable humorous columns for half a century. Art Gratia Artis. It was at one of these lunches on that wonderful watch-the-world-go-by corner of the Champs-Elysées and Avenue Georges Cinq, with Bea and Art holding forth about which were the most beautiful places in Europe, that Bea said whichever place was the winner was where we would go for the ten-day vacation between the end of the show's London run in the spring and the start of the national tour. After half-an-hour of hilarious repartee, during which nominees were discussed and discarded, it was unanimously agreed that the undisputed winner was Capri.

'So that's where we'll go!' declared Bea with finality. 'There's only one thing,' she added darkly. 'We have to get drunk in Marseilles on the way!'

I looked at her blankly. 'Why?'

'*Now* you know why,' said Bea as the huge aircraft headed straight for the cliff. I held my breath as the plane dipped lower and lower until it hit the choppy water as smoothly as it could under the circumstances. Fortunately, it was a flying-boat. We coasted slowly into the safe harbour of the Marina Grande. My first view of Capri was heart-stoppingly impressive. It was late April 1955.

'Remember, there's nothing to fear,' Bea had reminded us in her infinite wisdom a few hours earlier as we took off from the Solent near Southampton, 'provided you get drunk in Marseilles!' which we had all obediently done during the lunchtime refuelling stopover. 'Drink!' she had said, mysteriously but firmly. 'I'll tell you why later!' So we drank, and she spent the second half of the journey blissfully and immovably asleep on the spiral staircase connecting the two levels of the flying-boat. She awoke five minutes before landing and regaled us with a few chirpy bars of her current favourite Lillie lyric, '*I've got you under my sink...*'

Bea knew Capri well, and everything that was going on there. One morning she pointed down the hill from our dizzyingly high clifftop hotel to a pretty pink villa far below and said, 'Alan Jay Lerner's in there, trying to make a musical out of *Pygmalion*. Poor baby!'

One afternoon, she announced, 'We're having tea with Gracie today.' Gracie was Gracie Fields, Britain's great wartime singing heroine, who had been living in Capri since the war. Gracie owned the famed 'Canzone del Mare' (the Song of the Sea), Capri's most glamorous swimming pool-restaurant-hotspot on the Piccola Marina side of the island, where love came to Noël Coward's Mrs Wentworth-Brewster. It was protected by Emilio Pucci's exotic boutique to the north, disused German World War Two gun emplacements to the east and west (still there in the year 2000) and the sea itself to the south. Gracie lived simply and well with her (I think) fourth husband, a charming Italian ex-electrician called Boris, atop a high rock that towered over the Canzone del Mare. We went up to see her at four o'clock for tea, for all the world as though we were in England. We laughed 'til we cried, and we smiled when she and Bea sang fragments of bygone silly songs.

Gracie seemed both completely content and completely out of place. It was like being in Rochdale-Sulla-Mare, unfettered Lancashire in deepest Italy, except there wasn't an aspidistra on the whole island, and no cheering shiploads of British troops to remind me that this was 'Our Gracie', the great inspirational singing voice of the darkest Dunkirk days of the war, little more than a decade ago, second only to Winston Churchill in British national affection. Our Gracie was a wonder – and she made a bloody good cup of tea!

During the long summer of the national tour of *An Evening with...*, we had two pleasant weeks in Dublin. Bea, like myself, was part Irish. We had supper every evening after the show in the dining room of the Sherborne Hotel on St Stephen's Green. Staying in the hotel was the fabled film director John Huston, who had just completed principal photography on his mighty sea epic *Moby Dick*, starring Gregory Peck as Captain Ahab. I assumed he was editing in Dublin.

On the first evening, he saw Bea across the dining room as he entered. He was alone, and asked if he could join us. Now, if there is one thing that John Huston could do better than direct films, it was tell stories. He was a raconteur without equal. For 12 consecutive unforgettable evenings, as we dined together, in his unmistakable, deliberate and distinctive, slow American–Irish drawl, he held us spellbound as he regaled us with a thousand wonderful tales from his endless repertoire.

Only through Bea could experiences like that have befallen me at that age. She was like a magnet to whom the most wonderful people in the world seemed drawn. As indeed was Huston. Bea was as besotted by him as I was. We sat there like a couple of alcoholics, drinking in his magic. Seldom did I ever know her to be as silent as she was during those extraordinary evenings. But it takes a star to know a star, and she willingly gave the tiny stage of our dinner table over to John.

Suddenly, on the second Saturday, he was gone. I never saw or spoke to him again. In a strange way, I didn't need to, having drunk so deep at his Pierian spring. But I think of him every time I see a bottle of 1982 Mouton Rothschild, for which he designed the label. His movies ain't bad either.

We performed *An Evening with Beatrice Lillie* 400 times, which drove me so close to the borders of insanity that I carried my passport at all times. The only thing that stopped me from crossing the border and taking out full citizenship was Bea herself. She would play evil games with me on stage to avoid either of us getting bored. She would bet me she could corpse me (make me break up laughing) during the Double Damask Dinner Napkins sketch. Halfway through it, she would pull terrible faces, with just the upstage half of her incredibly mobile face, and suddenly go cross-eyed, leaving the downstage half looking perfectly normal from the audience's point of view. It was explosively funny, and I would crack up in front of 1,000 people for no apparent reason, causing them to do the same, whereupon Bea would fix them with a stern and unsmiling gaze.

The entire second half of the show was Bea, in all her glory, being wildly funny. The living proof that she never did the same show twice is myself, because I watched every performance she gave during that year, from the wings, from a box, from the stalls, from the circle, stage left, stage right. She was comedic perfection on the move, constantly reinventing herself. As Noël Coward constantly pointed out, she was the funniest woman in the world.

Finally, like a dream, the year of enchantment with Bea was over. The tour ended, and the threat of a return to the real world and a normal life hung heavily in the air. She invited me to return with her to America, to tour *An Evening with...* in Florida and across the United States. I was sorely tempted to go, and maybe I should have. It would have undoubtedly continued to be as fantastic a joy-ride as the year that had just ended. And much as I loved my own mother, Bea and I existed on an altogether different Auntie Mame–Patrick Dennis level of mutual adoration, one of the greatest blessings of my life. Tempting as it was, I didn't go. It was a tough choice, the known versus the unknown but, in the end, my love of writing knocked out my hatred of performing in the fifteenth and final round of that particular title fight. Apart from missing Auntie Bea, I had no regrets. Other than TV talk shows and documentaries and interviews, and a few recordings, I am happy to say I have never performed again. My loss, I assure you, is the world's gain.

So it was back to square one. Once again, I was homeless. With my Aquarian flair for solving any problem in the least practical way known to man, I acquired a pretty apartment in the seaside town of Brighton, facing the glorious rainbow-coloured flowerbeds of Preston Park. For someone seeking a career in the throbbing heart of London, this was a monumentally dumb move, the first of many such idiot manoeuvres dotted across the landscape of my life. The daily commute to London was a 120-mile round trip, absorbing five hours a day, but I bore it stoically because I loved driving my shiny, new white Ford Zephyr convertible. The engine of that car consumed approximately the same proportion of my now-diminished income as the Inland Revenue. My agile mind quickly leaped upon the fact that I needed to earn some money.

My resident guardian angel at the Department of Fate promptly filed this information under Urgent because, the following week, I received a charming letter from a lady called Joyce Briggs, who was Head of the Script Department at Pinewood Studios, offering me a lucrative one-year contract at that esteemed temple of British film production.

Rightly at the time, wrongly in retrospect, I loyally offered half the deal to Freddie Raphael, thinking we would settle in at Pinewood and instantly be hailed as Britain's Billy Wilder and Charlie Brackett. Wrong. I didn't take into account Freddie's own agenda. Even more of an intellectual snob than Robin Beaumont, he had the same attitude to Pinewood as Robin had to Max Bygraves. He had absolutely zero desire to go there. That made me the lowbrow of the group. I would have taken the office, met all the people, especially the hordes of glamorous young starlets who reputedly roamed the Pinewood corridors, and learned as much as I could along the way. Instead, our total Pinewood output for the year was a fast rewrite on a dire low-budget Norman Wisdom comedy and one original screenplay for a film that actually got made.

The producer of that film, Vivian Cox, was a fascinating man, a contract producer at Pinewood who had made a couple of classy films with Alec Guinness, *The Prisoner* and *Father Brown*. Vivian was a Renaissance man, with a spectacular story-so-far past. He had played two international sports for Cambridge and England, knew all 37 Shakespeare plays *by heart*, and had had 'a pretty good war' as a young lieutenant commander in the Royal Navy, accompanying Churchill as an intelligence aide to Washington for his meetings with President Roosevelt in December 1941, when the Japanese bombed Pearl Harbor, and the United States officially entered World War Two, after which FDR 'borrowed' him from Churchill to go and live in the White House for six months, setting up Roosevelt's map rooms. Post-war, he had joined forces with film producer Sidney Box at Pinewood, where they were not surprisingly known as Box and Cox.

The film which Freddie and I wrote for Vivian was intended to be a comedy about Cambridge University. In our story, a clever young Cockney lad – in our imagining the still-baby-faced Richard Attenborough – gets a scholarship to Cambridge, where we follow his subsequent hopefully hilarious adventures. What we ended up with, the film they actually made a year or so later, appeared to be Pinewood's personal apology to Germany for our having won the war. It starred a Teutonically handsome leading German actor, Hardy Kruger, and was directed by a somewhat solemn and serious German director, Wolf Rilla, in a vaguely related but not surprisingly heavier-handed version of what we had written. Every subtle English comedic nuance was lost and, though the final film was far from being a disaster, it became what I can most charitably describe as a romantic non-comedy. Charming and talented as both Hardy and Wolf were, a comedy about U-boats rather than Cambridge might have been more appropriate – *Carry on Torpedoing*. Our humiliation was completed by an embarrassing 'find a name for the movie' competition which provided the eventual stomach-turning title *Bachelor of Hearts*.

Freddie and I were also called in to try to fix an unfixable stage musical called *Jubilee Girl*, which had been co-written, overwritten and underwritten by a ridiculously rich young playboy of our acquaintance. We journeyed down to the Pavilion Theatre in Bournemouth and spent a brave few days struggling to salvage what we could and rewrite what we couldn't. But there's a limit to what you can do with a comedy that isn't funny and a score that you would pay good money never to hear again. The cast was talented, as casts invariably are, but the odds against success were about the same as Butch Cassidy and the Sundance Kid's in the final scene of that movie. The show nonetheless transferred into the West End, to the Victoria Palace Theatre, thanks mainly – if not only – to our rich and untalented friend's big fat chequebook. Fittingly, the show was a big fat flop and, like the noble Queen after whom the theatre was named had done on the Isle of Wight in January 1901, it quietly died.

We still had hopes that *Lady at the Wheel* might resurface in the West End. Various proposals were floated, only to gasp briefly for air and sink without trace, par for the course, I was to learn, for that exercise in perpetual frustration known as 'putting on a musical'. The show was on and off half-a-dozen times. What had been hot and unobtainable in Cambridge was hot no longer because it was available in London. So, while Freddie wrote a novel, I wrote the book, music and lyrics for a new musical called *The Boy on the Corner*, intended as a stage vehicle for Max Bygraves, who agreed to star in it. Producer Bernard Delfont gave us the London Hippodrome as a theatre and the multi-talented Wendy Toye as director and choreographer. Everybody loved the score, but, 12 good songs and as many months later, shadowy figures around the producer started to express what I regarded as unneeded and hysterical concern over what they saw as the show's racy, but in actuality mild, anti-Russian political content. Most of the world was nervous about Russia at that time, as the Cold War got chillier, but that shouldn't have been allowed to influence innocuous theatrical satire. If anything, it should have encouraged it. But it didn't. The vapid excuse I was given was that anything controversial might prove damaging to Max's wholesome family image. 'God forbid,' I said, with my finger down my throat.

If I couldn't get *The Boy on the Corner* produced starring the biggest box-office name in England, which Max had now become, I knew it would be pointless to start working my way *down* the ladder of alternatives. So I abandoned the project, which meant that I now had *two* unproduced musicals to my credit, or rather debit. I envisioned a bleak future, starring myself as a broken old man hobbling down Shaftesbury Avenue and St Martin's Lane, peddling a wheelbarrow full of dog-eared scripts and yellowing scores, representing several decades of unproduced shows, the sum total of my pathetic life's work, and finally being buried with them in a pauper's grave in Preston Park, Brighton.

Moving to London was suddenly a necessity. I reluctantly realised and accepted that I had to live nearer the action. Thanks to my ever-dependable Julie, I found a small but cosy pied-à-terre in a big apartment block in St John's Wood, right around the corner from where the Foot family were living in their brand-new house at 32, Abbey Road, a few yards from the famous recording studio. I was happy still to be spending time with them. They had become my surrogate family, and always surrounded themselves with interesting people, not just politicians – people like Wolf Mankowitz, the hot young novella author, whose early books *Make Me an Offer* and *A Kid for Two Farthings* I knew and loved, and Ronald Neame, David Lean's early cinematographer colleague when Lean was an editor, then his producer when Lean turned director for their great Dickens collaborations on *Great Expectations* and *Oliver Twist*. Ronnie was now himself a director, currently filming Mark Twain's *The Million Pound Note*, starring Gregory Peck, out at Pinewood, for which Julie's mother Jill had written the screenplay.

I kept Brighton for weekends, so, with my new central London pad and a highly desirable home-from-home right around the corner in Abbey Road, and not five but one London-to-Brighton commutes per week, I suddenly had the best of both worlds. Professionally, some slight but welcome consolation for my musical disappointments came in the form of the title songs and other production numbers that I was asked to write for a series of Bernard Delfont's big, splashy and spectacular London Palladium revues with pre-chosen icky titles like *We're Having a Ball* and *Swingin' Down the Lane*, which starred the biggest names in contemporary music hall, like the wholesome family Max and a lovable but insane Welsh tenor called Harry Secombe, who had made his name in BBC radio's funniest-ever comedy series *The Goon Show*, alongside two other equally insane, up-and-coming young comics, Spike Milligan and Peter Sellers, with whom I also became friends. They were all stark, staring mad.

As though I didn't already have enough lunacy in my life, I decided to spread my wings a little wider in this strange new world, and started writing with yet another slightly potty young comedian called Benny Hill, who, like almost everyone else in my life at that point, lived just around yet another corner, this time in Maida Vale. This dismayed both my musical snob Robin and my intellectual snob Freddie ('What *is* Leslie *doing*?') but my theory was, and remains to this day, that any writing is more rewarding than no writing.

Benny Hill, whom I absolutely adored from the outset, was, surprisingly, the meanest man I ever met in my life, which I found out, of all places, in his kitchen. 'Let's eat in the kitchen,' he said on the first evening we worked late at his flat. We trooped out to the seemingly foodless kitchen. The fridge was empty.

'What would you like?'

'What have you got?'

For answer, making 'Ta-da!' fanfare noises, Benny opened wide all the 15 kitchen cupboards, to reveal row upon row of neatly stacked and severely rusted cans of every shape and size. There were literally hundreds of them, and they bore no labels. Benny beamed with pride.

'*Voilá! Le dinner est servi!* Help yourself!'

'W–what are they?'

My jaw dropped as he started reciting his menu with the fervour of a maître d' in a top restaurant. 'The rectangular ones are sardines and the oval ones are pilchards. The flat round ones are pineapple, the short round ones are baked beans, and the tall round ones are mushroom, tomato or mulligatawny soup!'

It slowly dawned on me that what Benny had done was to buy up vast quantities of canned food salvaged from the wrecks of American Liberty Ships torpedoed in the Atlantic during the war. I had seen such cargo washed ashore during my wartime holiday in Bude, North Cornwall, which was on the Atlantic coast. I asked Benny if this was the case. He replied with the glee of the man who had just broken the bank in Monte Carlo.

'Absolutely. Two cans for a penny... 500 cans for a pound. I bought 1,000 cans. I can eat from now to 1960 for two quid!'

'But the war's been over for more than a *decade*! You're going to kill yourself! You'll die of food poisoning or ptomaine wotsit or salmonella... probably all three!'

'So far, so good.'

With this blithe philosophy and his infectious trademark grin, Benny opened up a large tin of rusty pilchards and tucked right in. I watched aghast, then cautiously peeled back the corner of a small tin of sardines and sniffed within. They seemed OK. Miraculously, they *were* OK, though they defied every preconception I might have had about the durability of canned food stored at the bottom of the Atlantic. For all Benny knew, this stuff could have been on the *Titanic*. And so, for the duration of our collaboration on a random bunch of stage and TV comedy sketches, I gambled my life each time Benny's equally rusty can-opener was plunged with relish into yet another World War Two food relic. As often as possible, I tried to end our work sessions by 7.00pm in order to escape and enjoy some post-war sustenance and, as often as not, I failed. But I lived to work with Benny Hill on many another day, as he did with me.

These diversions were always fun, but they were also frustrating side-tracks and cul de sacs, well away from the main musical highway I wanted to travel, as indeed was my next endeavour, co-hosting an early-evening BBC TV show called *Line Up for Tonight*. This was the brainchild of my friend Ned Sherrin, who had been my Footlights equivalent, if there was such a thing, at Oxford, where we had met when the Footlights stormed their showbusiness battlements. It was a generous offer and a pleasant summer-long job, which I accepted, guiltily aware that I was again betraying and delaying my long-overdue onslaught on the musical theatre. But I got to interview quite a number of fascinating people, including a promising young actor from the Bristol Old Vic called Peter O'Toole.

Finally, that winter of my discontent, things started to stir at long last in the theatrical forest. First, my music publisher decided to assemble the finance for a small West End production of *Lady at the Wheel* and, second, I was invited to work on the English adaptation of the Parisian Folies Bergère show *Ah, Quelle Folie!* that was coming to London the following summer. It was hardly *Cyrano de Bergerac*, but it was at least musical and it was French, and would involve making several trips to Paris. So, naturally, I said 'Yes'. I would have said yes to *anything* that involved several trips to Paris, including becoming a train driver.

Neither show was due to happen 'til the following spring, so I accepted an offer from a well-known BBC radio producer called Roy Speer, who happened to have seen some of my summer TV interviews and asked me if I would like to interview any and all of the Hollywood movie stars working on films in England for a brand-new five-times-a-week radio show he was planning called *Roundabout*, and write the title song for the show. It didn't involve any trips to Paris, and no one gets rich working for the BBC, but it sounded like as good a way as I might ever get to meet some of my Hollywood heroes. So an acceptable if not remarkable winter fell gently into place.

One of the extremely few good things, and in retrospect maybe the only one, that had happened when Freddie and I were working on the doomed *Jubilee Girl* had been befriending a lovely, slightly eccentric and wildly funny girl in the cast called Vilma Ann Leslie. She was a very appealing honey-blonde with a Joan Greenwood voice and a wicked sense of humour; she never stopped talking and she was quite divine. We had all stayed friends and kept in touch, seeing one another from time to time when we could.

One morning in late February, the first day for the better part of a year since London had glimpsed the sun, the phone rang in my tiny St John's Wood flat. It was Vilma, and she was about to utter the sentence that would forever change my life. 'Dahling!' she said. 'Dahling... I started work on a film today, and in it is the girl of your dreams and I'm bringing her round to tea!'

And promptly at five o'clock, the doorbell rang. I had spent the greater part of the day buying enough cucumber sandwiches and cream tea biscuits and Dundee cakes and fruit tarts and silver-wrapped chocolate mini-Swiss rolls to set up in serious competition to Fortnum and Mason's. Trying nonchalantly to look as though this kind of massive spread was an everyday event in my life, I opened the door. There was Vilma Ann, and there beside her was the absolutely most beautiful girl in the world – indeed, the girl of my dreams – the most gorgeous, delectable, ravishing, luscious, exquisite, heavenly creature I have ever seen in my life, delivered right to my door.

'Dahling, this is Yvonne!' gushed Vilma, and to Yvonne,

'Dahling, this is Leslie! Ooh, chocolate swiss rolls! My favourite!' she said, swooping down on them like a diving pelican.

Yvonne temporarily blinded me with her dazzling whiter-than-white smile as she entered the flat, apologising for her intrusion. Apologise? Intrusion? She had the warmest and most mellifluous natural speaking voice I had ever heard. I started trying to remember what happened to Ulysses when he heard the Sirens, and it wasn't good, as I recall.

The next hour passed in about three minutes, until Yvonne, looking considerably prettier than the first day of spring, asked me with great politeness if I could possibly help her get a taxi, as she had to be in Piccadilly sharp at seven. I would gladly have carried her on my back to Piccadilly, but I had an even better idea. I had that very day taken delivery of my latest car, a turquoise-and-white Nash Metropolitan with a black interior. It was a very snazzy little town car, and I warmed to the thought that its first-ever passenger would be the delectable Yvonne.

The trendy Nash Metropolitan was the heaven-sent vehicle to transport the heaven-sent Yvonne on its maiden voyage to Piccadilly. For 20 sublime never-to-be-forgotten minutes, I was a resident of Paradise – in the perfect car with the perfect girl. With outstanding clumsiness, I tried desperately to steer the conversation around to the subject of telephone numbers. With moments left, as the little Nash drew up outside the big, smart Piccadilly Hotel, Yvonne gave me the treasured phone number without which I feared I might never see her again. She gave the number without a second asking, innocently almost, with the easy, open, friendly charm that was one of her more devastating weapons.

In the last 30 seconds, I also learned that she lived with her mother in the village of Stanmore, only two miles from Pinner, that she was 19 years old and about to be 20. She was so perfect in every way I wanted to scream. But the scream choked in my throat when she alighted from the car and I saw her waiting escort step forward to greet her. He was easily the most handsome man in England, if not the world – the actor Richard Greene, whose famous dimpled smile and shiny hair glared constantly out at an adoring world from a hundred million Brylcreem billboards and newspaper adverts. Not only that, he was also a gigantic film and television star, currently appearing in the hugely successful *Robin Hood* series.

I drove off in my suddenly miserable little Nash Metropolitan. What hope in hell did I have against Robin bloody Hood? On the way home, filled with malice, I thought that, if I had only known that I was going to deliver the girl of my dreams into the arms of the legendary hero of Sherwood Forest, I would have run him over.

Her mother's name was Adelaide... Adelaide Warren. Which made her daughter Yvonne Warren. I established this sharp at nine the next morning by calling the Stanmore phone number to confirm that it was real. Like Yvonne, it was real. She had already left for the studio at 6.00am, as she did every day. I was impressed. That's really early, I thought. Adelaide sounded a great deal like her daughter on the phone, and was very sweet and patient with me as I fumbled clumsily around, using all my natural stupidity, trying to find a way to ask the most beautiful girl in the world's mother if I could take her daughter out to dinner. All I learned was that Yvonne's family nickname was BonBon, because her younger brother Beverly couldn't pronounce Yvonne when he was a baby. I liked BonBon, an appropriate name for such a delicious confection, though I had been a fan of the name Yvonne since the days of my teenage devotion to Miss De Carlo.

Adelaide was patient, charming and adorable throughout my desperate campaign for the dinner date with the divine one. We spoke at length every day for the following two weeks, by which time she had become my agent in the quest for Yvonne's attention. Finally came the message I was waiting for – Yvonne would finish her film on Friday and have dinner with me the following Tuesday, Adelaide announced triumphantly. Jock Jacobsen himself never closed a better deal.

Where do you take the absolutely most beautiful girl in the world to dinner? I nominated five restaurants, as though I was planning to give an Oscar to the winner. And the winner was... Le Matelot, in Belgravia, a particularly charming little bistro, *très, très, très Français*, run by three Frenchmen in sailor-suits, who all seemed to be called André. Le Matelot was gayer than Christmas. Yvonne walked in wearing black velvet huggy pants and a white angora sweater that rocked the restaurant, turning every head in the room, including the three sailors.

We chose escargots bourguignons, because I loved them and she had never tasted them but was keen to and, of course, the very first snail of her life flew straight out of the little clamp thing you hold them with into the delicious depths of the white angora sweater, creating a not unattractive garlic-strewn patch in a very strategic position. She did not panic. She did not scream or get upset. She laughed. She laughed the best laugh I have ever heard in my life. Her coolness in the face of what many ladies would have considered disaster was exemplary. We drank plenty of wine to compensate for and help forget the little drama, and the evening revealed many things. She had the quickest and most delicious sense of humour of any young lady I had ever met. She was a brilliant mimic and explosively funny in her own right. Revelling in the luxury of her laughter, I suddenly realised that I now had both the first and the second funniest ladies in the world in my life. I couldn't wait for her to meet Bea Lillie.

And I didn't have to. The second date was no problem... nor the third, fourth or fifth. We were instantly together every evening after work, but I always drove her home to Adelaide in Stanmore at the end of it. I found myself committing the diminutive sins of my parents by wanting to call her Eve or Evie rather than Yvonne. Yvonne sounded too grand, too formal, for the sweetness of her character. She was the ultimate woman-child. She had been born on Adelaide's seventeenth birthday, which put Adelaide in her mid-thirties, and a great beauty herself, though more in the Elizabeth Taylor mould. They were like two loving sisters, and every year on 17 February they were each other's best possible birthday present.

We drove down to Henley to see Bea, who had just returned to England to play – what else? – Auntie Mame in the West End later in the year. Bea and Evie were like kindred spirits from the moment they met. Being with both of them filled me with joy, and I suddenly had two soul-mates from two different generations. Bea took me aside during a walk in the glorious riverside garden with a flotilla of her Pekingese dogs, and tapped her forefinger wisely against the side of her nose as she looked at me and said softly, 'That's the one, kiddo. *That's* the one!'

'I know!' I said deliriously. 'I *know!*'

My humble little Nash Metropolitan now became our golden coach as I drove Evie down to Brighton to see my flat, up to Cambridge to show her its beauty and why I had been so happy there, across to Warwickshire to meet my parents. Dad fell instantly in love with her, as did every man. Even my mum approved, the sternest critic of all, who, when I once told her that I was having dinner with Princess Margaret, made the memorable comment, 'What do you want to go out with *her* for?'

Young and beautiful as she was, Evie seemed to possess a deep inner wisdom. Bea said she was an old soul. She had been here before. She had an uncanny knack of assessing people, a built-in radar that instinctively guided her. It was amazing to observe, because she was charming to everyone, but sensed infallibly who she could be close to and who not. I was glad to be in the former category.

I was in love, by which I mean IN LOVE, for the first and only time in my life. I wanted to be with her every moment of every day. The Folies Bergère show was looming. I asked her if she would come to Paris with me. She said she would. I was invited by friends to the World's Fair in Brussels. I asked her to come with me. She said she would. The year was shaping up as prettily as Evie.

Lady at the Wheel went into production a couple of weeks later, and opened at the Westminster Theatre, near Buckingham Palace. Andrew Broughton's glorious girlfriend Lucienne Hill, known for her beautiful translations of the plays of Jean Anouilh, took over the now Freddie-less book, and I added two new songs to the now Robin-less score. The cast was bursting with talent. But the inexplicable something that had worked so well with a group of happy amateurs up in Cambridge somehow got lost in the hands of a group of experienced professionals in London. I think it is called lightness of touch. The show never quite recaptured the spontaneous humour, sparkle and freshness of the original 1953 undergraduate production. It had taken four long years to stagger into the West End, and predictably perhaps, the magic had been lost. Or, equally likely, the world of the musical had moved forward a couple of small paces in the interim. Had the show moved into London when it should have, as *Out of the Blue* did, there might have been a different tale to tell. Three successful recordings of songs from the show were the only consolation. After the fact, I wondered whether the massive quantities of time and energy expended in the long struggle would have been better devoted to another newer project, but that was spilled milk.

My natural optimism was quick to bury the past. After all, I still had my Folies Bergère show and my BBC *Roundabout* movie-star interviews ahead of me, plus several trips to Paris and, above all, the ravishing Evie shining on my life like a summer's day. It was Evie's first ever visit to Paris, and I had the sublime chore of showing the world's most beautiful girl around the world's most beautiful city. The City of Light was on her best behaviour. We ate at my favourite Saint-Germain bistro, Au Vieux Paris, and strolled along the Left Bank of the Seine on a perfect moonlit evening. It was the lyric of 'April in Paris' come to life.

And, of course, she wiped out Paris. It made me slightly self-conscious and not a little smug to have this definitive head-turner on my arm, but I soon got used to it when I realised that she never seemed to be even aware of it. I was in awe of her natural lack of vanity and in love with her bubbling enthusiasm for everything around her. From that day forward, Evie made every Paris trip. We did it all. Lunches up the Eiffel Tower and in the Bois de Boulogne, visits to the Folies Bergère to see *Ah, Quelle Folie!* (All Folies Bergère shows, I learned, had 13 letters in the title, a long-observed superstitious custom.) We befriended the show's star, Gérard Séty, whose complex and hilarious act I was adapting into English, a trickier task than it sounded. He and his lovely young wife, a delightful Vietnamese model called Maguy, took us to wonderful Asian restaurants in Montparnasse and Montmartre. If the Department of Fate was looking to cheer me up after the disappointment of *Lady at the Wheel*, it was doing a damn fine job.

The Brussels World's Fair was fun for a few days, full of great restaurants that we could neither get into nor afford. But Brussels wasn't Paris. Nowhere is. By the end of the third Paris trip, knowing that the fourth would be the last before the Folies show moved across to London, I had made up my mind to do what I had known I would do from the very beginning – ask Evie to marry me. I had only known her for a couple of months, but there were unspoken depths to our relationship that defied explanation, and every time I looked at her I could hear Bea Lillie's voice in her riverside garden whispering, '*That's* the one, kiddo!' I knew I had found the ideal girl. What was I waiting for? I was waiting for the ideal moment.

I prepared my plan in considerably greater detail than D-Day. It was now late May. I chose Bea's birthday, 29 May, as my talisman date to take Evie for a late sunset stroll along the Left Bank of the Seine beside Notre Dame and the Ile de la Cité, and basically relive the Gene Kelly–Leslie Caron 'Our Love Is Here to Stay' sequence from *An American In Paris*, but without the dance. I would then ask her the Big Question, pray for a 'Yes', climb the riverside steps and whisk her across the street to sit in the window table at La Tour d'Argent for dinner overlooking the river and the cathedral. I had the table booked and everything. Perfect. Perfect? Here's what went wrong. It went *too* perfectly. Everything about the evening was *so* enchanting, magical as only a Paris spring night can be, that, by the time I finally plucked up the courage to ask Evie to marry me and she said, 'Yes', the Tour d'Argent had stopped serving. It was after midnight.

Happily, the Department of Fate revels in situations like this, and provided the following scenario. We heard car-horns tooting in the distance. Toot-toot-ti-toot-toot. Hundreds of them. I knew a lovely late-night champagne and oyster place on the Champs-Elysées, Le Marigny. We agreed that would be as worthy a substitute as we were likely to find at that hour. We hailed a taxi, and drove into an almighty traffic jam that was clogging central Paris at one o'clock in the morning. We walked the last couple of hundred yards to the restaurant, sat outside under the red-and-gold awning, opened the champagne and watched half a million people march down the Champs-Elysées a few yards in front of us, shouting and cheering, accompanied by the cacophony of thousands of toot-toot-ti-toot-tooting cars. I said to Evie I thought it was gratifying of Paris to react so emotionally to the news of our engagement, especially as we hadn't yet told anyone. The waiter arrived with the oysters and explained. The voting polls had just closed, and General Charles de Gaulle, France's great wartime hero and Leader of the Free French, had tonight been elected the new President of the Republic! I didn't have the chutzpah to tell Evie I had planned it. Toot-toot-ti-toot toot, we learned, translated into '*De Gaulle au pouvoir!*'

Ah, Quelle Folie! opened at the Winter Garden Theatre in London and settled in for a comfortable run. The Folies Bergère is not the kind of show that needs to worry about critics and notices. It would run until all the people who wanted to see it had seen it, and then go back to Paris and start all over again, as it had done for over a hundred years, and open yet another variation of exactly the same show, with yet another 13-letter title.

I was 27. So much for my 'bachelor 'til I'm 35' bravura. If you are lucky enough in life to find an Evie, you tear up the calendar and the long-term planner and rethink your life all over again. I was ecstatically happy to do exactly that, because I knew it was the sort of situation the Department of Fate completely understands, and would deal with accordingly. And here's what the D of F did.

The producer of *Ah, Quelle Folie!* was a black-bearded man called James Lawrie. He had the look of a pirate, and I could easily picture him in the full Long John Silver kit. He sounded Scottish, but was, in fact, Australian, and after the show had opened in London he put to me the following proposition: Would I be interested in going to Australia and finding an indigenous Australian subject to make into a musical? He would give me a round-the-world air ticket, a suite in his sister's hotel in Sydney for three months, and a weekly per diem. Hmmmm, I thought.

I promptly asked Evie if she fancied the idea of a round-the-world honeymoon. She said she'd think about it, and when do we leave? We had planned to marry on Saturday, 18 October, four years to the day after I had opened with Bea Lillie at the Royal Court Theatre in Liverpool. So we'd leave late on 18 October. I asked Jim Lawrie if instead of one round-the-world ticket I could have two one-way London to Sydney tickets, and we'd find our own way back to London in the spring, God knows how. Here was my reasoning. While Evie and I didn't have the money to go on a six-month, round-the-world dream honeymoon, we did have the time, and by the time we had the money, we wouldn't have the time. And so it proved. For all our travelling in the interim, we didn't actually go around the world again until 44 years later, which we are doing now as I write this in Mexico. We complete the final leg of our second circuit next week.

The deal with Jim Lawrie was closed. The bad news was that Evie had a longstanding promise to fulfil to Adelaide, to take a lengthy summer trip to Malta, where Adelaide had been born and grown up. You don't get to look like that unless you start in Malta. They would be gone two months, July and August. As I was about to steal Evie away from her beloved mother-sister for all eternity, I could hardly complain, so I didn't. I determined instead to fill in the time by doing as many of my BBC *Roundabout* movie-star interviews as I could possibly cram into those two endless months, for both diversionary and fiscal reasons.

And I did. The interviews were being organised for the Beeb by a feisty PR lady called Freddie Ross, who was also shortly to marry Britain's favourite TV comedian Tony Hancock. And Freddie certainly knew her PR stuff and how to set up interviews with movie stars. I did over a hundred interviews in eight weeks. I didn't even know a hundred movie stars existed. But none of the interviews was as terrifying as the first one, at Elstree Studios.

I set up my heavy green BBC reel-to-reel tape recorder on a table. I knew I was going to do three interviews. What I did not know is that I would be doing all three at once. Freddie omitted to tell me that bit. Imagine the scene: you are sitting at a table, nervous as a kitten that you are about to chat face to face for the first time with a major Hollywood movie star, and into the room walk Kirk Douglas, Burt Lancaster and Laurence Olivier and sit three in a row facing you across the table like a firing squad. It was like seeing Mount Rushmore come to life before your eyes, or having a coffee break with the Father, the Son and the Holy Ghost. All three were on a break together, between set-ups. The three superstars were co-starring in a film adaptation of Shaw's *The Devil's Disciple*. Freddie said afterwards that she thought it would be novel to catch this unique trio all at one time, as indeed it was. She'd decided not to tell me in case I seized up, which of course I did. I remained partially paralysed throughout the interview. But, once we got started, the interplay among the three of them was so spontaneous and amusing that it more than compensated for my temporary loss of the power of speech.

I interviewed Tyrone Power in his suite at the Connaught, the most handsome and charming man I ever saw in my life. More than handsome – stunningly beautiful. He made that Robin Hood actor, whatever his name was, look like a delivery boy. Tyrone Power was 44, and three weeks later he was dead of a heart-attack in Spain while filming *Solomon and Sheba* with Gina Lollobrigida. My interview with him was one of his very last.

I interviewed Julie Andrews, surprisingly in her tiny single bedroom in the Savoy Hotel, sitting at the end of the bed. She was an adorable 22 and about to open as Eliza Dolittle in *My Fair Lady* at the Theatre Royal, Drury Lane. Although *Mary Poppins* hadn't been made yet, that's exactly who she was. 'Enchanting' is a word that sits well on extremely few people. Julie would own that word throughout her life.

Our wedding took place at the imposing St James's Church in Spanish Place, a large Catholic bastion just off Baker Street, the service conducted by a very young, enthusiastic, ginger-blonde priest called Father Keep. Julie Hamilton took our wedding pictures, having by now become a successful photographer. She had also found a nice new boyfriend, a young actor called Sean Connery, and they, too, were thinking about marriage. Or rather, Julie was...

Next morning, there were large photographs of Evie all over the front pages of every English Sunday newspaper. Not a sign of me anywhere. I had to check with Evie to confirm that I had been at the wedding. She assured me that I had. Many of the pictures were extreme close-ups of the beautiful bride, focusing on the unusual antique heart-shaped crystal pendant, surmounted by a pearl and platinum crown, that she wore in the centre of her forehead at the wedding. It was perceived as a fashion statement. It was much more, but no reporter or photographer at the wedding had thought to ask her *why* she was wearing it. The true reason would have made a very pretty press story.

When the first Sir Robert Peel, who was England's Prime Minister in the 1840s and the reason London's policemen became known as Bobbies or Peelers, married, his mother gave the crystal heart pendant to his bride, just as her husband's mother had given it to her at *her* wedding. The crystal had been in the family since the 1700s. Thereafter, from generation to generation, the crystal heart had been passed down from the eldest son's bride to *her* eldest son's bride. Thus, the heart always stayed within the Peel family, but was handed on to the first bride of each new generation to welcome her into the family, a highly romantic gesture. All the first sons had been named Robert. Bea had married the last-but-one baronet, Sir Robert Peel, and had herself received the crystal heart from his mother at her wedding 40 years before. The fifth baronet, like several other people in this book, took himself out with the demon drink, and the title passed to Bea's son Bobby, to whose bride Bea intended to hand on the crystal heart. But young Bobby, as we know, was tragically killed in the war, the last of the Peel line.

At the conclusion of telling us this lovely story in her Park Lane apartment two nights before our wedding, Bea pressed the crystal heart and its long platinum and enamel chain into Evie's hands and said brightly as she kissed her face, 'So now you're my new daughter-in-law. Keep it in the family.'

Forty-one years later, on Saturday, 22 May 1999, Evie duly handed over the crystal heart to Ms Sarah Woodhead, the beautiful, blue-eyed blonde who married our son Adam on that lovely day. Fittingly, Sarah wore the heart on her forehead, exactly as Evie had done. On Saturday, 22 December 2000, our beautiful, blue-eyed, blond grandson Roman was born, and somewhere around the third decade of the new millennium, Sarah will have the joy of handing on the crystal heart to Roman's bride. Vivat Beatrici!

On the last evening before our epic Around the World in 180 Days circumnavigation of the globe began, I gave Evie and

Adelaide the best going-away treat I could think of. I acquired three front-centre stall seats for *My Fair Lady*, the theatrical rage of the century at Drury Lane, which, as performed by Rex Harrison, Julie Andrews, Stanley Holloway and Robert Coote, remains the greatest evening of musical theatre I have ever seen or ever hope to see. Whatever Alan Jay Lerner had been up to in that pink villa in Capri four years before, he was definitely *not* wasting his time!

Supper at Le Caprice afterwards was the only way to maintain the standard of the rest of the evening, and to thank the beautiful Adelaide for the greatest gift of my life, the beautiful Evie.

New York was the first destination on our epic honeymoon. The triple-tailed TWA Super Constellation that chugged us endlessly across the Atlantic was a major stylistic step up from my hair-raising Flying Tiger Airlines saga of five years before, but, at 300mph, Australia seemed an unimaginable number of propeller turns away. Evie had the magical gift of being able to sleep like a baby throughout the entire duration of any air journey.

For our ten days in New York, Bea had given us her glorious 1930s-style apartment on East End Avenue, overlooking the East River at 80th Street. I was the wide-eyed Evie's tour guide to Manhattan, showing off my own very limited knowledge of the magical city. The undoubted highlight of our stay was our first-ever Broadway musical – Rodgers and Hammerstein's *Flower Drum Song*, which had opened the night before at the St James Theater. We saw the Wednesday matinee, an ocean of blue hair and a noise like the world's biggest parrot cage as 1,500 ladies-who-lunch provided the capacity audience.

There was a heart-stopping moment for me at intermission. As we were returning to our seats, 10 feet away from us, I saw the mighty Rodgers and Hammerstein, standing side by side chatting at the back of the stalls. It was my first and only glimpse of these two gods of the musical theatre. I was so impressed that it never occurred to me 'til we got back to Bea's apartment that I could oh-so-easily have asked them both to sign the cover of my programme. Two years later, Oscar was dead, shortly after the opening of their final and most beloved collaboration, *The Sound of Music*.

We spent Christmas in Canada with the Harcourt Eldon Greening Bulls. A lunch with the ever-kindly editor of the *Hamilton Spectator*, Tom Farmer, secured me a roving reporter commission to write for the Southam Press group while on our travels, which would contribute handsomely towards our journey home in the spring. After Christmas, we flew on across Canada via Vancouver to an unscheduled bonus two-day holdover in San Francisco. Then two days in Hawaii, a glimpse of Fiji, and we finally arrived in Sydney on New Year's Eve. We were relieved to discover that Jim Lawrie's delightful sister Rhoda did indeed own a pleasant small hotel in Point Piper, high on a hill with a stunning view across the bay to Sydney Harbour Bridge. Even better was the fact that Jim's genial best friend, Sonny Marshall, lived in an astonishing penthouse next door and, forewarned that we were coming, his generosity ensured that we saw Sydney in style. He made us honorary members of the glamorous Glen Asham Club, set on a bluff over the sea, where we would spend most of our days while I pondered further how to plumb the unfathomable depths of the as yet undiscovered Indigenous Australian Musical.

I bought books about Sydney and Australia, plus Ozzie films and plays, to see if anything ignited a spark. I studied Sidney Nolan's art and Ned Kelly and the legend of *Leda and the Swan*, and read myself silly for weeks on end, sitting in the shade by the Glen Asham pool while Evie read and sunbathed and acquired a glorious darker-than-Tondelayo tan. Her smooth, olive Mediterranean skin enabled her to absorb endless sun without a glimmer of a burn, unlike my paleface self, who existed in the shadow of a vast umbrella and could cope with maybe one hour a day of the merciless Sydney January sun, capable of deep-fried temperatures up to 120°F, and no negotiating. I became a Mastermind on all things antipodean *except* Indigenous Australian

Musicals. Jim Lawrie would have done better to send me prospecting for gold.

At five o'clock one morning, there was an urgent tapping on our hotel bedroom door. Blearily, I staggered out of bed and opened it, to find myself staring at Ava Gardner. 'Can I come in and hide,' she asked, 'just for a few minutes?'

'Of course,' I said, as though this sort of thing happened to me at five o'clock every morning.

She came in and hid. 'Fucking photographers,' she said. I agreed, and pointed out that we had a door in our living room that led out to and down a fire escape. 'Perfect,' she said, 'you're a doll.'

She kissed me and fled, and we never saw her again. She was starring with Gregory Peck in *On the Beach*. It occurred to me that, every time I met anyone connected with the film business, they were making a picture with Gregory Peck. Clearly, Mr Peck was constantly working, because it seemed no one could make a film without him.

Evie slept through the whole incident and didn't believe me – why should she? – when next day I said to her, 'Guess who came to see us at five o'clock this morning – Ava Gardner!' But a not very good picture of Ms Gardner legging it at Olympic speed appeared in one of the Sydney newspapers the next afternoon, with our hotel clearly visible in the background.

Evie was impressed. 'Why didn't you wake me?' she said.

It is given to comparatively few men to have the privilege of throwing his wife's 21st birthday party, and I was one of that lucky few, with the generous help of the magnanimous Sonny Marshall. I bought Evie 21 birthday presents, and Sonny and his blonde green-eyed girlfriend Miriam provided a sumptuous feast, a fireworks display and a guest list featuring everyone we had met in Sydney... except Ava Gardner.

Throughout our Sydney stay, I wrote what I hoped were amusing articles about our adventures and airmailed them to Tom

Farmer in Canada, who promptly airmailed cheques in return. It was a felicitous arrangement and, together with my carefully safeguarded per diem from Jim Lawrie, guaranteed that we would not be marooned in Australia for the rest of our lives. I reserved a cabin on a P&O liner leaving Sydney in mid-March for the six-week voyage home to England.

The nearest I got to an Indigenous Australian Musical was a treatment about the Snowy River Project, the least I felt I owed Jim Lawrie. But my heart wasn't in it and, to Jim's credit, he gracefully accepted that it was perhaps too tall an order. In my defence, 44 years on, Indigenous Australian Musicals are sadly still high on the list of The World's Shortest Books.

The good ship *Strathaird* was hardly the pride and joy of the P&O line. At least I sincerely hope not, for, although it was officially ranked as a passenger liner, it had been used as a wartime troopship and gave the firm impression that the P&O line were not yet aware that the war had ended some 14 years earlier, and that our side had won. But beggars can't be choosers. If I had to give *Strathaird* a place in the history of seafaring, it would be as a cross between *The African Queen* and the Bombay Brasserie.

In Ceylon, now Sri Lanka, we made a sentimental journey on behalf of Bea to try to find Bobby Peel's grave. And after a long search we finally found it, in a small military cemetery outside the town of Kandi. We placed fresh flowers on it and photographed this poignant but missing memory to take home to our beloved Bea.

The ship's 'cinema' was a laundered (sometimes) white-ish sheet awkwardly strung up between a ship's funnel and various capstans on the top deck, where P&O proudly presented a series of really low-brow British film comedies. The best of a bad bunch, with certainly no Oscars at risk, were the first of what would become the endless *Carry On* series – *Carry On, Sergeant* and *Carry On, Nurse*. The ship's tannoy recording system was also considerably less than world-class, the music played on it having a hollow, tinny sound, as though it were being played inside a submarine while you were listening underwater but *outside* the submarine. Despite this significant quality hazard, I heard a vaguely familiar voice singing a quasi-rock'n'roll song as we were wandering through the ship's lounge one day. 'My God, that's Anthony Newley!' I said to Evie. 'He's a friend of Julie Hamilton's. His wife Annie Lynn's her best mate.'

I had written a number of individual and unconnected songs in my spare time in Australia, my favourite being 'Tumbarumba', with a lyric made up entirely of aboriginal place names, which I had written in the remote hope that it might somehow lead me into the elusive original Indigenous Australian Musical through the back door. It didn't. The back door, like the front door, was firmly locked. In fact, the whole house was boarded up. Max Bygraves would eventually record the song and use it in his act when he toured Australia, where he was a huge star.

But there were a couple of other songs I thought might be suitable for Newley, who had suddenly become a major recording star in the UK through the success of a small movie called *Idol on Parade*, about a rock'n'roll star drafted into the Army. I resolved to track Newley down via Julie Hamilton when we got back to London.

Evie landed a leading movie role about three minutes after we got home, and I took just a little longer to find Newley, but find him I did, late one night, in a Decca studio in central London, where he was recording his new album. Between takes, he heard a couple of my songs, and promptly agreed to record one of them, which was in retrospect a somewhat turgid ballad called 'A Boy without a Girl', which duly ended up on that album. More importantly, Newley and I immediately hit it off and became instant friends. We had a rare rapport, a wavelength all our own and, above all, we made one another laugh. Evie promptly became the third corner of that triangle, and the time the three of us spent together was always, from day one, special and precious and hilarious.

Within days, Tony and I had decided to write together, having no idea what we would write, or indeed whether we could. Tony had never written a song, but he had an instinct, a rare feel for a song that a small handful of singers possess better than the songwriters who supply them. Right back to his child-actor days playing the Artful Dodger in David Lean's masterly film of *Oliver Twist*, Newley was a performer with a unique and eccentric style all his own. His star was in the ascendant, thanks to his newfound acclaim as a singer, and I was not slow to appreciate the built-in potential of having an established star performer on the writing team. It soon became evident that some kind of vehicle specifically tailored to Newley's diverse and formidable singing and acting talents was what was required, a search I was confident would be infinitely more fun than my recent failed hunt to find the Indigenous Australian Musical.

During our six mad months wandering around the planet, Evie and I had lent our Brighton apartment to my parents. They loved it down there so much that they had decided to get a place of their own. I discovered there was an available flat in the same block as mine, and put a hold on it. Two days later, I went over to Max Bygraves's home to work on the 'Tumbarumba' song with him. He opened the door to tell me he had just received an urgent call from my mother. Would I go to Brighton immediately? My father was extremely ill.

In less than two hours, Evie and I were at the Preston Park flat. Dad, who was suffering from advanced arterio-sclerosis, had had a stroke. Evie comforted Mama while I sat the night vigil in my bedroom with Dad, and I was alone with him, holding his hand, when he died at 3.30am the next morning. He never recovered consciousness.

It was time to take stock of my life. Both the 1950s and my twenties were drawing to a close. Evie's twenties were just beginning. With Mama widowed, I now had two ladies to look after. I promptly acquired the twin apartment to ours for my mother. I was at the beginning of my married life with the divine

Evie, and I was about to enter into what I sensed would be a second successful professional marriage with Newley.

I was suddenly acquiring a selection of new responsibilities, which I realised placed me at a career crossroads. I had had five years of fabulous fun since I left Cambridge, and gained a fair amount of theatre and musical experience as a Jack-of-All-Trades. I now needed to become Master of One.

3rd Key: C Sharp

We were going to write a musical. On that much, Newley and I were agreed. And we wanted it to be different, so we started looking in less obvious places for source material, starting with the films of our cinematic hero, Ingmar Bergman, as Stephen Sondheim would do more successfully a dozen years later with *A Little Night Music.* We ran full-tilt into a slew of Swedish copyright problems and swiftly withdrew, taking with us one significant souvenir, Bergman's name. Newley took the Berg and I took the Man, so that we became Brickman and Newberg, the nicknames that would stay with us among family and friends throughout our lives. There was a smart ethnic motive behind the move, not so much Swedish as Jewish. We were both well aware that almost every great songwriter in our lifetime was Jewish; ergo, we were convinced that two Jewish songwriters called Brickman and Newberg were more likely to write a hit musical than two Gentiles called Bricusse and Newley.

For our next musical attempt, we brought Jesus Christ back into today's world, placing the Second Coming in contemporary London's sleazy Soho district. That didn't work, either. By page

27, both Jesus Christ and ourselves had had enough, so we abandoned the project and had Our Saviour call a cab and disappear into the West End traffic sunset. I must admit, I did wonder a decade later, when *Jesus Christ Superstar* became a huge international hit, whether we hadn't been a little hasty in allowing Our Saviour to hail that taxi.

While Brickman and Newberg continued to stumble around looking for a kindly light to lead them out from amidst their encircling gloom, young Evie skipped merrily from one movie to the next, working pretty well non-stop. Newley was recording, filming occasionally, and doing TV and variety stage shows. I continued to write for various TV shows, which I really didn't enjoy any more. I felt I was marking time. I worked with Benny Hill on another big West End revue called *Fine Fettle*, which did well enough. Benny, as always, was funny, but that kind of show was rapidly becoming a dinosaur. And Benny was *still* eating out of those rusty cans, the gastronomic equivalent of Russian roulette.

The St John's Wood flat was too small for us. No self-respecting cat would wish to be swung there. We quickly found a brand-new, modern apartment in Stanmore, close to Adelaide, which I knew would make Evie happy. We still commuted to our flat in Brighton or to Bea's house on the river at Henley at weekends, and I had to admit that, for someone who was barely better than unemployed, we had a pretty sophisticated three-home set-up.

True to form, Evie landed another movie role as soon as we got home, opposite Oliver Reed in Hammer Films' *The Curse of the Werewolf*, which was shot at Bray Studios on the River Thames, 25 miles outside London. Some mornings, I would drive Evie out to the studio by the dawn's early light, at around 6.00am or something equally obscene. On one particularly beautiful summer's morning, after I had dropped her off, I had an idea for a song for her. I parked the car by the river. It was one of those songs that write themselves. Less than 30 minutes later, I had completed both the words and the melody. I returned to the studio, found Evie still in make-up and presented her with the first of what would become known as the Evie-songs. It was called 'My Kind of Girl'. We both liked it, and a few days later I submitted it for an upcoming international song contest. In the competition, the song was allocated to a young singer who until recently had been a bus driver. His name was Matt Monro. He was unknown, but not to me. I had heard him do an uncanny impression of Frank Sinatra on a Peter Sellers comedy album for which Peter and I had written some stuff together.

'My Kind of Girl' did not win the song competition, alas. It was leading by nine votes with one city, Dublin, left to phone in its ten votes. All ten votes went to the winning and − in my highly prejudiced view − extremely average song entitled 'And You Will Marry Me', which as I dimly recall through the mists of time, sported lyrics like:

This is our playtime − Let's have a gay time...
This is the way our lives will be −
And you will marry me!

and carried off the first prize of £1,000. On national television, no less. I received the runner-up prize of £500 from the show's hostess, none other than Our Lady of Rochdale and Capri, Miss Gracie Fields. I told her I had written the song at 6.30 in the morning. Gracie replied, 'Well, you see, that's what happens when you sleep in like that!'

By way of consolation, 'My Kind of Girl' went on to win a much bigger game, becoming a major hit record for both Matt and myself in both the UK and the United States. It later received the ultimate compliment of three separate recordings by the members of the Rat Pack − Dean Martin, Sammy Davis Jr and Frank Sinatra. Sinatra recorded it with the Count Basie Orchestra. Velvet-voiced Nat King Cole added yet another classic recording to the growing collection.

Sammy Davis Jr made his first-ever London stage appearance

that summer, at the Pigalle Club. Evie, Viv and I were among the first to see him. I had been listening to Sammy Davis recordings for some years. His highly individual versions of songs like 'That Old Black Magic' and 'Hey, There!' were the most original treatments those songs ever received. His appearances at the Pigalle created the greatest sensation since Danny Kaye's tour de force at the London Palladium a decade before.

To my astonishment, I had an even bigger number-one record at that time. My music publisher asked me if I would collaborate with a popular young skiffle singer named Lonnie Donegan. Thus, I came to write the lyrics of 'My Old Man's a Dustman' with Lonnie. The record went straight to number one in its first week of release, the first song ever to do so, as duly recorded in the *Guinness Book of Records*. I was so paranoid doing something that far out that I used the *nom de plume* of Beverly Thorn for the occasion. A number-one song by any other name... There are those of my acquaintance who still regard 'My Old Man's a Dustman' as my finest achievement. Hmmm.

With Bray Studios being close to Henley-on-Thames, I would collect Evie after shooting on Friday evenings, and we would spend the weekends at Peel Fold with Bea and John Philip and the great and the near great who would stop by. One weekend houseguest was the acerbic American actor Clifton Webb, whom I had admired ever since his explosive screen performance as the astringent news columnist Waldo Leideker in the classic thriller *Laura*, opposite the sublime Gene Tierney. He had starred with Bea in a long-ago Rodgers and Hart musical on Broadway. Clifton was inconsolably mourning the recent death of his renowned mother Maybelle, apparently one of the all-time great showbusiness Mamas, at the age of 98. Over drinks before dinner on the Saturday evening, he decided he wanted to share his grief with Noël Coward at his home in Vevey in Switzerland. We all got on to various telephone extensions, Evie and I in our bedroom, The Swan Room, to speak with the master. Once again, Clifton poured out his broken heart. Noël listened patiently to the lengthy outpouring of emotion, then said crisply, 'My heart goes out to you, dear boy, but you know it isn't exactly abnormal to be orphaned at 72!' I have heard various versions of this story in the years since, but that is what actually happened, and such was Coward's wit, I don't think he ever needed to repeat his *bons mots*.

Bea told me she was planning to put together an autobiographical show made up of the best of her revue material, from the André Charlot revues of the 1920s up to the present day. The show would be called *Beaography*, and she would like Evie and me to go and stay with her in New York in the early spring, where Bea and I could go through all the material together. John Philip would assemble it all, and Bea and I would make the final selections, to which I would add any necessary linking material. To be in New York with Bea was too good a treat to miss, so we promptly signed up.

In the meantime, Bea was to star in *Auntie Mame* in the West End. The show was a personal success for Bea, though not as big a hit in London as it had been on Broadway. David Pelham, its young producer, was an astute PR man and organised a highly newsworthy stunt by having Auntie Mame, alias Bea, invite all the stars of all the other shows running in London for a weekend in Paris. Evie and I went with them on the midnight chartered plane. Being Bea, it was, of course, a BEA flight (British European Airways, for you young ones). We arrived in Paris around 1.00am and proceeded to a late supper at Fouquet's. Charles Laughton went to bed, so that he could be up next morning to go in search of Impressionist paintings, which were still buyable in that era. Trevor Howard went in search of all-night saloons. We and Trevor's beautiful red-headed wife Helen Cherry made the mistake of going with him, and arrived back at the hotel towards dawn, considerably the worse for wear, with Trevor singing 'Men of Harlech' at the top of his stentorian voice.

The weekend was a huge success, especially in terms of David Pelham's quest for publicity. He brought the Monday-evening curtain-up of *Auntie Mame* forward by half-an-hour, so that, in the play's opening cocktail party scene, Auntie Mame's usual party guests were augmented by all the stars of the other shows in London, unannounced, in full make-up and costume for the roles they would be playing on other stages 30 minutes hence. The audience's gradual realisation began as a low buzz and ended up an ovation. When Bea saw Charles Laughton grinning at her, she was on it in a flash, and got great mileage out of the moment on stage, as well as great press mileage out of the next morning's news pictures.

Evie and I couldn't wait for the New York trip to roll around. We had had no reason to return there since our honeymoon, and New York is even more appealing if you're going there with a purpose. The night before our departure from London, with the suitcases half-packed, the telephone rang. It was Newberg. 'Brickman, great news! Bernie Delfont's offered me a summer season at the Brighton Hippodrome, and says I can do anything I want. I told him I want to do a one-man revue with ten beautiful girls. And I want *us* to write it together, starting tomorrow. We've got to have it ready to rehearse in one month!'

My mind flashed through the possible options, seeking a solution. There wasn't one. I knew the one thing I could *not* do was let Auntie Bea down at the last minute. With a heavy heart, I told Newberg that, while I wanted more than anything for the two of us to work together, I had a longstanding promise, which I couldn't break, to work with Bea on her project, and we were leaving for New York in 12 hours' time.

Reluctantly, he understood. Next time, we agreed. We wished one another luck, and I hung up the phone feeling like the direct descendant of Quisling and Laval. I told Evie what had happened. She didn't hesitate. 'That,' she pronounced, 'was a mistake. A big mistake. There's a simple answer. Call him back and tell him to come with us.'

'What, all the way to New York?'

'If he really wants you to do it, he'll come.'

'But I'm working with Auntie Bea!'

Top left: The future. Sister Pat and I (aged ten and four).

Top right: Schoolboy (aged fourteen).

Centre right: Defending the realm (aged eighteen).

Bottom: From left to right: Cedric, Ann, Patricia and myself.

Top: The first musical – *Lady At The Wheel* (Cambridge University). From left to right: Frederic Raphael, myself and Robin Beaumont.

Middle left: Evie.

Middle right: Adelaide.

Bottom right: The luckiest man alive.

Top left: Beatrice Lillie – "C'est lady parle qui Peel"

Top right: Adam in the bath and 'Auntie Bea' fulfilling her godmotherly duties.

Middle: Dinner with Van Johnson in New York.

Bottom: New Year's Eve in London. From left to right: Newley, Collins, myself, Evie and Bea.

Top: Writing *Stop The World*.

Middle left: In Las Vegas with Sammy.

Middle right: The Famous Four on the beach at Montauk. From left to right: myself, Joanie, Tony and Evie.

Bottom right: Dinner at the Pickwick Club in London.

Top left: We hit gold with Shirley Bassey and *Goldfinger*.

Top right: Evie has trouble with Oliver Reed in *The Curse of the Werewolf*.

Middle left: David Merrick being adorable.

Middle right: Sean Connery being suave in *The Frightened City*.

Bottom: Adam Cedric Bricusse takes over our lives.

Doctor Dolittle: *Top left*:
Mia Farrow and friend on
the set.

Top right: Rex Harrison
and friend, also on set.

Middle: Evie and I at the
London premiere.

Bottom right: I am
surrounded by loveliness.
From left to right:
Joan Collins,
Evie and Samantha Eggar.

Top: The Richard Attenboroughs and the Steve McQueens at the Los Angeles premiere of *Doctor Dolittle*.

Bottom left: The Gregory Pecks at the same event.

Bottom right: Sammy Davis Jr receives my Best Song Oscar from Barbra Streisand.

Top: Elvis and Evie in *Double Trouble*.

Bottom: Oscar night in Beverly Hills with Hank and Ginny Mancini.

'Look, I love Auntie Bea as much as you do. But Newberg is your future.'

'What's that supposed to mean?'

'It's supposed to mean you work with Auntie Bea in the mornings and Tony in the afternoons.'

'He'll never do it.'

'He'll do it.'

'No, he won't!'

Tony met us at Heathrow at 10.00am the next morning, and the three of us flew together to New York. Auntie Bea took the unexpected change of plans in her stride, gave the three of us John Philip's apartment across the street from hers, and moved John into her guest room. And, exactly as Evie predicted, for the next three weeks I spent my mornings across the street with Bea and John, wading through the massive stacks of old scripts and recordings that John had pulled out of archival storage, and my afternoons and evenings on the other side of the street with Newberg, trying to figure out what we were going to do. The beauteous Evie selflessly shopped and cooked for us, and generally played den mother and housekeeper.

One amazing thing I had not discovered about the amazing Evie until after our round-the-world honeymoon had ended was that she was a phenomenal cook. Her Mediterranean cuisine matches the best of the *Michelin Guide*. Talk about the girl of your dreams! All this and gigot, too! I have always felt about Evie as Truman Capote did about Barbara 'Babe' Paley: 'If she has a fault, it's that she's perfect. Other than that, she's perfect!'

With Auntie Bea, the trick was to try to sense whether comedy material from the 1920s, '30s and '40s had passed its sell-by date. Bea and I were pretty much in accord about what had been funny once and what was funny now, but for the doting John Philip, who had suddenly become a self-appointed creative co-ordinator of this potential show-to-be, everything Bea had ever done was, by definition, a timeless classic and could not possibly be omitted from the final show. John's qualifications in these capacities were considerably limited by the fact that he had zero sense of humour, except to laugh automatically at every single thing Bea ever said, even when she was telling him to fuck off, which was frequently.

John was an awkward mix of a Golden Labrador puppy with the hide of a rhinoceros, and he was determined to prevail. Cabaret sketches, revue sketches, radio sketches, some of them considerably older than John himself, were all regarded by him as absolute 'musts'. He had no critical faculty to go with his zero sense of humour. Bea drifted in and out of our daily morning meetings like the ghost of Elvira in *Blithe Spirit*, cool as a box of cucumbers, always in a benign mood and singing her latest lyrics like '*I hate to see my eldest son go down*'. But poor old John just didn't get it. To him, jokes about the Wall Street Crash of '29 were still a barrelful of big laughs that would lay any audience in the aisles as performed by the peerless Miss Lillie. After a week, we had assembled a seven- or eight-hour show, and we had only gone through about a third of the material.

Things were better across the street. Newberg and I were acutely aware that time was of the essence on our project. We had just three weeks to write the whole thing if Tony was to have time to cast and rehearse whatever it was we ended up with. We were the theatrical equivalent of Kamikaze pilots, planning to crash whatever we were flying on to the Brighton Hippodrome stage about eight weeks hence. This show *had* to open in June, and this was April. I put it to Newberg that we should be looking for a musical rather than a revue. Having worked on more than my share of the latter, from the three Footlights shows to Bea Lillie to Max Bygraves, Harry Secombe and Benny Hill, to say nothing of *Ah! Quelle Folie!*, I gave Newberg a crash course in the advantages of a cohesive song score built around a simple storyline, as opposed to a banal series of disconnected sketches and, perish the phrase, 'production numbers'. A musical would have longer-term value for us as authors and composers. The name of the game was copyright and, if dear old Bernie Delfont was going to put it on anyway, what did we have to lose? Having served my years in the

Palladium trenches writing for Bernie's music hall stars, I felt he owed me one, and, if we emerged winners, so would he.

Newberg was sold. For our simple storyline, we chose Jacques's 'All the world's a stage' Seven Ages of Man speech from *As You Like It*. With Shakespeare as a collaborator, we were already three steps up from the Palladium and on our way. We would take a Newley-like character on a two-hour journey through a man's life, a contemporary comedy with, say, a dozen songs about the trials and tribulations a contemporary Everyman might expect to encounter along the way. We named our character Littlechap, and we wrote the book in seven sections, four in the first Act, three in the second, according to the pattern set out by Jacques in seven or so sentences. And the deeper in we got, the funnier we realised it could be.

But with all Evie's tender loving care, we were 15 days in before it occurred to us that we only had eight days before Newberg had to be back in London, and no score. We had taken on a vastly more ambitious project than Bernie Delfont was expecting and he would probably hate it. To his later credit, and true to his word to Tony, he said, 'I don't wanna *read* it, I wanna *see* it!' He was maybe expecting half-a-dozen new sketches and 15 famous standard songs.

As I was working from ten every morning 'til after midnight seven days a week on the two shows, with only a daily walk back and forth across the street for exercise, I insisted on one evening a week off, for my sanity and in fairness to Evie, though having propelled me into this Box and Cox situation, she never once complained. Bea loved organising these evenings, and the weekly formula was dinner at Sardi's before the show, followed by the biggest hit musical we could find, followed by several nightcaps at The Stork Club, where Bea's old friend Sherman Billingsley, the owner, treated us royally and always gave Bea and Evie big bottles of Sortilège perfume as we were leaving. The shows we saw were *The Music Man*, with Robert Preston's dazzling performance as Professor Harold Hill; Lerner and Loewe's *Camelot*, starring Julie

Andrews, Richard Burton and Robert Goulet; and Rodgers and Hammerstein's monster hit *The Sound of Music*, where Auntie Bea took us backstage to meet Mary Martin.

Back across the street, things weren't getting any better. If I timed my trip exactly at ten o'clock each morning, I more often than not had the heart-lifting experience of riding down the 20 floors in the elevator with the exquisite Loretta Young, who lived in John's building. But my heart dropped back down about two minutes later when I entered Bea's apartment to find John beaming at me over a new pile of even older material that he had unearthed from Bea's distant past, such as sketches from the early André Charlot revues in which Bea had starred with Gertrude Lawrence in 1920–21. We were almost back in World War One at a time when America, led by its new and youthful President, Jack Kennedy, was far more concerned about the looming prospect of World War Three.

Still not a word or a note had been jettisoned. *Beaography* was now considerably longer than Wagner's *Ring of the Nibelungen*, weighing in between 12 and 15 hours of material that was officially dead before World War Two. The truth was that Bea had already done what *Beaography* was intended to be in *An Evening with Beatrice Lillie*. She and I knew that by the second week. We exchanged meaningful glances, but she continued to indulge John because he saw this as his moment of becoming Florenz Ziegfeld, which is the moment where most of this material came from.

Poor John. He had no idea about the realities of the theatre. The rules don't apply to Beatrice Lillie, he proclaimed three times a day. John had made himself indispensable by becoming a major-domo in her life, or 'manager', as he titled himself. He was loud, brash, pushy, abrasive and devoted, and had doubled his weight in her service. He was disliked by almost everybody, especially Bea's contemporaries, who couldn't stand him. But Bea needed him, and I understood from the beginning his place and his value in her existence, so Evie and I tolerated him for her sake. The cruel truth was that a 35-year-old John Philip Huck – you can imagine the Noël Coward limerick – was hard to find if you were a pushing-70 Bea Lillie.

I became increasingly frustrated, having seen the current crop of Broadway smashes, becoming more and more excited by what Newley and I were doing, knowing I was wasting my precious mornings on this sad voyage to the past. Mercifully, Bea knew it, too, and suggested that we call it a day and leave it to John to put together what he saw as the best final choices – i.e. every word she had ever uttered or sung on stage, screen or radio.

Back across the street, Newberg and I had a completed script, and 14 indicated song-spots. We knew what each song had to achieve in terms of storytelling, and we also knew we had never written one single song together in the two years since we met. We had never even tried. We just knew we could. And we did. Starting at the top, we wrote the 14 songs in the eight days at our disposal, working from 10.00am 'til 2.00am every day. A kindly muse was sitting on our shoulder for those eight days, for we never changed one note or one word of any of those songs. I still have the piece of paper that has 'Once in a Lifetime' on one side and 'What Kind of Fool Am I?' on the other.

Because Evie was our heroine, our Woman of the Year, without whom the show would never have been written, we named the show's heroine Evie in her honour, and wrote Littlechap's love song about her, 'Someone Nice Like You', as our tribute to our Evie. Over the years since, hundreds of people we know and hundreds more we don't, the moment they learn who she is, start singing, sometimes all the way through, while Evie stands smiling and listening:

Why did someone nice like you, Evie,
Have to fall in love with me?
When I think of all the men
You could have loved –
The men you should have loved –
Who would have loved you.

You're worth so much more than me, Evie —
Believe you me, Evie —
You know it's true.
And if we could live twice
I'd make life Paradise
For someone really nice
Like you.

The night before Newberg left for London, we went into the midtown New York Decca studio, where his record company had arranged for him to record a couple of songs with the all-powerful Jerry Lieber and Mike Stoller, songwriters supreme who had written pretty well every great hit that Elvis Presley had ever had. The 'A' side was their contemporisation of Debussy's 'Claire de Lune', a stomach-turning lyric attached to the classic melody. Newley insisted that 'What Kind of Fool Am I?' be the 'B' side of the record, and paid for an arrangement to be prepared that day. Lieber and Stoller pooh-poohed the idea, because the song wasn't commercial. No 'Fool', no 'Claire de Lune', said Newley. They gave in, and at the three-hour midnight session they allocated two hours and fifty minutes to 'Claire de Lune' and ten minutes to 'Fool'. They were so pleased with 'Claire de Lune' they never even bothered to play back Tony's two takes of 'Fool'. They made no comment at all on the song or Tony's performance, little knowing or caring that they had just been the first to record the following year's Grammy Award-winning Best Song, which would subsequently be recorded by more than a thousand singers. Mind you, we didn't know it either. We were just desperately happy to have the first recording of any song we had ever written together.

Newley left for London. I left it to John Philip to edit or not to edit what had now become the world's longest-ever show. He was thrilled and proud of what he now called 'my baby', and told us at length of the millions we were all going to make. Needless to say, *Beaography* was never heard of or mentioned again.

Bea always delighted in surprising me. One day she said to me out of the blue, 'Be free at five o'clock. I want you to meet someone.' Just that. No further information, no clues.

Bea, Evie and I, leaving John to his whatever-is-the-opposite-of-editing, got in the car and were driven uptown, then across town, to our mystery destination, with not a word from Bea about why, where or who. We arrived at a hospital called The Harkness Pavilion, facing the Hudson River. We entered the building, took the elevator to the seventh floor, where we were met by a white-jacketed butler, who led us along a wide, windowed passageway, like that of a giant ocean liner. Still not a word from Bea. At the far end of the passageway, lying on a chaise lounge with his back to us, was an elderly gentleman in a silk dressing-gown. We drew up alongside him. Bea turned to me, smiled her most wicked and triumphant smile and said, 'Leslie, this is Cole Porter.'

Meeting God without being forewarned is a pretty shabby trick to perpetrate on an impressionable young songwriter, but, since I have spent much of my adult life trying to pull comparable stunts on Evie, I could not blame Bea, but just stand there and hyperventilate. And Cole – 'Please call me Cole,' he said – was as elegant, witty and charming as anything he ever wrote, and for two hours of total enchantment, plus a huge tub of Beluga and two bottles of Roederer Cristal, Evie and I sat spellbound as he and Bea reminisced and we all talked about the world of musicals past and present.

Bea told the story of a struggling songwriter called Herman Hupfeld, who had offered to sell her for $200 the copyright of a song he thought might work in her cabaret act. Bea tried it, and said, 'Thank you, but no.' The song was called 'As Time Goes By', and a few months later it found its way into a B-movie called *Casablanca*.

At the end of the two hours of our enchanted evening, Cole handed me the recently published *Cole Porter Songbook*, with its internal white spiral binding, so that the book would lie open flat on the piano. He inscribed it simply 'For Leslie From Cole'.

Little did I know as he did it that he was laying the foundation stone for my subsequent lifelong passion for collecting rare and inscribed books.

Bea had arranged that the four of us − herself, John, Evie and myself − would sail back to Europe. The *SS Constitution* was the vessel of choice. I remember that we sailed from New York on the day that Bea's friend Gary Cooper died. We spent two weeks getting back to London. A stormy Atlantic crossing ended in Casablanca, where Bea got more than slightly drunk and sang, '*You must remember this… That Auntie Bea is pissed… Which no one can deny…*' as we guided her gently back to the ship. Naples gave us a brief sentimental glimpse of Capri, and Genoa of Portofino, before we disembarked at Marseilles and drove back to London via the Atlantic coast of France and the Normandy beaches and war graves.

Newley had used his two weeks far more creatively than I had. Not only had he completely cast the show − it was still Newley and ten girls, but oh-so-different from what he had originally intended − he was directing it himself, and he had persuaded Bernie Delfont to forget about the summer season in Brighton and to open the show as a musical at the Palace Theatre, Manchester, and, if successful, bring it into the West End.

The show didn't have a title 'til the third week of rehearsals, when we finally hit upon *Stop the World − I Want to Get Off*, which gave me the further idea of the Littlechap character freezing the stage action any time he wanted to by shouting 'Stop the world!' and stepping out of the play to comment to the audience. This device worked beautifully. It produced a number of big laughs, and it gave the title more meaning, since Littlechap was the narrator of his own life story, and therefore had the licence to break the fourth wall.

What Anthony Newley achieved in the ten weeks between our starting to write and the finished show opening to the public in a 2,000-seat theatre is little short of miraculous, the most diversified, creative tour de force I have ever witnessed by one man. Everything he was ever meant to do or be came together in those two-and-a-half months. The natural spontaneity that existed between us from day one exploded into life. Good songs had fallen on to the page one after another. Tony's instincts as a performer led him to inspired casting as a director, and the teenage girls who made up the ensemble were to include three future stars. Ian Fraser, Newley's arranger and conductor, became the guiding light of the show's musical presentation, and Sean Kenny, England's leading young stage designer, fought and won the battle over the look of the show, a classic small circus tent set, which we later learned was an old design he had never been able to unload. But it worked. My God, how it worked! I concluded that it was all meant to be.

Manchester was successful beyond our dreams and, four weeks later, *Stop the World* opened at the newly rebuilt Queen's Theatre on Shaftesbury Avenue, next door to the Globe Theatre where my professional life had started with Auntie Bea seven years before. The first 20 minutes of the opening-night performance seemed to my cat-on-a-hot-tin-roof mind to be interminably dull and boring, and my heart stopped when four people in the middle of Row E got up and walked out, arguing volubly about what I assumed was their disgust with the show. I sank lower into my seat, waiting for the rest of the audience to follow them. They didn't, and three minutes later Newley brought the house down with 'Gonna Build a Mountain'. From then on, the show was flying. 'Once in a Lifetime' and 'What Kind of Fool Am I?' also stopped the show, and Evie and I were suddenly in floods of tears in the middle of a standing ovation. Bernie Delfont, looking like the cat that got the cream, gave us a stylish first-night party at the Society Club in Jermyn Street and, before it was over, the morning papers confirmed that we were indeed a big hit. Newley's career and mine were off to the races. Our lives changed overnight. On the brink of the ripe old age of 30, we had arrived.

David Merrick, Broadway's leading producer, flew over from New York and promised to take the show to Broadway in the autumn of the following year, as soon as Newley's one-year West End commitment was completed. The reason for Bernie Delfont's cat-like grin was that the total budget for the show, with one set, a cast of 11 and no costume changes, was £6,000. Bernie would net over £1 million, some 200 times his investment. More power to him. He allowed us to do our thing the way we wanted, and never interfered at any stage of the process. I bought Evie her first car as a thank you for causing it all to happen, and taught her how to drive into the bargain, a gallant but necessary added bonus.

The tempo of our lives increased perceptibly. Our circle of friends exploded like the Big Bang, and from that explosion came the inner circle of a dozen or so people who have remained the closest to us from that day to this, 40-plus years later. In the beginning, we would meet in twos and fours and sixes at a handful of favourite restaurants, chief among them our official group headquarters, The White Elephant Club on Curzon Street, followed by Alvaro's restaurant in the King's Road, Chelsea, and the Trattoria Terrazza in Romilly Street, Soho. And, of course, the grande dame of London watering holes, opposite my original digs in Arlington Street, the much-loved Caprice, still immaculately run by London's most celebrated maître d', the great Mario, continued to be the top of the list.

Vivian Cox, who for many years produced the annual Royal Film Command Performance at the Odeon Theatre, Leicester Square, asked me to help him out for a couple of them, writing speeches and continuity chit-chat for the glittering array of international film personalities who always showed up for this most glamorous event. I happily obliged. It was worth it if only for special moments like meeting and gazing at the delectable Kim Novak, or writing a speech for one of England's great movie stars, John Mills, with whose family Evie and I were to become close friends. Evie already knew Johnnie, because she had appeared in a film called *The Baby and the Battleship* with him and

Richard Attenborough and Bryan Forbes when she was 16, and they had all fallen in love with her. Dickie Attenborough and I had first met at another Royal Gala event, the annual *Night of a Hundred Stars* at the London Palladium, in the mid-1950s, when Bea was in the show. The Millses, the Attenboroughs and the Forbes were each other's best friends, and we happily became absorbed into their delightful little family clique.

The cast album of *Stop the World* proved highly popular, driven by the individual success of three or four of the show's songs and the ever-expanding list of new recordings. Tony had a successful single with 'What Kind of Fool Am I?', but the main cause of the score's long-term success came from a totally unexpected and exciting source. Sammy Davis Jr returned to London in triumph a month after *Stop the World* opened. His unique one-man show, its title simply his name, was a sensation and a sell-out at the Prince of Wales Theatre, a couple of blocks away from *Stop the World* at the Queen's. His singing, his dancing, his impressions, everything he did – and he did everything – was so dazzling that every time he stepped on stage he rejustified his reputation as the world's greatest entertainer. He came to see *Stop the World* just before he opened, and fell head-over-heels in love with the show, the songs and Newley's performance. Within days, the three of us linked up, and, from Sammy's first night at the Prince of Wales onwards, we saw one another almost every night for late suppers after the shows, either at The White Elephant or back at Sammy's huge sprawling Monte Carlo suite at the Mayfair Hotel. Sammy put together his London entourage, to add to the substantial American entourage that travelled with him, so that any meal to which we sat down would have an average cast the size of a major Broadway musical.

Sammy, like no one I have ever known before or since, knew how to enjoy himself. His life was a constant party, on stage and off. Deeply deprived as a child, he was surely making up for it now, celebrating every minute of every day, compounding endless acts of excessive generosity with outrageous self-indulgence. The chameleon in him decided he wanted to be more English than the English. Within days, he was wearing bowler hats, Savile Row suits, Turnbull and Asser shirts and ties, and Dunhill cuff-links, and carrying ebony, gold-topped walking sticks. He was David Niven. He was Rex Harrison. He was Ronald Colman. No question, Sammy was an entertainer and a life-force 24 hours of every day he lived.

He had recently married the beautiful Swedish film actress May Britt, a source of considerable controversy in the United States, where mixed marriages were still viewed with alarm, concern and even hatred. Their acceptance in London was far greater, another reason for Sammy's all-embracing passion for things English.

Sammy announced to us at supper one night that he had arranged with his record company, the Sinatra-owned Reprise label, to record four songs from *Stop the World*, and release them as a special extended-play mini-album. And, as we were to learn time and again in the years to come, Sammy never made us a promise he didn't keep. The songs were duly recorded and released not only in the United Kingdom but also in the United States. And it was Sammy's recordings of those four songs that blazed the trail to the torrent of recordings by every major American singer that created the unprecedented year-long build-up of interest in *Stop the World*, guaranteeing the show's success on Broadway.

It was around this time that Peter Sellers called me. Peter was a considerable distance from being the most emotionally stable person I knew, and, though he wouldn't openly admit it, I quickly gathered that he had fallen insanely in love with Sophia Loren, having just made a film with her called *The Millionairess*. No man can be blamed for falling in love with Sophia Loren, even though at the time Peter was seemingly happily married to a lovely Australian lady called Ann Howe, and indeed Ann Sellers, and they had two young children, Sarah and Michael. Peter told me that he had a wonderful idea for an album, to be cleverly entitled *Peter and Sophia*, because he suspected that Sophia had a singing talent. (Oh, sure, Peter!)

I drove out to Peter's magnificent Georgian home in Chipperfield to help him select material. By chance, I had recently written a song called 'I Fell in Love with an Englishman', purely because I had stumbled on a nifty rhyme for Englishman – 'a sweet and simple singlish man'. Peter loved the song, because it said exactly what he wanted Sophia to express, he being the Englishman. So intense was his ardour that he insisted we march out to his lavish games room, where a full drum kit and elaborate recording equipment awaited us. With Sellers as my drummer, I recorded the demo, which sounded a bit dubious sung *by* an Englishman and, in due course, Sophia did indeed record it. I also wrote Peter a though-I-say-so-myself funny sketch about Lawrence of Arabia after Peter, Evie and I went to see Alec Guinness in Terence Rattigan's play *Ross* at the Haymarket Theatre. Sellers doing Guinness was marginally better and infinitely more hilarious than Guinness doing Guinness. In Alec's dressing room after the play, Peter kept repeating everything Alec said, word for word, and you couldn't tell the two apart.

Peter and Sophia became a highly successfully album, the star track being a little duet entitled 'Goodness Gracious Me', a substantial hit single.

A few weeks later, Peter called me again. Spurred on by the success of the record, he had had another Wonderful Idea. He was now living in a superb penthouse in Oak Hill Park in Hampstead, yards away from my old school. He and Ann were separated and divorcing. I was to learn over the years that Sellers changed homes, ladies and motor cars as other men change socks. To my certain knowledge, he owned over 200 cars in a 15-year period. He sounded desperate, and had to see me that evening.

I arrived to be greeted by a wild-eyed Sellers, who introduced me to the other person present, film director Richard Lester. Peter announced that he had brought the three of us together because we were the perfect team to create the definitive romantic comedy for himself and... yes, Sophia. It would be, he assured us, Billy Wilder plus, the commercial hit of the decade, and Oscars for all. Every night for close to two weeks, because Peter was filming by day, Dick Lester and I allowed ourselves to be dragooned by this madman to create a storyline for a project in which Sophia would be Sophia and Peter would be Cary Grant, Jack Lemmon and William Holden irresistibly rolled into one. We actually ended up with quite a good treatment, which predictably did not go any further due to Sophia's in-every-sense unavailability. She was fond of Peter, but, at the height of her beauty and super-stardom, she was happily married to Carlo Ponti, so she charmingly and diplomatically wriggled herself out of a possible embarrassment. Dick Lester, as director-elect of the Romantic Comedy That Never Was, was as relieved as I was to be freed from Peter's crazed stranglehold, and starkly visualised to me the mayhem into which this project would have descended, with the three of us locked in adjoining cells in a madhouse.

Max Bygraves lived just a few hundred yards away from us in Stanmore, and one night he and his divine wife Blossom and Evie and I were having dinner and bemoaning the fact that there wasn't a decent restaurant within miles of our homes. So we decided to open one. Evie and I imagined a jolly little bistro called the Bistro Vino or the Café des Artistes, but Max had grander ideas. We should use his name and pulling power. OK, I thought, we'll call it Max's or Maxie's or even Maxie B's. 'Better than that!' cried Max. 'Maxim's!'

Max brought in a major film-set designer called Maurice Carter, who created a red, purple, black and gilt monstrosity that would have served well as Count Dracula's dining room, had we been making a movie. I wanted to cast Christopher Lee as the head waiter, with some of Evie's fellow thespians from Hammer Films, or the Addams Family, as the customers.

A couple of months later, Maxim's opened its fairly forbidding doors to the stunned suburban Stanmore public. It was impossibly pretentious and extremely expensive, catering to a clientele about as far removed from Max's wholesome family audience as can be imagined. It projected the warmth of a graveyard. Nonetheless, against the odds, it had a following of sorts. A few well-to-do local businessmen, a retired Air Marshall who insisted on calling his favourite wine 'Geoffrey Chambertin', as though it were an old school chum, some wealthy retirees and a smattering of snobs. Amazingly, Maxim's survived for four years, and we did not have to sell the plantation when we disposed of it.

We took lots of pals there in the early months. Evie played a leading guest role in *The Saint* TV series opposite Roger Moore at nearby Elstree Studios, and brought Roger and his brand-new girlfriend, a beautiful young Italian actress called Luisa Matteoli, to Maxim's for dinner at the end of the last day of shooting. Roger was still married to but recently separated from his second wife, a famous and tempestuous Welsh songstress called Dorothy Squires.

Early in the dinner, clearly wishing to get it off his chest, Roger confessed to me that it was one of his many contretemps with Madame Squires that had caused the precipitous departure of his party of four from Row E of the Queen's Theatre on the first night of *Stop the World*, for which he now wished to apologise profusely, and hope that one day I would find it in my heart to forgive him. I said I was just glad he wasn't a critic. Roger and Luisa were living nearby in Elstree, so we met regularly and integrated quickly into one another's circle of friends, which had a number of people in common.

Roger was a surprise. Extremely English and well mannered, he had a gentle self-effacing modesty, skilfully welded to a naughty schoolboy's dirty sense of humour. I suspected his self-deprecating manner was a defence mechanism to offset the impact made by his devastatingly good looks. Luisa spoke hilarious Chico Marx English, was deliciously and paralysingly funny, and seemed likely to become a worthy successor to her Welsh forerunner in the tempestuous department.

One Monday evening in late September, Evie and I were sitting in Newberg's dressing room after the show, waiting to go and have supper with Sammy at The White Elephant, when the theatre manager ushered in a couple of celebrities from the audience, the handsome American actor Robert Wagner and the extremely dishy Joan Collins. It was an instant classic Hollywood scenario. We had met Joan at the last Royal Command Film Performance a few months before, with her then fiancé, Shirley MacLaine's baby brother, Warren Beatty, who was all of 21 years old. Since then, Warren and Joan had broken up, and Warren was now with Natalie Wood, with whom he had been filming Elia Kazan's *Splendour in the Grass*. This had contributed handsomely to Natalie's divorce from Robert Wagner, thus removing their Hollywood's perfect couple tag. I recalled that Joan and Warren were being touted as Hollywood's perfect couple just a few months before, but that was now over. So now here were Joan and RJ, as he was known. I wondered whether they were contenders for *next* year's Hollywood's perfect couple contest. Apparently not. They were, I was informed, just a couple of old chums consoling one another while life's script department did a quick rewrite.

They both adored the show, Joan in particular. Just how much became evident two days later when out of a clear blue sky she called Evie, having got our number from God knows where, and announced that she had found out that this coming Saturday was Tony Newley's birthday, and she would like to give him a birthday supper at The White Elephant for about a dozen people after the show, and would Evie please assemble Tony's closest friends for the occasion?

Evie did so, we all enjoyed a jolly evening together, Joan moved in with Newley that night, and that was that. I don't think poor old Newberg ever knew what hit him. A truck could not have done a better job, but then very few trucks look as good or move as fast as Joan Collins when she has her foot on the pedal. And Newley, as I say, was run over in spectacular fashion.

Joan, then as now, was an irresistible force. Newberg, for all his blazing talents, was a docile soul at heart, and, if he had any thoughts about posing as an immovable object, he needed to start digging in fast. Together, they made a spectacular couple, and the four of us promptly embarked upon the best four-way friendship I have ever known any four people to enjoy. We were all the right age in the right place at the right time. It was the beginning of what we did not yet know was about to become the Swinging Sixties, although the signs were already there, and, with *Stop the World* a big West End hit and the two most gorgeous girls on the planet on our arms, Newberg and I knew we were in pole position to enjoy whatever lay ahead.

The four of us were as inseparable as our busy lives allowed. Joannie was filming, Evie was filming, Newley was doing everything under the sun, and Bernie Delfont invited me to collaborate with Wolf Mankowitz and Cyril Ornadel on a new musical vehicle to star Harry Secombe as Pickwick. It was an inspired idea. Harry Secombe *was* Pickwick and, although the show was more than a year away, I immediately started to tinker with possible lyric ideas. Dickens is my favourite English novelist, and I have always marvelled that he was able to weave so colourful and complex a tapestry as *The Pickwick Papers* at the age of 23.

In January, Joannie returned to California and, when Newley's two-week vacation from *Stop the World* rolled around in February, she invited him to spend it with her out there. Evie and I saw him off at London Heathrow, Newley grumbling that we should be going with him and, ten minutes after our emotional farewell, the expression on Tony's face when we walked on to the plane to join him was worth the price of the air fare.

It was our first-ever Boeing 707 polar flight, London to Los Angeles non-stop. It was Evie's 24th birthday, and what Joannie organised for us in the ensuing two weeks showed us more of the Beverly Hills and Hollywood lifestyle than we have witnessed in the 40 years since. Joannie loves and epitomises glamour, and she ladled it out to us in huge helpings. The four of us shared a gorgeous little Hollywood Hills house just off the Sunset Strip, and the three newly arrived, jet-lagged travellers sat open-mouthed listening to Joan rattling off our itinerary for the next

12 days. She then put us through the Hollywood equivalent of a Marine assault course, with herself as the drill sergeant. In those 12 days we had a welcoming dinner party at a beach-house in Malibu; a day at Disneyland; four days in Palm Springs, where Joannie and Evie fell in love with the innocent-looking pineapple rum drinks at Don the Beachcomber's restaurant, got completely legless and had to be carried home by their gentleman escorts; three days in Las Vegas as Sammy Davis's guests at the Sands Hotel, where each night he sang the songs from *Stop the World* and introduced us to his audience; then, after his midnight show, around 2.30am, he was joined on stage in the Copa Room by Frank Sinatra, Dean Martin, Joey Bishop and Peter Lawford, and we witnessed the now-famous Rat Pack Summit Meetings, where the ad-libs and the insults flew back and forth like zinging bullets, to the total delight of the ecstatic audience; dinners at Joan's favourite hot-shot Beverly Hills restaurants, Chasens and La Scala, as well as her cheap dives on Sunset Strip; and three parties at her house for her longstanding circle of Hollywood chums, which included Tony and Judy Franciosa and Paul and Joanne Newman.

When Joannie finally poured us back on to the London-bound plane 12 days later, we were considerably more exhausted than when we arrived. But the glow from that glorious long-ago Hollywood initiation of fire is still visible.

We returned to London to discover that Newberg and I had won two Ivor Novello Awards, the British equivalent of a Grammy-cum-Tony, for Best Musical Score − *Stop the World* − and Best Song − 'What Kind of Fool Am I?'. I also picked up a third one for the Most Performed Song of the Year, 'My Kind of Girl'. The awards show was televised by the BBC, and the finale of the show was to be a medley of songs from *Stop the World*, culminating in the appearance of Newley to sing 'Fool'. At the end of the song, I had to join him on stage from the audience to receive the handsome bronze statuettes of Melpomene, the Greek goddess of music. The medley sounded good, then Newley appeared to heavy applause to sing what was officially categorised as the Best Song of the Year, lyrically and musically. He then completely dried, his mind went blank and he proceeded to sing the melody accompanied by a lyric of total Jabberwocky.

Having sung the song to show-stopping effect some 300 times since the show had opened in Manchester the previous summer, Newley picked our moment of glory on national network television to dry like an Arizona riverbed and turn our beautiful song into 32 bars of unintelligible gobbledegook beamed to several million homes around the country. I got up on cue to join him on stage. Newley saw me out of the corner of his eye and, traumatised by what was happening, thought I was coming up there to kill him, which was not a bad idea. There wasn't a jury in the land that wouldn't have acquitted me on the grounds of justifiable homicide.

Lulled into a false sense of security by *Stop the World*'s smooth path to success, Tony and I started to think about our second show. Naively, we believed that, having written the first one in three weeks, we could knock off the second one in four, five at the most. We met every morning in the circle bar of the Queen's Theatre, whose huge plate-glass windows look out on to Shaftesbury Avenue and Soho. We were aware that Tony and Joan would soon be off to New York and Broadway for a year or more and, during that time, I would be working on *Pickwick*. We got as far as a working outline entitled *Mr Fat and Mr Thin*, and laid out first drafts of half-a-dozen songs, but somehow the show lacked the simple straightforward line of *Stop the World*, and we got bogged down in a no man's land somewhere between a Laurel and Hardy farce and *Waiting for Godot*. Finally, time ran out on us, Tony and Joan left for New York, inviting Evie and me to join up with them over there as soon as we could, and I turned my attention to *Pickwick*, which I had been anticipating with some relish. It would be the first time I had worked on a stage adaptation of a famous literary work. I found the idea appealing.

This, in turn, brought me back to my long-lasting, on-off romance with *Cyrano de Bergerac*. I determined to return to the pursuit of the rights if all went well with *Stop the World* on Broadway and *Pickwick* in London.

Wolf Mankowitz did a masterly job adapting and condensing the vast sprawl of *The Pickwick Papers* into the tight, workable, funny, two-hour musical book that Cyril Ornadel and I received shortly thereafter. With Evie and Cyril's lovely Israeli wife Shoshana, we rented ourselves a pink Mediterranean villa, Alan Jay Lerner-style, in the South of France for a month, then another on the Italian Riviera. Work on the score went well on the Côte d'Azur. The second villa, on the Italian Riviera, was less than a success. It was a modern white villa overlooking the Mediterranean in the town of Varigotti. It looked good in the brochure, and it was, except that what both the brochure and the agent omitted to tell us was that the Genoa–San Remo mainline railway tracks were right outside our front door, alongside the road. The result was that at all hours of the day and night there would be a sudden earthquake-like roar as a window-rattling express train exploded out of the mountain tunnel to our east and rocketed past us like an angry dragon on wheels. It was hardly the serene setting that Alan Jay had enjoyed in Capri. It was not conducive to the meditational calm required by the soul in the making of beautiful words and music. It was as soothing as a mariachi band at midnight. I swiftly renamed Varigotti 'Very Grotty'. But Cyril and I soldiered on. Compared to the electric tempo at which I worked with Newley, this was pretty leisurely stuff, but nonetheless enjoyable, and we liked what we were writing.

By mid-August, we could tolerate it no longer, and we agreed to part company and meet back in London. We were satisfied that we had a pretty good first draft score and knew where all the songs went, and agreed to send one another revisions, improvements and new ideas, long-distance if necessary. But, as we went our ways, I was acutely aware that there was as yet no sign of the big song for *Pickwick* and Harry Secombe's glorious tenor voice, nor any likely place for it.

In retrospect, the only good thing about Varigotti was its proximity to Portofino, an hour's drive away. We stayed in the beautiful small Hotel Paraggi on the sand beach at Paraggi, less than a mile from Portofino, which has no beach. Our love affair with Portofino deepened during the ten days we spent in this little bay, with its deep, turquoise-green waters reflecting the rich sub-tropical vegetation growing out of the lava-rock hills that loomed over it. Evie and I promised one another we'd come back for a longer stay.

A couple of weeks later, our Portofino tans still more or less intact, we found ourselves in Philadelphia, where *Stop the World* was to open at the Shubert Theater prior to Broadway. Our producer, David Merrick, who normally liked to project a mean and grumpy Groucho Marx image, was in rare high spirits and had nothing but good news to impart. The advance word on the show in New York, like the advance at the box office, was extremely encouraging. Sammy's recordings of the show's songs had sparked huge interest among other recording artists, and our music publisher Howard Richmond told us that he was hearing of important new recordings virtually every day. Everything about the Broadway production, including even the brilliant new poster design, pointed towards success.

Philadelphia was a triumph. The press and the public loved the show. It was a complete sell-out and, remarkably, recouped its entire Broadway investment in the first two weeks. Little wonder that David Merrick was smiling, or that the Famous Four were thus enabled to enjoy a blissfully happy stay in the City of Brotherly Love. We took a thousand photographs of one another, and could have been forgiven for assuming that the Broadway happy ending was now purely a formality. Wrong. We were about to learn that you never assume *anything* about Broadway.

Joannie led the social way, as usual. We spent the weekend before the Broadway opening, while the show was being moved into the Shubert Theater on West 44th Street, staying with the Paul Newmans and their three little daughters at their lovely, sprawling country home up in Weston, Connecticut, a most acceptable rural lull before the New York storm.

Our day of destiny was 3 October, an unseasonably sweltering autumn night in New York, so hot that, as the first-night curtain went up, the theatre management saw fit to turn on the Shubert Theater's air-conditioning system, a medieval device which made a sound reminiscent of the dreaded World War Two Doodlebugs. It was like watching television with the sound off while someone vacuumed the room. I dashed to the front of house and begged the box-office manager to get it turned off. He replied that this was not a box-office matter. I said it would become a box-office matter tomorrow when people stopped buying tickets and there *was* no box-office. Apparently, the air-conditioning was controlled from backstage. I ran down Shubert Alley to the stage door, and was informed I couldn't go on to the stage area because there was a performance in progress. I went anyway and got hold of the assistant stage manager. I explained that the air-conditioning was on in the auditorium, and was informed that, yes, 'it's because it's an unseasonably warm evening'. I pointed out that, while I was in favour of the audience being comfortable, I was even more in favour of them being able to hear the show they were watching, especially as tonight happened to be the first night, and about half the audience were critics, which made me think for a moment that maybe it wasn't such a bad thing they couldn't hear the dialogue. I'd sooner they blamed the air-conditioning than Newley and myself. The ASM said that at intermission she would get the stage manager to talk to the theatre manager, or even Mr Merrick himself, to get a ruling. I said that by intermission the theatre would be three-quarters empty, and it wouldn't matter any more. I suddenly wished I was back in Port Carling, Ontario, with The Straw Hat Players and dead priests falling out of the bottoms of coffins. At least they made decisions up there, even if they were mostly wrong ones.

At intermission, they turned off the air-conditioning, which earned one of the better rounds of applause of the evening so far. Newley was livid. The show proceeded, Act Two played beautifully and, at the end, Tony and his tiny team of players earned their customary standing ovation. Our dampened spirits rose again, and we all trooped across the street to Sardi's for the first-night party. The place was packed with glittery first-nighters, and we had a great time for an hour-and-a-half before David Merrick's general manager, Jack Schlissel, arrived with three newspapers under his arm and an expression on his face that made the Grim Reaper look like Bozo the Clown. He came up to Newberg and myself and addressed the following three memorable words to us: 'Leave... Now... Disaster.' David Merrick had already disappeared.

Tony, Joan, Evie and myself repaired to the Navarro Hotel on Central Park South, where we were staying. A handful of staunch loyalists came with us, my agent Richard Gregson, Sean Kenny, our designer, and Paul and Joanne Newman. And it was true, the three morning reviews, particularly the all-important *New York Times* review by David Merrick's bête noir Howard Taubman, were about as favourable as Caesar's thumbs-down at the Coliseum in Rome. We sat enveloped in gloom. Someone, probably Sean, mournfully suggested that we drink ourselves to death. The idea sounded good at the time, and copious quantities of booze were ordered up to Tony's suite, where we all conscientiously set to work to drown our sorrows. The evening became a cross between a wake and an all-night vigil. We decided to wait up for the next day's four afternoon newspapers, which would appear on the streets at dawn. We bravely made defiant and tasteless jokes. There was an excess of nervous and near-hysterical laughter, but deep down we were sick to our stomachs.

At 5.30am, Paul Newman announced that a new and more important emergency had arisen. We had run out of beer, and room service wasn't responding. Ever resourceful, Paul said he knew from experience how to solve this kind of crisis. It would require two fearless men, so he and I, both by now rather the worse for wear, descended to the street and walked the short distance to Sixth Avenue and 58th Street, through the first rays of dawn light. The beer trucks, he confided in me, made their deliveries to all the popular saloons at dawn, to avoid the rush hour. He also offered to share another New York phenomenon with me. If you lie down in the middle of the street at the intersection of Sixth and 58th and look east, he said, you get a perfect view of the sunrise. I volunteered that you probably also got killed.

I would venture to claim that I must be one of the few people alive today who have laid down dead drunk in the middle of the intersection of Sixth Avenue and 58th Street in New York City with Paul Newman at dawn on an October morning and watched a perfect sunrise. The huge red ball came up out of the road, dead centre between the buildings, exactly as Paul had predicted it would, and we lay there gazing at it seraphically until the big cop joined us and asked if he could be of any help. Happily, he recognised Paul, who happened to be the world's biggest film star that morning and a lot of other mornings. Even more happily, the first beer truck rolled into view right after the big cop, who generously helped us carry the beer back to the Navarro. I later wondered how many sunrises Paul had watched from that unique vantage point to be such an authority.

And I guess that was the turning point of my life. About ten minutes later, someone arrived with early dawn copies of the four evening papers and they contained four unanimous rave reviews for *Stop the World*. It was as though they had seen a completely different show from the morning critics. They had, in fact, all been sitting next to one another in the theatre. So, overall, we had a 4–3 edge with the Seven Butchers of Broadway, as they were then affectionately known. We finally went to bed, ecstatically happy, saved by the bell, as it were and, a few hours later, Newberg and I were standing with David Merrick in Shubert Alley looking at the long line of people queuing for tickets. David remarked dryly, 'That's one line I don't want cut from the show!'

I loved Merrick, unadulterated monster that he was. A lawyer by origin, he delighted in being a figure of controversy and playing the villain, but he was a fabulous producer and waged a brilliant ongoing war against the press. He filled the big *Stop the World* newspaper ads with the best of the critical quotes, and because Howard Taubman hadn't had one kind word to say about any aspect of the show, Merrick put in a huge quote in Ancient Greek alongside the raves, purely so that he could put 'Howard Taubman, *New York Times*' at the foot of it. The Greek quote probably said that this was the worst show in the history of Broadway.

Now at last we could enjoy New York. At least Evie and I could. We went to see Sammy Davis Jr knocking 'em dead at the Copacabana, New York's prime cabaret club, where a decade before he hadn't been allowed in the door 'til Frank Sinatra changed things. Again, as at every show, Sam sang our songs and introduced us to his adoring audience. We regularly went with Tony and Joan, late at night after the show, together with Joannie's closest New York chums, Peter and Linda Bren, to an amazing Italian restaurant called Chez Vito, where a dozen red-coated violinists wandered through the room, playing in unison favourite themes from operas and musicals. Seated at their tables, stars from Broadway and the Metropolitan Opera who happened to be eating there would sing their famous arias and showstoppers for the benefit and delight of their fellow diners. It was unique.

But all was not as well as Evie and I would have wished between Tony and Joan. One would have thought that Tony, acclaimed as author, composer, director and star of the big new Broadway hit show, with Joan Collins as his live-in lover, living in one of the largest and lushest penthouses in Manhattan on the 29th floor of Imperial House on East 69th Street, had at the age of 30 as much as any kid from the slums of London could reasonably ask for. But reason had nothing to do with it.

In the *Stop the World* company, playing Littlechap's two daughters, as they had done in London, were the most exquisite pair of identical, 16-year-old blonde blue-eyed twins, Susan and Jennifer Baker, of devastating appeal, and an enormous asset to the show. Only they and Tony's towering leading lady, Anna Quayle, who played the central figure of Evie, had come to Broadway from the original London production. We had known that there had been an ongoing thing between Tony and Susan Baker ever since the show had opened in Manchester, long before Joannie had appeared on the scene to rewrite Newley's life. And it seemed the Susan flame was still burning brightly whenever Joan wasn't around. Joan, never one to beat about the bush, gave Tony a clear-cut ultimatum – he had ten days to make up his mind what he wanted. In almost the same breath, ever the planner and the politician, she invited Evie and me to Jamaica for ten days to celebrate our upcoming fourth wedding anniversary on 18 October.

Forty-eight hours later, Evie, Joannie and I were at the Half Moon Hotel on the pink-sand beach of Montego Bay, in the villa where Princess Margaret and Tony Armstrong-Jones, now Lord Snowdon, had recently spent their honeymoon. The first evening there, I had the pleasure of escorting the two most beautiful girls in the world to the beach terrace for dinner. A Jamaican steel band played softly in the background, and the moon was reflected in the sea. A warm, balmy breeze gently swayed the palm fronds, and the food and the Jamaican rum drinks were appropriately exotic. Paradise, I thought, must not be terribly unlike this. Two minutes later, the hotel management turned their loud-speaker system up to full, and Paradise cooled rapidly as we sat and listened to President John Fitzgerald Kennedy's Cuba Crisis speech, which delivered to President Khruschev of the USSR an ultimatum even more far-reaching than Joan's to Tony Newley. Not only were we a few days away from the end of the world, but, Cuba being the next island to Jamaica, we would have front-row seats for it.

When the world is about to end, there's not a hell of a lot you can do except wait. We befriended James Jones, the novelist who had written the great World War Two saga *From Here to Eternity*, which also seemed a not inappropriate title for our present predicament. Jim was there with his delightful wife Gloria, and their gorgeous little two-year-old, blonde-ringleted daughter Kelly. He and I played some desultory games of tennis together, but our minds were elsewhere. The sense of worldwide tension was unbearable. Jim was convinced we were going into a nuclear war, and was desolate that he had survived World War Two 20 years ago to bring Kelly into the world for this. We would all eat together as the world held its breath, waiting to know whether Khrushchev's Cuba-bound ships would turn around or call Kennedy's bluff. And it was no bluff.

We all know how the story ended, or you would not be reading this. Evie, Joannie and I returned to New York, one world drama resolved, to await the outcome of the other. And we had two happy endings. Tony knew what he had in Joan, and how good they were together, so he vowed, as in a Barbara Cartland novel, to be true. And, more to the point, to marry the delectable Joan. Peace and calm were instantly restored in the Newley penthouse.

Evie and I returned to London with several sighs of relief, though I confess I remained acutely sensitive to the fact that, while order had ostensibly returned to East 69th Street, the cold reality was that Newberg and Susan Baker were still in the show together for the next year or more, performing, as it were, eight times a week.

Pickwick started to come together. Peter Coe, who had directed Lionel Bart's *Oliver!* with great panache a couple of years before, was brought on board to complete his Dickensian double, as was Sean Kenny, who had designed both *Oliver!* and *Stop the World*. Sean was by far Britain's best stage designer, as delightful an Irish leprechaun as you could ever wish to meet, and quiet, fine company to be around. Lovely, ebullient, rotund Harry Secombe, our star, was that rare theatre being who, apart from delivering a great talent on the stage, was beloved by everyone in the cast and crew off it. Harry's huge and generous personality was the cement that held the bricks of *Pickwick* together, creating the proverbial big happy family.

We were deep into rehearsals, everything was going well, but we still didn't have that big song for Harry. Nobody except me seemed too bothered by its absence, as the book and score were both playing well, and Harry, as the centrepiece of the show, had lots of other good material to perform.

Wolf Mankowitz and I had conceived and co-created a cunning, if not audacious, if not insane, extra-curricular activity for ourselves, to open a restaurant called The Pickwick Club, timed to the opening of the show. We offered to throw the *Pickwick* first-night party there, an offer Bernie Delfont was swift to accept. Wolf and I recruited London's American celebrity chef Robert Carrier to design a Dickensian menu of good old English dishes, and a very fine and tasty job he did.

The Palace Theatre, Manchester, was once again our out-of-town venue of choice. Evie and I arrived at our hideaway hotel just outside the city, a charming garden residence called Milverton Lodge, where we had stayed for *Stop the World*, to an urgent message from Peter Coe. He felt there was a song missing early in Act Two, when Pickwick gets caught up in a local political election in the town of Eatonswill. For a fleeting moment, I dared to hope that Peter had found an idea for the big song. Alas, no. His thought was for a patter song to be entitled 'If I Were Your Parliamentary Candidate'. I could hardly see this becoming a chart-topper, even if it were recorded by Prime Minister Harold MacMillan, but I promised Peter I would think about it overnight.

And I did. At four o'clock in the morning, I woke up, angry and frustrated, realising that we were running out of time, and knowing the value that 'What Kind of Fool Am I?' had brought to *Stop the World*. It had summed up the central figure of the show.

It went on to be a huge hit for Sammy Davis, spawned a thousand recordings, and won the American Grammy Award for the Best Song of the Year. So now step one was to find the song that summed up Pickwick. I went back to basics. Rule one, exemplified a thousand times in the great theatre songs, was to use the verse of the lyric to link the specific context of the story to the expression of a bigger idea with universal application, viz, the chorus of the song. I decided to try to apply this theory to Peter Coe's 'If I Were Your Parliamentary Candidate' at the moment in the show where Pickwick is unexpectedly asked to make a speech. I put the essence of Peter's title into a verse, to see where it would lead me. And it led me naturally to the bigger idea I had been seeking in a dozen discarded lyrics. The idea was 'If I Ruled the World'. I knew the moment I had the title that I had the big song, too. The lyric wrote itself after that, and the melody arrived with the lyric. I had the whole thing inside half-an-hour, and then I was too thrilled to sleep.

I awakened Cyril Ornadel at dawn and was round at his hotel 20 minutes later. We went straight to a piano and put it down. Cyril made some deft improvements, particularly a much better melody for the bridge, and at ten o'clock that morning Harry Secombe sang 'If I Ruled the World' for the first time. When the show opened a few days later, he sang the song not once but twice in Act Two, and for the next three years, in Manchester and at the Saville Theatre in London and across America and at the 46th Street Theater in New York, he stopped the show twice every night that he ever played Pickwick.

The remarkable thing about Harry Secombe, a distinction he shared with Victor Borge and Harpo and Chico Marx, not bad company to be in, was that he combined lunatic humour with exceptional musicianship. These two qualities, which had each worked for him separately with a high degree of success up 'til that time, now came brilliantly together in *Pickwick*. And Wolf and I pulled off our daredevil double. Not only the show, but also the club that bore its name became a big hit, and they both opened on the same night! The Pickwick Club was a special place. Situated in Great Newport Street, just off the Charing Cross Road by the London Hippodrome, it was a members-only club for showbusiness people. It was oversubscribed within the first week, and it was always packed. The famous faces who came there loved it because they were left alone and no one asked them for their autograph. It was a permanent party, by day and by night, because almost everybody knew almost everybody else.

Sammy Davis was back in town, this time at Vaudeville's world headquarters, the 2,500-seat London Palladium. London had no theatre big enough to contain this tiny man's gigantic talent, and tickets to see Sammy traded like gold ingots. I wanted Sammy to hear 'If I Ruled the World', to see if he thought it would give him a chance to repeat his gold record success with 'What Kind of Fool Am I?'.

So I went over to the Mayfair Hotel one afternoon to see him. His suite contained everything except a piano. 'Never mind, there's one in the suite next door,' said Sam. We walked down the hall. The suite next door was called The Mancini Suite, and not by chance, for it contained not only a piano but the great Henry Mancini himself, sitting on the sofa, quietly scoring a movie. Sammy introduced us, and I then had the excruciating and dubious honour of auditioning my brand-new song for the biggest star in London before the undisputed maestro of Hollywood film music, who in the preceding 18 months had won three Oscars and about a dozen Grammies. Those three minutes rank high on my list of most embarrassing moments, but my heart started up again at the end of it when Sammy grinned at me and said, 'I'll record it as soon as I get back to LA.' And the great Mancini looked up, smiled and said, 'So will I.'

There *was* a hit single recording of 'If I Ruled the World', but it wasn't Sammy's, nor indeed Henry's. Tony Bennett had received the song very early on from our publisher at Chappell's Music, Teddy Holmes. He loved the song and promptly recorded it, and deservedly had a big success in the United States, but not, alas, in

England. Compensation came in the form of Harry Secombe's own recording of the song, which was played constantly and very soon became identified as his theme song, which it would continue to be for the rest of his life, because its philosophy was as much a reflection of Harry's personality as it was of Pickwick's. 'If I Ruled the World' went on to repeat the success of 'What Kind of Fool Am I?', winning the Novello Award for Best Song of the Year.

Those of you who remember *The Saint* television series will also no doubt recall that, for reasons never explained, the Saint, in the 6-foot-2 form of Roger Moore, used to drive around in a funny little white hunchback car supplied by the Swedish automobile manufacturer Volvo. Even in this early James Bond era, when Roger's predecessor as 007, Sean Connery, was flashing around in Aston Martin DB3s with multiple machine-guns and ejector seats, I thought the producers of *The Saint* could have sprung for something a little more upmarket for their hero... a drophead Jaguar, say, or, at the very least, a decent, sporty-looking MG or Morgan.

Anyway, Roger called us one gloriously sunny Saturday morning and announced that Volvo had graciously offered him the use of the Volvo yacht for the weekend, and would Evie and I meet him and Luisa at such-and-such a boatyard in Marlowe at noon, and we would cruise the Thames together 'til sunset. It all sounded *très, très* glamorous, so Evie and I spent the next hour assembling suitable yachting outfits for the occasion.

We arrived in Marlowe sharp at noon, because Roger was never one second late for anything. He was born with not a silver spoon but a Swiss watch in his mouth. He and Luisa were already there, but there was no sign of the Volvo yacht. Roger, embarrassed the way polite Englishmen easily get, asked the boatyard owner, who scratched his head and then said, 'Oh, you mean the Volvette! She's over there!' He led us along the towpath. No yacht in sight. The boatyard owner pointed down to the water and said, 'There she is, sir!' We followed his gaze to a tiny white dinghy-sized open boat, maybe 10 feet in length. It was the maritime edition of the Saint's funny little white car. I could only conclude that the Board of Directors of Volvo were all dwarves.

Luisa vividly voiced the general view in her picturesque Anglo-Italian. 'I no a-go in thees fuckin' rowin'-boat, Rogero! Yacht, my ass-a-hole!' Poor Rog, humiliated, put a brave face on it, and sensibly suggested that, having come this far, we should not ruin our day. He volunteered to navigate this splendid little craft to Maidenhead, where we would have lunch at the ever-popular Skindles restaurant, and thus save the situation in the finest Simon Templar tradition.

It is redundant to point out now that we could have driven from Marlowe to Maidenhead by car in less than ten minutes, but try telling that to a determined Roger Moore. Give Simon Templar a river with a boat on it, and he will sail to his destiny. The Volvette had a single, low-powered engine and a steering wheel, making it far less manoeuvrable than a twin-enginned craft, where the engines do all the work. In our case, Roger did all the work, cursing and cajoling the little boat, mostly sideways, to the first lock-gate.

A busy Saturday morning in midsummer is not the quietest time on the Thames. A jam of boats waiting to get through any Thames lock-gate is a mind-draining experience, and after five of them you long for the comparative luxury of London traffic gridlock. Hundreds of people, all in bigger boats than ours, recognised Roger, and gazed down cheerily at us, sitting cramped together like four people on a bus, from the chaises-longues on the sun-decks of their cruisers. Some wanted autographs, which the ever-obliging Roger provided. One cheeky fellow asked Rog which boat our dinghy was from, and Roger had the face-saving presence of mind to answer suavely, 'The Volvo yacht. It's too big to get through the locks.' Luisa sat alone at the back, furious and humiliated, clutching her handbag like Grandma Giles and muttering dark Italian threats, among which occasional words like 'stupido' and 'cretino' were vaguely audible.

Suffice to say that we arrived safely at Skindles punctually at three o'clock, exactly one hour after the kitchen had closed. I can only add that the return journey wasn't half as much fun, and the sun was setting when we arrived back in Marlowe shortly after 7.00pm, tired, irritable and hungry. Luisa was by now threatening divorce, which was a tad premature in that she and Roger were not yet married. On the way home, we had fish and chips at a pub in Henley, easily the high point of our day. I made up my mind to re-read *Three Men in a Boat*. *Four Friends in a Boat* seemed a likely sequel.

Tony Newley and Joan Collins were finally married. The world heaved a sigh of relief, and Evie and I returned to New York to spend Newberg's summer break from the show with them. Tony had agreed with Merrick that, if he got a four-week break instead of the contractual two, he would extend his Broadway stay by an extra few weeks before handing the role of Littlechap over to Joel Grey.

Joannie had found us a pretty house called The Davis Cottage on the beach in Montauk, on the northernmost tip of Long Island. Joannie was to enjoy the opportunity to take things a little easier now, as she was already well pregnant, and due to deliver the next generation's first baby Newley in October.

After four or five days of sunbathing, swimming, playing badminton and Scrabble, building sandcastles and watching Fred the crazed Abyssinian cat, Newberg and I both began to get a little restless. Whenever we were together, we were used to being creatively productive, so we started to look around for something to do. We opened the next morning's newspaper and there it was, staring us in the face. The juiciest political scandal of the century was unravelling in England, and Harold MacMillan's Tory Government with it.

John Profumo, the Minister of War, it emerged, had been playing naughty party games at the Astor family's stately home, Cliveden in Berkshire, involving two 'party girls' called Christine

Keeler and Mandy Rice-Davis, while Miss Keeler was simultaneously playing more party games with a London-based Russian naval attaché believed to be a Russian secret agent. The security implications were manifest, and all hell broke loose as story built upon story and scandal upon scandal. The British press, character assassins and people-eating piranhas at the best of times, fell upon this heaven-sent feast and were having a field day every day of the week, tearing apart the private lives of leading political figures and hitherto respected members of the aristocracy. The Government was on the ropes and tottering. Newberg and I looked at one another and smiled. Perfect.

Within five or six days, sitting on the beach under a giant umbrella with our toes in the Atlantic, we had completed a dozen wickedly satirical sketches based on various aspects of the scandal. We entitled the piece *Fool Britannia* and arranged to record it live the following week at London Records' largest studio in New York, from midnight on, inviting the casts of all the Broadway shows to be our audience.

Having seen him in London the week before, I knew that Peter Sellers was also on Long Island, about to make a film called *The World of Henry Orient*. His limitless range of comedy character voices and perfect mimicry were exactly what we needed. I tracked him down in an hour, and the four of us drove over to Sands Point to see him. Over lunch by his pool, we read through the sketches with him. Peter convulsed with laughter from the first page, and I knew we had him. We cast him to play seven or eight wildly different characters, ranging from Prime Minister MacMillan himself, trying clumsily to cover up the scandals in an old-school-tie House of Commons speech, down to a tacky London agent trying to make a cheap deal for the scandal's film rights from a Soho telephone booth.

That Saturday night, at midnight, five of us recorded the album – Peter, Tony, Joan, Daniel Massey (a Cambridge Footlights contemporary, no less, son of Raymond Massey, no less, and appearing on Broadway at the time) and myself. The star-studded audience of 300 included Vivien Leigh, Sammy Davis and Richard Harris, and they screamed their heads off all the way through. Sellers was spectacularly funny. His virtuosity and versatility never ceased to amaze me. In a couple of hours, we had the whole thing.

Through a PR friend in London, I sold the album to a label called Ember Records, owned by our film composer friend John Barry. It was released within days, while we were still on our holiday, and became a top comedy album in London that summer. More than that, the whole experience gave Newberg and myself enormous pleasure and the urge to start writing again. We resolved to exhume *Mr Fat and Mr Thin* the moment he and Joannie returned to England in the spring.

And, speaking of urges, Evie observed Joannie's great contentedness and started to get nesting instincts of her own. She had been so young when we married that we agreed we would enjoy our lives and get on our professional feet as much as possible before starting a family. Evie had just finished shooting a film with Sean Connery called *The Frightened City*, and had a completed television series yet to be shown, so maybe the time had finally come. As went the Newbergs, so went the Brickmans. A month later, my brilliant beloved was pregnant, and the two babies were born within six months of one another. Theirs was Tara, ours was Adam, and Tony and I named our new music company Taradam in their honour. We made Tony and Joan Adam's godparents, adding Auntie Bea and Vivian Cox.

An interesting proposition was waiting for us when we returned to New York for Tony to resume his role in the show. Two California film producers, Jerome Hellman and Arthur P Jacobs, made us a firm offer to film *Stop the World* at the same studio where Sellers was making *Henry Orient*. It would only take 16 shooting days, they calculated, and they wanted to start as soon as possible.

Jerry Hellman was small, tough, cool and smart in an upmarket John Garfield way. Apjac, as Arthur P Jacobs was known, was a leading Hollywood press agent in the throes of transition to film production, and the most hyper-tense human being I had ever seen in my life. He chain-smoked little brown Sobranie cigarillos and wrote down everything everybody said on the rectangular pink, blue, green, yellow and white cards that he appeared to be carrying on every part of his body. Each card colour represented the degree of urgency of whatever he would write on it. As something became either more or less urgent, it would be upgraded or downgraded to a new colour.

I personally liked both Jerry and Arthur, but the decision about the film I left to Newberg. He was the one doing eight tough shows a week. And, alas, he decided against it. He reckoned that to shoot all day every Monday, Tuesday, Thursday and Friday for four consecutive weeks, commuting out to Long Island every day, on top of his present killer workload, would completely finish him off. So, although there were to be two subsequent movie versions of *Stop the World*, neither one would star Newley and his dazzling performance, which is therefore lost forever. We both regretted his decision for the rest of his life. I would still be showing it to young performers as a masterclass.

With the better part of an empty year ahead of me, my creative focus immediately returned to *Cyrano*. I knew I could not even think about getting involved in this massive project without acquiring the underlying rights to the famous English translation by Brian Hooker, but my agent Richard Gregson and I, thinking that would be no problem, confidently advanced on other fronts at the same time. Evie and I had long been friendly with the Canadian actor Christopher Plummer, who was a regular weekend visitor at Auntie Bea's house at Henley, and Chris, who had already played Cyrano at the Stratford, Ontario, Theatre Festival, was enthusiastic about tackling the role again musically. Gregson entered into negotiations with David Merrick, who had just agreed to take *Pickwick* to Broadway, about presenting *Cyrano* in America first, before London, and made the mistake of telling Merrick that he had not quite closed the deal for the translation rights. And Merrick did a Merrick. He called Richard the next day to say that *he* had acquired the translation rights by the simple means of gazumping Richard. Since he now controlled the project, he would naturally expect me to accept a much reduced royalty deal... shall–we–say half? Bye-bye, David Merrick. I was not about to be blackmailed by the demon bastard producer. So the curtain came down on my dream and, perversely, need I add, Merrick never produced the show, with me or anyone else. Somebody ought to write a song called 'There's No Business Like Show Business'...

Evie and I stayed in New York for our fifth wedding anniversary, seeing our friends and most of the new shows, then sailed back to England on the magnificent *SS France*. I did not want to take any chances with Evie's early pregnancy. The Atlantic Ocean, however, judging from the almighty storm it threw at us, did not agree with my judgement and, by the second day, nor did I. By the third day, we both devoutly wished we had flown home. Despite everything, it was the most luxurious ship with the most exquisite floating restaurant in the history of maritime travel. The mighty vessel being tossed around the great ocean like a rubber duck in a jacuzzi brought out a few ribald comparisons to Noah's Ark, which, in turn, reawakened in me another idea which I had toyed with a year or two before, to make a musical built around that most vivid of all Biblical tales. It was a story the whole world knew and loved. There were no underlying rights or translations to enable David Merrick to screw up the whole project. It was as public domain as you can get. It had drama. It had spectacle. It had animals. So why not add a little music and a dab of comedy, too?

I had six months to wait for the Bricusse–Newley team to reunite to try to stop the world a second time, so *Noah's Ark* it was. I had converted part of our second Stanmore apartment to provide a work studio for me by day and a TV sitting room for Evie and myself by night. It was known and labelled as the Newberg Memorial Wing. We had also bought twin apartments nearby for our respective mamas, so a cosy family atmosphere was established at just the right moment in our lives. And the rest of that winter was devoted to laying out the storyline and writing the first draft music and lyrics for *Noah's Ark* and watching the ever more beautiful and contented Evie's tummy grow. We had the most divine grey Persian cat, cleverly named Persia, who would sit on Evie's stomach and purr from dawn 'til dusk. The whole thing was quite sickeningly perfect.

At 8.31pm on Saturday, 4 April 1964, the day that the Beatles made musical history by filling all five top places in the US Singles Chart, Adam Cedric Bricusse weighed in at 6 pounds 14 ounces, at the Royal Free Hospital in London. He took a monumental 27 hours to arrive, during which I sat holding Evie's hand and reading Moss Hart's autobiography *Act One* from cover to cover.

I then acquired the apartment on the *other* side of our original flat, making three in a row, so that we now had something like six bedrooms, three bathrooms, three kitchens and three reception rooms. It was more than adequate space for our immediate needs, but Evie and I were both starting to think increasingly that it was time we looked for a house. Otherwise, I could see us living out our lives in an ever-lengthening labyrinth of interconnected apartments.

Who was going to play Noah? That was the key question. My first and probably best thought was Harry Secombe. I was both happy and unhappy to know that I would have to wait two or three years for that to become a possibility. Peter Coe and Sean Kenny agreed to become director and designer-elect, and Bernie Delfont was content to continue the roller-coaster ride with me and produce. But no Noah meant no show. We had a series of brainstorming casting sessions, and a number of interesting ideas emerged, but no spine-tinglers. Then somebody mentioned the name Tony Hancock, and everybody went crazy. Of course, Britain's longstanding number-one Everyman comedian and biggest TV star would be perfect. I voiced my slight concern that I had never heard Hancock sing, which was eventually explained by the simple fact that he couldn't, but, for the time being, I allowed myself to be swept along on the sudden tidal wave of enthusiasm, and was quite excited to learn that Hancock's perennial and brilliant scriptwriters, Ray Galton and Alan Simpson, would be interested to meet with me, and indeed to collaborate. And they did and they did.

Sadly, it all led nowhere, and sadder still the so-talented, lonely, confused, erratic, alcoholic and non-singing Mr Hancock would eventually elect to end his life in a hotel room in Sydney, Australia, at the unnecessarily early age of 44. And the funny script that Ray and Alan had tailored so beautifully to Hancock's special and eccentric comedic talents could not be adapted to anyone else's. It was small comfort to me that the whole Hancock undertaking was in retrospect a total waste of time, because no one but myself ever faced up to the fact that he would never have been able to sing it, anyway. So *Noah*, at least in my life, remained all at sea.

I called Peter Sellers. I had long wanted to do a comedy album with The Goons – Peter, Harry Secombe and Spike Milligan – Britain's prime trio of crazed anarchic comics and our nearest equivalent to the Marx Brothers. A general election was fast approaching in Britain. With the MacMillan Government still reeling from the pounding it had taken with the Profumo scandal, a Labour victory was likely, and that was my pre-selected target. I wrote a dozen sketches and entitled the album *How to Win an Election – Or Not Lose by Much*. Peter and I met for dinner. He loved silly projects like this, and agreed at once to do it.

For some never explained reason, he was staying at the Dorchester Hotel. As I have said, Peter bought houses as other men buy ties, and I knew he had recently purchased a beautiful Tudor property in Elstead, Surrey. As we were going to his suite, the elevator doors opened and a staggeringly pretty, definitive Scandinavian blonde beauty emerged. We watched her walk down the corridor and enter a room at the end. I looked at

Peter. We raised our eyebrows. For the first time in three years, I was confident that at that moment Peter was not thinking of Sophia Loren.

Harry Secombe was in *Pickwick*, and Spike Milligan was a friend who lived near us in Mill Hill, so they were soon safely on board, too. I had already presumed to book the studio.

Peter called me the next day in a state of seismic excitement, speaking inexplicably with a heavy Welsh accent. 'This is it, boyo! I tell you, this is fuckin' *it*!' Her name was Britt Ekland, she was 21, she was Swedish, she was a definite 10-plus, and she had no idea who Peter was. He told her he was a photographer, which he was, and a good one; he had already taken pictures of her that morning, and he was having dinner with her that night.

I invited Peter, Harry and Spike to Friday lunch at The Pickwick Club prior to recording the album in the afternoon. Spike and Harry duly turned up, and Peter duly didn't. Instead, there was a long, complex message telling me that he and Britt were getting married tomorrow, and would I please record his tracks for him. Would I then please meet him and Britt at London Airport the day after, give him the master tapes, and he would replace my voice with his as soon as he got settled in Los Angeles. He had to be there by Sunday because he was starting work on a Billy Wilder film on Monday.

Spike, Harry and I, slightly stunned, went ahead with lunch anyway, during which Spike personally put away about three bottles of top-quality Bordeaux. At about four o'clock that afternoon, I arrived at the recording studio with no Peter Sellers, a giggling Harry Secombe and a legless Spike Milligan, who had absolutely no idea why he was there. Undaunted, we went ahead, with me doing Sellers' stuff and Spike ad-libbing like the inspired madman he was. Astonishingly, four or five nerve-racking hours later, we emerged with what was potentially a pretty funny album, which was going to be completely useless, of course, unless the erratic Peter added his brilliance to what we had. On Sunday morning, I duly met the newly wed Peter and Britt, blissfully happy and surrounded by photographers, at London Airport, and Peter flew off into an unknown future with my masterpiece and the second Mrs Sellers, whom he had now known for all of 20 days.

Weeks went by. Total silence. Then early one evening, I got an emergency phone call from Peter's PR man, Theo Cowan, with devastating news that Peter had suffered eight massive heart-attacks in California and was not expected to live the night. I arranged for Theo to gather all of Peter's friends together at The Pickwick Club, closed the restaurant for the evening, and about 30 or 40 of us sat there all night, swapping Sellers stories and with an open phone line to Cedars Sinai hospital in LA, with Peter Lawford at the other end, waiting for the inevitable news that never came. Sellers held on, rallied and miraculously survived. The next day, Britt called me with the good news that Peter was making a remarkable recovery and that, on the day he had the heart-attacks, he had gone into a studio and completed his *Election* album tracks, replacing my voice with his, just a couple of hours before he was stricken. The tapes were airmailed to me the next day, and three weeks later, nicely in time for the election, the album was in the Top Twenty.

I had a regular boys' lunch at The Pickwick Club every Friday, with John Barry, actor Terence Stamp and a hilariously funny, unknown Cockney actor who lived in Terry's spare room, by the name of Michael Caine. Mike had just finished shooting a film called *Zulu*, in which he had his first featured role, and he was hoping it would finally get his career moving. When Tony Newley returned at last from 18 months on Broadway, he made up what became the regular Friday lunch quintet.

Life with the newly returned Newley was all babies and nappies and nannies and grannies, so Tony and I gratefully locked ourselves away in the Newberg Memorial Wing to continue writing *Mr Fat and Mr Thin*, our second show-to-be. We had barely restarted work when we received a phone call from John

Barry. He was delighted with the success of *Fool Britannia*, and as the newly appointed resident composer for the James Bond movies, he wanted to know whether we would like to write the title song for the next one with him. 'It's called *Goldfinger*,' he said.

I shrugged and replied, 'Catchy title,' and arranged to meet him at his Cadogan Square apartment at eleven the next morning.

We arrived promptly, and John proudly sat down to play us his melody. After the first three notes, Newley and I both instinctively sang '*Wider than a mile*', which went down like a ton of hot lead. But we loved the melody, took it home with us and went straight to work. Now I have written some pretty unlikely lyrics in my time, and that one ranks high on the list, but none of us was prepared for what happened to that song when the film of *Goldfinger* opened a few months later. Because our attention was focused elsewhere that summer, we not only didn't see the movie, we didn't even know that Shirley Bassey had recorded the song, until we returned to New York in October and received a call from United Artists Records to say that they had a couple of framed soundtrack gold records for us, waiting to be collected.

The cause of Newberg's thoughts and mine being elsewhere that summer was our second-born musical, which frankly was giving us a bit of trouble. The songs, as before, were no problem. They just happened, one after another, and we were quickly aware that we were writing a better score than *Stop the World*. The title changed to *The Roar of the Greasepaint – The Smell of the Crowd*, and we liked that, too. But the book was hard work, i.e. it had problems. There was no nice and easy adaptation of a Shakespeare soliloquy available to us this time around. This time we set the scene after the nuclear holocaust that most of the Western world was confidently expecting, and played out the battle between the surviving haves and have-nots as a board game, with the odds heavily manipulated by the Have, the former Mr Fat, at the expense of the Have-Not, the former Mr Thin. It was a good structure, more complex than *Stop the World*, and by no means the three-week job we had arrogantly hoped.

Bernie Delfont, busy counting money from both *Stop the World* and *Pickwick*, couldn't wait for us to finish it. He had already booked the Palace, Manchester, for the third time in three years, and wanted urgently to know who the two stars were going to be. Everything was going a little bit too fast. This time, we were looking for Bigchap as well as Littlechap, a sort of atomic age Laurel and Hardy. The perfect choice for Sir, as Bigchap was called, born to be cast in this role, was the incomparable Robert Morley, whose face and fat were his fortune, and who beyond his many well-chronicled movie character roles was an authentic West End box-office star in his own right, with a long string of theatre successes to his credit, some of which he had had also written. Dickie Attenborough kindly arranged a lunch between us at the 500 Club in Albermarle Street, at which Robert hilariously laughed and joked his way out of the project. As a play, perfect. As a musical, disaster. He assured me categorically that he couldn't sing a note, even more than Tony Hancock couldn't sing a note.

We then heard that the formidable and ferocious Rex Harrison was in town. We went to see him at the Connaught Hotel, where happily he had forgotten that I had met him exactly ten years before, at a dinner with himself and Auntie Bea, plus his beautiful then-wife, Lili Palmer, and his even more beautiful wife-to-be, Kay Kendall, in the Connaught's celebrated restaurant. The three of them were starring together at the Phoenix Theatre in John Van Druten's play *Bell, Book and Candle*, during which Rex was having an affair with Kay. Lili knew about it, and Auntie Bea called it *Bell, Book and Kendall*.

At the dinner, they were all as drunk as skunks, howling abuse, laughing, roaring, clawing and fighting like hyenas. Fortunately for their fan clubs, it was 2.30 in the morning and the restaurant was otherwise empty. Not surprisingly, Rex had successfully eliminated all memory of the occasion. He was now married to neither of them, Lili having divorced him and Kay having died tragically of leukaemia at the age of 32.

To my pleasant surprise, given the above anecdote, Rex was charm itself, greeting us warmly and saying how flattered he was to be asked and all that, but unfortunately he was about to start shooting a film by Terence Rattigan called *The Yellow Rolls-Royce*. 'But hopefully we'll work together another time,' he said with engaging insincerity. And with that, out the door.

Littlechap, this time called Cocky, was easier to cast. Newberg had made himself categorically unavailable for the role, having just completed three non-stop years in *Stop the World*. That gave us one obvious choice, if he was interested – Norman Wisdom, for more than a decade Britain's most popular and lovable film comedian clown, with a penchant for singing awful, cloying, self-pitying songs like 'Don't Laugh at Me 'Cos I'm a Fool'. But, having written 'What Kind of Fool Am I?' and now 'The Joker' and 'Who Can I Turn To?' for *Greasepaint*, who were we to talk?

Newberg and I wrote the second half of the *Greasepaint* score in a Hampstead house that he and Joannie had rented from actor Keith Michell. Joan Collins moving into a house is like relocating Harrods. On the day of the move, trying to write, Newberg and I ended up marooned in a back bathroom, and it is a tribute to our powers of concentration that we wrote and composed the heart-rending ballad 'Who Can I Turn To? (When Nobody Needs Me)' with Newberg lying in the empty bathtub and myself seated on the john!

Norman Wisdom *could* sing, and he *was* funny, as Evie and I witnessed when we went up to Liverpool to see him starring in *Sinbad the Sailor* at the 3,000-plus-seat Empire Theatre. The place was packed, the audience loved him, and he tore the place up. But how would he feel about *Greasepaint*? The role of Cocky was a radical departure from his usual knockabout slapstick routines, but to our surprise and delight he was up for it and ready to take the big risks that went with the territory.

With a Robert Morley lookalike called Willoughby Goddard as Sir, Norman Wisdom embarked on an extended provincial pre-London tour of *The Roar of the Greasepaint – The Smell of the Crowd*, directed by Anthony Newley and choreographed by Gillian Lynne. And everything about the show was not quite... The musical numbers were well staged, but not quite showstoppers; the book was amusing, but not quite funny; the audience wanted to like the show, but did not quite like it enough. And Norman Wisdom was good, but not quite good enough.

On top of this, Newberg and Sean Kenny had given the production a minimalist look of all-pervading gloom, with virtually no set and miserable-looking, end-of-the-world costumes. I knew the show was in there somewhere, fighting to get out, but it could not quite make it. The critics, like the audience, to say nothing of the authors, were somewhat bemused by it all. It was what the King of Siam would have called a 'puzzlement'. And the great Norman Wisdom public stayed away in droves. Norman not being Norman as they knew and loved him, in his too-short trousers and his errand-boy cap, doing funny walks and pratfalls, was not Norman, so there was no point in going to see him. The same 3,000-seat Liverpool Empire that Evie and I had seen Norman pack to capacity less than six months before had maybe 30 people at a Wednesday matinee. Newberg caustically observed that the nearest thing to the sound of applause was the pit-a-pat of upturning seats as people got up to leave.

The final out-of-town date was the Palace, Manchester, home of our previous two triumphs. But there was to be no hat-trick. Newberg and I agreed with Bernie Delfont that the reaction of the critics there would determine whether or not the show should go to London. So Newberg, Evie and I sat in the depressing Midland Hotel TV room after the opening, alone except for a solitary fat Norwegian businessman, to watch the verdict of the five Manchester critics, deciding our fate one by one in a thumbs-up or thumbs-down display worthy once again of the Roman Coliseum. And, in solemn succession, every thumb went down, much to the chuckling delight of the fat Norwegian businessman, and our dark despair.

Still Bernie was reluctant to post the show's final notice to close the show at the end of our Manchester run. Instead, he did something much smarter. He telephoned David Merrick. And suddenly, out of the darkness, light. Merrick flew over from New York the next day to see the show. We met afterwards in the circle bar. And here, word for word, is what David Merrick said. 'Don't go to London. Close the show in Manchester. Get rid of the little guy. Newley play the role. We redesign the whole show. We rehearse in New York in January, and I guarantee you a success.'

Music to my ears, but not to Newley's. I didn't have to do the show eight times a week. He did. He told Merrick he'd think about it and give him an answer in two weeks. Evie, Joannie and I promptly suggested we should all take a relaxing little holiday.

For the post-*Greasepaint* vacation, we decided to return to the same little beach hotel in Paraggi, next to Portofino, where Evie and I had stayed two years before with Joannie. Baby Tara was now nine months old and Adam four months, and he had been on the road with *Greasepaint* for most of that time. Paraggi was peaceful and perfect for the babies. The tranquillity gave us time to assess the *Greasepaint* situation realistically and objectively and, in a couple of relaxed days, our beloved Newberg made the wise and noble decision to go forward with the show with Merrick and return to Broadway in the role of Cocky just one year after he had left it in the role of Littlechap.

Two shows simultaneously criss-crossing America prior to Broadway was pretty heady stuff. *Pickwick* was still playing in London, and *Greasepaint* was set to rehearse in New York in the first week of January. So the Newleys and ourselves rented a house on East 63rd Street for Christmas. The four of us, plus the two babies and two nannies, were joined by Joan's younger sister Jackie Collins with her baby daughter Tracy. We flew to New York and moved into the house on the evening of 20 December, and discovered that the entire place was infested with cockroaches the size of Volkswagens, thousands of them. We moved swiftly out after about an hour, Tony saving the day with a phone call to his pal Milton Berle, whom he had befriended during the run of *Stop the World* at Danny's Hideaway, a popular New York watering hole where all the stand-up comics used to congregate. Milton and his wife Ruth were staying at the Gotham Hotel on 55th Street with their baby son, Billy Berle, and they somehow managed to get us all into the hotel at a time when Manhattan was overflowing with Christmas-rush tourists. There we stayed for two days until the fumigated Cockroach Towers was ready for our return.

Since there was little for us to do during *Greasepaint's* first weeks of rehearsal, Evie and I, now addicted to the Caribbean, took a trip to the Virgin Islands, where we celebrated my birthday at the Cane Bay Plantation on the island of St Croix. My birthday was marred by the news of the death of Winston Churchill at the age of 90. How that great old lion managed to live to that splendid age, fortified by his doctor-damning diet of brandy and cigars, is yet another of the many mystiques surrounding this protean figure, with his Nobel Prize for Literature to cap the mountain of laurels poured upon him by a grateful world. He was the great hero of my lifetime. Without his monumental man-of-the-moment courage and fortitude and gift for language in 1940, we would most likely be living in a very different world today. No man on earth contributed more to the half-century-plus of world peace that followed World War Two than Winston Leonard Spencer Churchill.

Greasepaint opened in New Haven in February and *Pickwick* in San Francisco in April. Tony and I added into the *Greasepaint* score four new songs that we had written for Norman Wisdom in Nottingham, all of which he had gracelessly refused to sing. They all worked beautifully, and Tony stopped the show with two of them. Sean Kenny created an ingenious new multi-level platform set, which gave the show some height and dimension. David Merrick brought in the Tony Award-winning costume designer Freddie Wittop, who created gloriously ragged outfits for Tony and his co-star Cyril Ritchard, who brought to the character of Sir his many years of experience, wit and revue performer style. He was splendidly arrogant and outrageously camp. He got all the laughs that were there to be got, totally missing in the English production, and delivered his songs with a fine edge and a high polish.

And then there was Newley. It isn't easy to convey the elusive magic that was Newley the performer. He brought a natural ease and grace to everything he did, a deep inner knowledge, an old wisdom, a masterly body language of such humour and beauty that illustrated and illuminated every lyric he ever sang, that took an audience by the hand and led them unerringly and mesmerically through the story he was telling. At his best, he was unequalled. Sammy Davis told me that Tony was the only performer other than Sinatra that he envied. There can be no higher praise than that.

With Newley as Cocky, picking all the flowers that Norman Wisdom had left by the wayside, *The Roar of the Greasepaint – The Smell of the Crowd* became another show on another level. It opened sensationally in New Haven. I couldn't believe the transformation. Everybody was thrilled. All we needed to do was to leave the show alone and allow the performers to play themselves in and give it the final pace and polish that only they could give. Merrick had been true to his word, and we were all set to return to the Shubert Theater on West 44th Street in mid-May, air-conditioning and all.

Evie and I flew back to London for a couple of weeks for a last look at *Pickwick* in the West End before it moved to San Francisco. I discussed a few possible improvements with Peter Coe and Wolf Mankowitz, but the show was playing so well we decided to leave it pretty much alone.

By April, I was commuting backwards and forwards between San Francisco and Toronto and the two shows, travelling with David Merrick every Tuesday and Friday. I got a very unpleasant shock when I saw *Greasepaint* after one month away from it. Merrick had made the disastrous decision that if he made a few more 'improvements' he could turn *Greasepaint* into a mega-hit.

He had clearly never heard the adage 'If it ain't broke, don't fix it'. The good news was that the score was working brilliantly, carrying the show along at a cracking pace. The bad news was that Merrick and Newley weren't talking. As director, star and co-author, Newley had a lot of power, but, as producer, lawyer and megalomaniac, Merrick didn't much care what the contracts said. In flagrant violation of the written agreements, he had brought in a couple of 'show fixers' during my absence, one English and one American, perfectly nice young men who had not an idea in hell what the show was about, let alone what they could fix. The immediate effect of their tinkering was that the show started to lose the natural rhythm that had been its greatest asset in New Haven. I tried to mend the rift between Tony and David before it escalated into something more dangerous. But I didn't, and it did.

Merrick wanted to cut one of Newley's most successful songs, 'The Joker', near the end of Act One, because it was bang up against his Act-closing big ballad 'Who Can I Turn To?' It was true they were back-to-back, but, since they both worked and, in my view, 'The Joker' was the rocket-launcher that enabled the big ballad to stop the show, I sided with Newley. Two against one was all the motivation that mad Merrick needed. The next day, before the Saturday matinee, he personally went down into the orchestra pit and removed all the band parts for 'The Joker', and didn't tell anybody. When the show reached that point, the musical director found himself looking at 'Who Can I Turn To?', and that's what the band played and, having no option, what Newley sang. Merrick came smugly backstage to Newley's dressing room at the end of the performance, and they spoke for the first time in two weeks. Newley was surprisingly calm and unruffled. Merrick said, 'The show played better without the song. I think you'll agree after tonight's performance.'

There was a long pause, Newley turned, looked up at Merrick, smiled and said, 'I'm not doing tonight's performance. Read my contract.'

The band parts were safely back in the orchestra pit in good time for the evening performance, Newley put a little extra something into 'The Joker', stopped the show with it, and four minutes later stopped it again with 'Who Can I Turn To?'. Talent is its own security system.

Pickwick was part of the San Francisco and Los Angeles Civic Light Opera summer season, successfully run for many years by a delightful old-world gentleman called Edwin Lester. Four shows each played eight weeks in each city to full, oversubscribed houses in two major theatres. As a result, as with *Stop the World* and *Greasepaint*, Merrick was guaranteed to take *Pickwick* to Broadway already in profit. And he was about to embark on even greater acts of skulduggery on *Pickwick* than those he had committed on *Greasepaint*, and this time fatally.

Without our knowledge, he was inciting outside writers to come and look at the show and contribute songs at random, telling them that if he liked anything they wrote he would try it in the show. It was like some crazy country fair song competition and, of course, there were plenty of budding songwriters out there who would do anything for a shot at having a song in a show on Broadway. I was obviously unaware of this, and the Department of Fate was about to engineer a totally unexpected development in my life that would further deflect my attention away from what was going on behind the scenes on *Pickwick*.

Arthur P Jacobs – Apjac – the nervous one of the two PanArts producers who had wanted to make a film of *Stop the World* a couple of years before, he of the many-coloured notepads, had stayed in consistent touch with both Tony and myself. He was genuinely interested in everything we did, separately and together and, in the last two years, he had succeeded in his own aim to become a film producer. Darryl Zanuck had regained power at Twentieth Century Fox from the minuscule Spyros Skouras, of whom Billy Wilder famously said, 'Beware of Greeks wearing lifts', after the vastly expensive *Cleopatra* had all but bankrupted the studio. Apjac had made a deal at Fox with Zanuck to make a film called *What a Way To Go!*, intended originally as a vehicle to star Marilyn Monroe, whom Apjac had represented as her press agent. Marilyn's untimely death in 1962 had surprisingly not caused the film to suffer a similar fate, and it was finally made starring Shirley MacLaine and six big-name actors. It proved a huge success, making Apjac *persona molta grata* at Fox. He was now planning other projects at Fox, including a film of Pierre Boule's *Planet of the Apes*. Apjac knew about *Noah's Ark*, and asked if he could hear it. I gladly sent him the demo tape, which he thought was 'fantastic'. He then started to drop mysterious hints that he might have something important to discuss with me soon, depending on developments. I was appropriately intrigued.

A few days later, he called from Los Angeles to say he was coming up to San Francisco, would be there in a couple of hours and had to see me URGENTLY. Everything Apjac ever did had to be done URGENTLY. Evie took his call, told him I was at the theatre and she wasn't sure whether she could find me. Knowing nothing of this, I returned to our hotel, where Evie, Adam and Bobbi the nanny were out by the pool with Harry and Myra Secombe and their little boy, David. Out of the corner of my eye, I saw a frantic Apjac emerge from the shadows on the far side of the pool and hurry towards me, slim brown Sobranie cigarillo as always in his hand. He was on the brink of a nervous breakdown because he had been waiting for me for nearly TWENTY MINUTES. I explained that I had not known he was coming, and tried to calm his desperate nerves, which was like trying to swim the Bosphorus with your hands in your pockets. He finally stammered, 'B–B–Brickman,' (he loved calling us Brickman and Newberg) 'y–you d–d–don't understand. I am here to change your LIFE!' And he was. And he did.

This was the story, like something out of a cheap showbiz novel. Apjac and Fox had been trying for some time to reunite Rex Harrison and Lerner and Loewe, the triumphant triumvirate of *My Fair Lady*, in a film version of the *Doctor Dolittle* children's books by Hugh Lofting, about the country doctor who learned to talk to animals. It was on. It was off. It was on again. And now finally it was off, because Fritz Loewe had retired, and nothing would persuade him to re-emerge from the luxurious cocoon of self-indulgence and laziness that he had spun around himself since the intolerable pressures of the final collaboration on *Camelot* had killed Moss Hart and nearly wrecked the health of both Alan Lerner and Fritz Loewe into the bargain. Life was too short. So Apjac had flown up to San Francisco to ask me whether I would like to write the screenplay, the music and the lyrics, all three, on my own, for the big-budget musical that Twentieth Century Fox were planning to make, starring the formidable and ferocious Rex Harrison. I thought it over for point four of a second and said, 'Yes, I would.'

The Roar of the Greasepaint – The Smell of the Crowd opened at the Shubert Theater in New York in early May. My favourite first-night telegram came from Stephen Sondheim and read, 'Dear Leslie, Good Luck, but I think you should know that the second and seventh words of your title have been interchanged accidentally. Love, Steve Sondheim.'

And, speaking of the great man, Evie and I had got to know Sondheim through mutual friends, notably a *très* trendy and popular New York socialite called Didi Ryan. *Stop the World* had opened on Broadway when Steve's first solo words-and-music score, *A Funny Thing Happened on the Way to the Forum*, had become the big new hit of the season. We were in competition for Best Score in the Tony Awards, and we both lost to Lionel Bart's *Oliver!*. That created a bond of sorts.

Sondheim, as the world knows, is a brilliant composer and lyricist, the best of his generation, but a complicated man who was not easy to get to know, so Evie and I felt it was something of an achievement that we did, and we became very fond of him. One famous evening at his house on East 49th Street, our friendship established, he felt comfortable enough with us to volunteer a private preview of his new score, *Anyone Can Whistle*.

He played and sang the whole thing to just the two of us, and if I didn't know it already I realised that night what mighty things would surely come from him. He was still in his early thirties.

Later the same evening, after a long, chatty dinner, Steve took us to a late-night piano bar called Goldie's on East 54th Street. The owner, Goldie, and his piano-playing partner had just finished a set of songs. Evie, in a frisky mood, told Steve that we had not been in New York when Ethel Merman had starred in *Gypsy*, which Steve had written with Jule Styne, and which surprisingly ran little more than a year. It had been our favourite Broadway score of recent years, so Evie asked him if he would play a little of it, just for her. Steve obligingly sat at the piano, played the famous opening four chords of the *Gypsy* score, the door of Goldie's opened, Ethel Merman walked in, accompanied by two gentlemen, and right on cue belted out 'I Had a Dream'. True. For the second time in one evening, an enchanted audience of two sat in awe for a private performance of a Sondheim score as Merman's mighty voice bounced off the walls of the tiny club. As Irving Berlin once observed, 'If you are going to write lyrics for Miss Merman, they'd better be good, because everybody gets to hear them!'

Stephen Sondheim was also a Beatles fan, and wanted to meet his heroes. In a moment of New York madness, I promised Steve that I would somehow arrange this great musical summit conference. I went to enormous trouble and, after a lot of back-and-forthing, I finally got Paul McCartney to undertake to deliver the entire Fab Quartet to the Ad Lib Club, London's hottest discotheque, in Leicester Square, at midnight on a specified Saturday night. Evie and I duly turned up there with Steve a few minutes before twelve. The Ad Lib's popular manager, Brian Morris, gave me a 'You'll be lucky' look when I told him that the Beatles would be joining us in a few minutes. We ordered drinks and, as midnight struck, with Cinderella-like punctuality, the four young cult icons trooped in, stopping the place in its tracks, and joined us at our booth. They were as impressed to be meeting the mighty Sondheim as he was to be meeting them. John Lennon sat next to Steve, and I remember thinking that I would be unlikely to see so much musical talent assembled at one small table ever again. Stupidly, none of us thought to have a photograph taken. I sat there glowing like Edmund Hillary. This was the top of the mountain.

There was one problem. The decibel level at the Ad Lib was like putting your head in the mouth of a bellowing bull elephant. We sat there, deafened and smiling stupidly at one another for about five minutes, mouthing unheard niceties. A couple of minutes more, with no signs of noise abatement, and John turned to me, grinned and said, 'Well, that's that, then!' Everybody shook hands and hugged, Evie got kissed a lot, and the Beatles trooped out, exactly as they had trooped in, and Steve was left sitting there denied the in–depth intellectual exchanges he obviously craved. I would have enjoyed listening to Sondheim versus Lennon in musical debate, and I would have hesitated to pick a winner.

As for our current production of *Greasepaint*, I personally don't think the show was ever as good again as it had been in New Haven, and for that I blame the villainous Merrick. If he had left well alone, I think he might well have got the major hit he was after. But he had delivered on his promise made amid the debris of Manchester nine months before. The show was a hit, but a base hit, not a home run. Financially, it cleaned up, but the reviews were again mixed. I took issue with one lesser critic who had murdered *Stop the World* three years before and now wrote that *Greasepaint* had none of the wit and style that made *Stop the World* such a runaway success three seasons ago. I sent both his reviews to a rival newspaper, who gleefully published them side by side and condemned the evil critic for 'self-promoting hindsight'.

As with *Stop the World*, what made *Greasepaint* a hit were the songs. There is no question that that score was the best that Newley and I ever wrote. Apart from the success of the big ballad 'Who Can I Turn To?', on which Tony Bennett again delivered the definitive recording and a big hit single, nearly a dozen other songs 'got up and walked', as Newley and I used to say, to create a life of their own outside the show. Sammy Davis recorded half-a-dozen of them, and the likes of Lena Horne, Ethel Merman, Judy Garland and hundreds of other theatre and recording stars did their versions of the songs. And as with *Stop the World*, the driving force behind this avalanche of recordings was a dapper, dynamic little Damon Runyan character who just happened to be the greatest old-fashioned Tin Pan Alley song plugger in the history of the world. His name was Happy Goday, a name that fitted him like a glove. Happy was always happy, and Goday could go all day. I never knew of anyone in the music business who could get records like Happy could get records. A force unto himself, he was incomparably the best in the business, and he stands alongside Sammy Davis as the man who did most to promote the songs of Bricusse and Newley.

All seemed well on *Pickwick*, still in San Francisco before moving down to LA. In early June, we decided to drive the 400-plus miles down the California coast, via the Monterey Peninsula, prior to my starting work on *Doctor Dolittle*. I still could not quite believe this was all happening, but, by packing all our luggage and Adam and nanny Bobbi into the car and driving into town like the Beverly Hillbillies in the TV series, Evie and I felt about as down-to-earth as the circumstances would allow.

As an audition, admittedly a most handsomely paid one, I had agreed to Apjac's diplomatic proposal, to calm whatever Twentieth Century Fox nerves other than his own needed calming, that I would write two songs and the first 20 pages of a screenplay, to give everybody, including myself, some idea of how I intended to approach what was clearly going to become a mammoth project.

Imagine the situation – Apjac had lost the mighty Lerner and Loewe team, and was pitching me, whom Fox had almost certainly never heard of, to replace *both* of them. I heard from one reliable studio source that he had used my *Noah's Ark* demo as a persuader on the flimsy pretext that he had 'found a guy who writes great songs about animals'. Fox were feeling pretty pleased with themselves at this moment in time, riding high as they were on the phenomenal box-office success of *The Sound of Music*, with Julie Andrews consolidating her huge personal triumph and Best Actress Oscar for *Mary Poppins*. If *Mary Poppins* was a home run, then *The Sound of Music* was surely a Grand Slam.

I was introduced to the new head of the studio, Darryl Zanuck's 30-year-old son, Dick Zanuck, whom I liked instantly, an experienced head on young shoulders. I also met the key people who would be working on the *Dolittle* project, and it did not help my sang-froid to be constantly told that this was going to be the most expensive musical ever made. I also met Arthur Jacobs's associate producer, Mort Abrahams, an amiable fellow whom I promptly dubbed 'Mort d'Arthur', a neat little joke that unfortunately nobody got.

We were installed in a stylish little house in Beverly Hills, on Linda Crest, just off Coldwater Canyon. Shining new copies of the 12 Hugh Lofting *Doctor Dolittle* books were delivered to the house on the first morning, and I was left alone to get on with it. Before I started reading the books, I sat in my study that first day, considering my game plan. I came to two conclusions. Although I was free to write any songs I wanted, that might end up anywhere in the film, I decided to write the first 20 minutes of the film, and incorporate whatever those first two songs might become into the 20 pages of screenplay, so that the reader would have a cohesive feeling of the style of the movie to come. Conclusion number one.

Conclusion number two was that, before I immersed myself in reading the three to four thousand pages of the 12 books, no doubt confusing myself to the point of madness, I wondered how Rex Harrison as Doctor Dolittle would view the situation. There stood his monumental portrayal of Henry Higgins as my role model. And, while Rex Harrison suggested much more a Harley Street specialist than a West Country village doctor, I suddenly realised that Doctor Dolittle had something else in common with Henry Higgins other than Rex Harrison, namely that both men were philologists, students and lovers and explorers of language. Which led me to wonder how Henry Higgins would tackle Dolittle's problem. Which led me to write the root song of the score, 'Talk to the Animals', that first morning, before I ever opened or read any of the books. And it was that starting point that made me feel as confident as I could in this unknown wonderland that I knew where I was going. To this day, I am not sure whether I wrote that song for Doctor Dolittle or for Henry Higgins, but, since they were both Rex Harrison, it didn't much matter.

Reading, more reading and making endless pages of notes took up the daytimes of the next two to three weeks, and getting to know our way around Southern California took up the weekends and the evenings. Apjac was wonderfully attentive to our every need, the residue, I assumed, of his days as a top press agent, catering to spoiled, demanding movie stars. Through him, we met all sorts of fascinating people in the film business. Sammy and May Davis were also in town, in their new house up in the Hollywood Hills, and, knowing that Sammy would have ten to fifteen thousand close friends drop by most evenings, we rationed our visits to about one a week.

We took Hank and Ginny Mancini to the Los Angeles opening of *Pickwick* at the Music Center a few weeks later, if only to remind Henry of our first embarrassing meeting with Sammy Davis when 'If I Ruled the World' was premièred in the Mancini Suite at the Mayfair Hotel a couple of years before.

The show was still playing well, but not as well as it should have been. The overall rhythm of the piece was less smooth, and Peter Coe, without being specific, told me it was because Merrick was still wanting to experiment with further changes. He reassured me that all would be well in the end. I had my doubts, but I now had *Doctor Dolittle* to worry about and, as only the lyricist on *Pickwick*, there was really nothing I could do. I wished it well and I walked away.

From the 12 *Dolittle* books, with their thousands of pages, I constructed a story outline that incorporated all the key characters, animal and human, and some of the good doctor's more entertaining adventures. I wrote the first 20 pages of the screenplay easily and quickly, adding a second song entitled 'My Friend the Doctor', which set up the character of Dolittle before we met him, and ending the 20 pages with 'Talk to the Animals'. I delivered everything to Apjac the following day, and I told him that I would like to sing the two demos of the songs myself, so that we got the mood right. Apjac agreed and said he would arrange a recording session with Lionel Newman, Fox's perennial and avuncular Head of Music.

Three days later, Apjac informed me that the recording would be at ten o'clock the next morning. I met him at his bungalow on the studio lot at 9.45am, and together we walked across to the recording studio. Not *a* recording studio, *the* Recording Studio, the Big One where they recorded all the movie soundtracks. I was expecting a piano, and Ian Fraser to play it. That was my idea of a demo. Not this time. Waiting for me there was a beaming Lionel Newman, the genius-arranger Alexander Courage and a 75-piece orchestra. For a *demo*? Apjac's straightforward philosophy was easy to comprehend. Big-Budget Musical Movie equals Great Big Demos. And, when I heard that orchestra play what Sandy Courage had done with my two simple little songs, I realised why. It was so stunning I was almost in tears. I had never had an orchestra that big play anything of mine. Apjac's job was to sell this movie, and he was leaving nothing to chance, and he was right. It was a near-overwhelming experience. So, trying not to sound too much like Rex Harrison doing Henry Higgins, but enough to make the point, I sang the two songs in something approximating to Rex's unique *Sprechgesang* style, though singing the melody a little more than I imagined he would do.

The 20 pages of screenplay and the two lyrics were put into spiffy script form, with *Doctor Dolittle* logos and copyright warnings and Property of Twentieth Century Fox plastered all over it in big letters. 'Now what?' I asked Apjac. The scripts and the demos were being flown to Darryl Zanuck in Paris and Rex Harrison in Portofino, Italy, today, he told me, and we were going over to Europe to see them both at the beginning of next week. As indeed we did.

How you run a major Hollywood studio from the Georges Cinq Hotel in Paris was something I assume only Darryl Zanuck himself understood. The probable answer was that you have your son do it for you, and you telephone him a lot. Anyway, Zanuck Senior was certainly feeling no pain living in his sumptuous penthouse quarters in the great hotel, with his large cigars and his extremely young and glamorous French companion of the moment, Mlle Genevieve Gilles, in constant and devoted attendance. And Mr Zanuck was simply terrific. The same sharp-eyed enthusiasm displayed by Richard Zanuck was in no way diminished in his dad, who apparently loved what he had heard and read. The otherwise warm meeting ended with the chilling words, 'Now it's all up to Rex, and good luck to you!' I felt that some sort of gladiatorial reply like 'We who are about to die salute you' was in order, but refrained from actually saying it.

It was a pleasant surprise and unexpected bonus to learn that the ferocious and formidable Rex Harrison lived in Portofino, but, sure enough, a couple of days later, we were staying at the incomparably beautiful Splendido Hotel. Rex Harrison's imposing Villa San Genesio, named after the patron saint of actors, was perched on the pinnacle of the hill behind the Splendido, with spectacular views down on to Paraggi and across the bay to Santa Margharita and Rapallo.

Just as at the Connaught Hotel in London with Newley the year before, Rex was charm itself to my face and as trustworthy as a crocodile behind my back. Mind you, had I been Rex Harrison, which thank God I wasn't, I would not exactly have been turning cartwheels of joy either at the prospect of losing Lerner and Loewe and having them replaced by Leslie Wotsisname...

Exulting in his role of playing hard-to-get, Rex toyed with Apjac and Dick Zanuck, not being quite sure if he could make the final commitment (which his agent already had)... other offers, you know, and, of course, he hadn't yet got around to reading the pages, so many other scripts, you know, or playing the ditties, but of course he would, just as soon as he found the time. I felt not unlike I had felt on my way to my pre-Cambridge interview with Francis Bennett, insecure as a falling rock, but, whereas Francis Bennett had uplifted me as he assessed me, Rex was much more into the assessing business than the uplifting business. I, too, was charm itself, and extremely aware from that moment on that I was going to have a tough and tricky customer on my hands if this thing was going to go forward. On the plus side was Rex's latest wife, the vivacious Rachel Roberts, whom I had interviewed on the TV talk show *Line Up for Tonight* a few years before. She was bright, funny, open and playful as a puppy, had too many glasses of wine at lunch, and by the time we left she was barking like a dog, insisting that she do the animal voice-overs for the movie.

Back in London, Apjac kept me up to date with daily bulletins. Rex was concerned that I was too young, too inexperienced, too overloaded by being asked to write the screenplay as well as the score, too Cambridge University and, apart from all that, in the lyric of 'Talk to the Animals', 'rhinoceros' did not rhyme with 'of courseros'. Despite his incessant nagging, he had liked what he had read and heard, knew he would be good in the role, and graciously relented and agreed to play it and allow me to write it. General elation erupted on all sides, and would I now please go straight back to Portofino and 'work' the first two songs with Rex? I read something sinister into the use of the word 'work' in connection with the ferocious and formidable Mr Harrison. I was not wrong.

I had contrived to get Ian Fraser, musical director of my three Broadway shows, on to the *Dolittle* music team to co-ordinate what I did with Lionel Newman and Sandy Courage. So Ian it was who accompanied Evie and me back down to Italy to teach Rex the songs. I found it a quaint conceit that a man who professed to be unable to sing should have a music room the size of Wigmore Hall in his garden, but such was the case. It was an enormous wooden edifice reached along a cliff path around the back of the villa, and a good place to work. Rex belittled it, as he did almost everything in life, by calling it 'the garden shed', but it could comfortably have garaged half-a-dozen London double-decker buses.

'My Friend the Doctor' was not to be sung by Dolittle in the film, so, in fact, we had only to work on 'Talk to the Animals'. Rex expressed grave doubts about it. 'It's such a *silly* song,' he opined.

'That's because it comes from a silly story,' I pointed out.

'And you are aware, of course, that "rhinoceros" does not rhyme with "of courseros",' he added.

'It does if you pronounce it "of cos-eros",' I said.

'Well, I don't,' he said. 'I pronounce it "of course-eros"... because that is English, you see, and Doctor Dolittle and I happen both to *be* and to *speak* English.' He sounded like Henry Higgins at his most waspish and cantankerous, in a scene cut from *My Fair Lady*.

'It's a humorous song,' I ventured.

'A humorous song is meant to be funny,' countered Rex. '*This* isn't funny.'

'We're playing with words,' I said.

'Oh, God protect me from fucking puns,' he snorted. 'Silly schoolboy stuff. Anyway, that's not the point. The point is that it doesn't fucking *RHYME*!'

That sort of thing. Rex Harrison single-handedly raised nit-picking to a high art form. But, by God, he was good. Once he started to find his way into the song, which he quickly did, you realised how incomparably accomplished and funny he was. Performance artistry at its best. And nit-picking was the price you paid for it, Rex's infuriating rate of exchange. Alan Jay Lerner later told me that if he, Alan, had not already been a complete nervous wreck before he met Rex Harrison, he would most certainly have become one immediately afterwards. Alan attributed seven of his ten chewed fingernails to Rex Harrison, and the other three to having been married eight times.

Anyway, we were finally in business, and I had the job. Before I settled down to work, we returned to New York for the Broadway opening of *Pickwick* at the 46th Street Theater. Then, and only then, did I witness the full horror of what Merrick had done to the show, and what Peter Coe, as the director, had allowed him to do. Three or four anonymous new songs, with Americanised lyrics that displayed zero understanding of the style or the cadences of Dickensian speech, in flagrant violation of our contractual rights, had been interpolated into the show. They had replaced perfectly good story songs and comedy songs, in the misguided hope of producing a long-shot show-stopper. What they produced instead was the opposite, a surefire show-closer. The storyline had become disjointed as a result of these intrusions, and even Harry Secombe's balanced central performance, which had always held the ship steady, had taken on a touch of discomfort and despair.

I left town without even speaking to Merrick. There was nothing to say. The show staggered to a close in eight weeks. Merrick was probably content, since the production showed a profit, and, for him, 'in the black' equated with success. But for all his San Andreas-size faults and Machiavellian methods, David Merrick at the end of the day did deliver, on paper at least, what he had promised – three out of three in three years.

Now *Dolittle* began in earnest. The Beverly Drive house had a wonderful upstairs library-study as part of the master bedroom suite, and that was where I would spend between 12 and 15 hours of every 24 for the next several weeks, trying to break the back of the screenplay before it broke mine. Apjac and Fox had allocated me a huge corner office in the main studio executive building, complete with a smart and shiny secretary called Patti in the outer office and a parking space with my name on it right outside the door, but I have always been allergic to offices, preferring the comparative safety of working at home.

Nevertheless, the office and the parking space did get used, all too frequently, because of the unbelievable number of *Dolittle*-related meetings that took place every week. This was partly due to the complexity of the project, involving as it did hundreds of animals, wild, domestic and fantasy, a situation further aggravated by Apjac's near-paranoid passion for meetings. His 3-by-5 cards, in pink, lavender, blue, green, yellow and white, neatly arranged in racks, were never more than 3 feet away from wherever he happened to be. Only Apjac himself fully understood how his card system worked, and he was constantly reshuffling his deck like a demented Las Vegas dealer, upgrading, downgrading, introducing new cards, eliminating old cards, driving his large and overworked secretarial staff and Mort d'Arthur to distraction. 'The blue one on *Dolittle* should be pink, and the yellow one on *Planet of the Apes* should be green!' he would scream hysterically across his bungalow office through a cloud of Sobranie cigarillo smoke.

Nor did it end there. Apjac had recently purchased a big Spanish hacienda-style house on Beverly Drive, a block-and-a-half away from us, and not only did his study and his living room contain the omnipresent card racks, but his bathroom, too! The toilet actually had a fold-down, white formica desk built over it, with four phone lines, notepads, card-racks, pens and pencils, calculators and enough hi-tech office stuff that I am sure that, had the need arisen, Apjac could have produced a major motion picture with his trousers down and without ever getting off the john. This was a man who did not have a *moment* to spare.

Evie created a wonderful family atmosphere for us all in the Beverly Drive house. She found a Mary Poppins-calibre young English nanny called Wendy, the daughter of an old friend of the family, to look after Adam. I think that all nannies should be called Wendy, so that you can actually address them as Wendy

Darling and thus recreate the realm of Peter Pan that should be present in every young household. Evie also brought her mother Adelaide and younger brother Beverly over from the drizzle and gloom of a London winter, consequently placing Adam at 18 months in total command of a doting family. That done, she promptly got herself a leading role in a movie called *The Swinger*, starring Ann-Margaret and Tony Franciosa and directed by George Sidney at Paramount.

Writing the screenplay of *Dolittle* first enabled me to find my way in and out of the song ideas as I went, and I was comfortable with the story setting in the imaginary English West Country village of Puddleby-in-the-Marsh. And here began a problem. I delivered the first half of the screenplay of what Fox intended to be a three-hour 'roadshow' movie. Everybody liked it, but as the box-office gross of *The Sound of Music* soared, so did Fox's aspirations for *Doctor Dolittle* soar with it. 'Open it up,' was the studio cry. 'Make it bigger.'

More meetings took place, from which emerged the unanimous decision that, in the second half of the film, Dolittle's sea voyage in search of the legendary Great Pink Sea Snail should be the last word in eye-popping fantasy. One tiny anecdote best illustrates the soaring budgetary costs that ensued from that decision. In the early part of Dolittle's voyage, as his boat passes a small tropical island, I wrote a ten-word descriptive stage direction to set up the mood. It read, 'The trees are filled with thousands of multi-coloured songbirds.' At our next production meeting, Fox's worried-looking production manager, Stan Hough, said to me in all seriousness, 'Leslie, about these thousands of multi-coloured songbirds. Do you realise how much multi-coloured songbirds *cost*?'

Keeping a straight face, I suggested amending the offending stage direction to read, 'The trees are filled with *three* multi-coloured songbirds,' expecting a big laugh, but instead received the po-faced reply, 'That would be much better.'

The film was scheduled to be made on location in England and the Caribbean, with the studio shoot to follow on the newly built Stage Twenty, all of which made me realise how intricately and how far ahead this thing was being planned. Apjac and Dick Zanuck and I also did a great deal of flying back and forth, to New York, to Paris and to Portofino, keeping Zanuck Senior constantly updated and Rex Harrison constantly mollified.

The casting of the film's main roles was a source of endless fascination. Apjac's bizarre first choice for the role of the aristocratic English rose, Emma Fairfax, for example, was Barbra Streisand, the greatest young singing talent on the planet. Barbra was in her mid-twenties and playing Fanny Brice in *Funny Girl* on Broadway. I flew to New York to visit her at her apartment on Central Park West, to discuss the role. She was enchanting, she was funny, she was adorable, but we both agreed that the one thing she wasn't, any more than Fanny Brice, was an aristocratic English rose. Three or four years later, I helped her to become one by working with her on the English accent that she needed, and achieved brilliantly, in 'On a Clear Day You Can See Forever'.

Although slightly suspicious of Apjac's casting instincts, I was nevertheless totally unprepared for his next choice to play the role of the Irish Cats' Meat man, Matthew Mugg, Dolittle's unlikely best friend. Standing alone at the top of a list of one was the name Anthony Newley. Visually and musically perfect as Newley was for the role, I was probably the only person alive who knew that one of the few things Newley could *not* do was an Irish accent. But I was so thrilled at the thought of having Newberg and Joannie with us in California for the next year or more that I kept my mouth shut and determined to help him become an Irishman, even if it meant dubbing his voice myself.

The fourth and final principal featured role, that of the circus owner, Albert Blossom, was going to be offered to the eminent Welsh character actor Hugh Griffith, until we learned that, apart from being one of only three Welshman on earth who couldn't sing a note, Mr Griffith was also reputed to be heavily involved in an ongoing romance with a vodka bottle. We decided to leave that one for later.

Apjac consoled himself by the apt casting of our lovely green-eyed, red-headed chum from London, Samantha Eggar, as Emma.

The mid-Sixties were in full swing. The Beatles ruled the world, and the world loved every minute of it. The social life in Hollywood was sybaritic, hedonistic heaven. There is now something almost surreal about my memories of our early and frequent dinner parties at the house on Beverly Drive; Yvette Mimieux arriving with a fully grown female jaguar, which lay contentedly like a big fur rug under the grand piano and peed copiously when it was time to leave; Sean Connery sitting way up in the branches of the big pepper tree in our backyard, chatting up Adelaide, who had somehow got up there with him; walking Natalie Wood out to her car, always alone and otherwise unescorted; Roddy MacDowall telling me that our handyman at the Beverly Drive house was his father, John MacDowall... and he was; Ryan O'Neal sitting at our kitchen table when he was 23, trying to remember how many women he'd had; escorting a far-from-sober Warren Beatty off the premises after he saw Joan Collins was with us and alone, and followed us home with a 'for-old-times'-sake' gleam in his eye.

Our social lives apart, being around the studio, which became increasingly necessary as pre-production on *Dolittle* gathered momentum, introduced me to all manner of fascinating new people, especially music people. Prime among them was composer-conductor André Previn, whose name, fame and accomplishments were already well known to me. We struck up an instant friendship, and, while I wasn't exactly expecting him to be a sprightly octogenarian, I was severely stunned to learn that he was only about a year older than myself. He had the look of a trouble-making choirboy, had been a wunderkind, a fully fledged musical director at MGM at the age of 15, was now 35 and had won four Oscars and received over a dozen nominations. He was seriously thinking of leaving Hollywood, where he had nothing left to prove, and moving across full-time to the world of classical music. I met André, as I did most people, through Apjac, because André and his lyricist wife Dory were writing the song score to Apjac's intended *Goodbye, Mr Chips* musical.

André was and is a special human being, with a wonderfully amused and cynical view of the world. He had a devastating sense of humour, a full deck of charm cards and a wonderful speaking voice that reminded me of Alastair Cooke. His intellect was daunting, but his natural warmth protected lesser mortals from being cut by its razor-sharp edge.

André it was who promptly proposed me for membership of the Academy of Motion Picture Arts and Sciences, to give it its full and highly impressive name. Hank Mancini seconded me and, with those two musical heavyweights in my corner, I was an Academy member before you could say 'Moon River'.

Twentieth Century Fox had the number-one TV series at that time, *Peyton Place*, which starred a delicious wide-eyed, 19-year-old, fawn-like creature called Mia Farrow, and a talented cast of young actors. But Mia Farrow was the show's representative image. She was special and she was different, for many reasons, because she was enchanting, because she was beautiful, because she was newsworthy and, above all, because she was about to become the third Mrs Frank Sinatra, with a 30-year-plus age difference for the gossip-mongers to feed on.

Evie and I met Mia late one night at The Daisy, the legendary Beverly Hills discotheque, just before my birthday, through our mutual friend, writer and lyricist Leonard Gershe. Evie invited Mia to my birthday party, and she, a fellow Aquarian, invited us to *her* birthday party that Frank was giving at Chasen's a week later. All of which would eventually lead to several beautiful friendships, but in a somewhat unexpected way.

Mia duly came to my birthday dinner, which was memorable for one other thing. Evie had told me it was for a very small group. I arrived home late from the studio after a particularly prolonged Apjac multi-coloured-card meeting, and was told to hurry up and shower and change because the guests would be here in a few minutes. I dashed upstairs, threw off all my clothes in the master bedroom and rushed into the bathroom to find 30 people in there, glasses raised, with Mike Nichols directing them in singing 'Happy Birthday to You'.

Mia Farrow and I met every day for lunch in the Fox commissary, just the two of us. We indulged in intense private conversations and conspiratorial gigglings, which created fierce speculation about what we were up to at the tables around us, an intrigue we blithely encouraged. I knew more about *Peyton Place*, on stage and off, than all the gossip columnists of Hollywood combined. Mia became more and more part of our little group. Evie and I would regularly take her with us to the Previn evenings. Prior to marrying Frank, Mia had a small apartment on La Peer Drive in Beverly Hills. Evie and I went over to see her 'pre-Daisy' one evening, to meet her closest childhood friend and near-contemporary Liza Minnelli. Liza was still only 19, but we had seen her perform at the Persian Room at the Plaza Hotel in New York when she was 18, and she had already won her first Broadway Tony Award in the title role of 'Flora the Red Menace', which marked the beginning of her brilliant lifelong collaboration with songwriters John Kander and Fred Ebb. Just as Sinatra had Cahn and Van Heusen, and Sammy had Newley and myself, so Liza had Kander and Ebb. No one has ever managed to explain how or why these powerful singer-songwriter relationships developed, but it was simple things like hanging out together and being friends. Certainly, Jimmy Van Heusen could match Sinatra Jack Daniels for Jack Daniels down in Palm Springs. Certainly, the Bricusses and the Newleys could *not* match Sammy in the stay-up-all-night stakes, yet we managed to hang out together for most of *our* waking hours, if not his. And, certainly, Liza's greatest song successes, and Tony and Oscar triumphs, all came via Kander and Ebb, who became her mentors, as Bea Lillie became mine. Sammy Davis recorded 60 of my songs, and I don't doubt that both Frank and Liza had done their favourite chosen songwriters equally proud.

At the end of the year, after *Greasepaint* closed on Broadway, Newberg, Joannie, daughter Tara and their new baby son Sacha came out to the West Coast and moved into the house we had found for them in Bel-Air. Our Hollywood era had officially begun. By now, I was well into the score of *Dolittle*. I had completed about half of the 14 songs that would end up in the movie, plus a few more that wouldn't. Apjac put together the next round of symphonic super-demos, with Newberg singing his own songs and me talk-singing Rex's. Rex continued to give both Apjac and Dick Zanuck a long-distance roasting from Rome, where he was making a film called *The Honey Pot*. He wasn't enjoying it very much, and he was taking out his bad humour on any target he could find. And *Dolittle* became his favourite target, at a range of about 6,000 miles. He complained about 'the Cambridge undergraduate writing the score', and about the casting of Newley, calling him 'a little Jewish East End music hall comic'. He complained about Darryl Zanuck allowing 'his teenage son' to run the studio. He complained about Apjac producing the movie on the grounds that 'I'm fucked if I want some second-rate, self-promoting press agent furthering his shabby little career riding on *my* coat-tails.' Rex's charm was all-embracing. No one was spared. Finally, having wound himself up into an almighty tantrum, he announced through his agent, Laurence Evans, that he was not going to do the picture.

Dick Zanuck had had enough. He called Rex's bluff. The next morning, Dick, Apjac and I flew to New York to have lunch with Christopher Plummer. Chris's star was rising with the stratospheric success of *The Sound of Music*, although the movie had been a little sugary for Chris's tart taste. He told me his private title for the film was *The Sound of Mucus*. Anyway, by 3.00pm that day, the erstwhile Baron Von Trapp had officially become Doctor John Dolittle. Rex's agent was informed accordingly. By 5.00pm, Rex called Darryl Zanuck in Paris, full of remorse, profusely apologetic and pleading temporary insanity. By 6.00pm, a Zanuck-to-Zanuck phone conversation reinstated him. Christopher Plummer was paid in full for the movie, so lunch that day cost somewhere north of $350,000.

While I was in New York, staying at The Plaza, I bought from Doubleday's Bookshop the newly published Rodgers and Hart and Rodgers and Hammerstein songbooks. Since the magic moment five years before when Cole Porter had inscribed 'For Leslie From Cole' in his songbook, I had put together a respectable and ever-growing collection of inscribed film, theatre and music books, and was always on the lookout to widen it further. I called the Rodgers and Hammerstein office in New York and asked the lady there whether, if I were to drop off the books, Mr Rodgers would kindly find a moment to inscribe them for me. She asked me to hold on for a moment, then the great man himself came on the line. It went like this. 'Where are you?'

'I'm at The Plaza.'

'Are you free for lunch?'

'Yes.'

'Meet me in The Oak Room at 12.30.' Click.

It all sounded a bit John Le Carré, but an hour later there I was having lunch with Richard Rodgers at the famous table in The Oak Room where he had sat with Oscar Hammerstein a thousand times. Steve Sondheim, who had been a protégé of Hammerstein and loved him dearly, did not like Rodgers, and had collaborated with him unhappily on *Do I Hear a Waltz?*. But, in the best Rex Harrison tradition, Dick, as he insisted I call him, was charm itself to me and asked me whether I had in mind any musicals I would like to do. It quickly emerged that a collaboration was there for the taking, and we started to talk in earnest. A second lunch followed, and a third and, by the end of day three, he was very taken with two projects dear to my heart.

Noah's Ark appealed to him greatly, and so did the idea of a musical play about King Henry VIII and his six wives, a concept I had been flirting with for some time. We parted company, planning to stay in close touch, and I returned to California with my two lavishly inscribed songbooks and serious thoughts of being a participant in Volume Three, 'Rodgers and Bricusse'.

I couldn't wait to telephone Richard Gregson and tell him the great news. He listened, impressed, to my story. There was a long pause. I knew instantly that something was wrong. And Richard said quietly, 'I don't know how to tell you this, but you are exclusive to Fox until *Dolittle* opens, and that's 18 months away.' And that is the tragic story of why I had to say 'No' to the chance of collaborating with Richard Rodgers, the man whose theatre music I admired above all others.

The footnote to the tragedy is that, in the rest of his life, Richard Rodgers only wrote two more stage musicals. One was a version of *Noah's Ark*, called *Two by Two*, and the other a version of Henry VIII, called *Rex*.

One of the advantages of being the only person on the Fox lot writing a musical was that I soon became regarded as 'the resident songwriter', with a steady stream of directors and composers coming by my office asking me if I would like to write the lyric to the title or theme song for their new movie. This is without doubt the jammiest job in the entire film industry. The film has been lovingly and expensively completed after maybe a year in the making, the title and release date long since set, the movie is being scored and the composer, producer and director suddenly decide that the beautiful main theme deserves a lyric. They show you the film, they play you the music, they offer you money and they ask for the lyric by Friday. You know the story, the style and the context. They place the whole thing in your lap. The film opens three weeks later, with hopefully a major recording to back it up, and every radio or TV performance is a money-earning commercial for both the movie and the song. It is a highly civilised process that deserves its own creative category, under the heading 'Money for Old Rope'.

André Previn, having married his lyricist, was an unlikely collaborator, but he marked my card, recommending that, if the opportunity arose, I should work with a gifted young film composer friend of his, 'a charming guy and the best of the bunch. His name is Johnny Williams.' I wrote the name down, and the Department of Fate promptly saw to it that the opportunity arose.

It's a strange thing about the lasting impact of screen images. Whenever I see a famous stage actor, I register that it's a famous stage actor, but whenever I see a famous *screen* actor, my mind immediately relates to the giant screen images with which I associate him or her. I didn't realise this until the morning Gene Kelly walked into my office at Fox, said, 'Hi, Leslie, I'm Gene Kelly,' and asked me if I'd like to write the lyric for the title song of the new movie he was directing. I gaped. This was my hero, GENE KELLY, whom I had watched a hundred times in my childhood at the Empire, Leicester Square, and another hundred times at the Rex Cinema in Cambridge. He was wearing a flat cap and an open-neck sports shirt, but all I could see was the shore-leave sailor from *On the Town*, the artist singing and dancing with Leslie Caron beside the River Seine in *An American in Paris*, and the soaking-wet genius with the umbrella in *Singin' in the Rain*. There was no way he could know how well I already knew him.

I tried to look and sound as cool as my fluster would allow, as though I were used to having my MGM musical gods drop in to see me and ask me to write songs for them. Sweet Lord, I was sitting there talking movie songs with GENE KELLY! The film, and the song, were to be called *A Guide for the Married Man*. Walter Matthau was the star, and to score the movie he had this great young composer called Johnny Williams. I smiled. 'You know him?'

'I know *of* him.'

'He's the best of the bunch.'

'That's what I hear.'

Then, one night at Jack Haley's house, producer Arthur Loew Jr, scion of the famous Loew's group, told me he was about to produce a new film at MGM, starring Natalie Wood and entitled *Penelope*, and perhaps I might like to write the title song with this terrific young composer he had engaged, Johnny Williams.

I was well aware by now that a number of cinematic giants walked the corridors of the Fox Executive Building. My next surprise visitor, a couple of weeks later, was small, but a giant nonetheless. William 'Call me Willy' Wyler, who had directed no fewer than three Best Picture Oscar-winning movies, *Mrs Miniver*, *The Best Years of Our Lives* and *Ben Hur*, suddenly popped his head round my door one morning. I had not realised his office was only a couple of doors down from mine, because the elevator was in the other direction. A sprightly, Irish, Marc Chagall-like leprechaun of a man with a killer smile, he was shooting an art heist suspense comedy starring Audrey Hepburn and Peter O'Toole, entitled *How to Steal a Million*, and he wanted a set-up song over the main titles. He had already selected his composer for the score, a brilliant young fellow called Johnny Williams.

Thus was I thrice more made vividly aware of the omnipresence on the Hollywood music scene of the young John Williams. He was scoring every movie being made. Thirty-five years later, the same is true. As I write this, John Williams has just received his 45th Oscar nomination, the most of any man alive. His remarkable ongoing collaboration with Steven Spielberg has single-handedly raised the quality of the motion-picture musical score to a level no one would have thought possible when he began his spectacular career. The film score today can stand alone as a separate artistic achievement in its own right, a far cry from the sillier movie theme songs that John and I wrote together in the Sixties.

To most of my celebrated friends in the music business, especially the younger ones, my greatest claim to fame is that I am married to a beautiful lady who once made a movie with The King, Elvis Presley. This is entirely true and, to this day, I continue to bathe in Evie's reflected glory. The film was called *Double Trouble*, and it was made at MGM. On the last day of shooting, at the wrap party, Elvis gave Evie a farewell present, a gleaming red Ferrari sports car. Gentlewoman and idiot that she is, the embarrassed Evie politely refused the gift as being overly generous and undeserved. Disappointed, but not wishing to offend his leading lady, Elvis had the car sent away. That was in 1967. I won't go so far as to say that Adam and I have exactly forgiven Evie for this lunatic transgression. We still love her very much, and we are slowly beginning to come to terms with the full impact of this mindless tragedy, and somehow learning to live with it.

Richard Fleischer was appointed director of *Doctor Dolittle*. A calm, mild-mannered man, he was Dick Zanuck's insurance policy against any future unpredictable outbursts by the formidable and ferocious Rex Harrison. Dick Fleischer, though he had never made a musical, had an impressive string of directorial credits, including two major movie successes starring the notoriously demanding and tough Kirk Douglas, *The Vikings* and *Twenty Thousand Leagues Under the Sea*. He had also directed the young Dick Zanuck's first film as a producer, *Compulsion*, and was Dick's loyal friend and ally. A leading Broadway choreographer, Herbert Ross, himself on the brink of a major directorial career, was brought in to stage the musical sequences. The time drew near for our hair-raising return to Portofino to discuss the screenplay and score with the formidable and ferocious Mr H, a daunting thought for all concerned.

Apjac, chain-smoking his little brown cigarillos, nervously shuffling his multi-coloured 3-by-5 cards and, his latest obsession, chain-drinking an obnoxious soft drink called Fresca, had one big problem. We still had no actor to play the role of Albert Blossom, the circus owner, who was required to sing the film's biggest production number, entitled 'I've Never Seen Anything Like It!'. I had recorded the song at yet another of our monster symphonic demo sessions, and Apjac insisted on singing it from morning 'til night, driving everyone around him to the edge of madness. But the Albert Blossom issue stubbornly remained unresolved, resisting even the best of Broadway, such as Stubby Kaye, the original Nicely-Nicely Johnson in Frank Loesser's *Guys and Dolls*. He was fabulous, but irretrievably American.

Then, one late spring morning, looking out of my Fox office window, I saw two sailors in white uniforms strolling across the parking lot towards the commissary. I instantly recognised the stockier of the two and flew downstairs and caught up with them. The second sailor looked on in amazement as I asked the first sailor if he would like to do a huge song and dance number as a circus owner in *Doctor Dolittle*. The stocky sailor grinned broadly and said, 'For you, Brickman darling, anything.' It was Dickie Attenborough. Indicating the other sailor, he added, 'By the way... do you know Steve McQueen?' They were starring in a Robert Wise film, *The Sand Pebbles*, having just returned from a diabolical location shoot in the Far East.

The three of us enjoyed a location-story lunch together in the commissary, we were invited to the McQueens that night for dinner, and I trotted happily over to Apjac's bungalow afterwards to inform him that Albert Blossom, the circus owner, was alive and well and available and dressed up as a sailor over on Stage Fourteen.

Our lease expired on Beverly Drive, and our new house, just north of Sunset Boulevard, behind the Beverly Hills Hotel, came with extremely glamorous neighbours. We were directly across the street from Danny Kaye, my childhood hero from the London Palladium. A few doors up on the left was Fred Astaire, and on the right Raquel Welch. These facts were confirmed by the endless trickle of 'Homes of the Hollywood Stars' tour buses that drifted down the street all day long. Danny Kaye's wife Sylvia Fine, who crafted the dazzlingly clever songs that were his trademark, heard of our arrival and promptly invited Evie and me across the street for dinner. This ranked alongside Gene Kelly's visit to my office as a major event in my life. There were eight of us for dinner, and we sat at a round table in a Chinese-style room that had been added as an extension to the Kayes' main kitchen. Three large Chinese stainless steel ovens, surmounted by huge woks, stood ominously at one end of the room. Danny, assisted by three Chinese ladies in white aprons, proceeded to cook a ten-course Chinese feast of surpassing magnificence. He did not eat with us, but sat at the table, watching eagle-eyed as we savoured every succulent and fantastic dish. It was the first of many such fabled meals that Evie and I would enjoy at that magic table.

Danny's star performance as a chef was directly related to his perfectionism as an entertainer. He had an uncanny eye for detail, and a natural ability to learn. He had learned how to cook in his years as a young cabaret performer in the Far East in the 1930s, by going into the kitchens of the restaurants where he ate. He had an amazing ability to absorb and copy, as he showed in his great aptitude for mimicry. Everything Danny did was like that. When he guest-conducted the world's great symphony orchestras, although he did not read music, his flawless bravura performances were the result of listening to the great orchestras and watching the great conductors. He managed to marry his love for the music with his talents as a performer. And he donated all his fees to the orchestras' pension funds.

Similarly, his years of tireless work for UNICEF, who made him their first and most celebrated international ambassador to the children of the world, were further evidence of his great generosity of spirit. And over the years, that unique and tiny round table in the Chinese kitchen, acknowledged by those who knew it to be the best restaurant in Beverly Hills and possibly the United States, would receive well-deserved recognition when the three-star Michelin chefs of France awarded Danny their ultimate accolade, 'Ouvrier de France', whose small framed certificate hung proudly but modestly on the kitchen wall. At that table, Danny not only fed every great name in Hollywood, but distinguished guests from all over the world, heads of government and members of most European royal families. The kitchen, like Danny, was one of a kind.

We returned to Portofino. Whether it was the balmy climate, the Zanuck threats, the phase of the moon or a combination of all three, Rex was a different man. He actually liked the script, or professed to, and he loved his songs, albeit with the old rerun reservations like 'You do know, Les' – he now called me 'Les' – 'that "of cos-eros" doesn't rhyme with "rhinoceros".' But apart from that he was lovely. I had somehow magically survived my baptism of fire. From that day forward, for reasons never explained nor understood, and certainly never questioned by me, Rex Harrison became my friend, and my good friend, which he remained for the rest of his life, a rare accolade, I promise you, and one accorded to very few, if only because very few wanted it. Beneath that nearly impenetrable, cantankerous façade, he knew that, deep down, both Evie and I were fond of him, admired him and cared about him. And the more time we spent together with him and Rachel, the more the four-way friendship was cemented.

Rex Harrison and Rachel Roberts were an unlikely pair, Rex with his ultra-smooth veneer of sophistication, which blithely belied his humbler Merseyside beginnings, and Rachel with her broad, open, Welsh peasant style. She was a warm and affectionate creature, in complete contrast to Rex's diffidence and aloofness. She was a fine actress in her own right but, in her private life with Rex, she seemed destined to play an ever-weakening supporting role. She could be wildly funny, and her powerful personality worked both for and against her. She called me 'Cambridge' and I called her 'Aberystwyth', after our respective universities. I always sensed a tinderbox tension just below the surface with her and Rex, especially when they were drinking too much, which was most of the time.

That was a major Portofino problem. There wasn't much to do on that heavenly little dead-end peninsula. Once you had drunk your fill of the glorious views, there was nothing to do except drink your fill. Rex and Rachel had become seasoned campaigners in this area. Before lunch and dinner, we would descend the hill in Rex's old white Jeep, then walk through the village to the port, to a floating bar called La Gritta, owned by a piratical rascal called Lorenzo Raggio. We were accompanied on these outings by Rex's basset-hound, Homer, who bore an uncanny resemblance to his owner, and had an unfortunate short-sighted habit of walking off the quayside into the port, from which he was regularly rescued by the local fishermen, who would return him to Rex and Rachel, who by then would have had too many drinks to notice that Homer was missing.

Rex was a generous host, a ruthless and seasoned raconteur with devastating delivery and an endless fund of evil stories, nearly all of which ended up insulting and demeaning, if not totally wiping out, his nearest and dearest friends and colleagues. He was hysterically amusing company, and he delighted in his wickedness.

We worked each day on the *Dolittle* songs, Rex talk-singing along to the piano tracks that had been laid down for him. His reading of the songs was dazzling, combining masterly timing and unique phrasing of Swiss-watch precision, creating minor miracles of character invention interlaced with the subtle underlay of humour that was his trademark. As an actor, he brought more to any song, musically as well as lyrically, than any songwriter had a right to hope for. All this rubbish about Rex Harrison being unable to sing, I soon realised, was a self-perpetuated myth. His infallible sense of rhythm enabled him to slip in and out of the melody whenever he wished, always on the right note, which gave him the rare ability to *act* a song, to give it a dramatic interpretation that no singer staying on the melody could ever hope to achieve. Rex Harrison was, I promise you, a highly accomplished musical performer.

Doctor Dolittle soon started shooting in England, and everything seemed to be going surprisingly smoothly. Rex was behaving, and Dick Fleischer kept everything firmly on schedule. There was nothing for me to do except stand by and execute the occasional minor rewrite, a line of dialogue here, a phrase of lyric there. So I began to think about what came next for me, when, if ever, the seemingly endless *Dolittle* did finally end.

I continued to be the 'songwriter in residence' at Fox. The quality of movie songs seemed improved from the year before. Composer Jerry Goldsmith brought me his gorgeous main theme for Robert Wise's *The Sand Pebbles*, to which I wrote a lyric entitled 'And We Were Lovers', which Andy Williams sang to a fare-thee-well. It was beautiful, with a stunning arrangement.

Then, wonder of wonders, I got to write my first song with Hank Mancini. He showed me Stanley Donen's newly completed film, *Two for the Road*, starring Audrey Hepburn and Albert Finney, in Dick Zanuck's screening room at 8.30 one morning. Freddie Raphael had written the acidly funny, sweet-and-sour screenplay. I loved it, and Henry's main theme captured its ultimately poignant mood to perfection. Two things stay in my mind from that film – the brief and telling first appearance of a gorgeous young English girl called Jacqueline Bisset, and the equally powerful first appearance of the white two-seater Mercedes SL convertible that marks the Finney character's arrival at success. I had taken delivery of the identical car the night before, and the first time I ever drove it was to see *Two for the Road*. It felt like a bizarrely oblique personal message from Freddie to me, warning me of the dangers of success.

The lyric to 'Two for the Road' was a joy to write. Certain melodies simply tell the lyricist what to say, and all he has to do is write it down. I dedicated the song to Evie. Its content qualified it for inclusion in the growing 'Evie-song' collection. *Doctor Dolittle* contributed three more – 'When I Look in Your Eyes', 'Where Are the Words?' and 'Something in Your Smile'. 'Two for the Road' was special for one other reason. It became Hank and Ginny's personal favourite of all his many songs, an unspoken indication that, when the opportunity arose, we would write together again.

To complete a rather nice hat-trick, John Barry called me from London to collaborate on the title song for the next James Bond movie, *You Only Live Twice*. After *Goldfinger*, John had told me the next Bond song title would be 'Mr Kiss-Kiss Bang-Bang', the nickname for James Bond in Japan, where the films were hugely popular. So we wrote a song called exactly that and, in John's view and mine, it was the best of the three Bond songs on which we collaborated. The lyric and the music were tough and smart and sophisticated, and the song was about the 'love 'em and leave 'em' Bond character, which no other Bond song ever was until 'Nobody Does It Better' more than a decade later. John made a marvellous recording of 'Mr Kiss-Kiss Bang-Bang' with Dionne Warwick, and we were convinced we had a big hit. We sat back and waited for the film *Thunderball* to be completed.

At the last minute, the film's producers, Cubby Broccoli and Harry Salzmann, decided to stay with the existing formula of giving the song the same title as the film. So 'Thunderball' it was. By that time, I was far away and up to my neck in *Dolittle*, and John asked Don Black, his long-term collaborator-to-be, to write the lyric. Now John was back, with another classy Barry melody for 'You Only Live Twice', and he wanted the lyric within days.

Evie and I had been invited down to Palm Springs for the weekend by Kirk and Ann Douglas, whom we had met at Danny Kaye's magic Chinese dinner table. I took the music of 'You Only Live Twice' with me and, on a glorious autumn Sunday morning, I wrote the lyric in Kirk's study, The Marc Chagall Room, in their beautiful desert home. I remember smugly thinking as I sat there, how good can it get? I was being handsomely paid to spend the weekend in the home of one of my favourite movie stars, writing the title song for a movie of one of my favourite heroes of fiction. I was the houseguest of Spartacus, writing for James Bond. It was

Top left: Anouk Aimée, Albert Finney, and myself at the London premiere of *Scrooge*.

Top right: Natalie Wood, myself, and Petula Clark at a *Goodbye Mr Chips* party in New York.

Middle: Myself with Evie, Sammy, and George and Alana Hamilton at the Hollywood premiere of *Scrooge*.

Bottom: Princess Margaret at the London premiere of *Scrooge*.

Top: David Niven reads me his latest pages from *The Moon's A Balloon*.

Bottom left: Champagne with Michael Caine at our Beverly Hills home.

Bottom right: An all-star gala of our songs in Hollywood.

Top: Dudley Moore and George Hamilton recuperating from their divorces with me in Acapulco.

Middle: Evie suffering at Casa Adan y Eva.

Bottom: Adam Bricusse yawning with boredom to be in the company of Lerner and Loewe, aboard Fritz's yacht, *Giriz II*.

Top: The three Es: Elizabeth Taylor, Elton Hercules John and Evie.

Middle left: Gregory Peck's infamous 'wine tasting' at Cap Ferrat.

Middle right: Liza and I having lunch at La Colombe D'or in Saint Paul de Vence.

Bottom left: Staying with five Lizas at their New York apartment (four Warhols).

Bottom right: Elton gives Evie his phone numbers.

Top: Adam Cedric Bricusse at Merton College, Oxford.

Middle: Greeting the divine Shirley MacLaine in London.

Bottom: Connery and Caine try in vain to cheer up Evie.

Evie reviews her Bond investments! *Top left*: Sean. *Top right*: Pierce. *Middle left*: Roger. *Middle right*: Niven.

Bottom left: Sex God Sellers.

Bottom right: Evie on a bad day!

Top: Newley, Mancini and I congratulate Sammy for *Stopping the World*.

Middle: Cher and Placido Domingo make my and Mancini's day at the Oscars!

Bottom: Congratulating Dickie Attenborough on his double Oscar win for *Gandhi*.

Top: Christmas in Gstaad with the Frank Sinatras and the Roger Moores.

Bottom: Sunday brunch at the Brickmans'.

unreal, a symbolic fulfilment of all my Cambridge daydreams of a decade before. And the resultant song wasn't bad, either.

My pondering on my professional future was resolved by a phone call from a gentleman called Gabriel Katzka. He had co-produced a Broadway musical called *Baker Street*, based on three of Sir Arthur Conan Doyle's Sherlock Holmes short stories. It was the first musical to be directed by Broadway's hottest young producer, Hal Prince. But it had not succeeded. What Gabe Katzka wanted to do was turn it into a major screen musical at MGM, and would I like to write a brand-new screenplay and score, keeping only the three short stories as the core of the piece?

My heart leaped at the mention of the three magic letters M-G-M, and my childhood dream of working on an MGM Hollywood musical came roaring back into focus. I asked Richard Gregson, my agent, who had moved his offices to Los Angeles, whether my *Dolittle* deal would preclude this, too, as it had done with Richard Rodgers. Richard said he'd talk with Dick Zanuck, and it was amicably agreed by all that I could start the project the following spring, as soon as *Dolittle* finished shooting, and a handsome deal was agreed.

Now that Gregson was LA-based, it occurred to me that he and Natalie Wood might enjoy one another's company. Richard was recently divorced and, although Natalie was always filming and constantly surrounded by people, she was still living alone in her pretty little house at 191, Bentley Avenue. Evie and I took the two of them to dinner at our and Natalie's favourite restaurant, La Scala, and invited them both to whatever else we were doing. They needed no prompting, and soon they were constantly together. Richard had been a loyal friend, as well as a world-class agent, for a decade now, and was extremely solid and stable. He was highly regarded in the industry, and even more so by Natalie Wood. Evie and Natalie and I had always been close, and the four of us now spent more and more time together, as the Sixties continued full blast.

There were so many exciting and beautiful people in everyone's lives we hardly knew which way to turn. It was Palm Springs or

Malibu every weekend, or Las Vegas if Sammy or Frank was playing there. It all seemed too good to be true.

It was...

I made one of my smarter career moves when I persuaded Apjac to take on Happy Goday to promote the *Dolittle* score. The little wizard song plugger took those 14 songs to every singer in the United States who was alive and had a recording contract, and beat them up one by one until they agreed to record something. My contribution was to try to get Sammy Davis to do the same. I called Sam and told him I wanted to play him something. He invited Evie and me to spend the weekend with him in Lake Tahoe, Nevada, where he was performing at the sumptuous Harrah's Hotel. Since we'd first met him five years before, we had seen Sammy perform something like a hundred times, in London, Paris, Las Vegas and New York, and every time we saw him he was the best he'd ever been. There was no other way to describe his ever-burgeoning magic.

In Lake Tahoe, Sammy had taken the lakeside villa provided by that most generous of hotel-owners, Bill Harrah, for his star performers. It had once belonged to Judy Garland, and would in time be bought by her daughter, Liza Minnelli. We watched Sammy's show Saturday night and, around midday on Sunday, we met in the living room, and I played him the recorded soundtrack-to-be of *Doctor Dolittle*. He didn't speak one word for the entire hour that it lasted, just stared his concentrated one-eyed stare at the vaulted ceiling as he listened.

When it finished, there was a long silence. I knew he hated it. Suddenly, he said, 'I'll do it!'

Relieved, I said, 'Which one?'

He put on his Stan Laurel face and, in exactly Stan Laurel's voice, scratching the top of his head, said, '*All* of it, silly!'

That was the good news. The bad news was that Sammy's marriage to May Britt, after six or seven hectic years, was drifting apart. No one but Sammy himself could sustain the non-stop pace and pressure of his always-on-the-road, all-night-partying, seven-days-a-week existence, with the entourage and the ever-changing assortment of hangers-on. May was a down-to-earth Swedish lady who simply wanted a quieter life than Sammy would ever be able to offer. She settled in Lake Tahoe and remarried. When Sammy told me this news, he added with dark, venomous humour, 'And wouldn't you know, she had to marry Doctor *White!*'

Jack Haley Jr, who produced many of the best big musical TV specials of the 1960s, asked me whether I'd like to do a two-hour special in Rome with Sophia Loren, and one or two guests singing a bunch of my songs. It sounded pleasantly escapist and relaxed, and the thought of three or four weeks in the Eternal City did not exactly upset Evie, who was good at adapting to such hardships. To celebrate, I wrote a rather nice ballad called 'Summertime in Rome' especially for Tony Bennett to sing to open the show.

The *Doctor Dolittle* film unit, having completed shooting in England, where the village perennially voted the nation's most beautiful, Castle Combe, in Wiltshire, had doubled as Puddleby-in-the-Marsh, now moved across the Atlantic to the Caribbean island of St Lucia, to film the sequences of Doctor Dolittle's famous sea voyage in search of The Great Pink Sea Snail. Shooting at sea is a costly business at the best of times, and taking hundreds of people on an extended stay in the Caribbean tends to further complicate an already complicated situation. Rex was becoming testy and, when Rex became testy, testy became a totally inadequate word. Blinding rage would be nearer the target. He and Rachel had chartered a yacht, moored out in the beautiful bay where the principal scenes were to be shot. But, beautiful as it was, the bay contained the one beach on St Lucia that had no sand. Days of delay ensued as thousands of truckloads of sand were hauled across the island, and the sand they imported happened to come from the one beach on the island that had sand-fleas, which promptly bit everyone to death.

Both Rex and Rachel were drinking too much and fighting too much. These fights usually ended with Rachel howling like

Homer, the basset-hound, and the sounds of conflict drifted across the beautiful bay, which had the acoustic perfection of a concert hall, so that everyone could hear every word, especially since Rex and Rachel, with their lusty, theatrically trained voices, knew how to project to the back of the hall, and therefore halfway across the island, too.

Getting daily bulletins from Ian Fraser about the rapidly deteriorating situation on flea-ridden St Lucia, Evie and I kept our cowardly distance and, instead of going there as originally planned on our way to Rome, we diverted our trip to Puerto Rico, where we stayed at the luxurious Dorado Beach Hotel. I was not keen to become the newly arrived target for Rex's testiness. I had not had any form of holiday since I had started work on *Dolittle* 20 months before. All we wanted was ten days of peace and quiet, playing on the beach with Adam. We arrived, unpacked and let go.

One hour later, the phone rang. It was an urgent call from Dick Zanuck in Hollywood, asking me if I could return to California the next day, as he urgently needed me for another project. He was unhappy with the screenplay of Fox's next big movie, *Valley of the Dolls*, based on Jacqueline Suzanne's monster bestseller. It was due to start shooting in eight weeks' time, and would I write a new screenplay? Evie had read the book, but I hadn't, since absorbing the works of Ms Suzanne was not high on my list of things to do. Dick said, 'Please read it and call me tomorrow.'

I reluctantly agreed to do so. Paperback copies of *Valley of the Dolls* were never more than 50 feet from any living human being on the planet at that time, so next morning I picked one up from the hotel gift shop and waded through its hundreds of pages from cover to cover. The temptation to which I might have succumbed, that might have tipped the balance, was that I knew there were songs in the film. I also knew that André and Dory Previn had already written them. I suppose, in retrospect, Dick Zanuck would have let me write my own songs as part of my screenplay, but those were games I didn't want to play with friends.

Richard Gregson made it worse by calling to say that Zanuck

had spoken to him, too, and that financially it would be extremely worthwhile, as well as further cementing my good relationship with Fox. I was, to an extent, perversely tempted by the challenge, just to see whether I could do well something I would normally not have done at all. Evie and I batted it back and forth, discussing the pros and cons. I didn't want to let Dick Zanuck down but, on the other hand, I was amazed that he was offering this highly sexed, drug-ridden, all-American saga to a boring and bespectacled Cambridge-educated English songwriter. I didn't have enough time to think it through and, at the end of the following day, I called Dick back and told him, probably mistakenly, that, flattered as I was, I wasn't sure that I would do as good a job as an American writer, who might be better suited to the basic material than myself. Evie let the decision be mine, but I think she would have preferred me to take the challenge and say 'Yes'. Evie is usually right about these things. Dick Zanuck was, as always, the perfect gentleman, accepted my reasoning, thanked me for my frankness and didn't try to persuade me further. End of story.

The diverse attractions of Rome, Sophia Loren and Sherlock Holmes were to prove a substantial consolation during the months ahead, which we planned to spend in Europe. We had a wonderful stay in Rome. Sophia and Carlo Ponti's classical villa at Merino, a few miles outside the city, where the two-hour special was to be filmed, was a remarkable setting, and Sophia herself collaborative and delightful to work with. She and Jack Haley and Ian Fraser and I cobbled together the musical layout of the show, a bizarre and eclectic selection of my songs that included 'Out of Town' from *Charley Moon*, 'Siesta' from *Lady at the Wheel*, 'Look at That Face' from *Greasepaint* and 'Talk to the Animals' from *Dolittle*, all of which she sang in the attractive voice that I had first heard singing 'I Fell in Love with an Englishman' on the *Peter and Sophia* album.

More than anything, Sophia wanted to start a family. She had

had a number of miscarriages, and greatly envied Evie having the blond and beautiful three-year-old Adam bouncing around the place. She offered to buy him. I was prepared to negotiate a deal, but for some reason Evie thought we should hang on to him. Sophia eventually produced two beautiful boys of her own, Carlo Junior and Eduardo.

Back in LA, we rejoined *Doctor Dolittle* for the studio shoot at Fox, which progressed comparatively smoothly, a phrase that unfortunately didn't apply to the state of some of our closer friends' marriages. Tony and Joan Newley were entering an increasingly bumpy phase of their marital roller-coaster ride, as were André and Dory Previn, Frank and Mia Sinatra, and Rex and Rachel Harrison. It was still calm on the surface, but storm signals were being hoisted and, sadly, all these seemingly perfect partnerships were destined to disintegrate within the next 12 to 18 months. On the flipside of this eternal dating game, other seemingly perfect couples, like David Hemmings and Gayle Hunnicutt, or George Hamilton and Alana Stewart, were preparing to enter the marital arena. It was like keeping score at a never-ending baseball game. And the go-go Sixties rolled relentlessly on towards their conclusion.

We did impromptu, silly things. One night at dinner at our house, Candice Bergen and I were bemoaning the fact that we hadn't seen a single one of the five films nominated for the Best Picture Oscar. We had both been too busy. We therefore rashly decided to see all five, back to back, the next day. Everybody said that (a) it wasn't possible, and (b) we were out of our minds. Candy and I regarded this as a head-on challenge, and promptly took it on. We met in Century City for breakfast sharp at 9.00am the next morning, movie schedules at the ready, to work out our game plan, which required masterly timing, meal breaks, car trips to Westwood and back, and so on. We calculated the Movie Marathon would take around 16 hours, door to door. By 10.00am, we were seated in our first movie house. Predictably, we constituted the entire audience. Who goes to see movies at ten o'clock in the morning? We segued to our second nominee around 12.30pm, and broke for a late lunch at 3.00pm. We were back inside for number three by 4.00pm, and in Westwood for number four by 7.00pm. We treated ourselves to a lavish Polynesian dinner at Trader Vic's around 9.30pm, before braving number five around 11.00pm. By 1.00am, mission accomplished.

Drunk with success, we proceeded to get ditto with white wine over a 2.00am supper cabaret show at the Century Plaza Hotel, listening to a celebrated, tone-deaf lady singer, who shall remain nameless. We considered submitting our achievement to the Movie Buff section of the *Guinness Book of Records*, but modestly decided to refrain. Like other great adventurers and pioneers before us, it was enough for us to know that we had done it.

We recorded the title song to *You Only Live Twice* in London. John Barry had found a sensational young black girl singer for the song, but, because she was unknown, Cubby Broccoli and Harry Salzmann rejected the idea. Pursuing their policy of associating the James Bond songs only with whoever was hot, they chose Nancy Sinatra, who had just had a big number-one hit with 'These Boots Are Made for Walking'. So Nancy it was who recorded the song. The unknown black girl was Aretha Franklin, who burst upon the scene a few months later with a string of number-one hits of her own. She became so hot that naturally Cubby and Harry wanted her for the next Bond movie a couple of years later. They were amazed and outraged that she didn't want to know about it.

Nancy Sinatra and her younger sister, Tina, soon became our close friends. They knew about us from Mia, who was their friend as well as their stepmother, even though she was younger than Nancy. We had known lovely Nancy Sr, their mother, since our first Christmas in California. The Sinatra family gave memorable Christmas Eve parties every year, and continue to this day to do so.

When we returned to LA, Evie and I took Nancy Jr and Mia

to dinner at Chasen's one evening. A few minutes after we arrived, Nancy Sr took a nearby booth with Tina and a couple of friends. With two Mrs Frank Sinatras present, there was a palpable tension in the restaurant. And it didn't help the situation that Tina Sinatra, Nancy Jr's sister, has always reminded me strongly of the young Ava Gardner. Later arrivals were agog to see what some thought were all of Frank's present and ex-wives on parade simultaneously. Also at our table was Larry Harvey, who had recently married Joan Cohn, widow of the former despotic Head of Columbia Pictures, Harry Cohn.

For reasons not too difficult to figure out, Nancy Sr was not exactly close to Mia, but the rest of us were all good friends. The embarrassment, deliciously electrifying to other diners in the restaurant, resolved itself in an awkward succession of visits from our booth to Nancy Sr's. We understood the situation, and so did she. She knew we had been friends of Mia before she married Frank, and had remained so.

There was an underlying humour to this '*très* Hollywood' situation, and the other diners lapped it all up faster than their soup. I started to think of what situation could possibly have been worse than this, which led me to concoct and sketch out on our tablecloth The Ultimate Nightmare Hollywood Dinner Party, comprising eight people who had been married to the person on either side of them, all the way round the table. It looked like this:

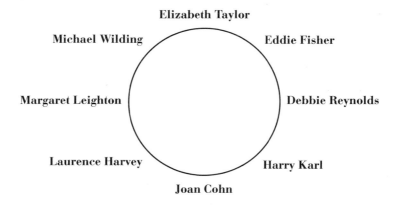

I had known George Axelrod since the day he burst into our first little house on Lindacrest in Beverly Hills, a restless, big bundle of nervous energy with a mind as sharp as a prosciutto slicer. His early successes as a Broadway playwright, especially *The Seven Year Itch*, had brought him to Hollywood, like myself, in his early thirties. He was a hugely successful screenwriter, with a great string of credits, including *Itch*, directed by Billy Wilder, *Breakfast at Tiffany's*, *The Manchurian Candidate*, *How to Murder Your Wife*, *Paris When It Sizzles*, and on and on and on. The reason for his first visit was to ask me to write a title song for a film he had written and directed, *Lord Love a Duck*, starring Tuesday Weld and Roddy MacDowall.

George and his A-group wife Joan were large on the Hollywood social scene, and wildly generous hosts. They knew everybody. My heart stopped on my first visit to their huge Holmby Hills house on Carolwood Drive when the first two guests I saw chatting together at the bar were Billy Wilder and Ira Gershwin. I called George 'Sir George', and he called me 'Lord Brickman'. George loved the odd libation, and didn't necessarily believe in waiting 'til the sun was over the yard-arm to enjoy it.

Dolittle had finished shooting. It seemed to have been going on for most of my adult life. Wonderful as it had been, our return to Europe was like The Great Escape. I was now officially free to start work on *Sherlock Holmes*, and promised Gabe Katzka that I would deliver a completed screenplay and 15 recorded songs by the end of the year, as he planned to shoot the film the following summer, in England and Europe. MGM gave it their blessing. I couldn't believe it. I was actually going to write an MGM musical, exactly a quarter-of-a-century after I had first seen one at the Empire, Leicester Square. I couldn't wait to start. We enjoyed a few lovely weeks in London, then made our way back down to Portofino, where, with the help of the film company, I had made a deal to spend several weeks at the sublimely located Splendido Hotel. And every morning, I would sit on its glorious near-deserted terrace, ecstatically happy, writing my screenplay while Evie and Adam went off on their adventures.

Evie and I drove into the nearby town of Santa Margharita one morning. Opposite the port was a boat showroom, and filling its giant window was a spectacular, gleaming, brand-new, updated model of next year's Riva Aquarama – a thing of rare beauty, a speedboat, dubbed by Mediterranean boat-lovers 'the Rolls-Royce of the sea'. We stopped and gaped. It was one of the most seductive sights we had ever seen in our lives. By the end of the afternoon, she was moored at La Gritta, Portofino's floating bar, where, like us, she would spend the rest of the summer. And glittering on her stern in chrome in the late-afternoon sun was her name, *Evie*, in honour of the other most seductive sight I had ever seen in my life, her namesake and new co-owner.

Sherlock Holmes was going well, so I didn't want to move as mid-summer approached. I had finished the screenplay and started the score. Adam, Evie and I were all in love with *Evie* the boat and content to be in Portofino – why wouldn't we be? It *is* the prettiest place on the planet – so we decided to stay on all summer.

Our first side-trip, expected, was to Rome, where Jack Haley Jr was now shooting the *Summertime in Rome* Sophia Loren TV special. It was all highly glamorous. Sophia was in sparkling form, and upped her offer for Adam. Evie still wouldn't sell, so I faced up to the fact that I would have to go on working for a living. The Hassler Hotel seemed to be inhabited by the population of the Beverly Hills Hotel. Half of Hollywood was there filming. It was still the good old days.

I had several unexpected lunches with Audrey Hepburn's genial then husband, Mel Ferrer, who had acquired part-ownership of the complicated film rights to *Peter Pan*, which apparently also involved Disney, the James Barrie Estate, London's Great Ormond Street Hospital for Sick Children, and other mysterious, lesser-known elements. I said that, if the present thick fog hanging over the rights ever cleared, I would love to be a part of the project. I doubted that I would ever hear from Mel about it again. I didn't.

There was a first-rate comedy sketch in Sophia's show about the Gestapo commandant who had occupied the house in Merino during World War Two. They couldn't cast the part, and Jack Haley was running out of time. I mentioned that we had seen Sellers in Portofino two days ago. Five minutes later, we were on the phone. The lure of Sophia was undiminished. Peter was there the next day, and no German Gestapo officer was ever funnier.

Tony Curtis was the big surprise of our visit. He was in Rome making a film with Claudia Cardinale. He was there with his two lovely young daughters, Kelly and Jamie, from his Hollywood's most glamorous couple marriage to Janet Leigh. Tony was currently married to the beautiful German actress, Christine Kaufman, and the four of us had had a few dinners together, mainly at Tony's rather grand house in Bel-Air. I have always thought him to be one of the most underestimated actors in Hollywood. He survived his Bernie Schwartz from Brooklyn beginnings, his pretty boy looks, his 'duck's ass' hairdo, and classic clinker lines like 'Yonder lies da castle of my faddah' in *The Black Shield of Falworth* to deliver a wide range of top-quality star performances in such superior films as *The Vikings, Spartacus, The Defiant Ones, The Sweet Smell of Success* and *Some Like It Hot*. To me, Tony has always been an authentic movie star, and I have always admired his work. True, he went through a series of strange phases and, at that time, he was deeply into his English aristocrat phase, wearing English tweed jackets, Ascots, jodhpurs even, with a British accent that put Olivier to shame, all of which I attributed to his playing opposite Christine in real life. She was an authentic aristocrat, daughter of a German contessa.

Tony Curtis loved clothes. He really did, and he wore them well. And he told me that the best tailor in Rome was Angelo Vitucci, at 34, Via Bissolati, and I had to meet him. Before I knew it, there we were at 34, Via Bissolati, and Tony was doing a sales pitch of such enthusiastic intensity to both Angelo and myself that an independent observer would have been forgiven for thinking he was on double commission. Angelo, a Paul Henreid lookalike, was a delightful man of immense charm, and he did indeed make stunning clothes.

Tony was a world-class salesman, and within three-quarters-of-an-hour I had ordered half-a-dozen suits, as many cashmere sports jackets, with delicious silk scarf linings, and a truckload of trousers. Tony commanded Angelo to have everything finished by Friday, because I was leaving Rome on Saturday, and set an arduous three-fittings-a-day schedule, at all of which he would personally be present. And he was. And let us not forget that the man was starring in a movie at the time.

What he did was most endearing. He didn't start shooting 'til mid-morning, so right after breakfast each day we were in the car to Via Bissolati... and again at late lunchtime... and again each evening around eight, before dinner, even if Angelo had to stay open and wait for us. Tony oversaw every detail of every fitting, changing a detail here, moving a pin there. He should have been a tailor. He was an obsessive, meticulous perfectionist when it came to clothes. He even turned up with Claudia Cardinale at one fitting, because we were all having dinner together later. By Friday night, I had the best wardrobe of my life, was considerably poorer, and returned to Portofino as the undoubted Beau Brummel of Liguria.

Our second side trip, unexpected, was to London. One Friday morning, we received a phone call from Sammy, who was back at the London Palladium, this time starring in the musical *Golden Boy*, which he had played on Broadway. 'We start to record *Dolittle* tomorrow night,' he announced, and added threateningly, 'You'd better be there!'

Evie flew to London from Genoa the next morning. I, alas, could not, because Apjac was on his way over from LA to see Rex and myself about the premières and publicity campaigns and music promotion for *Dolittle*, all of which were now seriously in the works.

I was awakened by a phone call at 4.00am on Sunday morning.

It was Evie and Sammy in London, in a mood of glee-ridden delight. They were in the control room of the Olympia Recording Studios. 'Listen to this, listen to this,' they clamoured, and for the next 15 minutes I heard for the first time, over the phone, Sammy's definitive recordings of 'Talk to the Animals', 'When I Look in Your Eyes' and 'Beautiful Things', superbly orchestrated and conducted by Marty Paich. They were to die for, even at long distance. What Sammy had done was to plan to record the 12 songs of his *Dolittle* album at four consecutive Saturday midnight recording sessions that became the hottest ticket in London. Remembering how Newley, Sellers and I had recorded the *Fool Britannia* album in New York, Sammy decided to turn the event into a series of catered parties, inviting friends and members of the casts of other West End shows to be his guests and audience. The big Number One Studio at Olympia was perfect for this, because you could accommodate a sizeable crowd behind the plate glass of the viewing room.

Needless to say, the following weekend I was there with them in London, and over the next three Saturday midnight recording sessions, probably the most exciting of my life, because of the amazing carnival atmosphere, the album was completed. Here was my first big Hollywood movie score being recorded by a megastar at the peak of his powers, orchestrated by a world-class arranger conducting a fabulous big orchestra made up of London's top session musicians, playing songs I was proud of in front of an audience of my friends and peers who were the first people on the planet ever to hear them. It doesn't get much better than that.

The highlight of an experience that was all highlights came at the fourth and final session. Sammy knew full well by now that he was making one of the outstanding albums of his career, and he was determined to give it a grandstand finish. The viewing room was crammed to overflowing, including our chum Richard Harris. Sammy decided to get the party started with 'After Today', an up-tempo love song with an exciting underbeat that Newley sang in the film. When the Twentieth Century Fox symphony-sized orchestra played Sandy Courage's explosive arrangement of this song for the first time, they put down their instruments at the end and applauded. There is no greater compliment from musicians. It was quite overwhelming. There is so much emotion involved between the revelatory moment when you first create a song and the fulfilling moment when you hear the best in the business perform it. It was a moment I felt could never be topped, but Sammy topped it now. Marty Paich had written a dazzling arrangement that was fully the equal of Sandy Courage's. Sammy nailed the song with a show-stopping performance on the first 'take'. It was greeted with roars of applause from everyone present. Sammy couldn't resist that reaction. 'One more time!' he commanded. They kept the tape running, and he did the song *11* times in a row, each time better than the last, just for the sheer joy of doing it.

The exultation I felt at Sammy's grand finale to the album dissipated sadly and swiftly at the end of the session when Richard Harris took me aside to tell me that Vivien Leigh had died earlier in the day. Evie and I knew Vivien well through Johnny and Mary Mills, her closest friends throughout the golden years of her marriage to Laurence Olivier, when the two of them were quite simply the most glamorous couple on earth.

At Apjac's urgent request, Evie and I returned to California. We were flying back and forth across the Atlantic more than most airline pilots. A frantic, chain-smoking, Fresca-guzzling, more-nervous-than-ever Apjac, covered from head to foot in multi-coloured notepads, was mounting a monster publicity campaign for the various upcoming international premières of *Doctor Dolittle*. Happy Goday, song-plugger supreme, had surpassed himself. By the time the film was to open worldwide, he had assembled somewhere north of *600* recordings of the songs, including over 20 complete albums of the score, by artists as varied as Sammy, Newley, Bobby Darin, Mantovani and The Chipmunks. The soundtracks I actually saw were in English,

French, Spanish, Italian, German and Japanese, and there were many others – Dutch and Greek and Swedish and so on.

We went to Paris to meet with the wizard French lyricist Eddie Marnay. Over a leisurely three-hour lunch aboard a Bâteau Mouche cruising serenely up and down the Seine, I realised how much tougher his job was than mine. He not only had to translate my lyrics and make them make the same sense in French at any given screen moment, which he achieved with great wit and style, he had the additional near-impossible task of trying to find French vowel sounds that would cause the lip-synching to match the English mouth movements. But, since Eddie had successfully achieved precisely this on every major film musical of his time, I knew the job was in the best possible hands. The thought of Dutch, Greek and Japanese lyricists trying to do the same was something I decided not to worry about.

Back in London, Ian Fraser was supervising the arrangements for the big orchestra demos of the 15 *Sherlock Holmes* songs which had to be completed before the flurry of *Dolittle* premières started in December. We arranged to trade homes with Peter Sellers. He was coming to California to make a movie, having just returned from Switzerland where, he informed me, his financial advisers had come up with a brilliant new scheme for him to commit suicide for tax purposes. He took our house, and we took his latest spiffy apartment in Clarges Street, Mayfair, about 10 feet from the delectable Mirabelle restaurant.

The night before we left LA for London, we had a farewell dinner at Chasen's with Steve and Neile McQueen and told them of our plans. Jealous, they announced that they were coming with us. We pointed out that with Adam and his nanny there, the flat would be full, except for the maid's room. Steve said, 'Fine, we'll take the maid's room.' And they did. So, for the three weeks of our London stay, we had a live-in couple who did nothing but go shopping and to restaurants with us, and keep us in party mood all day every day. Steve contrived to keep us on California time for the entire duration of our stay, so that we were up all night

28

and asleep all day. He would keep us up storytelling 'til dawn, so that we could go out to breakfast and be the first customers at Cartier's round the corner in Bond Street when they opened. One morning, the four of us bought a total of seven Cartier watches right after breakfast, and then went home to bed. It was obscenely decadent.

The *Sherlock Holmes* demos, which were recorded during all this lunacy, were, though I say so myself, sensational. Ian Fraser assembled a soundtrack-quality recording with 35 top session musicians and an impressive array of London character voices. I sang the role of Sherlock Holmes myself, first because I knew how I wanted it to be approached, and second because Rex Harrison was now keen to play the role. He was a little old for it, but he would bring other qualities to it that no one else could match.

We recorded the score at Chappell's Studio in Mayfair and, by the time we finished three days later, we were in a high state of excitement. Then the bomb dropped. On the day we finished mixing the record, Apjac called from LA to tell me that MGM had just been taken over by two gentlemen called Edgar Bronfman and Bo Polk, and they were dumping all the projects that their predecessors had in development. I sat dumbstruck as seven months of concentrated work got flushed down the MGM toilet, and marvelled anew at film companies' ability to squander unlimited sums of money. It was a terrifying waste of time and talent.

But there was no time for mourning. The whirlwind tour of *Doctor Dolittle* premières was upon us – four in eight days, in London, Paris, New York and Los Angeles. The royal world première, in London, at the Odeon Theatre, Marble Arch, attended by Her Majesty the Queen, was the grandest by far. The Queen was dazzling, and Evie and I were presented to her along with Zanucks *père et fils*, various Fox bigwigs and the stars of the film. As it was what was called a 'roadshow' production, there was a 20-minute intermission halfway through the film. The Queen and her party were ushered into the special area reserved by Zanuck for VIP refreshments. Everyone stood a respectful distance from Her Majesty, unsure of the protocol. She then moved towards us, smiling, and for some reason targeted Evie and me. She said how much she loved the sequence in which Doctor Dolittle gives Toggle, the local, short-sighted plough-horse, an eye-test, and fits him with an enormous pair of reading glasses. The ice broken, and knowing of HM's great love of animals in general and horses in particular, I told her some of the funnier moments we had experienced with Rex and the animals during the shooting of the film. She was highly amused, and so engaging that the three of us were deeply into a laughter-filled conversation about animals. Her legendary sense of humour was fully on display, she was extremely and wittily chatty and, before we realised it, the 20-minute intermission was over. The Queen had spoken to no one else except Evie and me. We were flattered, honoured and not unaware of the jealous glances being thrown at us by some of the film industry VIPs as we trooped back in for the second half of the movie. We didn't make too many new friends that night.

Dick Zanuck woke me up at five in the morning. He was ecstatic, and read me an unexpectedly glowing set of reviews from the normally truculent English press. 'Better than *My Fair Lady*' was one over-the-top quote I shall not easily forget. Premature euphoria spread quickly through the Fox camp, and we all left for Paris the next day filled with high hopes. No one goes to Paris without having a good time, so by the time we left for New York 48 hours later, after a spectacular party given by Darryl Zanuck at Maxim's, we were as close to over the moon as we were ever likely to get. There was a music party given for me by Fox Records in midtown Manhattan the night we arrived, attended by lots of old pals – Petula Clark, Natalie Wood, Eddie Fisher, Sammy Cahn, David Frost, David Merrick and Cyril Ritchard among them – at which I was presented with a gold record for the *Doctor Dolittle* soundtrack album, which had apparently gone over the moon ahead of us.

But the New York press seemingly didn't see the same movie as their London *confrères*, and we had a strange mix of love-hate notices in the United States, reminiscent of that long, long first night of *Stop the World* five years before. They either adored it or they didn't get it all. I attributed this inexplicable dichotomy of reactions to the extreme Englishness of the film's humour, that some people embraced and others didn't. Like most things, it's a matter of taste, and God knows few, if any, tastes are universal.

There was no time for rejoicing or for mourning. In any case, it was premature. Time alone would tell. The next morning, Apjac hit me with a new proposal that was totally unexpected. One project MGM were *not* abandoning, apparently, because it had been in the works for a long time and was too far advanced, was the musical remake of *Goodbye, Mr Chips*, one of their most prized titles. The lovely Terence Rattigan, now known to us all as Terry the Rat, which was Rachel Roberts's pet name for him, was still inexplicably turning out rewrites of the screenplay. I asked him why. He said, 'I can't stop!' The film had been written, screenplay and score, and was already in pre-production when I had first arrived in California for *Dolittle* two-and-a-half years before, and had been going round in circles ever since. Apjac, who had produced both *Dolittle* and *Planet of the Apes* in the interim, was now ready to bring *Chips* to the top of the heap, and planned to shoot the film that coming summer.

He got straight to the point. MGM weren't happy with the song score, principally because they felt the idiom of the lyrics was not sufficiently English, giving a stilted effect to the language. Apjac wanted me to write a brand-new score, and for Herb Ross, *Dolittle*'s choreographer, to direct.

I met with Herb. We both had the same problem. We were both close friends of the Previns, especially André. The situation was further complicated by the fact that André and Dory were drifting apart. I knew the score of *Chips*, because Dory had suggested that we have a dinner at their house at which we played and sang the *Chips* and *Dolittle* scores to one another, which we had done. I was aware of the *Chips* problems. Herb and I went to

Apjac. I offered to be Dory's back-up lyricist, to make the songs 'more English'. MGM refused, and said that, if Herb and I didn't accept the project, they had plenty of others who would, which I didn't for one moment doubt. There was only one thing to do. Talk to André. And that's when we found out that André and Dory were parting.

André had accepted a firm offer to become resident conductor of the Houston Symphony, and was planning to leave Hollywood for good. The Hollywood phase of his golden career was ended. He had all sorts of good reasons to move on, and gave Herb and myself his blessing, believing we would do a good job on *Chips*.

That was fine. André was André, the best in the business, whichever arena of the world of music he chose to bless with his protean talents. What was not so fine was Dory. Dory, the talented but insecure, nice but neurotic, complex and complicated Dory. The loss of André was devastating to her, and the consequent loss of *Chips* a further aggravation. Far worse was the reason she was losing André, which ultimately was Mia Farrow.

Frank Sinatra and Mia had also split around this time. Like Dory, Mia was very much the junior partner in her marriage. She had been close to completing principal photography in New York of the most important film of her young career, *Rosemary's Baby*, which was about to make both her and Roman Polanski bona fide star names in the industry. She was commuting each week between New York and Los Angeles, because she was simultaneously playing a role in Frank's current Fox movie, *The Detective*. Inevitably came the moment when she was needed in both places at the same time, at which point Frank told her she had to walk from *Rosemary's Baby*. Mia refused, and she told me that Frank delivered the ultimatum that, if she didn't, the marriage was over.

So *both* marriages were over, and suddenly André and Mia were together. Sad as it all was, there was no doubt in my mind that those two were the most viable and perhaps the only possible permutation in that particular quartet. Frank and Mia remained friends. André and Dory didn't.

It got worse. Apart from the drama over *Chips*, Evie and I were in the awkward position of being friends of all four combatants. It was Evie and myself who had introduced Mia into the Previn household in the first place. Dory was on the brink of a nervous breakdown, and who came to her rescue? Evie. Dory moved into our house, and Evie was a true friend to her. Dory's homemade therapy was writing, which ironically resulted in the most successful work of her career. She wrote a devastatingly self-analytical series of songs, entitled *On My Way to Where?*. Among them was one written in our house, called 'Beware of Young Girls', a thinly veiled indictment of Mia, warning married women to beware of wide-eyed and innocent young girls of 24 who bring flowers and friendship to your door and then leave with your husband. Dory's songs became a bestselling album, performed by herself, and the only positive thing other than André and Mia's subsequent marriage to come out of this whole sorry mess was that, through it, Dory Previn found her own voice and her artistic independence.

I am not by nature a cynic, though I am well aware that the same man who created the Nobel Peace Prize also invented dynamite. Doors opened and closed, I was learning, in the strangest of ways. But I continued to believe deep down that the Department of Fate knew what it was doing, and I agreed with Doctor Pangloss in *Candide* that all was for the best in the best of all possible worlds. Time would tell if Doctor Pangloss knew what he was talking about.

3rd Key Change

4th Key: D Major

The pre-production wheels began to turn on the movie of *Goodbye, Mr Chips*. I had 14 songs to write, and not an overabundance of time in which to write them. Herb Ross was already in Europe, scouting locations in England, Italy and Switzerland with his wife and choreographer, the ballerina Nora Kaye. It was decided that I, too, should base myself in Europe, spending time with Terence Rattigan in Bermuda en route, to make sure we were both writing the same movie.

Evie was pregnant again. She was in gloriously good health, and radiantly beautiful. Full of beans and the joys of spring, she friskily accompanied me on a long-weekend PR jaunt up to San Francisco, where I had to do some TV, radio and newspaper interviews. It was our first time back there since the good old bad old days of the David Merrick era. We stayed at the Fairmont, where Lainie Kazan was singing up a storm in cabaret, and eagerly revisited our former favourite haunts. It was a hectically happy three days.

We returned to LA on the Monday morning, and two days later the trouble started. Evie was rushed into Cedars Sinai Hospital and, within a week, had lost the baby. No one had said, 'Don't go to San Francisco', but we both wondered whether the two short air trips had contributed to the tragedy. We were both devastated, and withdrew into our shell until Evie had time to adjust to the loss, and her doctors said it was OK for her to resume normal activities. Sadly, it was *not* OK.

Our delayed trip to Bermuda was more eventful than we had planned. Evie felt unwell again on the plane from LA to Miami and, by the time we landed there, she was quite alarmingly sick. There was no question of taking the connecting flight on to Terry the Rat. I remembered that Frank Sinatra was in Miami making a film called *Lady in Cement* with Raquel Welch. I called him at the Fontainebleau Hotel, where I knew he always stayed. Like Superman, faster than a speeding bullet, he had a car at the airport to collect us and whisk us to the Fontainebleau, where he had doctors waiting to examine Evie. Post-pregnancy complications were diagnosed, and ten days of bed-rest recommended. Frank had pre-arranged our lavish accommodation, and there we stayed for over a week. I called Adam, who was now four, in California, to tell him we were not in Bermuda as planned, but in Miami, and I would call him each day. Next evening I called, Adam's nanny put him on the phone and he said, 'Hello, Daddy! Are you still in Your Ami?'

Frank being Frank, he was not content merely to be starring in a movie each day. Exactly as he had done during the making of *Ocean's Eleven* in Las Vegas a few years before, he was also performing at night, singing as only he could in the Fontainebleau's sumptuous showroom. After eight days, Evie was well enough to move on to Bermuda. Frank saw us off. We were not allowed to pay for anything. The best I could do was install an industrial-strength row of chrome Jack Daniels' dispensers in the much-used bar area of Frank's boat, moored across the way from the hotel on the Indian River.

If there was a more charming or wittier man than Terence Rattigan alive on the planet at this time, I certainly did not meet him. His tax exile in Bermuda was a source of constant bemusement to him – 'like living on an enormous Cunard liner moored in the middle of the Atlantic', as he described it. Mindful of Bermuda's British heritage, he called the vast terrace of his house 'the parade ground', and toasted the Queen in Dom Perignon at sundown each evening, pointing out the inescapable irony that it was only his tax-free exile from Her Majesty's kingdom that enabled him to afford to toast her in top-quality champagne. Having written the hugely successful play *French Without Tears*, which brought early fame and fortune to both Rex Harrison and himself, and having been Rex's best friend, 'if Rex has a best friend', for three decades, Terry had accumulated over the years a vast fund of stories about Rex's appalling behaviour in every conceivable circumstance, which he delighted in telling to anyone who would listen. In us, after three years in the Rex trenches, he had a heaven–sent audience, which was hard to come by in Bermuda at the best of times.

We laughed all the way to Paris, where we were greeted at the Lancaster Hotel by Apjac and Herb Ross with the news that they had that very day cast Peter O'Toole as Mr Chips. A great acting choice for Terry the Rat as screenwriter, I thought, but hardly a top-of-the-charts singing coup for me as composer and lyricist. Not that I was expecting or wanted it to be Howard Keel or Mario Lanza either. I just wanted someone who could carry a tune. I knew that Peter could carry a bottle of Scotch with no problem, but if he had a musical background it was even further in the background than his first sighting of Omar Sharif in *Lawrence of Arabia*.

Apjac was no fool. He knew that Robert Donat had won the 1939 Best Actor Oscar for *Chips* over Clark Gable in *Gone with the Wind*, and they were *both* MGM movies. So, of course, a fine actor was the first essential. He had also made John Williams the film's musical director, which was a massive plus. I had further persuaded him to promote Ian Fraser from number three on *Dolittle* to number two on *Chips*. There was, from my point of view, no stronger musical support team imaginable. Even so, John and Ian and I faced the formidable potential problem of a completely non-singing Mr Chips in the title role of a big-budget MGM musical of *Goodbye, Mr Chips*, which I likened to Apjac casting an organ grinder's monkey for a remake of *King Kong*.

But that wasn't my biggest problem. My biggest problem was that I didn't yet have a score. I knew that I would now have to trim the wings of my dreams of a highly romantic and lyrical score. My guess was that the O'Toole musical range was at best four or five wobbly notes, and time quickly proved that my guess was overly optimistic. Far more than with Rex, we would be depending on the strengths of the actor to salvage the shortcomings of the singer. I demanded of Apjac that he at least provide me with a top-notch singing *Mrs* Chips, around whom I would still have a slim chance to build a vaguely singable score... otherwise we were doomed.

To everyone's surprise and delight, not to say amazement, *Doctor Dolittle* received seven Oscar nominations, including one for Best Picture. I got two nominations, for Best Score and Best Song, 'Talk to the Animals'. But the film was a far cry from the box-office sensation that Darryl Zanuck had craved and predicted. It had cost far too much money, and I think its leisurely paced Englishness, warmly embraced at the royal première in London, lacked in-depth appeal for American audiences, especially the younger generation weaned on fast-moving TV shows. The film was destined to achieve an enduring popularity later in life, via its frequent and perennial TV and music performances, plus enduring video sales, but what *Variety* would call 'boffo' – i.e. a box-office smash hit – alas, it definitely was not.

Fox wanted us to return to Hollywood for the Oscars, but Apjac and I both knew that *Chips* was now our priority. I asked Sammy to sing 'Talk to the Animals' on the Oscar show and, in the unlikely event that I got lucky, to accept the award for me. I felt I had a stronger chance with the score than the song, especially since the opposition included Burt Bacharach and Hal David's 'The Look of Love' and Sammy Cahn and Jimmy Van Heusen's 'Thoroughly Modern Millie'.

I got my top-notch female singer when Petula Clark was cast as Mrs Chips. She and I had been friends since my first days in the business, and she had recently provided the definitive recording of one of my favourite *Dolittle* songs, 'At the Crossroads'. I knew the *Chips* score would be safe in her capable hands and delectable larynx. I also knew that her principal challenge would come from the considerable dramatic range demanded by the role of Catherine. To be a show-stopping musical Greer Garson was a tall order for any talent.

I completed all the songs except one, 12 of 13. And number 13, true to form, was destined to be unlucky, driving me to the very gates of the funny farm. It was the first time in my writing life that I ever got stuck on a song. It would haunt my entire summer. I wasn't stuck for writing songs. I was stuck on *that* song, Mrs Chips's most private moment, in which she had to express her deep and lasting love for Chips. Over those months, I would write *18* songs for that single infuriating spot, as opposed to 12 for the rest of the movie. Some of the 18 were good songs, but none of them exactly what I was after. Thus do songwriters acquire an ever-expanding 'trunk' of unused material.

Happily, there was more than enough completed material for John Williams to get started, and oh my God, did he make me sound good. At the famed CTS Studios in London's Notting Hill, he recorded the string of glorious arrangements that flowed from his unerring pen, setting the unmistakable style and creating the unique and distinctive sounds that were to become his signature in the 1970s, making him the greatest film composer of all time.

These pre-recordings, to which the actors add their singing voices, are called 'playbacks'. They then lip-synchronise the lyric when the scene is shot, which is as tricky as it sounds and a skill all its own. If you are a Julie Andrews, it is no problem. Your innate musicianship allows you to achieve perfect synchronisation every time, even while twirling on top of an Alp. Thus it was with Petula Clark, another natural. Thus it was not with Rex Harrison in *Dolittle*, whose unique and wondrous brand of *Sprechgesang* demanded that he record live while shooting, which is even trickier, especially for the sound engineers, and calculated to fray tempers, especially Rex Harrison's.

And thus it most particularly was not in the case of the endearing but musically hapless Mr Peter O'Toole, whose supreme capabilities as an actor were, to put it as politely as 30 years of retrospection allow, in no way matched by his contributions to the world of music. If the actor was Everest, the singer was Harrow-on-the-Hill. To Ian Fraser, having survived two years of the musical wrath and testiness of Rex Harrison, now fell the thankless task of trying to bring together the completely non-existent singing talents of Mr O'Toole and my musical expressions of Arthur Chipping's character and points of view, a marriage made in Hell. Ian later told me that Peter's first completed playback was the result of cobbling together individual syllables from countless different 'takes', the musical equivalent of a 10,000-piece jigsaw puzzle of a cloud formation.

But Ian Fraser's legendary musical patience ultimately won out, and Peter's playbacks were slowly and agonisingly completed. But if Peter was the agony, Pet Clark was the ecstasy. Two takes maximum, usually one, she sailed through song after song in minutes, so effortlessly that the all but tone-deaf Mr Chips soon longed to strangle his adored songbird, Mrs Chips.

Happy Goday woke me up at six o'clock in the morning and said, 'You won!' He didn't say exactly *what* I had won, and then his voice cut out. I was not to find out which Oscar I had won 'til late that afternoon, but I assumed Best Score, for the previously mentioned reasons. Not that I minded. To have won at all on my very first Hollywood film was more than good enough for me. I called Sammy, to find out more, but needless to say he wasn't home. I couldn't have cast anyone better in the entire world to celebrate on my behalf in my absence.

My next phone call was from Roger Moore, who'd already heard I'd won for something and was coming to collect Evie and me to take us out to a special celebratory luncheon. 'Be ready at eleven and don't argue,' he said. And special it certainly was. Sharp at eleven, and I mean sharp, because, remember, Roger was never late for anything, a huge Rolls-Royce arrived at Park Street, containing Roger and Luisa, and Ruth and Milton Berle, and swept us out of London on a perfect spring day into the glorious Bedfordshire countryside, to Woburn Abbey, the stately home of Ian, Duke of Bedford, and his French film producer Duchess, Nicole Milinair. The eight of us lunched in the fabled Venetian dining room where, unbelievably, 22 Canaletto scenes of Venice of breathtaking beauty hang in the only home they have ever known since a far-sighted family forebear bought them from Canaletto's studio some 200 years before.

Upon our return to London, I learned from the *Evening Standard* that I had, in fact, won Best Song and not Best Score, as I had thought. I pointed out a strange fact to Evie. I had possibly achieved something unique in Hollywood history, winning an Oscar on my first ever day of work in Hollywood, because that was when I had written 'Talk to the Animals', as the opening endeavour of my *Doctor Dolittle* audition for Twentieth Century Fox three years before.

Sammy had accepted my Oscar from presenter Barbra Streisand. I was fleetingly sad that Evie and I had not been there, since to accept an Academy Award from Barbra Streisand is the dream of any songwriter. I now learned via Apjac that Sammy had left town on an extended tour, and taken the Oscar with him. I was not to hear from either of them for several weeks, until Apjac finally turned up in London with my gold statuette and a lame excuse from Sammy that he couldn't let the little fellow go because 'he matched my jewellery'!

I received many lovely letters and phone calls from all over the place, as friends and people I did not know responded to the strange mystique of Oscar. He is touched with a rare and special magic. Oscar is probably the most famous and certainly the most photographed of all trophies of achievement. His aura of iconic power is such that the most frequently asked question about him is 'May I touch him?' as though the enquirer expects to receive a cure or a lifespan extension as a result of the hallowed experience.

Among many of the delightful messages I received, a couple live particularly long in the memory. A three-page handwritten letter from Darryl Zanuck telling you how wonderful you are is probably more than any man has a right to expect from any term served in Hollywood, but, memorable as it was, it had to take second place to the most treasured fan letter I ever received from anyone in my life – a four-page, again handwritten, thoughtful and beautifully detailed letter, analysing and complimenting my songs one by one, comparing them to Irving Berlin (ye gods!) and, at the foot of page four, the signature of the one human being above all others whom I would have wished to like my songs – Fred Astaire. I regret to add that both these letters were stolen by my then-chauffeur, a small-time crook of considerable ingenuity. 'Nuff said.

Throughout the 1960s, whenever we were in London, the two friends with whom we spent the most time, shared the best adventures, ate the best food and undoubtedly laughed the most were Britain's leading film hyphenate screenwriter-director Bryan Forbes and his angel-hyphenate-wife Nanette Newman.

Forbesey called one day to announce that he was off to the South of France to direct the film of *The Madwoman of Chaillot*, which he had taken over from John Huston. He was shooting at France's oldest film studio, La Victorine, and he had taken a large villa on Cap Ferrat for Nanette and the children, and would Evie and I like to bring Adam down there and spend some time with them? Always willing to sacrifice ourselves for the good of others, we graciously concurred.

The following week, Forbesey started shooting *The Madwoman of Chaillot*. The cast he had inherited from John Huston was stellar to the point of creating its own galaxy: Katherine Hepburn, Yul Brynner, Charles Boyer, Danny Kaye, Richard Chamberlain, Paul Henreid, Edith Evans, Guilietta Massina, Margaret Leighton and Oscar Homolka were among them. Ms Hepburn was playing the title role and she was living nearby. She would cycle heartily across Cap Ferrat most days to discuss her complex role in detail with Forbesey, so that we all got to spend lots of delicious time with the Great Kate.

Evie and I decided to stay in the South of France and look around for a longer-term summer home. The all-knowing Newman told us of a small new hotel that had just opened in the village of St Jean Cap Ferrat. It was called 'La Voile d'Or', a delicious, deluxe small hotel on the south side of the port of St Jean. It was a storybook setting, and we swiftly took the two best rooms, overlooking the whole coast from Beaulieu to Cap d'Ail and on down to Monaco and Italy, for the next two months, installing Adam and his nanny in one and ourselves in the other. It was the most romantic place on earth. If I can't find the elusive missing *Chips* ballad here, I thought to myself, I shall hang up my songwriting spurs and join the Foreign Legion. Evie agreed this was a good idea.

Snugly settled into the exotic splendours of our luxurious surroundings, Evie and I promptly corrupted the film's title *Goodbye, Mr Chips* into the much more elegant and expressive fractured French of *Au Revoir, M'sieur Pommes Frites*.

Evie the boat arrived from Portofino the next morning, navigated by our two old friends Mingo and Manuel, who constituted the entire naval strength of Portofino. Jeannot, the village sailor who constituted the entire naval strength of St Jean Cap Ferrat, agreed to take care of the boat for the summer. He moored her invitingly right below our window, like a beautiful 30-foot dog waiting to be taken out for a run.

Danny Kaye called us from the Negresco Hotel in Nice to

invite us to dinner. I suggested he come to us instead. I described the intimacy and the setting of the Voile d'Or, and the high quality of the kitchen, which had already achieved a Michelin star in its first year. Sight unseen, Danny moved in, and stayed with us throughout the movie. By the second night, he had moved into the kitchen and, by the fourth, he had pretty well taken it over. Franco–Chinese dishes unknown to the Michelin Guide started to appear on a fairly regular basis for the privileged few, which included Richard Chamberlain and Maggie Leighton, as the good word on the Voile d'Or spread among the *Madwoman* company.

I continued my struggle and search for the missing *Chips* love song. On average, I completed two new songs a week. I had love songs like other people have mice. But the more I wrote, the further away I got. I decided to wait for the Department of Fate to do something about it. I knew I wouldn't have to wait long, because the film was ready to start shooting, and Apjac, a nervous wreck at the best of times, was contemplating suicide, though not for tax purposes, unless something happened soon. And it did. MGM, in the best traditions of studio loyalty, brought in another songwriter. Mr Rod McKuen, famously labelled 'the world's bestselling poet' at the time, was asked to take a shot at the elusive love song and, in a memorable display of arrogance, proceeded to write a complete new ten-song score for *Chips* in one weekend.

At Apjac's urgent request, I returned to London. Together, we played the ten songs, which happily were so unsuitable that I have Mr McKuen to thank for removing not only the crisis but himself as well from the scene. His big love song, entitled 'Mr and Mrs Chips, Esquire' (pronounced in three syllables 'Es-quiy-ah') was, in my opinion, a particular dilly.

I was so incensed that I sat down in the Park Street apartment later that day in a cold fury, reached into my heart for what I, in Mrs Chips's place, would have said about Evie, and inside 30 minutes I had completed the words and music of my favourite of all my songs about Evie, 'You and I'. Everybody loved it, the score of *Chips* was complete, and life could now move on.

Thanks to the Forbeses' fabled hospitality, we spent many evenings with the Great Hepburn, who was quite terrific to be around with all her quaint New England eccentricities and that wonderful speaking voice. Kate had recently won her second Best Actress Oscar for *Guess Who's Coming to Dinner?*, her final film with her beloved Spencer Tracy. She would win again the following year for *The Lion in Winter*, and again in 1985 for *On Golden Pond*, to become the only actor or actress in cinematic history ever to win four Academy Awards, spread over more than half-a-century.

We planned a belated celebration for her. By chance, the following Sunday was Kate's birthday. Evie and I asked Forbes and Newman, given all their and Kate's kindnesses to us, whether we could have the privilege of hosting her birthday lunch, and invite all the actors. It was agreed. As a venue, Forbesey suggested a lovely old restaurant up in the hills, in the ancient village of Saint-Paul de Vence.

Thus it was that Evie and I marched into the famed courtyard of La Colombe d'Or at 1.00pm that Sunday, followed by the Forbeses and this jaw-dropping stream of some 20 movie stars, and arrayed them around the largest two tables on the premises, laid end to end. Even Francis and Yvonne Roux, the proprietors, who were used to distinguished guests from the film world, because Yves Montand and Simone Signoret lived in the hotel, were impressed. Even more impressed were Evie and I, who both fell head over heels in love with both the Colombe d'Or *and* Saint-Paul de Vence. It is a place of rare enchantment, a little piece of Paradise that has smiled down on the Mediterranean virtually unchanged for close to a thousand years, the sort of thing guaranteed to get the attention of someone born and bred in Wandsworth and Pinner.

Natalie Wood and Richard Gregson had got engaged in California, and sent a signal to forewarn us that they were coming to the South of France, where they would be staying with David Niven, who conveniently lived in St Jean Cap Ferrat, the tip of his wonderful waterfront property just visible across the bay from the Voile d'Or, about 400 or 500 yards away. We met there for lunch the day after Richard and Natalie arrived, and Evie and I, like the rest of the human race, were instantly captivated by the legendary Niven humour and charm. His house, Lo Scoglietto ('The Little Rock'), occupied the most exquisite position on the entire Cap, with its own mini-peninsula, surrounded on three sides by the sea and situated exactly halfway between the ports of Saint-Jean and Beaulieu, looking down the Riviera coast to Italy on the left and along Cap Ferrat itself to the right. His statuesque second wife Hjördis was an archetypal Swedish blonde beauty, one of those extremely rare creatures, a Scandinavian with a sense of humour, so, all in all, the Niven household left little to be desired in the glamour department.

There were six of us at the delicious al fresco lunch in the garden. The atmosphere was a mirror reflection of David's easy, relaxed, informal manner, and the food was lavishly lubricated by ample quantities of fine white Burgundy. In Niven's crystal-clear parlance, a drink was a 'beaker' and a friend was a 'chum'.

We sat there at the table for several magical hours, not yet knowing that we would do so hundreds of times in the years to come, basking in the glow of the unstoppable stream of enchanting and hilarious Niven stories that flowed as endlessly as the wine from this master storyteller. He was Hans Christian Andersen for grown-ups.

He explained the vastness of his swimming pool, which he had commissioned to be 8 feet deep. He went off to make a film, and when he returned he found this vast, gaping crater over 20 feet deep, the contractor having misunderstood his brief and creating a pool eight *metres* deep. The cubic capacity of the resultant lake was so colossal Niven had to fill it with seawater. You could have hidden submarines down there.

Natalie wanted to go to St Tropez. We decided it would be quicker and more fun to go in *Evie* the boat, and thus avoid the midsummer traffic snarls that plague the coast roads between

Sainte Maxime and St Tropez itself. Halfway there, on a blazing day, we decided to stop for a quick swim. The sea was as calm as a bowl of blue soup. Suddenly, Natalie screamed and panicked, thrashing around in the water. Richard and I grabbed her and took her back to the boat. She was terrified. She lay on the back of the boat, sobbing, and said to me, 'I have this terrible dream that I'm going to die in dark water.' We went on to have a wonderful day in St Tropez, but Natalie's deep-rooted fear stayed with me, and I never forgot that ominous moment, so tragically destined to turn a bad dream into a worse reality 13 years later.

John Williams and I had not yet recorded the elusive 'You and I', so a session with Pet Clark was promptly arranged. I had also written yet another ballad for the 'You and I' spot, even though it was no longer needed, probably because, after 18 attempts, like Terry the Rat, I couldn't stop. The song was called 'Tomorrow with Me', and I think I preferred it to 'You and I'.

I persuaded the ever-sanguine John to write arrangements for both songs, and Pet to sing them both, on the understanding that the priority be given to 'You and I' on the single three-hour recording session allotted to us. John pre-recorded the orchestra. Predictably, the 'You and I' arrangement was top-class vintage Williams. The orchestration for 'Tomorrow with Me' was something more, quite simply the most stunning chart for any song I have ever written.

Pet Clark joined us at the stroke of three o'clock. We had until six. She sang 'You and I'. Then she sang it again. And again. And again and again and again. I sat in patient silence. An hour passed. Two. Two-and-a-half. I gradually saw my beloved 'Tomorrow with Me' disappearing without trace as time ran out. At ten minutes to six, Pet finally nailed it 100 per cent, on-the-nose perfection, as in my view were the 27 other takes. At five minutes to six, I begged for just *one* take of 'Tomorrow with Me', which is all we had time for, before we all went home. Pet was tired, having sung 'You and I' until she was blue in the face, but, God love her, she agreed.

Well, let me tell you, that Miss Petula Clark hit the bull's-eye of that song with her first and only shot, like Annie Oakley with a sniper's rifle. Even super-calm maestro John paused to raise an eyebrow. What he and Pet Clark brought to that song that afternoon elevated its status and made it the best song I have ever written. And no one else has ever heard it, save the three of us and Evie.

'You and I' was the song used in the film, and very pretty it was. Lots of lady singers − Shirley Bassey and Liza Minnelli among them − recorded beautiful versions of it. Michael Feinstein made it the title track of one of his best albums. *Goodbye, Mr Chips* was nominated for Best Score in the Oscars, but *not* Best Song, and I've often wondered whether 'Tomorrow with Me' would have made the difference.

It is a particularly lovely day when a major movie project drops out of the sky and lands in your lap. I don't know what the word is to describe the arrival of *two* major movie projects dropping out of the sky on the same day. But that unlikely and ecstatic event did occur in my life about a week later. A young American producer named Robert H Solo, who was living and working in London at the time, asked me to lunch at The White Elephant to discuss an idea he had. I loved The White Elephant so much that I would have gone for the lunch *without* the idea, but the idea, when I heard it, made the food taste even better.

Bob Solo wanted to create a definitive musical film version of Charles Dickens's *A Christmas Carol*, which the great author had dashed off in a matter of days as a means of paying off a bunch of bills owing in 1843. The project would be financed by Cinema Center Films, and open in New York at Radio City Music Hall for Christmas 1970, to mark the centennial of Dickens's death. Bob then became the first person in my life ever to offer me four jobs at once, those of screenwriter, composer, lyricist and executive producer, to which I said, 'Yes... yes... yes and yes!' I was elated at the chance to 'collaborate' for a second time with my favourite English author.

I couldn't wait to tell Richard Gregson the news. I called his LA office. His opening line was, 'I have some good news for you!' And before I could tell him *my* good news about *Scrooge*, he told me that *he* had just received an offer from a film company called Commonwealth United for me to write a projected mammoth American–Russian musical co-production of *The Nutcracker*, to star Natalie Wood and be directed by Gene Kelly, and involve the Kirov and Bolshoi Ballets, the Moscow State Circus and other world-famous Russian performing troupes.

I had to return to California immediately, leaving Adam and Evie in the Chester Square house in London, to try to work out a schedule for this bizarre new double-header. As I flew to LA to meet with the head of Cinema Center Films, Gordon Stuhlberg, Richard flew from LA to London to meet with the young head of Commonwealth United, Ilya Salkind. Natalie, who had stayed on in London, flew back with me and, as I had had no time to organise LA accommodation, at Natalie's suggestion I stayed with her at her pretty house on Bentley Avenue, while she had a series of meetings with director Paul Mazursky, with whom she was about to start a new movie called *Bob and Carol and Ted and Alice*.

I guessed correctly that *A Christmas Carol* would be the more immediate of the two projects, because it had already set its dates, so I reacquainted myself with the delicious little Dickens Christmas novella. Its five-stave structure lent itself perfectly to a musical book structure, and I decided to title my version *Scrooge*, seeing no reason to break the mould of Dickens's recent musical successes bearing one-word, main-character titles – *Oliver!* and *Pickwick*.

The *Scrooge* and *Nutcracker* deals were successfully concluded, and I got started right away on the *Scrooge* screenplay while Gene Kelly flew to Moscow to try and to co-ordinate the availability of all these gigantic, world-touring Russian ballet and circus companies with the complexities of a huge motion picture. It was a massive and unenviable undertaking.

Gene and I talked about it in bizarre circumstances when he got back. Evie had rejoined me by now, and she and Gene and I took Adam and Gene's two young ones, Bridget and Tim, trick-or-treating up and down Rodeo Drive early on the evening of Hallowe'en. With our children dressed respectively as a skeleton, the Devil and the Wicked Witch of the West, we wandered up and down the beautiful tree-lined boulevard, discussing the potential hazards of what we calculated would become the most expensive movie ever made, while our children loaded us down with the candy and Hershey bars they had looted on their door-to-door chocolate scavenge.

Liza Minnelli, who was leaving town, asked us if we would 'spend some time with Mama' while she was away. This was not a great time in her mother's life, and we promised we would. We had met Judy Garland a few times in London, but she was always surrounded by hangers-on and sycophants. I called Judy and asked whether she would like to join Evie and myself at the Coconut Grove for Tony Bennett's opening night. She said she would love to. She arrived at our house more on time than I had been led to believe, and she had clearly taken on board a few fortifying beverages beforehand. She consolidated the fortifications considerably at our bar, but she was in an effervescent mood and hilariously funny. More drinks followed at our ringside table at the Grove, and I noticed that Judy barely touched her food.

Our table was set against the stage, so Judy had the stage on one side, me on the other, and Evie opposite us. Tony Bennett came on stage to great acclaim and proceeded to give his usual flawless performance, in which I was happy to hear he included both 'Who Can I Turn To?' and 'If I Ruled the World', our two hits together. The audience loved him. I checked to see whether Judy did, too. She was fast asleep, her head against the side of the stage. She was gone for the night.

Tony closed his act, as always, with 'I Left My Heart in San Francisco'. A few bars into the song, he came to the front of the stage, leaned forward and placed his microphone in front of Judy's face, unaware of the unflattering circumstances. I panicked at the thought of the impending embarrassment, gave Judy a mighty nudge that nearly knocked her off her chair and, trying to sound as much like a discreet wake-up call as I could, yelled in her ear, 'Judy, sing with Tony!' She awoke with a start. Tony was up to the bit where *'little cable-cars climb halfway to the stars...'* and it was clear that darling Judy was somewhere over the rainbow and halfway to another bunch of stars in a completely different galaxy. She gradually focused, smiled up at Tony, still groggy and finally took the proffered mike. They duetted for about four bars, as Tony let go the mike like a relay runner passing the baton. I held my breath, then watched in wonder at what happened next. I helped Judy stand on her chair, then step up on to the table. By now, she had a firm hold on both the microphone and the song. The little sleeping giant was now wide awake, realised who and where she was, and became Judy Garland at her breathtaking best, singing the rest of that song better than it has ever been sung before or since, during which brief time she went from a deep sleep to an even deeper emotional show-stopping performance that tore the roof off the Coconut Grove. Her reading of the line *'When I come home to you, San Francisco...'* was so moving that people were applauding and shouting, 'Go, Judy!' The final line *'Your golden sun will shine on me!'* tore out every heart in the place so completely that the capacity audience rose to its feet as one with the kind of mighty cheer that you only ever hear when the nation's favourite running-back scores the winning touchdown in the Superbowl in the last minute of the game, or when the World Heavyweight Champion retains his title with a knockout, as Miss Judy most certainly did that memorable night.

Evie was in London visiting her mother. Nancy Sinatra invited me to take Adam down to Palm Springs for a four-day weekend to houseguest at her dad's extraordinary desert compound, and to watch the World Series baseball, on which he planned to place some fancy bets. Nancy came with us. Adam received his four-year-old best-behaviour speech with wide-eyed attentiveness and three or four well-timed 'Yes, Daddys', which made me think that everything was going to be all right. When we arrived and he was introduced to Frank, Adam pronounced 'Franksinatra' as though it were one word, and persisted in this throughout our stay. I wondered whether I had misled Adam to believe that Franksinatra was a place rather than a person. 'We're going to Frank Sinatra for the weekend,' I had said.

Adam also met Jilly Rizzo, Frank's nearest and dearest old friend, who was down there and, together, Frank and Jilly spent the first hour attempting to corrupt Adam's impeccable four-year-old British accent into broad Brooklynese, by teaching him choice phrases like 'I'm wit youse, baby' and 'Who are dese bums?' all of which received Adam's enthusiastic co-operation and lasting admiration.

There was an atmosphere of rare tension in the usually relaxed household that weekend, due to the fact that the World Series was on television quite early each morning, by Sinatra standards, and had developed into a protracted cliff-hanger. Despite the lateness of the nights before – movies in the Great Hall until either the last of us fell asleep or Frank threatened to show *Lady in Cement* to clear the room – Frank, Jilly and I would religiously assemble in the Chinese Room each morning in time for NBC's TV coverage of the new game. We would stare blankly and unspeaking at the screen until either hot coffee or an exceptional play sparked us into life.

Frank's fancy bets were at the root of the tension. He had bet heavily on the first game for his favoured team. They lost. He had doubled his bet. They lost again. He doubled again. They lost three in a row. To give himself a chance of coming out even, he now had an astronomical short-odds bet on the other team, three up in the best-of-seven. No wonder he was so well loved by Nick the Greek, Las Vegas's premier odds-maker. The other team promptly lost games four, five and six, Frank was demented, and here we are for game seven on the edge of our seats, knee-deep in coffee and praying Frank hasn't gambled away the plantation.

Adam had been up for hours and had breakfasted and explored the estate with another newfound friend, Frank's young black houseman, Joel, who for Adam was the real king of the place, because it was Joel who fed Adam and played all sorts of games with him, and, when you're four years old, that's all that matters! So he had three super new friends, plus Nancy, whom he already knew and adored.

Anyway, in the middle of that crucial seventh game, Adam wandered into the room and stood right in front of the television set on the play that Frank thought might send him into bankruptcy. Frowning, Adam asked, 'Where's Franksinatra?'

Frank responded, 'Hey, Adam, you bum. I'm *here*!'

Adam shook his head. 'No, not you,' he said. 'The black one.'

Frank's original team won the seventh and final game and the World Series by four games to three. Since Frank had doubled and redoubled his original bet on games one, two and three, he came out of the whole nerve-racking mess comparatively unscathed since, more by good luck than good judgement, that team eventually won. Just how astronomical his about-face, back-up bet on the *other* team had been I never found out precisely, but it certainly confirmed why the Las Vegas odds-maker Nick the Greek was famous for his smile.

The Hollywood marriage-go-round continued to spin. David Hemmings and Gayle Hunnicutt, probably the prettiest couple in all of California, got married in the beautiful Beverly Hills garden of Jack Hansen, owner of The Daisy discotheque, with Adam Bricusse, as their ring boy, making one of his rare personal appearances. David and Gayle invited us to go with them on their honeymoon to Peru, but we counter-proposed Acapulco, and they gamely joined us there. A two-week, non-stop party featuring armies of your friends in a heavenly setting is not a bad kick-off for any marriage, and certainly one you are unlikely to forget.

Evie and I had been invited to the Acapulco Film Festival, a classic Mexican excuse for the glorious two-week party. We flew down with a bunch of friends from Twentieth Century Fox, Mia Farrow, Roman Polanski, Sharon Tate, Raquel Welch, Jim Brown, James Coburn and Tony Randall among them. I took the screenplay of *Scrooge* with me, a foolhardy move. Trying to write a screenplay during a two-week Mexican party is not unlike trying to swim up the Niagara Falls, as I was about to learn, since the only slight lull in the average day of non-stop celebrating seemed to occur somewhere between 9.00 and 11.00am. Such was the sybaritic scenario for the Hemmings honeymoon.

On the last evening of the festival, we attended an all-night farewell party and, as the first crimson rays of the dawn light peeped over the Acapulco Bay, I drove Mia home down the hill to Casa Sinatra. On the way, she said, 'Brickman, it's going to be such a swell sunrise.' She actually said 'swell'. 'Let's go somewhere where we can watch it.'

I saw a big empty driveway and drove in. We walked into the newly completed and deserted house, out on to the gorgeous pool terrace, with its staggering view across Acapulco Bay, and watched the best sunrise in the history of the world, which is what happens every morning in Acapulco. Six hours later, I bought the house, and named it 'Casa Adan y Eva' – The Adam and Eve House. Adam and Evie and I still have it.

We spent Christmas in LA, and Mia invited us to a small but magical Christmas Eve dinner party at the house of Roger Edens, the doyen of MGM musical directors. Also there were Mia's great pal Lenny Gershe, and Kay Thompson, who was Judy Garland's vocal coach, Liza Minnelli's godmother, a musical powerhouse in her own right and the authoress of the classic *Elöise at the Plaza* books. Kay was an eccentric in the Edith Sitwell mould, with a crackling wit and an evil sense of humour. Wondrous inside stories of the MGM musical era abounded throughout the evening, and I was like a cat lying in a vat of cream listening to them. Roger, an enchanting host, took me aside and paid me a compliment to rank alongside Fred Astaire's fan letter. He said that, when he first heard my song 'Where Are the Words?' from *Doctor Dolittle*, he thought Cole Porter had written it, to which I could only reply, 'He probably did.'

I noticed a huge, fat leather-bound volume lying on Roger's grand piano. Embossed in gold on the cover were the words *The Songs of Irving Berlin*. I opened it. Inside, bound together, were individual song copies of all the innumerable Berlin standards that that phenomenal songwriter had spread across most of the 20th century. The book was handsomely inscribed to Roger by Berlin. I realised that this most prolific of all songwriters was the only one of the top echelon who had never released a *Best of...* songbook.

First thing the next morning, I wrote Mr Berlin a letter asking whether, if I were to gather together his most famous songs, bind them and mail the resultant tome to him in New York, he would grace the book with his signature.

A month later, a great big box arrived at my office. I opened it, and there smiling up at me with the gleaming golden words *The Songs of Irving Berlin*, was the twin to the leather-bound volume on Roger Eden's piano. Together with a generous inscription on the first page was a covering letter from Mr Berlin explaining that he had had a limited number of these books – 25, I was told later – made up to give to his close friends in the music business, to mark his recent 80th birthday. Sadly, one friend was no longer around to accept it, but he believed that I would give it a good home, so... *voilà*! I was overwhelmed by this wonderful gesture from a notoriously generous man, the songwriter's equivalent of a gift from God.

The David Hemmings, the Steve McQueens and the George Hamiltons, as beautiful and entertaining a sextet of friends as anyone has a right to ask for, were our first houseguests at the Adam and Eve house in Acapulco, a pretty glamorous houseful. Before they arrived, we needed a few days to get the six-bedroom casa functioning, and received extravagant help in this endeavour in the delectable shape of Merle Oberon, an Indian-born

British film star who had a superb villa 300 or 400 yards away, with an exotic swimming pool with full-sized palm trees growing out of it.

Merle, once married to the mighty film tycoon Sir Alexander Korda, was presently married to a seriously wealthy Mexican businessman, Bruno Pagliai. She became our immediate best friend when I told her at our first meeting that we had David Niven in common. Merle and Niv had co-starred together in *Wuthering Heights* with Laurence Olivier for Alex Korda in 1938–39. Merle was Cathy to Olivier's memorably handsome and moody Heathcliffe.

Niv and Merle had enjoyed a major romance during and after filming, and planned to elope together. They made off across country from California as soon as shooting was completed. An indication of how young Merle was at the time, as Niv told it, was that the studio were desperately trying to find the pair of them before the police arrested and prosecuted him under the Mann Act for transporting a minor across a State line, hardly calculated to blend in with the film company's massive promotion of Cathy's timeless romance with Heathcliffe. Even allowing for raconteur's licence, I was suspicious about certain aspects of Niv's runaway romanticism in this tall tale, so I checked the facts and found that Merle the Pearl was born in 1911, which made her just one year younger than Niv and therefore around 27 or 28 at the time. But a nice try, Niv.

None of this detracted from Merle's enduring beauty and kindness 30 years later in Las Brisas. She delegated her highly efficient secretary Elisabeth to us for a month to co-ordinate everything that needed doing, with the result that the house was up and running in record time.

The Hemmings, the Hamiltons and the McQueens, as I say, were the best of all possible houseguests. Evie, Gayle, Alana and Neile were all gorgeous and compatible. Each of the men, however, had a personal agenda. George Hamilton was determined to have the deepest suntan of any man in Mexico, not too difficult to achieve, since he had already arrived with it. But there he was, sharp at 9.00am each morning, stretched out by the pool with a lifetime supply of coconut oils and sun reflectors, roasting himself until he was as deep fried as anything served by McDonald's. David Hemmings was researching with equal intensity and dedication the possibility of setting a new Mexican and world record for the number of margaritas consumed by a Caucasian male before noon, while Steve McQueen's equally admirable quest was to find the fastest and most powerful motorbike west of Mexico City on which he would have the best possible chance of ending his life before he was 40.

I, head and shoulders the most boring one in the group, was having as good a time as any of them and maybe better, sitting on the terrace all day, supremely content, writing the score of *Scrooge*, working on a project that I loved in a house that I loved full of people that I loved. Golden days with golden people, especially George, who, by the third evening, had acquired a mega-tan that made him look not unlike Al Jolson in *The Jazz Singer*.

Steve's motorbike looked ready for a remake of *The Great Escape*, but the greatest escapade he could dream up in that peaceful paradise was to indulge his passion for his favourite dessert, Cherries Jubilee. He had found a downtown restaurant that served them and, towards the end of dinner at the house, he would volunteer to provide Cherries Jubilee as dessert, leap on to his bike and zoom off up the perilously winding hill of Las Brisas, the challenge being to get the Cherries Jubilee back to the house before the ice cream melted. We would hear the approaching roar of his return, and he would arrive back at the house holding the big platter on the flat of his right hand, like a waiter, steering the bike with his left down the tortuous roads, just to make it more difficult, and grinning like a demented Cheshire Cat. Needless to say, the ice cream was always intact.

Our restaurant-owning friend Carlos Mendoza would provide sunset suppers for us on the beautiful beach south of Acapulco Bay, where the Acapulco Princess Hotel now stands. He would bring a couple of large trestle tables, chairs and a couple of waiters, then cook the most succulent sea bass, shrimp and calamari while we had a sunset swim. One particularly glorious evening, Steve and I unthinkingly swam out further than usual, admiring one of those beyond-belief Acapulco sunsets of such unimaginable glory and ridiculous colouring that only a really bad artist with a particularly gaudy palette would have had a hope in Hell of capturing it. We turned to swim back in, and found ourselves caught in a powerful undertow. The harder we swam, the further from shore we found ourselves. For what seemed an eternity, but was in fact a quarter-of-an-hour, we struggled to get back to the beach, which we finally did by swimming parallel to it until we found a calmer spot where the undertow felt less vicious. I was terrified, and it was comforting to know that the screen's great fearless hero McQueen was, too! A month later, a Beverly Hills dentist, standing waist-deep in the water in the same spot, enjoying a margarita, was killed by a shark.

George Hamilton was and is extremely handsome. Not only that, he could easily have rivalled Tony Curtis as the best-dressed man on earth. Only the fact that he was also one of the funniest made it tolerable to be around him. He had outfits for every occasion, by which I mean *every* occasion, as he amply demonstrated on the evening I heard Alana suddenly scream, 'Snake!' Alana's Nacogdoches accent naturally elongated the word to 'Snay-a-ake!' which was even more effective.

I dashed in the direction of her voice, grabbing en route the only snake-fighting weapon that came to hand, which happened to be my totally inadequate badminton racket, and arrived at the terrace of their pool-level bedroom, where Alana, rooted to the spot in horror, continued to scream 'Snay-a-ake!' at the top of her surprisingly substantial lungs. Inside the bedroom, I could hear George, her would-be rescuer, getting dressed to be suitably heroically attired for the moment. I heard his voice from inside their room calling out, 'Alana, where are those brown riding boots I like to wear with my khaki safari suit? And that matching safari hat that you like? The one with the eagle feather?' All this while his damsel in distress cowered in terror against the outside wall screaming, but finding the time to reply, 'Fuck your eagle feather, George! Come an' kill this fuckin' snay-a-ake!'

Her screams were fully justified when I saw on the wall about 3 feet from her head a lethal-looking coral snake, its red head weaving as though preparing to strike. He was probably more terrified of Alana's screams than she was of him. As the snake was on my left, my only available shot with the badminton racket was an upward-angled left-handed backhand, not a textbook shot, I admit, but one which I must say I executed perfectly, decapitating the coral snake and smashing my racket to smithereens against the stone wall in the process. A moment later, George came out on to the terrace, spiffily attired, every detail perfect, eagle feather at an appropriately jaunty angle, looking like Al Jolson imitating Stewart Granger in *King Solomon's Mines* and saying gallantly, 'Right. Ready. I think this outfit kinda works, don't you, Alana?' as his beloved and beautiful wife fell limply into his arms.

George Hamilton was also a frustrated singer, and his next-door neighbour in Palm Springs, Colonel Tom Parker, who was Elvis Presley's manager, was always encouraging him to do something about it. Things came to a head one morning when George called me in a panic and said, 'Brickman, I need your help. I have a crisis. Tom Parker has got me booked for a week in the Big Room at the Las Vegas Hilton for a ton of money!'

I asked him when.

'In three weeks' time,' was his strangled reply.

'Doing what?' I asked.

'I haven't the faintest idea. Why do you think I'm calling you?'

I told him to calm down, and we met an hour later to start to figure out a game plan.

My first call was to Sammy Davis. I told him George needed immediate help, *now*.

'Come on over,' said Sam instantly.

'To your house?' I said, Sam's house being 200 yards from George's.
'I'm in Chicago,' said Sam.

'We'll be there,' I said, and hung up. I suddenly saw this thing taking over all our lives. Our next call was to Hugh Hefner, to see if he would put us up at the Playboy Mansion in Chicago. Hef said, 'I'm flying in this afternoon in the Big Bunny,' as he referred to his all-black DC9 with a white bunny on the tail. 'Come with me.'

Thus it was that, less than eight hours after I received George's panic phone call, we were Hef's guests both on the Big Bunny and at the Chicago mansion, George in the Red Room and myself in the Blue Room. Sammy joined us right after his show, and we all had supper together.

By the end of the evening, Sammy had cast himself not only as George's saviour, but also his director, choreographer, production co-ordinator and first-night introducer.

A month later, George called me in London.

'How did it go?' I asked.

'Sammy was fabulous to me!' he raved. 'What a pal! But on the opening night, if you had been the audience, how would you have felt if the greatest nightclub performer in the history of the world, Sammy Davis Jr, suddenly walked out on to the stage unannounced. He lifted the roof off the place. Now the audience is anticipating this great extra bonus, an unscheduled appearance by Sammy Davis Jr. They know that Sammy has never set foot on a stage in his life without performing, right? Until that night. And what does he do? Not only does he *not* perform, he introduces as the star of the evening someone else who has never done a nightclub act in his life! Right away, I knew the audience wanted to kill me. They wanted Sammy to stay and me to go, or their money back! I could sense it. When I heard the groan as he left the stage, I felt I was looking into my grave. It took ten years off my life and about fifteen off my career! But Sammy was right. If he'd done one single song, even the first four bars of "Birth of the Blues", and then left me there, they would have probably killed me on the spot. The only mistake he made was doing me the favour of introducing me!

'The first night was OK. I got away with it, the house was pretty full and the audience was kind to me. The second night, there were about half as many people. The third night, I noticed these huge drapes at the back of the room had moved in about halfway towards me, to make what was now a much smaller room seem fuller. Each night the drapes got closer, until by Saturday night I was in this small room full of drapes playing to two tables of four!'

It is perhaps superfluous to report that the otherwise multi-talented George swiftly abandoned his career as a nightclub performer. Nor was I aware of any subsequent 5.00pm Sunday dinners with Colonel Tom Parker.

Bob Solo, the producer of *Scrooge*, had shrewdly signed the celebrated Ronald Neame to direct the picture. Bob, Ronnie and I were in total accord that the perfect choice to play the title role was my old friend Richard Harris. Richard thought so, too, and the deal was duly struck. Further, thanks to Ronnie Neame's vast experience and unparalleled relationships within the industry, we swiftly cast Sir Alec Guinness, Dame Edith Evans and Kenneth More as the various ghosts of Christmas, giving us a highly distinguished cast.

The opposite was true of the problem-plagued *Nutcracker* project. Gene Kelly didn't have an overabundance of hair to tear out, as I learned to my public embarrassment one Sunday evening at Matteo's Restaurant in Westwood, when we greeted one another with a warm hug and my right hand caught the back of his hair, causing the front half of his toupée to stand on end like the lid of a convertible. But he was certainly ready to tear out what there was. The budget of the as yet non-existent project continued to mount in multi-million-dollar leaps and bounds, and it quickly became clear that this absurd and overblown concept would collapse under the mountainous weight of its own pretension. And that is precisely what happened, mercifully sooner rather than later. But, before it did, I suggested to the bemused young producer, Ilya Salkind, that lurking in the midst of this mega-budget mess was a low-budget version of the same *Nutcracker* idea, a simple original story built around Tchaikovsky's magical music, and I would happily write a screenplay and ten or twelve lyrics to prove the point. Since I was on a pay-or-play deal, Ilya accepted my offer with alacrity and, during the following months, I did indeed write both a screenplay and a ten-song score, based on the best-known themes from *The Nutcracker Suite*. The film, entitled *The Great Music Chase*, could have been made for under $5 million. Unfortunately, while I was writing it, Commonwealth United Films disappeared off the radar screen, and to the best of my knowledge were never heard of again.

Alan Jay Lerner selected and edited the contents of a major hardcover songbook entitled *Broadway's 100 Greatest Ballads*. Newley and I, flatteringly, were doubly represented in the tome by 'What Kind of Fool Am I?' and 'Who Can I Turn To?'. Alan sent me an advance copy of the book, inscribed: 'Dear Leslie – To Whom Can I Turn? Love – Alan.'

I wrote him a thank-you note, which read: 'Dear Alan – By rights you should be taken out and hanged, For the cold-blooded murder of the English tanged! Love – Leslie.'

Most of our California friends seemed to be working in London when we returned there. Dick Donner was about to direct a comedy called *Salt and Pepper*, starring Sammy Davis and Peter Lawford. He asked me to write a title song for it, which I duly did. Roman Polanski was there, discussing a new project, and his wife Sharon was extremely pregnant. Apjac called from LA to say he needed me there for PR stuff prior to the opening of *Goodbye, Mr Chips*, so I travelled back a few days before Evie and Adam.

Sharon Tate was on the plane with me, and the house she and Roman were renting, at 10050, Cielo Drive, looked across the hill on Benedict Canyon at our house. I knew that house well. It was the same one Samantha Eggar and her husband Tom Stern had rented during the filming of *Dolittle*. As she was alone, I invited the eight-and-a-half-month pregnant Sharon to toddle down the hill for lunch any day she felt like it. On Wednesday morning she called, and arrived for lunch, looking absolutely radiant, with her close friend, Abigail Folger, the young coffee heiress. We spent a giggly couple of hours together, and arranged to reassemble as soon as Evie returned a day or two hence.

Evie, in fact, returned the following day, and we fulfilled a longstanding promise to fly up to Las Vegas for the opening night of Tony Newley's first-ever Nevada nightclub engagement at Caesar's Palace the day after that. We were at a ringside table with a dozen of Newley's close chums. I noticed that two of the seats were empty. The missing persons were Tony's hairdresser, Jay Sebring, and Connie Kreski, the girl who had played Mercy Humppe in Newley's *Heironymus Merkin* movie. The evening was a great success.

The Charles Manson murders, which happened while we were watching Newley that night, were all over the newspapers and TV news when we awakened next morning. Sharon Tate was dead, horribly so. Abigail Folger was dead. Jay Sebring was dead. Connie Kreski, who had been at the house with them, was alive for the slender reason that Sharon had found a stray kitten on the hill by the house and given it to Connie, who had taken it home an hour or so before the killers arrived. Like all of America, we were in total shock. This was three days after my lunch with Sharon and Abigail.

Roman returned to Los Angeles, to the hideous glare of macabre publicity that attended the whole horrible affair. We saw him by chance the following Sunday at singer Mike Sarne's beach house at Malibu. Evie and I happened to be at the adjoining house with Roddy MacDowall and Sybil Burton. Roman was with Tommy Thompson, a celebrated *Life* magazine photographer, and clearly devastated, his face blank and expressionless. But I have never quite understood why he allowed himself to be photographed at the death scene. The cover of *Life* that week showed him sitting on the front doorstep of the El Cielo house, with the word 'PIG' scrawled across the door in Sharon's blood. I still shudder to think about that senseless destruction of life and beauty.

It was a major tribute to Peter O'Toole's charismatic talent that, following Robert Donat in his Oscar-winning role 30 years before, in a musical film in which he was not ideally cast, he was nominated for Best Actor in *Goodbye, Mr Chips*. John Williams and I were also nominated for Best Score. We lost to *Hello, Dolly*.

We attended all the obligatory major premières, Apjac again achieving the major coup of a royal première in London, attended by the Queen. The only other notable aspect of the premières was that, at the Gala party on Hollywood Boulevard after the LA opening, I was extremely taken with the music provided by the young group on stage. Unusually, the drummer was a girl, and she sang like an angel. I went over and introduced myself. She was 19, and her name was Karen Carpenter. Her brother John was playing the piano. It was The Carpenters' first-ever professional gig.

It is one of the many perversities of Hollywood that, having proved beyond all reasonable doubt that he should never go within 50 miles of a musical, Peter O'Toole was immediately asked to segue to the huge singing title role of Don Quixote in *Man of La Mancha*. If you're going to make a musical, the general idea is that the first consideration should be to make the music sound good, which requires singer–singers. *La Mancha*, a perennially great and durable stage show, predictably became yet another waste-of-time musical film.

Scrooge was all set to start shooting at Shepperton Studios. At least in Richard Harris we had not only a fine actor, but a performer who could creditably find his way through a song. So all was well... we thought. Then suddenly, six weeks before shooting, disaster struck, quite unexpectedly, as disaster tends to do. The film Richard was completing in Israel fell heavily behind schedule. He couldn't leave, and we couldn't wait for him, because of our Christmas opening commitment less than a year hence. We had to recast, and fast!

I had some say in the matter, as, in addition to being the film's screenwriter, composer and lyricist, I was also the executive producer. I suggested Rex Harrison. Everyone was ecstatic at the thought. The fact that I had survived three years on *Dolittle*, a month-long Mediterranean cruise and several seasons in Portofino in Rex's company encouraged the general feeling that we might survive this encounter, too. Rex was happy to renew our working relationship, especially as he was still hoping we might get the Sherlock Holmes project off the ground, as was I. Even though he was '*un peu agé*' for the role, Rex would have made a magnificent Sherlock Holmes. The only I-won't-say problem, let's call it a dauntingly omnipresent fact would have been my awareness of the basic similarities between Sherlock Holmes and Doctor Watson, on the one hand, and Henry Higgins and Colonel Pickering, on the other. They were the same two people, the brilliant, sharp-minded misogynist and his retired Indian Army sidekick. Having played Higgins to Tony- and Oscar-winning perfection, could Rex ever have played Holmes without the ghost of Higgins coming back to haunt him? Of which more later. Back to *Scrooge*.

At the time, Rex was appearing in an eccentric play called *The Lionel Touch* at the Lyric Theatre in Shaftesbury Avenue, playing, of all unlikely things, an ageing hippie. He liked the script of *Scrooge* and, over the next two or three weeks, we had a fine time developing ideas together in his suite at the Connaught in the meticulous, nit-picking way that Rex had raised to an art form, and from which, by now, I derived a certain masochistic pleasure. And, once again, I had my trusty musical shield, Ian Fraser, whom Ronnie Neame happily accepted as musical director and Rex now grudgingly respected, to help me ward off any foul blows that Rex might and occasionally did throw.

With every passing day, it became clearer that Rex was going to be fabulous in the role of Scrooge. He was about to marry Richard Harris's ex-wife, Elizabeth, a bizarre coincidence that irrationally bolstered my own confidence that in switching from Richard to Rex, as Elizabeth had, I was going to solve *my* problems, too! We were both wrong, alas!

For disaster was on a roll and, just two weeks before principal photography was due to start, it decided to strike again! Rex suddenly became sick, from overwork and bronchitis combined. The doctors opined he was close to pneumonia, with the result that he had to withdraw not only from the play, but from the film, too. Now our backs were really to the wall. It was just days before the Christmas holidays. Cinema Center Films were firm. They gave us three actors to choose from, and *three days* to get one of them to commit – Peter O'Toole, Richard Burton or Albert Finney.

The chances of any of them being available were slim to none. You know my views on O'Toole the singer. God knows, Peter would have been a wonderful Scrooge, but *not* in a musical. And, if there was one Welshman on earth who couldn't sing, I'll bet it would have been Richard Burton. And in those halcyon Taylor–Burton days, with Richard as Scrooge, we might well have ended up with Elizabeth as the ghost of Mrs Marley!

My gut instinct was for Albert Finney. By a happy chance, he was in London. I already knew him, since we had first ventured on to Broadway at the same time in the 1962–63 season, when he played John Osborne's *Luther* while Newley and I were doing *Stop the World*. We had spent good times together.

It is hardly flattering to any actor to learn that he is not the first, nor indeed the second choice for a role, but a practical actor – and God knows Mr Finney is that – understands the fickle unpredictability of the lunatic lottery called the film industry. *Getting* the right role is what matters, not *how* you get it!

Albert was about to marry, *not*, I was relieved to learn, Elizabeth Harris, but the exquisite Anouk Aimée. When I accepted a Best Actor Golden Globe Award for Albie just over a year later, I would make my first and only French pun. 'A French actress has to be very much in love to change her name from Aimée to Finney.'

I called Albert and explained the project, the situation and the urgency. He invited me for dinner the same evening. Anouk cooked a meal as delectable as herself, and the three of us sat and ate and talked way past midnight in the kitchen of their flat in Westminster, until I had run out of killer persuasive chit-chat. I left Albie with the script and score of *Scrooge*, and went home to pray.

Happily, God, Albert, Charles Dickens and the Department of Fate were all listening! Less than 24 hours later, Albie was having his first costume fitting. Disaster went away with its tail between its legs, never to return. We opened at Radio City Music Hall on schedule the following November, broke all their box-office records, and Albert was nothing less than sensational. The film still plays on television every Christmas and, whenever I see it, I remember what I now call 'The Three Scrooges' – Richard, Rex and Albie – my very own ghosts of Christmas Past!

I predicted to Evie when we arrived in California in 1965 that we would be lucky if the Hollywood craze for making musicals out of just about everything were to last another five years. Well, it did, but barely. It was becoming increasingly clear that film musicals were at their last gasp. The dinosaur was dying, to be replaced in the world's affections by low-budget, money-making phenomena like *Easy Rider*, which was already revving up in the wings, ready to drive on and take over the cinema screens and box offices of America.

It would soon be time to start thinking about the Tarzan-like pendulum swing back into the theatre, from one jungle to the other. Tony Newley and I met to consider the pros and cons of this move back to the future. I was more ready, perhaps, than he was at the time, to embrace the less luxurious but equally alluring hazards of putting together a stage show where, unlike a movie, you can continue to replace and improve the bits that don't work, and where the writer's opinions are the last things to be discarded, rather than the first. That said, my own experiences in Hollywood belied that perennial cliché. My producers and directors were always scrupulously fair to me in all creative areas, making me perhaps an exception that proved the rule.

Newley was at something of a crossroads in his career at this time. His recording career was past its peak, he had no plans, alas, to return to Broadway, his film career was in limbo after *Heironymus Merkin*, his marriage to Joannie was over, and his new management team of Raymond Katz and Sandy Gallin were encouraging him to devote all of his time to the lucrative Nevada nightclub circuit. That's where the big bucks are, they rightly said, and that's where you should be, too. While this was not wrong financially, and Newberg was a brilliant nightclub performer, it was not in my view the right move for him artistically. There was no question that he had been at the peak of his creative powers when he was on Broadway. There he was unique, with all his wondrous talent on full and vibrant display. In Las Vegas, he was a great performer, but so were Sinatra and Sammy and Dean Martin and Tom Jones and Lena Horne and half-a-dozen other people.

The question of what to do was put on hold by a phone call from producer David Wolper. He wanted to know whether Newberg and I would like to write the song score for his upcoming film production of Roald Dahl's children's classic *Charlie and the Chocolate Factory*, to be retitled, for no reason that anyone cared to explain, *Willy Wonka and the Chocolate Factory*. We met at David's house in Holmby Hills the following morning. Newberg and I said 'Yes' before he had even finished describing the project and, within a week, we went to work.

It was the first time Tony and I had written together for five years. It could as well have been five minutes. We fell, as always, instantly into the smooth and natural work rhythm with which our collaboration had always been blessed, and the songs appeared obligingly on the page within a matter of days, with one slight variation to our usual routine. I was now in France and Tony was in California. We fairly zoomed through the score, which was just as well, as the film was due to start shooting at the Bavarian Studios in Munich. Gene Wilder had already been chosen for the title role, which he was to play with his usual eccentric brand of humour, charm and lunacy. I wondered why David had chosen a 34-year-old actor to play an old man retiring from the candy business, but, as it didn't seem to worry anyone else, I let it go. The die and Mr Wilder were both cast.

It never worried me again until one evening a couple of years later, when Fred Astaire was at our house in Beverly Hills for dinner. Late in the evening we played pool, which he did about as well as he danced. Between games, he suddenly turned to me and said in that famous, shy, modest voice of his, 'Leslie, I've been wanting to ask you this for years, but I didn't like to mention it. Why do you suppose it is they didn't want me to play Willy Wonka?'

I did not believe what I had just heard. Here was the greatest song-and-dance man in the history of the world telling me that he had actually *asked* to play the role of Willy Wonka, and they had turned him down! He was the right age. He *looked* like he should be Willy Wonka! And my heart stopped when I thought of what he would have done with the musical numbers, which for the most part were cumbersomely staged in the film, containing none of the magic that was generated when Astaire was on the set.

But *Willy Wonka* ended up being kind to us all. Newley and I were nominated for a Best Original Score Oscar, 'The Candy Man' was a humungous, multi-million-selling number-one hit single for Sammy Davis Jr, the biggest of his career, and the frequently re-released, re-digitalised and repackaged *Willy Wonka* video became the perennial biggest-selling family film in the Warner Brothers vast catalogue. The film itself was re-released in 1996, and on it still goes. I'll always be grateful for it, except for two things. The score would have been better if we had been allowed to write the ten songs we wanted instead of the six to which they limited us, and the thought of that miraculous might-have-been, the golden opportunity to work with my magical genius neighbour up the street in Beverly Hills, the one, the only, the incomparable Fred Astaire!

Scrooge and *Willy Wonka* were shooting simultaneously, one in England, the other in Germany. I went down to Shepperton several times, where Ronnie Neame had everything immaculately on schedule, with Albie Finney, at 32 even younger than Gene Wilder as Wonka, giving a dazzling display as Scrooge in his late sixties, inventively acting the songs better than anyone since Rex Harrison. I also went across to the Bavarian Studios in Munich. Once again, non-singing actors infuriatingly inhabited and inhibited this production. 'The Candy Man' was irrevocably destroyed by the tuneless thespian who was allowed by the equally tuneless director to 'sing' it. Newley offered to redo the scene and the song gratis, replacing the hapless actor who had done the damage. The generous offer was refused, which made Sammy Davis's eventual massive hit record an even greater and more unlikely miracle.

I left the *Willy Wonka* sound stage in Munich and wandered across to the one adjoining it. Night and day, chalk and cheese. What did I find there? I found Bob Fosse directing Liza Minnelli and Joel Grey in the song 'Money, Money' from *Cabaret*, from which a year later all three of them would emerge with an Academy Award apiece. There they were, these two movies, side by side, an object lesson of how-to and how-not-to make a Hollywood picture. That both films, in their vastly different ways, would prove to be successful is a phenomenon on which I think it would be wiser not to comment further.

Newberg and Joannie divorced and sold the house at 1151, Summit Drive, just as Tony Curtis and Janet Leigh had sold it to them when *they* divorced. Its ill fate had earned the house the nickname of Heartbreak Hotel. And who would buy it? Sammy and Altovise Davis. Major expensive interior reconstruction and enlargement took place, providing a living room the size of Radio City Music Hall and a dressing room for Sammy's countless thousands of suits and stage outfits large enough to stable 40 horses. Joannie Collins moved back to London and, before we could blink, was engaged to a dashing young London-based American music executive named Ron Kass. Newberg bought himself a very handsome Normandy-style stone farmhouse off Coldwater Canyon, and life went on more or less as before. He and I agreed that we would definitely write a new musical, starting directly after New Year. I was delighted at the prospect that this might lure Newberg back to the Broadway stage, where he belonged, although I knew his new managers were not as enthralled as I was by the idea.

We had lunch with André Previn and Mia Farrow in the Edwardian Room of the Plaza Hotel in New York. They were now married and ecstatically happy. They arrived breathless with the news that they had just come from the doctor's office and Mia was pregnant with twins. Sacha and Matthew would be born a few months later. They, too, were going to England to live, as André had been offered the great musical prize of the London Symphony Orchestra. George Hamilton and Alana Collins also got married. Tony Newley seemed more than content to be a bachelor again. All in all, a major game of Change Partners was in progress, and there was little the rest of us could do except, like spectators at Wimbledon, watch.

Evie and I escaped down to Acapulco for some winter sunshine. More newlyweds came to join us at the house in the form of the brothers Gibb. Our adorable little Scottish chum from London, the pop singer Lulu, had recently married Maurice Gibb, and we invited them to spend part of their belated honeymoon with us in Mexico. They were there in a flash, and since big brother Barry Gibb had also just got married, he and his young bride also rendezvoused with us there. It was at the time of one of the Bee Gees' first big successes with their album *Odessa*. I can assure you that there are few things more romantic in this life than to sit on a terrace overlooking the moon–splashed Bay of Acapulco, after a delicious Mexican dinner, listening to an improvised Bee Gees concert.

Scrooge duly opened at Radio City Music Hall in New York, and across the country and the world. Princess Margaret attended our London première at the Dominion Theatre. The film was critically well received, and became a perennial '*succès d'estime*', which Alan Jay memorably defined as 'a success that runs out of steam'. I got two Oscar nominations, for Best Score and Best Song ('Thank You Very Much'), so Evie and I decided that this would probably be as good a moment as any to attend our first Academy Awards show. Having won in my absence three years before, I was totally anticipating that I would lose if I showed up. I was right. Twice. 'Thank You Very Much' was heroically performed in the show in four languages by Ricardo Montalban (Spanish), Petula Clark (French), Burt Lancaster (Italian) and Sally Kellerman (English), but lost to 'Shaft', which was 'spoken not sung', like a James Bond musical martini, in one. And I was surprisingly content to lose Best Score to the Beatles' *Let It Be*. Their first and only Oscar was long overdue, the hit-laden song scores of both *A Hard Day's Night* and *Help!* having both been spectacularly and unbelievably ignored by an Academy still languishing musically between the wars. Moviegoers all over the world bought the Beatles' soundtrack albums in their millions, yet the supposed arbiters of movie and musical taste sat there deaf, dumb and blind, oblivious to popular taste, in a desperate last-ditch stand in defence of an already dead 'Onwards to The Past' era. The Beatles had disbanded by now, so *Let It Be* was their last collaborative chance to win. Losing is seldom an honour, but in that instance it was.

It was finally time for Newberg and myself to sit down and write our new stage musical, to keep our longstanding promise to one another. Neither of us had the remotest idea what we were going to write about, but it was sure to be a great adventure. Just *how* great I was about to find out.

The advent of a new Bricusse–Newley musical was of little interest to Newberg's money-minded managers, especially Mr Ray Katz, whom we nicknamed 'Stray Katz'. Evidence of this came on the first morning of our renewed collaboration, when Newberg, consumed with guilt, confided in me that Mr Katz had booked him eight consecutive weeks of cabaret in Reno, Las Vegas, Lake Tahoe and Atlantic City starting the next Monday, and the only way we would be able to write the show would be if I were to travel to all these dubiously wonderful places with him. My first instinct, and probably the right one, was to walk away from the project. My second instinct, also probably the right one, was that, if I did so, I would most likely be presiding over the burial of our partnership. I pointed out to Tony that, with him doing two shows a night, at 8.00pm and midnight, seven nights a week, especially in these less-than-peaceful, not to say Godforsaken, venues, our work was bound to suffer. With the outraged look of a boy scout accused of kicking a puppy, he assured me it wouldn't. There was only one way to find out.

One week later we were installed in tacky mega-suite splendour at Harrah's Hotel in Reno, 'The Biggest Little City in the World', also the divorce centre of the world, also the left armpit of the world. Our workday went something like this: I would awaken around eight, shower, shave, breakfast, and read the ghastly no-content local newspapers, with names like the *Nevada News* or the *Reno Renegade*, filled with mind-numbing front-page stories like Andy Williams's brother Dick had a hole-in-one at Death Valley Country Club, or Tony Bennett's great-aunt Sarah celebrated her 88th birthday at 'The Hole-in-the-Wall' Bar, Grill and Discotheque in Carson City, or that, of the 12,757 out-of-town couples who got married at the 'I Love Elvis' Wedding Chapel in Las Vegas last year, more than half planned to return to Nevada to get their divorces in Reno. By 9.00am, I was ready for work. Newberg, on the other hand, whose midnight show ended around 2.00am, would by then be so full of adrenalin that he would sit around and eat and drink with the boys, or maybe the girls, 'til 6.00 or 7.00am, and leap into the new day around 2.00 or 3.00pm in the afternoon. We would meet around 3.30 or 4.00pm, by which time I was senseless with boredom, my eyes as glazed as glass marbles. At 5.30pm, Newley would eat, before resting for an hour to be ready for his dinner show at 8.00pm. That gave us, on a good day, a maximum of two hours to focus on the creation of an original idea for a Broadway musical.

Against all the odds, we finally evolved a concept and a storyline for our show. It was a simple little saga about Man, Life, Death, God and The Devil, with The History of the World thrown in. Nothing pretentious. The best thing about the idea was that the show had a potentially great role for Newley as the Devil, wheeling and dealing throughout history with an alternately benign and wrathful God, desperately trying to prevent the Lord from destroying the human race, without whose vulnerability to temptation the Devil would be out of business. We pursued the amusing premise with mounting enthusiasm.

That was the upside. The downside was that I was still in Nevada, without the consolation of the $100,000 a week that made life there tolerable for my old chum Newberg. We moved from Reno to Las Vegas. The heart-stopping horrors of the décor of Caesar's Palace made the tastelessness of the Reno hotel we had just left seem in retrospect like an architectural masterpiece by Nash or Wren. This time, I had a suite about the size and cost of Dodger Stadium, which gave the impression of being a rejected set design for a Cecil B de Mille big-budget musical production of *Scheherazade*. Crimson, fuchsia, orange, pink and gold featured prominently among the blinding clash of colours that screamed a welcome at you as you entered, battling for your attention. I escaped from the strident aggression of my surroundings at every opportunity, but Caesar's Palace, with its airport-size casino, its wall-to-wall one-arm bandits and its Las Vegas policy of 24-

hours-a-day eating, drinking, gambling and entertainment, is hardly geared to be a haven of peace or meditation. I usually ended up seeking and finding refuge with my notebooks either aboard an exotic Egyptian floating bar called Cleopatra's Barge, which really was surrounded by water, or, my favourite, the one truly quiet spot in the whole neon-lit lunatic asylum, a serene little Japanese restaurant called 'Ah-So'. By the time I met Newley mid-afternoon, I had invariably OD'd on sushi.

I knew I could not survive long in this ridiculous pseudo-world. Friendly faces would appear from time to time, and I greeted them like a man who had spent his entire adult life bereft of human company. John and Karen Carpenter were my particular life-savers. They were on a scouting trip to Las Vegas prior to performing there, a far cry from their *Goodbye, Mr Chips* première party gig in a converted Hollywood Boulevard parking lot little more than a year before. In the interim, they had become major recording stars with Herb Alpert and Jerry Moss's A&M Records, and had just had a massive number one hit with 'We've Only Just Begun'. We had a number of memorable dinners together in the mind-boggling Bachanal restaurant, Caesar's sumptuously over-the-top showpiece eatery, where extremely lavish Roman dishes were served by other extremely lavish Roman dishes, namely the scantily clad waitresses dressed in hot-pants togas and necklines plunging into the abyss. The food, if anyone noticed, was unusually good and, in my case, so was the company. Karen and John were remarkably sweet people, though I was always moved by the overwhelming inner sadness I sensed in Karen whenever I saw her. To this day, I am still affected by the haunting beauty and purity of her unique and unforgettable voice. She died at 32.

Deliverance from my Nevada nightmare was mercifully at hand. Our next port of call was Lake Tahoe, a place of unsurpassed natural beauty, which is perhaps more than can be said for the shadier casino characters who frequented it. Better yet, Newley's performing dates had been switched around, giving him a two-week hiatus. We grabbed the heaven-sent opportunity. Bill Harrah, by far the nicest and most highly regarded of the casino owners, offered Newley and myself one of his lakeside houses in a beautiful estate called Skyland. From the moment we moved in, the show finally took off. We had laid out a rough first draft of the book, enough to know where the songs would occur, and we were dying to get started on the score, so we did. Instead of working two hours a day, we were suddenly working 12, and sometimes 14 and 15 and, by the end of these two wonderful weeks in Tahoe, we had completed a 15-song score, the show had a title, *The Good Old Bad Old Days*, and a pretty nifty title song to go with it.

When Newley went off to warble in Atlantic City, I escaped from Nevada with the alacrity of the Count of Monte Cristo legging it from the Château d'If. Never had Los Angeles looked so good. Evie lovingly nursed me back to full mental health from my narrowly avoided Nevada nervous breakdown.

Jimmy Nederlander, a tough-talking, high-powered, chainsaw-voiced but always friendly Damon Runyan character, Broadway producer and theatre owner, showed strong interest in *The Good Old Bad Old Days*, and with him on board we would lack only a director. We contacted our hero, Bob Fosse, who came to spend a day with us at the Sherry Netherland Hotel. We read the book, played and performed the songs, and had a great time together. Fosse said he adored the whole thing and would *love* to direct it. We never heard from him again, except that a couple of years later he completely lifted the concept of our main Act Two production number, presenting the American Civil War as a minstrel show, and used it lock, stock and barrel in *Pippin*, his next production. So much for heroes.

In the end Newley agreed to direct himself in *The Good Old Bad Old Days*, Bernie Delfont gave us the Prince of Wales Theatre in London and, as they say in France, '*Robert est votre oncle*'.

I was left with one major problem to solve in New York.

Believing I was going to spend several months there, I had started looking for a suitable apartment. Over dinner with George Hamilton one evening at Lutèce, he convinced me that the other indispensable necessity of life in Manhattan was a chauffeur-driven limousine. I suggested that this could be more expensive than renting an apartment. 'Not,' countered George immediately, 'if you *own* the limo! It's the *car* they charge so much for, *not* the driver!' Knowing George to be a deal-maker among deal-makers, I accepted that the logic of this was unassailable. Furthermore, having himself just spent several weeks in the Big Apple, George said that having a limo at his disposal 24 hours a day had not only saved him time and money, but also added greatly to his prestige as well as sparing him the inconvenience and humiliation of constantly scrambling around for transportation.

By the end of dinner, I was sold. Not only on the deal, but also on the limo that George had no further use for now that he was returning to the West Coast. It was a beautiful, black stretch Cadillac, the length of your average train, with dove-grey velvet seats and sofas plus the essential walnut and crystal cocktail cabinet. And, above all, Bill the driver. Good old Bill. The Lutèce dinner cost me slightly more than $6,000, but I thought I had the bargain of the century. I was all set to become the definitive Englishman-about-town in Manhattan. If the worst came to the worst, I could always sleep in the car and save money on the apartment. There was certainly enough room. I was exhilarated. I felt like Fred Astaire in a Dietz and Schwartz musical, driving around Central Park at midnight, lacking only Cyd Charisse to duet 'Dancing in the Dark' with me.

Unfortunately, this transaction took place less than 24 hours before the New York plans for *The Good Old Bad Old Days* completely fell apart and we decided to move the show to London. So now I had a 200-foot-long limo for which I had absolutely no use whatsoever, and I was leaving New York in a day or two, probably never to return. Desperate, I made an insane deal with Bill the driver to drive the car across the United States to

California and leave it in Beverly Hills, to which I knew I *would* return in the not-too-distant future.

I was determined not to leave New York without at least finding an opportunity to show off my lavish limo just once. At short notice, I called Joan Crawford and invited her to lunch at 21. To my delight, she was available. As coolly as I could, I said I'd send the car for her, and I did, the limo's maiden voyage in my service. We had the identical lunch that we had had there before, the Joan Crawford salad at the Joan Crawford table, and talked of the good old, bad old studio days at MGM and Warner Brothers. When it was time to leave, I again smoothly offered 'the car' to run her home. I would like to think that she was impressed, but, remember, this was a woman, a film star for nearly 50 years, who had probably known no other form of transportation *except* limousines since the first one had been invented.

I stayed on at 21, chatting with old Walter, my favourite waiter, 'til Bill the driver returned. After about 15 minutes, there was a phone call for me, which I took in the Remington-littered lobby of the restaurant. A voice came on the line. 'Mr Bricusse? This is the concierge of Imperial House. I'm just calling to let you know that your limousine is on fire on East 69th Street between Third and Lex. You'll be pleased to know that Miss Crawford is safe.' And he hung up.

The George Hamilton Limousine Sales Service in Beverly Hills received a phone call from a less-than-satisfied customer later that afternoon, and George and I spent half-an-hour on the phone, helpless with laughter, while I explained to him how nearly we had conspired to incinerate one of Hollywood's most enduring Oscar-winning legends.

The end of the story is that Bill the driver did indeed drive the limo all across America to Beverly Hills, where fittingly, upon arrival, the car had a massive heart-attack and died. I asked George if he'd like to be buried in it, at no cost to himself, but my generous offer was declined with thanks. Bill the driver, lucky to have survived, flew back to New York in search of a newer, safer limo, and I hope to this day he regales his friends at the Annual Limo Drivers' Ball with the tale of how he once set fire to Joan Crawford.

Happily, Newberg at last found love again, at an altitude of 35,000 feet, in the person of a sparkling young American Airlines stewardess named Dareth Rich. Dee was a true delight, and a natural sunny antidote to the soft cloud of gloom that always seemed to be drifting across the Newley horizon.

They got married a few months later. Dareth Rich became Dareth Newley. I, prize idiot, could not resist the delicious pun of calling her Mrs Newley-Rich, and I regretted it, even though I still think it's funny! The Newley-Rich marriage was to last the better part of two decades and produce two exceptional children, daughter Shelby and son Tyler. Newberg was at the peak of his nightclub earning powers at the time, so he had reverted to his 'royalty never carry money' routine, but Evie and I both felt acutely that, from this point forward, life somehow wasn't as much fun for Newberg as in the giddy days of the Sixties. Maybe it was the glamorous life-force Joannie always brought to the party. Whatever it was, the equation had changed, and we were once again in the upside-down Wimbledon tennis tournament, where you start out with your two favourite players, the finalists, then – Boom! – divorce, and now there are four semi-finalists, and so on.

The Las Vegas boom years for Newley as a nightclub performer were drawing to a close as younger, hotter, pop music stars came on the scene. The big money well quickly started to dry up. Having turned his back on a potentially great Broadway career, and with both his movie and recording careers stagnating simultaneously, dear sweet Newberg, who hadn't a financially aware bone in his body, saw his years of prosperity coming to an end.

But that was still a distant cloud in the long-term weather forecast of Newley's life. When we started pre-production for *The Good Old Bad Old Days* in London, Tony was clearly happy to be back in the one arena where he could display the full remarkable range of his talents – the theatre.

Michael Caine was watching TV in his London home when he saw this commercial featuring a stunningly beautiful Brazilian girl. He was so smitten by what he saw that he decided then and there to go to Brazil to find her. His agent saved him the trouble by pointing out that the gorgeous girl was also in London, one mile away, in Fulham. Her name was Shakira Baksh, and she wasn't Brazilian at all. She was from Guyana, formerly British Guiana. Not one to be deterred by details, Mike tracked her down in darkest Fulham, and wooed and won her. She was sensational, and she was now Mrs Michael Caine. They were living in Mike's wonderful Georgian pile on the River Thames at Windsor.

Mike Caine loves the country. Among his proliferation of talents are his twin passions of gardening and cookery, which for four well-fed decades have combined to give Evie and myself more classic Sunday lunches than we have enjoyed from any other single source in life. The vegetables in a Caine Sunday lunch are all homegrown, fresher, more varied and more succulently perfect than those to be found in any restaurant on the planet. Mike is a world-class authority on potatoes, and can name more kinds of potato than you can name countries in Africa. He knows, as a surgeon knows his scalpel, which potatoes are the best roasters, and how to crisp them, which make the best chips, and why, and 15 different ways to mash them, and on which occasions relevant to the other vegetables one should do so. His roasted meats, beef, lamb, veal or pork, duck, chicken, turkey or goose, and his Sherlock Holmesian omniscience of the world of sausages, made it almost inevitable that he would eventually go on to own one of the most successful strings of restaurants in London. If Mike is a brilliant cook, it is the direct result of his being a brilliant gardener. When he has finished creating what he considers to be the perfect garden, he is quite likely to move house so that he can create another one.

On this particular Sunday, we arrived at the Mill House to find Mike in thigh-high waders, a roadworker's orange rain-jacket and a flat cap, busily planting rows of small evergreen trees along parts of his grassy river frontage. ''Allo, Les,' he said in the unmistakable voice, pointing proudly to the baby trees, 'I've planted nearly two 'undred o' these little sods since 'alf past seven this morning!'

I was impressed, but I still ventured the comment, 'Aren't they a bit close together?'

'By 1980,' he replied with satisfaction, 'it'll be like fuckin' Burma!'

We wandered through the garden with Evie. He pointed to an exotic-looking plant, unable to resist flaunting his vast knowledge. 'You see that,' he said with great authority. 'That is a *florabunda aurora borealis*. There's only two o' them in the 'ole of England. I 'appen to know that because the other one's over there!'

We passed the immaculate, newly completed tennis court, with its automatic serving machine. 'Why the serving machine?' I asked. 'You don't play tennis.'

'I know,' he said. 'I'm gonna buy another one, so's they can play each other.'

We walked back up to the house. There was a small political group from nearby Clewer Village at the front door, requesting Mike to sign a petition protesting the influx of Pakistani immigrants into the area. Mike was quick to react. 'Come an' look at this!' he said, pulling the leader of the group into the hallway. He pointed up to the curved stairway, where Shakira, draped in a purple and gold kaftan, a vision of beauty, was starting to descend the stairway, followed by her mother. 'You think *you've* got problems,' shouted Mike to the stunned little man. 'I've got 'em in the bleedin' *'ouse!*'

Michael Caine is quite simply the best company on earth, and Evie and I have laughed longer and harder and more frequently with him over our 45-year friendship than with anyone else, and that's against some pretty stiff competition. The long and winding pathway of our lives has been magically crazy-paved with an awesome wealth of wonderfully funny people, and if laughter be the best medicine, Evie and I are good for another couple of hundred years.

Newley, Ian Fraser and I recorded the demos of the songs for *The Good Old Bad Old Days* out at Denham Studios. We were pleased with them, but just down the hall, in the big studio, John Williams was scoring the movie of *Fiddler on the Roof* for Norman Jewison with a 75-piece orchestra. There they were, side by side, the two ends of the musical spectrum, the first tentative recordings of a new stage show not yet in production, and the huge-scaled Hollywood motion-picture version of the long-running Broadway smash. *Fiddler* would win John Williams his first long-overdue Academy Award for Best Score. *Willy Wonka* was among the nominees he beat. *Fiddler* went on to become one of the major commercial successes of the year.

Back in Denham, Roger Moore, after several arduous years of trying, had finally achieved his bitterly fought divorce from his previous wife, the Welsh singing star Dorothy Squires, and was now free to marry the lovely Luisa Matteoli, which he promptly did, because the lovely Luisa would have killed him if he hadn't. Roger and Luisa were knee-deep in domestic bliss, with two beautiful young children, Deborah and Geoffrey, contemporaries of our Adam, and they had just bought themselves a charming new home, Sherwood House, set in 15 sumptuous Buckinghamshire acres.

The adjacent property to Sherwood House chanced to be the magnificent Denham Place, owned by Michael Caine's *Ipcress File* mentor and Cubby Broccoli's partner in the James Bond movies, Harry Salzmann. Sean Connery, after playing Bond six times, found himself neither shaken nor stirred by the prospect of playing him again. The search for the new James Bond was on with a vengeance and, as we all now know, Harry Salzmann finally resolved the situation by casting his next-door neighbour, Roger Moore, in the most coveted role in moviedom.

Bryan and Nanette Forbes also had a new neighbour of some significance in the Wentworth Estate, in the larger-than-life person of a young singer-songwriter-piano player who had just bought a house down the street. Born Reginald Dwight, his first claim to fame from my point of view was that he had been born in Pinner, Middlesex, and had attended the same school as myself. Close second was the fact that he was a gargantuan talent, and his professional name of choice was Elton John, full name Elton Hercules John. His Wentworth house was also called 'Hercules'. With his lyricist-poet collaborator from Lincolnshire, Bernie Taupin, Elton had just achieved his first major hit record, 'Your Song', which already bore all the beautiful and unique trademarks of the many great Elton–Bernie songs to come. Completing this talented triumvirate was Elton's child-manager, a fiery teenage Glaswegian called John Reid. Together, this titanic young trio were about to turn a major page in pop-music history.

Elton's natural wit and speed of thought are as blinding as his musical talents are dazzling. He befriended the Forbes family with the all-embracing generosity of spirit that was his way with most things. Overnight, he became the fifth member of their family. If there was ever destined to be anyone on this planet named Hercules Forbes, here was the best chance for it to happen. Elton is a magic person. He swept them off their feet with his Gale Force Ten personality, and they were all besotted by him, and he by them.

Having done precisely the same ourselves many years before, Evie and I easily understood the magnetic force that drew Elton to them. The Family Forbes have always unfailingly projected as idyllic a family image as any on whom *Good Housekeeping* could slap their solid gold seal of approval. Elton, more than most, needed the comfort zone that all that stuff provided. For all his wonderful and frequently inspired generosity, I always felt that Elton received more than he gave from the Family Forbes, for the simple reason that you can't put a price on the indefinable gifts they bestow on their friends, a rare and ravishing combination of welcome, laughter, warmth, intelligence, peace, indulgence and contentment.

Elton, Evie and I, starting out with Pinner, Watford Football Club, songwriting and the Forbeses in common, got off to a flying start in a friendship that has spanned the decades and continues today in whatever far-flung corners of the planet our paths criss or cross, usually Los Angeles or the South of France, where we all spend enough time at the same time to link up on an irregularly regular basis.

Elton came to a small birthday dinner that the Forbeses gave for me at Les Ambassadeurs Club in Park Lane. He arrived at our apartment early in T-shirt and jeans, holding a large, menacing cream cake, sang 'Happy Birthday' to me and then swung the cream cake with full force into his *own* face! He took a quick shower, changed into an exotic and sequinned outfit that his chauffeur brought up from the car, and off we went for a hilariously funny, extremely well-lubricated dinner in the staid and respectable dining room.

Elton's chauffeur appeared again at the table, carrying a large, Santa Claus-like sack, which he placed on the floor between Elton and myself. From the sack, Elton withdrew an endless array of Pinner-related gifts, including four albums of romantic music played by the Pinner Starlight Orchestra – I kid you not – plus several boxes of elaborately gift-wrapped, rainbow-coloured condoms, nestled among an assortment of other hard-to-fathom sex toys and, as the centrepiece, a full-size, inflatable, blonde-haired sex-doll, into which Elton promptly breathed full and alarming life, asking the puce-faced maître d' for an extra chair at the table to accommodate our surprise extra guest. The rest of the room looked on with mounting horror and embarrassment, pretending it wasn't happening.

Finally, at the bottom of the Santa Claus sack, Elton unearthed a lavish Cartier gift-box containing an exquisite set of sapphire and platinum cufflinks. The combined lunacy, thoughtfulness, love and humour that made up both the gifts and the evening were a reflection in microcosm of the man who gave them, for Elton also stole the dinner bill away from Forbesey.

After dinner, Forbesey went upstairs to the casino to gamble for an hour, and lost quite heavily. Elton went up there at the end for two minutes to get him and won ten grand! There's a moral in there somewhere.

Forbesey loved and adored Les Ambassadeurs. It was his favourite club in London, combining in one dazzling setting so many highly desirable Forbes-rated elements – the perfect Park Lane location, the elegant architecture of a beautiful English building, the chicest clientele, the finest food, the immaculate service, the ultimate wine-list and finally, above all, upstairs, the ultimate temptation, the casino. Forbesey doted on Les A like a dog in kaka and had spent a considerable part of my birthday dinner evening singing its praises. So much so that he planted a truly evil thought in my normally pure and perfect mind.

I forewarned Elton of my wicked plan. He loved it. As we left Les A, I acquired a few sheets of the club's stationery and some matching envelopes. Early the next morning, I wrote a letter, typed it on to the stationery, signed it in the name of the Les A Club Secretary, Robert Mills, then organized a motor-cycle dispatch rider to ride it out to Wentworth and hand-deliver it to Seven Pines. The dispatch rider left London around 9am. Shortly before ten, my phone rang. It was Forbesey. If a voice can be ashen-faced, that was the sound Forbesey made at that moment.

'Brickman, dear,' he began, in a sepulchral, hollow tone that suggested his entire family had just been wiped out in a major bomb explosion, 'Did you get one?'

'One what?' I asked innocently.

'Letter,' he said. 'The letter from Les A.'

'No,' I replied, truthfully, because the letter wasn't from Les A, it was from me and I hadn't sent myself one.

'Brickman,' he said, the voice moving deeper into tragedy, the voice of a man well into Act Five of *King Lear*, 'They've cancelled my membership.'

'Who have? What membership?' I prompted, perversely wanting to keep it going.

'Les A. This letter. Are you *sure* you haven't received one? It's from the club secretary, you know, Robert Mills, and it says that our behaviour last night at dinner was, quote, raucous, excessive, offensive and unacceptable and unbecoming the high standards and best interests of Les Ambassadeurs, and that therefore the committee have reluctantly but unanimously accepted my resignation as a member. Are you sure you didn't get one of these letters from them, Brickman?'

I assured him that I had not. Happily, it had not occurred to him that the committee would have had to meet at around 6am to have passed this resolution and got the letter to him. He changed tack, seeking frantically to exonerate himself. 'It's all because the fucking table was booked in my name,' he said desperately, like a man fighting for his life in the witness box. 'It's victimisation. They're making an example of me. It's fucking fascism!' he declaimed. 'No, it's not, it's fucking Elton, that's what it is, with his fucking red suit and his fucking rainbow-coloured condoms and his fucking inflatable sex dolls! You don't *do* things like that at Les A, Brickman dear, do you?'

I assured him that I did not and that it was probably the first time in the club's long and distinguished history that either rainbow-coloured condoms or inflatable sex-dolls had put in an appearance there.

'Well, then,' concluded Forbesey vehemently, 'it's Elton who should get the elbow, not me! I should think they'd be bloody glad to get rid of him, anyway! He's always winning in their bloody casino, on top of everything. They *need* me, Brickman, because I always lose!' I did not dispute this alarming but well-established fact. Forbesey went on, planning his defense like a demented QC. 'I'm going to call Elton and ask *him* to do the decent thing and resign. He wouldn't even be a *member* if I hadn't proposed him. You've got to understand, Brickman, I've been a member of Les A since it opened!'

Distraught, he called Elton, who continued the game brilliantly, giving nothing away, eloquent in his sympathy, but reminding Forbesey that perhaps he did have a jar or two too many last evening, and that in retrospect trying to inflate the rainbow-coloured condoms like party balloons before a horrified crowd of respectable diners was possibly a mistake. 'That's probably what did it!' Elton philosophised. Forbesey groaned and said he had absolutely no recollection of this. 'Well, you don't when you're pissed, do you?' said Elton helpfully.

And so it went on through the morning, till Forbesey, on that knife-edge brink between suicide and despair, finally prepared to pluck up the courage to call the club secretary and plead his case. We could press it no further, so we let him off the hook and told him the truth. I expected him to kill us both. Instead, he was almost grateful, like a man given a last-minute reprieve on Death Row, but a man whose pride was such that he wouldn't want to live without his Les A membership, anyway. 'You are an unutterable shit, Brickman,' he declared. I agreed with him, and I invited him to lunch at Les A with me the next day. All was promptly forgiven.

For reasons I no longer remember, Forbesey and I were due to have lunch at Les Ambassadeurs one day with peripatetic American film producer Elliot Kastner. We arrived at the bar to be informed that Elliot had unexpectedly had to fly to New York, and would we be good enough to feed the foreign lady he had also invited? Forbesey and I looked at one another with deep suspicion, not wanting to be landed with any woman ugly enough to cause Elliot to fly to New York to avoid her. Forbesey was up the stairs into the casino like a rat up a drainpipe, leaving me alone and torn between staying and running for my life. Before I could make up my vacillating Aquarian mind, the maître d' whispered in my ear, 'Your lady guest is here, Mr Bricusse...'

Towards me, like Bo Derek or Ursula Andress respectively emerging from the Pacific and the Caribbean to wreak havoc on the lives of Dudley Moore and Sean Connery, came the most ravishing, tall, classic Nordic beauty I have ever seen in my life, and I have seen a few. Her face was instantly recognisable to me from a thousand Revlon advertisements that were in every magazine one opened. Her name was Maud Adams, her smile lit up the sky, and, when I told her that Elliot Kastner had had to fly to New York unexpectedly, she won my heart with her reply, 'Oh, that's good!'

Word of the arrival of a rare beauty flashed through the premises like a bolt of lightning, reaching up into the casino so fast that, before Maud even had time to sit down, Forbesey had rejoined us with the speed of Sylvester the cat pursuing Tweetie-pie in a Chuck Jones cartoon. A delightful lunch ensued, Maud swiftly proving herself to be one of only seven Scandinavians on the planet suspected of having a sense of humour. She is also the only person I have ever met who was born inside the Arctic Circle, and she went on to become the only person ever to play a Bond girl in *two* separate 007 movies, *The Man with the Golden Gun* and the title role in *Octopussy*.

Newley and I, deep in rehearsals for the London opening of *The Good Old Bad Old Days*, were vastly encouraged by the enormous success Sammy Davis's recording of our song 'The Candy Man' was enjoying in the United States. Sammy couldn't believe it. He called me every week. 'It's number 24 with a bullet...'

'It's number eight...'

'It's number five...'

'It's number three...'

'It's number *one!*'

He finally had a multi-million-selling number-one smash hit at the top of the American charts. We couldn't believe it, either. It was by no means one of the better songs we had ever written, and Sammy's monster hit came a full year after *Willy Wonka and the Chocolate Factory* had been and gone from the movie theatres. Nonetheless, we were delighted to accept both the kudos and the royalty cheques that came with it.

Sammy's next album not only contained 'The Candy Man' but also included six new songs from the score of *The Good Old Bad Old Days*. His follow-up single, 'The People Tree', from the show, also made it into the US Top Twenty, though lightning was not about to strike twice. As usual, our one and only hitmeister, Happy Goday, who was now running my music publishing company, Stage and Screen Music, was out there drumming up some great recordings for us and, once again, it was Tony Bennett who was our star turn with a stunning rendition of one of the show's big ballads, 'The Good Things In Life'.

The Good Old Bad Old Days enjoyed pretty good notices, and ran successfully at the Prince of Wales Theatre in the West End for the year that Newley was in it, although it was not a runaway hit. Newley was, *comme d'habitude*, unique, his performance a tour de force, delivering four or five show-stopping songs in the course of the evening. As usual with us, the score was better than the book. I put it to Newberg that, if we could only find a top-notch book collaborator or two, we could write half-a-dozen scores a year. But top-notch book-writers, I have learned, are, like perfect pearls, few and far between and, at the end of the day, DIY is the trustiest stand-by. Nothing has happened between then and now to change my opinion.

I was becoming acutely aware of major changes brewing in both my working life and our personal lives. The film musical had disappeared from the face of the earth as surely as the dodo and the pterodactyl. Stage musicals, whether for Broadway or the West End, were about as big a talking point in Beverly Hills as the sex life of marsupials. If you were planning a new musical around that time, you would have been as well off in Chernobyl as California.

Evie and I were again increasingly inclined to spend time in Italy or in the South of France. Europe was calling us home. We both wanted Adam, who at age eight now had an accent like Humphrey Bogart's, to be educated in England. My mother's health was failing. Everything pointed east, not west.

Professionally, since Richard Gregson had married Natalie Wood and had become a producer, I had been without an agent or any form of representation for nearly four years. That didn't worry me. I preferred to self-start my projects and, in the foreseeable future, that was precisely what I was going to have to do.

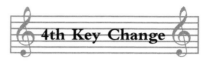

4th Key Change

5th Key: E Flat

Peter Sellers was about to re-enter the matrimonial arena. His third sashay down the aisle, this time with the daughter of a good old English noble family, by the name of Miranda Quarry, reflected Peter's upwardly mobile move into the higher reaches of society. The wedding reception was to take place in the South of France, and a few of Peter's old chums, including Roger Moore, Johnny Gold and myself, were invited to attend. Evie couldn't be bothered with all the packing and production that goes into a one-day trip, so I flew down with my old pal Johnny Gold, the much-loved proprietor of London's premier discothèque, Tramp.

We had an early lunch at Burke's, the celebrity restaurant in Clifford Street owned by everybody's favourite tailor, Doug Hayward, and his aristocratic partner and chum, the Queen's cousin, Lord Lichfield, which caused the restaurant to be known by local wags as Lord and Tailor. During lunch, a well-known trendy Clifford Street shirtmaker came over to our table and asked whether we would be kind enough to take his wedding present to Peter with us. 'A little goodie from Asprey's,' he smiled, placing the familiar purple-wrapped, green-ribboned box on the table.

We arrived at the Voile d'Or hotel in St Jean Cap Ferrat around six in the evening, to be told by Jean Lorenzi, the owner, that Peter and Miranda were on his boat in Villefranche, and would we join them there. Johnny and I zoomed off in *Evie* the Riva, waiting shining for us in the port of St Jean, and sailed around Cap Ferrat into Villefranche Bay, with the Asprey's box prominently displayed on top of the dashboard. As we passed the lighthouse on the end of the Cap, a siren sounded behind us and a French Customs patrol boat flagged us down. They drew alongside, and two uniformed men came on board. 'What had we been doing in Italy?' was their first question. I said we hadn't been in Italy. 'Where are the boat's papers?' was next. I said they were at the Voile d'Or. The two men were unsmiling and aggressive, and said they needed to search the boat. I invited them to go ahead, exchanging helpless shrugs with JG.

They proceeded to take the boat apart. They went into everything. They even picked up the little Asprey's gift-box and shook it cautiously, as though expecting it to explode. After what seemed like three hours but was probably six minutes, they let us go. As we approached Peter's boat, the *Victoria Maria*, I saw Sellers and Roger Moore standing together on the deck, pointing at us and falling about with laughter. I suddenly realised that the whole thing was a set-up. They had bribed the Customs boat to stop us, a big, fat practical joke. They confessed. I threw the Asprey's box at Peter. 'Here's your bloody wedding present from your fucking shirtmaker!'

Peter opened the box; it was filled to the brim with cocaine. We had carried it through London and Nice airports. Had the Customs men opened it, the practical joke would have been over, and Johnny Gold and I would still be in jail. I went to see the trendy shirtmaker when I got back to London. I won't say what transpired, but a little later he went out of business. So, sadly, did Peter and Miranda.

Richard Gregson bought a small terraced house in Westmoreland Street, a not-quite fashionable area on the southern tip of Pimlico, nominally part of Belgravia but on the wrong side of Buckingham Palace Road. Mrs Gregson, née Natalie Wood, had just flown over to London from Los Angeles to join him. On the evening of her arrival, the four of us went out to dinner at a popular Italian trattoria off Kensington High Street called 'Tratoo'. We were gone maybe two-and-a-half hours, cab rides included. Upon our return, we found a tall builder's ladder propped up against the front of the house, with the second-floor bedroom windows wide open. We rushed upstairs and, of course, all of Natalie's jewellery, which she had left in her still unpacked suitcases, was gone. Richard sold the house, which was worth considerably less than the jewellery, and moved to Mayfair.

Richard was never professionally happy after he sold his agency and became a producer. He functioned far better as the big fish in the small pond of his own making than as the small fish in the big pond into which he was thrown after he married Natalie. It started out well enough. Natalie teamed him up with her friend Robert Redford, and the two men co-produced the film *Downhill Racer*, with Redford starring. After that, it all started to go a bit pear-shaped. Whether or not it was a marriage death-wish on Richard's part, or a flashing sign of his unhappiness either with himself or the new life-role thrust upon him, Natalie found him *in flagrante delicto* with her secretary, and the marriage was instantly over. Richard was out the door. He called me in France to tell me that he and Natalie had split, without ever giving me the gory details, which Natalie supplied later, and asked whether he could stay in our home 'til we returned. Old friend in distress. Of course.

When we got back a couple of months later, he was still there, and stayed on. One evening, over drinks at the bar before dinner, I asked him what his plans were. He took a deep breath and agonisingly revealed that he was preparing a stage musical version of *Cyrano de Bergerac*, with Christopher Plummer as Cyrano. The project obviously did not involve me, whom he knew had been dying to do it, since he had represented me through all the protracted negotiations that had dragged on for the better part of a decade. Richard had Anthony Burgess providing the book and lyrics, and a comparatively unknown film composer called Michael Lewis, whose work was favoured by Dickie Attenborough and Bryan Forbes, two of Richard's former clients.

I did not regard this as an act of friendship, given my enduring passion for *Cyrano*. What irked me most was that he didn't tell me during the whole two years he had been developing the project, especially given that he had turned to me and I had come to his rescue in the Natalie wreckage and he had been living under our roof for a quarter of a year.

Richard went on to produce his *Cyrano* at the Tyrone Guthrie Theatre in Minneapolis; it went on to Broadway; Chris Plummer was predictably brilliant and won the Tony Award for Best Actor in a Musical, but the show failed, and the score bore the brunt of the blame. No comment.

My friendship with Richard faded after that, not acrimoniously, just drifting apart, which was regrettable, because Evie and I were fond of him. He moved to Wales and became a writer. Natalie moved to Robert Wagner and became his wife for the second time. I called her Mrs Wagner Gregson Wagner. The final shock came a decade later when I saw RJ and Richard standing side by side together at Natalie and RJ's pretty house on Canon Drive in Beverly Hills after her funeral. They looked like brothers.

We took Dudley Moore, Larry Harvey and 'Redbird' — our nickname for his stunning redheaded girlfriend, Paulene Stone, who was a top English model — to The Guinea for dinner. Dudley had parted from his first wife, Suzy Kendall. I thought they were perfectly suited and had an ideal marriage, but I also thought the *Titanic* would make it across the Atlantic.

The Guinea is a 17th-century coaching inn in Bruton Mews, Mayfair, that for many years has been a popular and upmarket steak-house. Across from us, Peter Sellers was having dinner with Princess Margaret, Tony Snowdon, and Bryan and Nanette

Forbes. Great hilarity was issuing from both tables, ours the more raucous on account of Dudley's outrageousness. He had perfected the super-slurred drunken voice that he was later to use to Oscar-nominated acclaim in the film *Arthur*, and he was on a deadly Dudley roll that had us convulsed with laughter throughout our meal. The more we laughed, the more outrageous he became. He was totally out of control, yet fantastically funny. We finished dinner ahead of the others, and went by to say hello as we left. I detected a slight envy that they hadn't been at our table, having the fun we'd been having. Dudley, drunk with success at his surefire humour, was on a high. He just wouldn't give up. He lurched over to their table, playing it drunker than ever, gave Princess Margaret a sweeping courtly bow and slurred, 'G'd evenin', your Royal Highness... I s'pose a blow-job is out of the question!'

We rented a pretty villa in the hills above Vence called 'Campobello', and I invited George Axelrod to write something in the villa's guest book. These were his words: 'The show we are going to write will be called *Feeling No Pain*.'

Since we had never discussed working together, it was an intriguing inscription. George and Joan were staying in a villa at the picturesque Château Saint Martin, also above Vence. The Axelrods had moved to Europe, a serious relocation for two people who defined New York and Hollywood. They had bought a major house in London, just off Eaton Square, and would shortly buy a second and bigger one in neighbouring Chester Square, in the heart of Belgravia, at a time when you could ask the price of a property in London without being struck speechless by the answer you received. The Axelrods, needless to say, had already become the hub of London literary society, with George Weidenfelds and Kenneth Tynans and John Mortimers lurking in every corner.

When Evie and I arrived back in London a couple of weeks later, George handed me a script. 'What's this?' I asked.

'Act One,' he replied.

I was impressed. The cover of the script read as follows: '*Feeling No Pain – A New Musical* – Book by George Axelrod – Music and Lyrics by Leslie Bricusse.'

George Axelrod placed comfortably among the top ten wittiest men on earth, not more than a couple of places behind his old friend and mentor Billy Wilder, with whom he had made Marilyn Monroe's spectacular success, *The Seven Year Itch*.

I eagerly read Act One of *Feeling No Pain*, which remains to this day the funniest first act of any musical ever to pass before my eyes. I was thrilled and exhilarated by it. I met with George at 9.30 the next morning at his house in Eaton Place South. Joan Axelrod, who was a world-class interior decorator, and a world-class everything, come to that, had converted the whole top floor into a wonderfully eccentric open-plan working space for her wonderfully eccentric open-plan George. George was a pacer. When he worked, he walked, back and forth, incessantly, a bundle of nervous energy, which his rare gifts enabled him to convert into pricelessly funny dialogue. He needed space, and Joan had cleverly provided it. On an average working morning, George would cover five or six miles, which was why Joan had shrewdly elected to put down no carpets up there, just a happy, sunny, bright yellow linoleum. She also kitted George out in a big pair of soft, black velvet slippers, embossed with 'GA' and a crown in gold brocade, from Burlington Arcade, to minimise noise below as George's considerable bulk moved back and forth above her head. I shuddered to think what size George would have become if he hadn't paced. I calculated that, over the 18 months it took to prepare a Broadway musical, he would put close to 3,000 miles on the clock.

We started to discuss the show. George was nursing a glass of white wine with his habitual Boxer-dog worried frown. He called me Lord Brickman, and he was Sir George. 'Lord Brickman,' he began, in a serious tone of voice, 'it troubles me deeply that, after many years of painstaking research, the perfect light, white breakfast wine still eludes me. But,' he cheered up, 'I am no quitter, and I want you to trust me when I say that, while we are working on this great show, the search will continue.' I applauded his resolve. 'You're lucky,' he added. 'It used to be vodka.'

Bursting with enthusiasm for our new project, we arranged to start work in earnest in California the following month. The weather in London was predictably lousy, and the thought of a quiet and peaceful hideaway in or near Palm Springs, where all-day, every-day sunshine is a given, became increasingly appealing. 'Leave it to me,' said Joan Axelrod, in her famously deep and decisive voice, which left nothing open to question.

Within a week, as we knew she would, Joan had it all figured out. Kirk and Ann Douglas generously gave us their house in Palm Springs, as Kirk was away filming. And so, six years later, I found myself back in Kirk's beautiful Marc Chagall study where I had written the lyric for the James Bond film *You Only Live Twice*. George and I, in separate areas of the house, got straight down to work, George more or less out on the terrace, where he could pace. The elegant, high comedic style of George's writing and the wicked charms of his wayward leading characters, offered me more opportunities to write songs of a more bitingly sophisticated and cosmopolitan nature than I had ever been given before. While I cracked into the songs for Act One, Sir George tackled Act Two of the book. We would meet at the end of each day to compare notes and report on progress over a bottle of Sir George's favourite light, white breakfast wine. Joan and Evie would soak up the many pleasures of desert life, and we would have cosy and hilarious little dinners for four, either at the house or in the local restaurants. The desert atmosphere was perfect, and we loved every minute of it.

The Axelrods threw me a New-York-chic-style birthday party in the third week of our stay, with an eclectic guest list ranging from Fritz Loewe to Lauren Bacall to Truman Capote, who was every bit as outrageous as I hoped he would be. By the time we came to the end of our enchanted desert stay and were ready to re-enter the orbit of the real world, we had two-thirds of a score and three-quarters of a book. And that was the problem. We didn't have *four*-quarters of a book.

For reasons neither Sir George nor I could comprehend, Act Two foundered about halfway through, and the previously debonair derring-do of our hero, Robert Bender, a thinly veiled carbon copy of his creator as a young man, suddenly ground to a shuddering halt halfway down page 74. The stream of creative brilliance that had carried Sir George through an Act-and-a-half of sustained comic invention had inexplicably dried up, and there they were, Sir George and Bobby Bender, marooned without a paddle half-an-hour from the final curtain.

Among the many problems that this presented, it was clear that, if Sir George couldn't finish the book, Lord Brickman couldn't finish the score. I suggested to George that he should maybe step away from the play for a bit, to recharge his batteries before returning refreshed to the fray. The proposal was adopted; we returned to LA and shifted our focus on to more practical matters. I started organising demo recordings of my two-thirds of a score with Ian Fraser, while George gave Jack Lemmon, his inspired first choice to play Bobby Bender, his three-quarters of a play to read.

John Uhler Lemmon III, in real life, *was* Bobby Bender. He knew it, and we knew it. Any part of the character of Bobby Bender that was not based on George Axelrod was based on Jack Lemmon. Jack, like George, was no stranger to the world of the light, white breakfast wine. The pair of them had been great drinking buddies for years. What Jack also knew was that, musical as he was when seated at a piano, and much as he identified with both Sir George and Bender, he could never begin to sing a full Broadway score eight times a week. Jason Robards, George's equally brilliant second choice for the role, declined for basically all the same reasons.

The three-quarters of a play next went to a slightly more off-the-wall but nonetheless intriguing choice, Jerry Lewis. George and I were both slightly concerned about whether or not Jerry would be willing to dock his notorious aircraft carrier-sized ego long enough to star in a project on which he was not also executive producer, director, writer, scenic designer and popcorn concessionaire. Surprisingly, and happily, he would, and did. In short, Jerry loved the play, and said he couldn't wait to read the rest of it. 'Nor can I!' George assured him.

Subject to the fourth quarter being as good as the first three, of which he had little doubt (glassy grin from George), Jerry was prepared to commit to the project. So there it was, and there, alas, it stayed. No amount of battery recharging, or any other form of creative rehabilitation, could refloat our three-quarters of a hit show. It was frustrating, especially as the demos of the songs were about the best that Fraser and I had ever done. George was beside himself, which was not a very good place to be and, although I knew that in the longer term it would not help our cause, I could not blame this lovely, hugely talented man for taking out quite a lot of his anger on the trusty light, white breakfast wine.

Despite his inner anguish, Sir George displayed a great fighting spirit on his substantial outer surface. Confident that what he regarded as our minor creative problems would somehow resolve themselves, he recommended that a few days in the Big Apple having preliminary talks with some Broadway big-shots might be a tonic for us both, and time well spent, so off we went.

Meetings were arranged with David Merrick, Hal Prince, Feuer and Martin, Roger Stevens and Alan Whitehead. The Axelrods were staying with their friends Arlene Francis and Martin Gabel on the East Side, and their ever-present chum Betty Bacall generously suggested that I should stay with her at the Dakota building on Central Park West. All part of the mighty Joan Axelrod New York network, I surmised.

Betty was wonderful. She and I pronounced ourselves founder members of the exclusive 'LB Club', and awarded honorary memberships to Lucille Ball and Leonard Bernstein, with Ludi Beethoven as president emeritus.

On Saturday, Betty had to go out of town. As she was leaving, she gave me a key. 'This,' she said, 'is the key to Bogie's cupboard. It's beside the bed in your room, Lesley's room,' meaning her daughter, Lesley Bogart. 'You might find it interesting.' And off she went.

That night, George, Joan and I had dinner at 21. I got back to the Dakota around midnight. I went to my (Lesley's) room, took out my magic key and opened Bogie's cupboard and, with it, Bogie's magic kingdom.

Before me, floor to ceiling, was a 12-foot-high, tightly-packed treasure trove of priceless memorabilia, letters, photos, contracts, the annotated scripts of *Casablanca*, *The African Queen*, *Treasure of the Sierra Madre*, *The Maltese Falcon* and *To Have and Have Not*, a movie buff's trip to Heaven. Apjac would have been up here in a minute with a handcart. I sat on the floor to sift through whatever came to hand. When I looked up, it was daylight. I went into the kitchen and made myself some coffee, and went straight back to Bogie's cupboard.

Thanks to Betty, I got to know the great man a little bit that night. What a pair they must have been, he and she, in that fabulous, black-and-white post-war era. And what a wonder she still is today, one of the few truly great, tell-it-like-it-is, legendary treasures of both Hollywood and Broadway.

The ravages of writer's block that were pulverising Sir George were an unseen enemy I had not previously encountered. Like a traffic jam, no one quite knows how it unravels itself, but somehow, eventually, it does. I could only pray that Sir George's personal creative traffic jam would also unravel itself before it unravelled Sir George.

It became a bizarre time for me professionally, in which I would collaborate with a succession of remarkably talented people on a series of ill-fated projects that seemed to have fabulous potential, but were somehow destined either never to see the light of day, or to end up with an indigestible mixture of ingredients that you only realised *were* indigestible when it was too late to do anything about it.

Thanks to the ongoing royalty flow from projects past, there were no financial problems, although friends outside the business invariably recoil in horror at the insanity of the months and years theatre writers gamble on the long shot of creating a hit show. Despite this, I had no plans to hang myself outside the Hotel du Cap as a warning to others contemplating writing a musical. One is hard-pressed to be suicidal about *anything* in the South of France, where the life on offer is the best available on this Earth. Evie and I were enjoying our lives so much that we were as good an argument as you'll get for *not* bumping yourself off.

David Niven, Gregory Peck and I decided to buy wine together. Greg started it and, therefore, at his Cap Ferrat doorstep must lie the ultimate blame. Greg was introduced to a Burgundian winemaker by the name of Bernard Grivelet, who owned the prestigious Château de Chambolle-Musigny. The eager-to-please Monsieur Grivelet proposed that he should provide a selection of superior wines for a special wine-tasting luncheon at Monsieur Peck's home, for a chosen handful of close, wine-loving friends.

There were about a dozen of us who sat down at the table on the huge terrace around 1.00pm on that memorable Saturday in early summer. I have no particular memory of a wine-tasting per se, nor of anything much else that took place between 1.00pm and 7.00pm that fateful day. Nor, I suspect, does anyone else who was present.

What I do know for sure, because I still have the luncheon menu provided by Monsieur Grivelet and signed by everyone present, is that our delicious and near-interminable luncheon was accompanied by seven different white and *14* different red wines, also provided by Monsieur Grivelet. Where it all went happily wrong was that this elegant gathering was never about wine-*tasting*, not for a single moment. This was about wine-

drinking and, in that capacity, it has to be said, everyone present put in an heroic performance.

Six hours and 21 wines later, as the sun and most of the guests were sinking in the west, Greg and I, like Wellington at Waterloo, surveying the battlefield that had been lunch, officially proclaimed Bernard Grivelet a national hero of France, and henceforth purveyor of wines to all our realms in Europe. We then proceeded to order from him insane quantities of fine wines that would 'in one swell foop' guarantee both the prosperity of his vineyards and the popularity of our wine cellars for years to come.

The next-to-last thing I remember is Greg and myself weaving our way unsteadily down the long lawn of 'La Doma' to play a jolly game of boules. And the final thing I remember after that is lying on my back in the boule pit, helpless with laughter, watching this most distinguished Oscar-winning movie-god icon, everyone's favourite American, the Abraham Lincoln of Hollywood, stretched out full-length on the grass and saying in that beautifully modulated world-famous voice, 'Leslie, that was one hell of a wine-tasting!'

Niven, as always the perfect gentleman, honourably undertook to buy one-third of the wine that Greg and I had so promiscuously ordered. What the three of us had agreed was that we would each be responsible for one-third of any shrewd and intelligent wine purchases that any member of the trio might make. What none of us had envisioned when the verbal agreement was made was that we would be buying up half of Burgundy in the first week. In fact, it proved to be a most felicitous investment, even though Greg and I never actually bothered to explain in detail to Niv, who was not present at the lunch, the exact circumstances of our very first 'shrewd and intelligent wine purchase'.

The Beverly Hills Wheel of Fortune continued to spin at a fair old clip. Steve and Neile McQueen, to our horror and deep sorrow, had parted, never to reunite. Big mistake. So had Larry Harvey and Joan Cohn. Not-so-big mistake. So had Peter Sellers and Miranda Quarry. No big deal. To balance the books, new marriages were forthcoming. Joan Collins had married Ron Kass in London and, on New Year's Eve, Larry Harvey married Paulene Stone at Harold Robbins's home on Beverly Drive. Evie and I attended this one, and afterwards flew up to Las Vegas with Larry and Paulene on George Barrie of Revlon's plane, to spend a bizarre New Year's Eve-cum-honeymoon celebration watching forgettable entertainment at the Las Vegas Hilton.

I decided to update the Beverly Hills section of my phone book. Of 105 couples, married or merely 'together' when we first arrived there, only *seven* were still together; 98 had 'moved on'. No wonder I needed to redo the book. All that crossing out. Nonetheless, a significant sign of those highly impermanent times.

Larry Harvey, at long last happily married to the beautiful Paulene – alias Redbird – picked this idyllic moment in his life to get sick. Seriously sick. The lethal quartet of his chosen indulgences – excessive smoking, excessive drinking, too little food and too little sleep – finally conspired to gang up on him and strike him down with cancer just a few months after the wedding. I flew over from London to LA to see him, spending every day with him and Redbird, but staying with my beloved fellow book collector Apjac at his newly expanded hacienda on Beverly Drive.

Roger Moore was also in town for a few days, doing publicity for his now-completed first James Bond film, *Live and Let Die*. On the Sunday, the day before the première, Roger came over to Apjac's to join us for lunch by the pool, a swim and a sunbathe. Apjac was spending the day, as he did most Sundays, feverishly working at yet another of his all-consuming hobbies, editing together recently acquired clips of great and not-so-great musical numbers from every musical film ever made.

At 5.00pm, the phone rang. It was Redbird. She was worried about Larry. He was deeply depressed. If Apjac wouldn't mind, would I please come over and stay with them for the last three or four days before I returned to London? Larushka – we called him that in deference to his Lithuanian heritage – badly needed my company, and to talk about the houses we were forever contemplating building in the South of France. I explained the circumstances to Apjac, who was most sympathetic. I said I'd pick up my things in the morning and, within the half-hour, presented myself at Larry and Redbird's ultra-modern palazzo overlooking the city of the angels from Cabrillo Drive on Coldwater Canyon.

The three of us enjoyed a quiet dinner on the terrace, and I proposed that I organise a dinner party here at their house for Larry's dozen favourite people, which I would enhance with the wines of the year of his birth. Immediately, Larushka's face lit up. He had been born in 1928, the wine year of the century. Wine-wise, this little dinner for a dozen was about to make my recent Burgundian acquisitions with Greg Peck and Niven look like a stroll through the Gallo wine-in-a-box section of Walmart. We made the phone-calls, and Larry ordered up from the vault, for its worthy world première, the solid gold dinner service, with matching golden goblets, that he had just bought from Sammy Davis Jr for an astronomical sum of money. We were all set.

The next morning, I drove back down the hill to Apjac's to collect my belongings. There were several cars in the courtyard of the house, which was nothing unusual, given Apjac's penchant for breakfast meetings and the virtuoso shuffling of his 3-by-5 multi-coloured cards. I walked into the house, where the first of the seismic shocks that were to be the indelible hallmark of that summer awaited me. Apjac had died of a massive heart-attack a couple of hours before. He was 51. His young heart doctor, Charlie Kibowitz, broke the news to me. As the word spread quickly around town, more cars started to arrive at the house in a steady stream – Dick Zanuck, Herb and Nora Ross, Roddy MacDowall, Edward G and Jane Robinson, Rosalind Russell and Freddie Brisson. Within minutes, the house looked as it usually did for a typical Apjac dinner gathering, except that this was 8.30 in the morning.

Apjac had had a heart condition for a number of years, but that didn't lessen the impact of the dramatic suddenness of his departure. We who knew him best surmised that he had died happy, with two new movies in production, and the 24th two-hour reel of edited musical clips neatly completed in the last 24 hours of his life. For all his quirky ways, Arthur P Jacobs was a forward-thinking and generous-spirited man who had always managed to harness his manic nervous energy and convert it into the power to make things happen, with spectacular benefits for everyone around him.

I stayed on in LA for the funeral, and served the 1928 Bordeaux as promised at Larushka's memorable dinner for a dozen. As I returned to London, so did Larry and Redbird, he for the last time. I reflected on my ten-day stay in Beverly Hills, first at Apjac's, then at Larry's, and concluded that I was unlikely that year to be voted America's favourite houseguest.

Larry died in London a few short weeks later. On our last visit to the house in Hampstead, Evie and I spent a couple of hours at his bedside with Redbird. They had been married slightly less than ten months. Redbird's stiff upper Roedean-educated lip kept her admirably strong throughout the ordeal. Elizabeth Taylor, Larry's longtime pal and co-star, was leaving as we arrived. Larry's spirit was intact, but his body, alas, was not. With a stream of bittersweet black humour on the subject of his imminent demise, Larry maintained his scathing wit to the last. To heighten the tragedy, Redbird had recently given birth to a baby daughter, Domino, to whom Evie and I became godparents. Dom was a mirror image of her father, a perfect female reflection of his beautiful, clean-cut Slavic features.

Wolf Mankowitz and I spoke the eulogies at Larushka's funeral, at St Paul's Actors' Church in Covent Garden, the first time I had ever been called upon to perform this overwhelmingly difficult emotional task. The jokes were particularly hard to deliver, but Larry would never have forgiven either of us for a po-faced performance at his final public appearance. We didn't let him down, thank God. The laughter and the tears were just about evenly divided.

The seldom-disputed cliché is that these things come in threes. My beloved mum also chose this less-than-wonderful time to leave us. Her health had been slowly failing for a number of years, ever since she had become diabetic. Her condition was now worsening rapidly, so I sought out a beautiful nursing home on the banks of the River Thames at Goring in Oxfordshire, where she spent the last three years of her life less than a mile from the home of her sister Jane called Gin, and an assortment of lovely and loving female cousins, who visited her every day and were loyal to the last.

There was no way I could ever repay the love and hard work that defined my mother's life throughout my childhood, except perhaps to match it with my own. That characteristic has remained with me as my work ethic throughout my life. My philosophy of life has always been to regard each day as a miniature lifetime, in which I have to achieve something and enjoy something. It has enabled me to sustain a sensible balance between work and play, the friend of both and the slave of neither.

We went with the Axelrods to the 21st birthday party of Kenneth Tynan's daughter Tracy, which was held at London's Young Vic Theatre on a Sunday evening. I was surprised to see Peter Sellers and Liza Minnelli sitting together, apart from the main group, so I went over to greet them. Liza, who had just won her Best Actress Academy Award for *Cabaret*, looked up at me with those huge brown eyes and even huger eyelashes, which Halston had made her trademark, and said, 'Les, darling, guess what? Peter and I are getting married!'

I slipped into the chair beside her, to avoid falling full-length on my face in horror, and came up with some brilliantly witty line like, 'Oh.'

Liza gushed that they had known each other a whole week now, and Peter had proposed last night, and Liza had, of course, said 'Yes.' Why wouldn't she? I mean, if you stopped for a moment to think about it, this was a natural, a marriage made in Heaven, and didn't I think so, and Evie and I, of course, would come to the wedding, wouldn't we?

The thought of these two card-carrying crazy people, both of whom I loved, forging a union that would have left the Marx Brothers looking like pillars of sanity by comparison, caused a glazed film of disbelief to form over my eyes and my brain. I mumbled a few incoherent words of gibberish which Liza interpreted as congratulations. She kissed me fervently. 'Isn't this *extraordinary*?' she said. I absolutely agreed that it was, *quite* extraordinary.

Peter just sat there with a huge fixed grin on his face, as though he had just been injected with a massive dose of Valium that had rendered him comatose, and I hurried back to Evie to report the news. Her beautiful jaw dropped open, further perhaps than I had ever seen it do in our 15 years together, as she absorbed this mind-bending and potentially cataclysmic titbit.

It was all over the front pages the next morning, as Liza and Peter chose the much photographed birthday party to hold an impromptu press conference. I said to Evie, 'I give it three weeks max! Ask Max what he gives it!' I was wrong by one day, the time it took our star-crossed lovers to figure out that, whatever else a marriage between their two towering talents might have been, it was definitely not a Heaven-sponsored product.

From time to time, Fritz Loewe, composer of *My Fair Lady*, *Brigadoon*, *Camelot*, *Gigi*, et al, the other half of the great Lerner and Loewe, invited us to join him for lunch aboard his yacht in Cannes. Fritz Loewe knew how to live. He had wisely chosen to retire after *Camelot*, which had devastated the creative collaboration of the legendary trio, Lerner, Loewe and Moss Hart. Moss had died, Fritz had had heart problems and decided that, at 60, he had more than enough money and hit shows, which would outlive him even if he made it to the select membership of the Cent'Anni Club. Only Alan Jay Lerner, the youngest of the team, had soldiered on, writing the screenplays for the film versions of *My Fair Lady*, *Camelot* and *On a Clear Day You Can See Forever*. Beyond his well-deserved celebrity as one of the great lyricists, plus his well-deserved notoriety for being married eight times, few people are aware that Alan is the only screenwriter in the history of movies to have written the screenplays of *three* Best Picture Oscar-winning movies – *An American in Paris*, *Gigi* and *My Fair Lady*, picking up three Oscars for himself in the process.

And good old Fritz, now in his seventies, was not travelling alone. He was accompanied by his new blonde fiancée, Francesca, a shy, quiet girl, who had recently celebrated her *19th* birthday, and who would go on to become Mrs Loewe, and eventually Fritz's widow. The age difference was more than half-a-century. I doffed my metaphorical cap to this maestro of the better-late-than-never good life.

Back in London, I spent a day with George Axelrod. While Sir George had not exactly been burning up the pages on *Feeling No Pain*, he had had one practical idea to help get us off the rocks before Jerry Lewis and our potential producers lost all interest in the show. George's idea was to bring in a fresh eye and a good mind in the substantial person of our old friend Burt Shevelove, a writer and director of great experience, a sometime Yale professor and Stephen Sondheim friend and mentor. Burt's main claim to theatrical fame was the book of *A Funny Thing Happened on the Way to the Forum*, which he had co-written with Larry Gelbart a dozen years before. Burt was another of those gravelly-voiced wits and pundits bred exclusively in New York. He had cheerfully agreed to work with Sir George on the fourth quarter of the play, convinced after reading George's first three-quarters that the piece was a winner. Burt confidently predicted that they would knock it off in a week, two at the most.

George suggested a small thimbleful of light, white breakfast wine to celebrate this breakthrough moment in our first collaboration. As we toasted Uncle Burt, the phone rang. It was Irving 'Swifty' Lazar, Hollywood super-agent of super-agents, fleetingly in London, and staying, of course, at Claridge's. Even more fleetingly in London was about to be the great Sir Noël Coward. Swifty had just learned that Noël was flying in from Geneva for a rare 24-hour stay in the city of which he once was king. Though king no more, Noël's legendary reputation had elevated him to the status of theatrical demi-god, a role he was happy to accept and to play. Accordingly, he had acquiesced to Swifty's request to put together 'a little gathering' at Claridge's at eight o'clock that evening, and would George and Joan and Evie and Leslie care to join the group?

Since nobody ever said 'No' either to Noël or to Swifty, the four of us were duly on parade as commanded. Only Swifty, alone among the human race, could have put together such 'a little gathering' at a few hours' notice. There were five tables, each of eight places, set around the small ballroom at Claridge's, with a grand piano on the dance floor. The guests included Laurence Olivier and Joan Plowright, John Gielgud, John and Mary Mills, David Lean, Alec Guinness, Lerner and Loewe, Burt Bacharach and Hal David, Maggie Smith, Vanessa Redgrave, and just about every distinguished above-the-title British film and theatre name you could possibly cram around five tables for eight at Claridge's. Noël, in frail health, walking with a cane, and accompanied by his ever-faithful Cole Lesley and Graham Payn, was ecstatically greeted by all his old chums and, in sparkling form, as he had been ever since that long ago December day in 1899 when he was born, nine days before Christmas, whence the name Noël.

Swifty, the consummate ringmaster, had the whole thing shrewdly figured out from the start. It goes without saying that the dinner was memorable. All five tables were rocking with laughter, mainly from Noël reminiscences, of which everyone in London had bucketsful. The atmosphere in the room was remarkable. This was as good as it gets. This was the best, and everyone present knew it. As the coffee arrived, Swifty stood up, made a brief but stylish speech of welcome to the master, and then said, 'Ladies and gentlemen, Burt Bacharach and Hal David.'

Burt and Hal went to the piano and played and sang three new songs from their score for the upcoming movie remake of *Lost Horizon*. Applause, applause.

Swifty stood up again and said, 'Ladies and gentlemen, Lerner and Loewe.'

Alan and Fritz followed suit, with the first public airing of three songs from their newly written reunion score for *The Little Prince*. Applause, applause.

Swifty stood up again and said, 'Ladies and gentlemen, Sir Noël Coward.'

Unprompted, everyone was on their feet, cheering, paying unspoken and perhaps premature tribute to a great career ended, and an amazing life nearly so. There was a sense of farewell surrounding the whole evening. Noël sat perfectly still for a few seconds, knowing, as we all did, that Swifty had cornered him perfectly. How could the two greatest songwriting teams alive perform before him without his responding? He got slowly to his feet and, leaning heavily on his cane, helped by Graham Payn, he half walked, half shuffled his way across the dance floor and sat at the piano. The cheering, which escorted him every step of the way, redoubled. It was deeply moving.

Noël sat immobile for several seconds more. His hands hovered over the keyboard. We held our collective breath. Was he all right? Was this a mistake? The silence seemed interminable. Then, hesitantly, Noël edged his tentative way into 'Someday I'll Find You'. The chords were uncertain, his voice was wavering. Worry was etched on every face in the room. Why didn't it occur to us that Noël was probably more moved by what was happening around him in this famous room on this famous night than the rest of us put together? He knew that he was doing this for the last time, performing for his oldest friends and admirers in the city

Top: Newberg and I in our usual deep depression when working.

Middle: Joan Collins, myself, Elizabeth Taylor and George Hamilton at Evie's Beverly Hills birthday party.

Bottom: At the Elyseé Palace in Paris with Elizabeth Taylor and Franco Zeffirelli on the occasion of Elizabeth's Légion d'honneur.

Top: The Swiss Family Edwards. In Gstaad,
Switzerland with Julie Andrews, Tony Adams, Blake Edwards, and Hank Mancini
preparing for the production of *Victor/Victoria*.

Middle left: 'You win some...'

Middle right: '...you lose some'. (Chateau d'Oex, Switzerland).

Bottom: Sean Connery silently seething over lost golf bet!

Top: A hundred and one Oscars. The Princess Royal hosts a gathering of British Oscar winners at Hampton Court Palace. (LB third from right, second row.)

Bottom: The old pals: Shakira Caine, myself, Evie, Joan Collins, Michael Caine, and Roger and Kristina Moore.

The Music Men:
Top: Myself with John Williams.

Middle: Myself with John Barry.

Bottom: Most of the music in my life and career is in this one photograph: Anthony Newley, Frank Wildhorn, Henry Mancini and Ian Fraser.

op: 'And she shall have music…' Without a doubt, when she has Elton and Quincy on
ther side of her.

iddle: Dinner in the South of France with the Greg Pecks, the Dickie Attenboroughs
d the Roger Moores.

ottom: Quincy Jones and Michael Caine are celestial twins – both were born at the
me hour of the same day of the same month of the same year.

Top left: Elton delivers my birthday cake!

Top right: Newley and I have Jackie Collins surrounded.

Middle left: Brickman and Bassey at Elton's house in the South of France.

Middle right: Rehearsing *Victor/Victoria* with Liza in New York. Take it as red!

Bottom left: With Polynesia the parrot and her voice-dubber during *Doctor Dolittle* rehearsals.

Bottom right: The ugly-but-kind Joan Collins lavishes affection at my humpty-fumth birthday.

Top: New Year's Eve at Valentino's chalet in Gstaad, Switzerland with George Schlatter and Francis Albert Sinatra.

Middle left: John Mill's 90th birthday party – Evie and myself with Andrew Lloyd Webber, Johnny, and Judi Dench.

Middle right: Evie and myself with the great Billy Wilder in Beverly Hills.

Bottom: My favourite sister act! Jackie and Joan Collins.

Top: Outside the London Palladium, Christmas, 2005.

Middle left: Still the luckiest man alive!

Centre: The future – Roman Bricusse (aged 5).

Middle right: Luca Bricusse (aged 3).

Bottom: Investiture at Buckingham Palace.

where it had all happened, from *The Vortex* to *Private Lives*, from 'London Pride' to the Café de Paris, from *Cavalcade* to *In Which We Serve*, from 'Mad Dogs and Englishmen' and 'The Stately Homes of England' and *Hay Fever* to *Blithe Spirit* and *Brief Encounter* and 'I'll See You Again', and on and on and on. He had given us all so much.

Suddenly, his voice built as the song progressed, his fingers found their way, and it was vintage Coward all the way from then on. The exchange of emotional energies between the master and his disciples had by now created a soothing sense of relaxation around the room. We knew that all was well. An uproarious rendition of 'Don't Put Your Daughter on the Stage, Mrs Worthington' was followed by a definitive 'If Love Were All'. When he got to the great understated line *'All I've ever had is a talent to amuse...'*, there was an almost audible sob from the entire audience, and an outburst of sustained appreciative applause. They were thanking him for a lifetime of gifts. A final standing ovation escorted him back to his table at the end of his trio of songs, which were instantly and forever indelibly printed among everyone's most precious and abiding memories.

Amid the exhilarated buzz of conversation that followed, with the great and the near-great all saying how privileged they were to have been a part of something so special, Alan Lerner wandered over to me, super-cynic that he was, and said, 'You know what's going to happen, don't you? We're all going to die off one by one, and Noël's going to keep coming back here once a year for decades to come and give annual heartbreaking farewell performances till he's 90!'

For once, alas, the cynic was wrong, as he knew he was when he said it. Noël took his final curtain call a few weeks later, but that magical evening remains very much alive.

Hank Mancini and I were still keen to do a show together, so we stepped up the search for a likely subject. André Previn, though now principal conductor of the London Symphony Orchestra, also wanted to find time to do another stage musical, having got his feet wet with Alan Jay Lerner on *Coco*. We too spent many hours together, deep in discussion about the elusive 'right property'. I was more than ready for a collaboration. Writing book, music and lyrics for a musical on your own is a bit like crossing the Sahara Desert on a unicycle. There are moments when you wonder if this was a good idea. There are moments when you crave company. I was starting to hate unicycles. What happened next gave me my collaboration. But it didn't involve Hank Mancini *or* André Previn; it involved *Mrs* André Previn, alias Mia Farrow.

The Hallmark Hall of Fame decided to celebrate their 75th anniversary with a major musical production of *Peter Pan*. They asked the prolific producer of TV film specials, Gary Smith, to produce it, and Gary asked Newley and myself to write the score. He chose my across-the-street neighbour Danny Kaye to play Captain Hook, and Mia Farrow to play Peter. No question, clearly the Department of Fate had a great deal to do with all of this.

Newberg and I were delighted to be reunited, especially as we didn't have to write the book. This tricky task was given to a young English screenwriter called Andrew Birkin, the baby brother of John Barry's then wife, Jane Birkin. Newley and I naturally asked for Ian Fraser as musical director. Gary Smith didn't want him. Because of Danny Kaye, Gary Smith hesitated. Gary finally relented, and the end of the story is that Gary Smith has never done another major project without Ian from that day to this, with Ian winning about a dozen Emmys from twenty-something consecutive nominations along the way.

Mia as Peter Pan was wonderful casting, but totally unknown territory as a singer. And looming over all of this, we were forewarned by a terrified production manager, was the giant shadow cast by Danny Kaye, whom I now learned had a Godzilla-like monster reputation, beside which Rex Harrison was up for the Angel of the Year Award. I found this hard to imagine, since I had only ever thought of Danny as the benign neighbour who cooked the best Chinese food I was ever going to taste, unless God is a Chinaman, which is quite likely these days. TV executives quaked at the mention of Danny's name.

Fraser darkly confirmed that Danny the performer, before a camera, was Mr Hyde to the Doctor Jekyll I knew in the Chinese kitchen across the street. Gary warned us further to prepare to have every song we wrote for the evil Captain Hook ripped to shreds. Newberg and I, confident bordering on arrogant about our abilities to write good songs, nonetheless braced ourselves for the onslaught to come.

Fortunately, we had a secret weapon, namely myself. My childhood devotion to Danny the performer, from his earliest movies – *Up in Arms*, *The Kid from Brooklyn* and *The Secret Life of Walter Mitty*, some 30 years before, plus his genius live performance at the London Palladium, when he had all of England at his feet – now stood me in good stead for the pending ordeal. My secret weapon was that I admired the songwriting of Danny's brilliant wife, Sylvia Fine, as much as I admired Danny, and I knew every word and every note of every fiendishly clever little song she had ever composed for him. I was quite certain I could create Captain Hook's songs in a style similar to Sylvia's, thus providing a comfort zone for Danny as a performer, and limiting his potential range of criticism.

The *Peter Pan* collaboration was far-flung, with Andrew Birkin writing in London, Newberg in California and myself in France, and audio tapes flying back and forth across the Atlantic. Over the years of our collaborations, we had become adaptable to any and all writing circumstances, so we were in no way fazed by these. In four weeks, we had our score. We arranged to meet with Fraser in London to do the demos. Peter Pan was to be filmed at MGM's Elstree Studios in England, although all the main production ingredients other than Newberg, Fraser, Andrew and myself were American. We managed to swing the balance England's way by persuading Sir John Gielgud to narrate, and Julie Andrews to sing the opening song.

Danny Kaye came to London. The moment of truth was upon

us. I am smugly happy to report that, to the amazement of the cowering cohorts surrounding him, he loved every song we gave him, and never asked us to change one single word or note of any of them. So I never saw the flipside of the Danny Kaye temperament, though I am assured by Ian Fraser that Danny found endless other ways to terrorise everyone around him during the shooting, and the general feeling in the company was that it was only when he was playing the cruel and heartless Captain Hook that they thought he was nice.

As for Mia, she was a trouper. Fraser found a small but strong boyish voice in her, which they developed to maximum effect, with the result that she gave an enchanting performance in a role she was born to play.

I had for a year or so been dabbling with a musical based on Jean Giradoux's *Ondine*, and Gene Kelly *loved Ondine*! I sent him the screenplay and score, because I knew that some form of dance and fluid movement, whether above or below water, was an essential part of the fantasy. I had written it as a screenplay primarily because of its visual needs, though I knew it would be an easy transition to convert it into a theatre piece if that proved to be a better way to go. I had guessed that *Ondine* would appeal strongly to Gene's sense of romanticism. He was also enthusiastic about the screen potential of *The Great Music Chase*, my low-budget version of our Tchaikovsky *Nutcracker* fiasco, so the pair of us now formed a partnership to try and make either or both of these projects happen.

When I returned to California, I went over to Gene's lovely old red–and–white Cape Cod-style house at 725, North Rodeo Drive, to discuss how best to move *Ondine* forward. His first choice to play the role, surprisingly, was Liza Minnelli, who was like a niece to 'Uncle Gene' after his long association with her parents, Vincente Minnelli and Judy Garland, at MGM. Certainly, Liza was currently a hot property after her Oscar for *Cabaret*, and she could sure as hell sing and dance. I could also understand

Gene liking her gamine look, as he had with Leslie Caron in *An American in Paris*, but Leslie was altogether a more delicate flower than Liza, and Liza was as different from Audrey Hepburn as Ondine as George Hamilton's Dracula was from Bela Lugosi's. For me, Mia was a more natural choice for the free-spirited water sprite, even though she lacked Liza's musical gifts.

Gene and I flew up to Las Vegas, where Liza was performing in cabaret. Not *Cabaret*, but cabaret. We went over to her house, and had a to-say-the-least interesting dinner in the kitchen with Liza and a trio of her fiancés past, present and future, Desi Arnaz Jr, Ben Vereen and Jack Haley Jr, who all seemed perfectly comfortable in one another's company. Liza and Gene had both recently appeared in Jack's dazzling and definitive anthology of MGM's greatest musical moments, *That's Entertainment*, which he wrote, produced and directed.

Later that night, Gene, Jack and I went to see Liza's show, which was a two-hour tour de force of powerhouse razzamatazz. Two things were certain. One, she was a great star and, two, she was not Ondine. Neither was our next choice, the delicious Diahann Carroll. Gene and I couldn't sell the concept of her in the role to anyone. The reasons? She was too old (in her thirties); she was too pretty (how ugly should Ondine be?); she was not a star (this would have made her one); she was black (so are the most precious and desirable pearls). Diahann in fact is a delicious sepia. The words 'talented' and 'perfect casting' never came into it. Gene and I found ourselves adrift in a sea of negativity, and *Ondine* was put 'on hold' – showbiz jargon for 'dead in the water'.

A few months later, Liza married Jack Haley Jr. 'DAUGHTER OF DOROTHY MARRIES SON OF TIN MAN' announced one *Oz*-oriented showbiz journal. Sammy Davis Jr was Best Man. The reception was at Jack's famous old eagle's nest headquarters in the Hollywood Hills. The house was bursting at the seams, as every single one of Jack and Liza and Sammy's 75,000 closest friends tried to muscle in on the party and wish them well. As Jack and Liza were both up to their ears in work, there was no time for a honeymoon. The plan was for them to come to us in the South of France where we had taken a house, a few weeks later, which they duly did.

You never really need to invite houseguests to the South of France. There is no shortage of good company. So many people find their way down there at some point in the spring or summer that the telephone stays as warm as the weather. More than one South of France friend had warned us never to take a house with too many guestrooms. 'Take the number of guest rooms and multiply by two,' they would say, 'and that's how many houseguests you will have.' A maxim to be carved in granite in every Côte d'Azur home.

We had one always-welcome houseguest during the school holidays, Adam's best friend, Sacha Newley, son of Tony Newley and Joan Collins. Like Newberg and myself, they were brothers, and we were Sacha's adopted family. He was a rather sad little boy at this time, missing his father, who was living in California, and not too ecstatic about his mother's new marriage to Ron Kass, especially since Joannie had just given birth to a new daughter, Katy Kennedy Kass, who had, not surprisingly, become the centre of attention and the apple of the new family's eye. So Sacha was happy to escape to us whenever he could.

It was a constant joy to me to see this inseparable second-generation Bricusse and Newley pair as close as their dads had always been. Sacha was a clone of his father, same facial expressions, same body language, same humour, right down to the timing, and even the same dark side. Evie once said to him, 'You seem a bit miserable, darling?'

He smiled and replied, 'That's all right, Auntie Evie. I *like* being miserable!'

Blake Edwards was shooting the new *Pink Panther* film in the South of France. Mrs Edwards, the divine Julie Andrews, came with him. Rather than submit to the rigours of hotel life, Blake had chartered an extravagant yacht, which most of the time was moored in the beautiful Bay of St Jean Cap Ferrat by the Voile d'Or hotel. Sunset dinners or weekend lunches on board, with *Evie* the Riva tied up alongside, became a feature of the summer. And, anywhere there is a *Pink Panther*, an Inspector Jacques Clouseau is never far behind. Sellers called to let us know that he knew that we knew he was there, and we were right. We invited him to dinner. He wanted us to meet Noi-Noi. I asked whether Noi-Noi was a giant panda, which is what the name suggested. No, Noi-Noi was his new Swedish girlfriend. So up they came, Peter giggling that he and Blake had spent the entire day without getting a single shot. In the scene they couldn't shoot, Clouseau was visiting his tailor in Rome, but they didn't have a name for the tailor. Blake came up with Pederasti di Roma, and that was it for the day, because, every time Peter got to the line where he had to say the tailor's name, he exploded with laughter. And if he didn't, Blake did. Sometimes they both did, a terminal double attack of the giggles, to which both were easy prey. They tried a different scene. It didn't help, because they were both still thinking about Pederasti di Roma. That shared streak of insanity that ran like a rich vein of gold through both Blake and Peter's humour, that made them the comic geniuses they were, was also capable of crippling them with uncontrollable fits of laughter for hours at a stretch. At the end of the day, all Blake had was 45 outtakes of Sellers laughing, so they packed it in and both went home giggling.

Peter fell in love with our house, our location and our sweeping panoramic views of the coast and the mountains. Mind you, Peter fell in love a lot, with cars, women, houses, boats and stereo systems, in approximately that order. But I had to assume he was serious when he called me the next morning to say he had just bought the piece of land next door. We arranged to meet again at the weekend and have dinner on Saturday night.

By Saturday, Peter's great romance with Noi-Noi had apparently run its course. We never saw her again.

Peter returned alone, this time dragging Ringo Starr and his pretty American girlfriend, Nancy Andrews, with him. Peter and

Ringo had become odd-couple friends ever since they had made the movie *The Magic Christian* together. Evie and I had been invited to dinner at Le Mas des Serres, a delightful, converted period farmhouse in the valley below Saint-Paul de Vence. Our host was the ever-charming John Pringle, an amiable hotel-owning friend from Jamaica, who was staying there. The imperturbable John accepted the three extra uninvited guests with trademark aplomb, much to the displeasure of the ferocious old dragon who owned the place and ran it like a concentration camp. She was in a permanently foul mood which worsened in the evenings. She glared in horror when Ringo appeared with a giant golden earring in one ear, having the night before shaved his head clean after a love affair with a bottle of grappa. He looked not unlike Doctor Evil in *Austin Powers*. Ringo decided the old dragon needed cheering up, and followed her out into the kitchen after she took our orders.

Five minutes later, for the first time in the restaurant's long history, music was heard, and romantic Spanish music at that, and into the room, to the stunned astonishment of everyone who knew the place, burst Ringo Starr and the old dragon, dancing a tango. The old dragon was laughing and clearly in seventh heaven. Ringo had a rose between his teeth as he twirled the old dragon around the tables and we all gaped in disbelief. Wild applause greeted their impromptu cabaret, and we wondered what the hell had happened in those five minutes in the kitchen to transform the old dragon into Rita Hayworth.

The answer was Ringo had happened. The least of the Beatles he may have been, but he was and is a huge personality in his own right, and to be number four in that quartet, the greatest of them all, is still pretty big stuff.

The old dragon was a creature transformed, beaming benignly on her guests and doting on Ringo as her Prince Charming. The Mas des Serres diners looked like concentration-camp prisoners at the moment of liberation. It was the happiest evening in the history of the hostelry, and in the life of the old dragon, too.

We thanked John Pringle for a rare evening, and Ringo for liberating the Mas des Serres. For the drive back up to our villa, we joined Ringo in his unnecessarily large limo, which just succeeded in negotiating the narrow country lanes. We sat around the house, and Peter said he'd like to watch a movie. The motion was approved, and Peter browsed through our collection of three-quarter-inch tapes, that size-wise were to today's DVDs what LPs are to CDs. From among the tapes available, Peter selected, not altogether surprisingly, *Dr Strangelove*, in which he had played three different major roles. 'Famous for his modesty,' muttered Ringo.

We settled down to watch, Peter leaning forward in his chair, fascinated, as though seeing it for the first time. About 20 minutes in, Ringo, to needle Peter, yawned loudly and said, 'Load o' bloody rubbish!' in fluent Merseyside.

Peter was on his feet in a flash, genuinely outraged. 'Well, you don't have to bloody watch it if you don't want to!' he screamed, and stormed out of the house, got into Ringo's limo and drove off into the night, never to be seen again, leaving Ringo and Nancy as our unexpected houseguests. They stayed the whole weekend, and we had a lovely time.

I suppose his unpredictability was part of Peter's fascination, but it was also the key to why nothing of real importance ever stayed in his life for long. My own analysis of that particular evening was that Ringo was its undoubted star, and Peter, used to being the centre of attention, resented it, which is why he put on *Dr Strangelove*, to restore the balance, and why, when it was criticised, he had stormed out like the only, lonely, spoiled child that he was.

Julie Styne called me from New York. The great English-born Broadway composer of a boxful of major hit shows, among which he numbered *Gentlemen Prefer Blondes*, *Bells Are Ringing*, *Gypsy* and *Funny Girl*, was now in his early seventies, but retained the youthful energy and enthusiasm of a Tin Pan Alley kid hustling to get his first song published. We had talked of collaborating some day, but he had been writing with Betty Comden and Adolph Green, and with Sammy Cahn, when I was doing my stuff with Newley. So now here he was on the phone, and would I please come over to New York as his guest, as he had acquired the perfect project for us, Tennessee Williams's *Rose Tattoo*. It sounded good to me and, since the teaming of Sir George Axelrod and Uncle Burt Shevelove on *Feeling No Pain* had so far produced nothing except the discovery of three brands of hitherto unknown vodka, I flew to New York.

Julie installed me in splendour in the Plaza Hotel, and we met each morning in his offices, which were located in the upper reaches of the Mark Hellinger Theater, off Seventh Avenue at 51st Street. He shared the offices with his long-time associate, Dorothy Dicker, and going there was, for me, like a descent into some sort of Dickensian hell. The offices could as well have been occupied by Scrooge and Marley. There were no windows, every available surface was stacked high with leaning towers of yellowing papers, but the hell element sprang from the fact that both Julie Styne and Dorothy Dicker were chain-smokers.

Large, unemptied ashtrays festooned about the place contained acrid pyramids of long-dead cigarette butts, as healthier premises might display cashew nuts. Since there was no air whatsoever circulating in the large gloomy room, a heavy pall of days-old smoke hung permanently in the air like Mexico City smog on a bad day. How Julie and Dorothy had sat there as they had, year after year, cigarettes drooping from the corners of their mouths, like Marge Simpson's twin sisters, coughing in unison as untapped columns of ash fell from their stained fingers on to the piles of paper in front of them, without succumbing, and both living well into their eighties, remains to this day beyond my comprehension. How they had managed not to incinerate the entire building with their highly combustible lifestyle of carelessly flung matches, open cans of lighter fuel and abandoned burning cigarette ends, was a miracle that will never be explained. One can only conclude that God needed more hit musicals.

Julie had successfully co-produced a number of his own shows, and it was his intention, he announced with massive confidence, to produce *The Rose Tattoo* himself, and turn it into the biggest musical hit of the decade, thanks in no small part to the amazing score he and I were going to write together. I was impressed. I had never met anyone quite like Julie Styne. It was hard to believe he had started out English. He was by now pure Damon Runyan Broadway, part Happy Goday, part Nathan Detroit, with a 100 per cent Tin Pan Alley approach to the musical. And, despite all that, he had written, especially in *Gypsy* and *Funny Girl*, some of the most vibrantly brilliant theatre music of the past 25 years.

Like Nathan Detroit, Julie was also a legendary gambler, reputed to have lost the fortunes he had made on Broadway on the racetracks of Belmont and Aqueduct. But he constantly bounced back like the little rubber ball that he resembled and went on to the next thing. Right now, the next thing was *The Rose Tattoo*.

We were having dinner tonight, he announced, with Tennessee Williams at Billy Barnes's apartment. Billy Barnes was Tennessee's agent, a ferociously social animal who inhabited a particularly luxurious penthouse on the Upper East Side, proving the old saying from the Hollywood Bible that the agents shall inherit the earth.

Tennessee Williams was a pleasant surprise. He was quieter than I had expected, probably because he was in a non-drinking phase of his life, and was affable and amusing company, with more than his fair share of Southern charm. We talked about everything except *The Rose Tattoo*, which Julie said was a *good* sign, since it indicated that Tennessee had no problems with our doing the project, a shining example of Styne logic with which I sometimes had trouble coming to terms.

There would be a number of such dinners over the ensuing weeks, during which I made half-a-dozen trips to New York to work on the score with Julie. We placed 15 songs in the play. Julie started composing some pretty nifty melodies, and from his music 'trunk' I retrieved one melody from *Gypsy*, another from *Funny Girl*, and two from the score of *Sugar*, his show based on Billy Wilder's *Some Like It Hot*. I put lyrics on all four of them. Julie loved them, and they stayed in the score.

We completed our first draft score. We were extremely happy with it. Julie wanted to call the show *Serafina*, the name of the principal character in the story, the role that had won the Italian actress Anna Magnani the Academy Award for Best Actress way back in 1955. I preferred the idea of keeping the title of the play. Julie was the producer, and so it became *Serafina*. I proposed we now set about making the best song demos ever assembled, which, with all the great, usually unemployed Broadway voices at our disposal right here in New York, would be a truly exciting experience. 'No, no, no!' said Julie. 'Nobody sings songs as well as the guys that wrote them, and that's what we're gonna do!' I knew this well-aired theory about songs and songwriters. Occasionally it worked. Nobody ever sang a Johnny Mercer song better than Johnny Mercer. Nor a Hoagy Carmichael. Nor, indeed, an Anthony Newley. On the other hand, I had heard both Sammy Cahn and Frank Sinatra sing the songs of Sammy Cahn and Julie Styne, and in that race the songwriter came out of it like a three-legged horse in the Belmont.

All of which brings us to the singing talents of the otherwise fabulous Mr Julie Styne. Beside him, Sammy Cahn was Luciano Pavarotti, and Jimmy Durante was Mario Lanza. The root of the problem was ego. Julie thought all his songs were so wonderful, as indeed most of them were, that they would sound just as wonderful even when *he* sang them. Not so. Chalk across a blackboard was more musical. But there was no shifting our Julie. He had written the goddamn songs, and no one was gonna stop him singin' 'em! And singin' 'em while he was playin' 'em on a piano, fortissimo or forget it, like his voice.

The whole experience was a world-class nightmare, because Julie didn't plan to play these songs for just anybody. They were intended only for Broadway's finest, the heaviest of the Great

White Way's heavyweights. And so this hideous, cacophonous two-hour audition, conducted at Julie's sprawling Fifth Avenue apartment, was inflicted first on no less a master than Jerome Robbins, whom Julie wanted to direct the show, then Angela Lansbury, whom he wanted to play Serafina, then Arthur Laurents, whom he wanted to direct the show if Jerome Robbins didn't, then Brenda Vaccaro, whom he wanted to play Serafina if Angela Lansbury didn't. And so on shamelessly down the line. My choices would have been Hal Prince to direct and Liza Minnelli to play Serafina. Neither appealed to Julie. The fact that both Liza and Hal were collecting Tony Awards on an annual basis didn't change his opinion. Julie wanted to control the project, and he felt he would lose control of both the show and Liza to Hal if Hal got involved. And he was probably right.

Overall, we did that benighted audition a dozen times, each one worse than the one before, when a simple set of demos with first-rate young Broadway singers would have done the job ten times more efficiently and 20 times better musically. As it was, anyone who wanted to hear the songs would have to fly to New York and endure two hours of Julie singing 15 consecutive ear-cracking solos in order to do so.

Worse was to come. I discovered, via a London agent who knew nothing of my involvement in the project, that Julie Styne did not in fact have the stage musical rights to Tennessee Williams's play, despite all the protracted negotiations and social hobnobbing with Billy Barnes and Tennessee. He had allowed us to go through all the months of work without telling me, gambling, I suppose, as usual, that everything would work itself out and he would emerge a winner in the end. How many gamblers, I wonder, have gone under and stayed under following exactly that formula?

I stayed in touch with Julie, because I liked him and his lovely English wife Maggie a great deal. Periodically, he would call me out of a clear blue sky in Micawber-like anticipation that something big was about to happen on *The Rose Tattoo*. Nothing ever did, of course. Like the opening song in Nathan Detroit's show, it was just another 'Fugue for Tinhorns'. Pity, because it was a good score. In fact, it was more than that – it was bits of *four* good scores.

André Previn and Mia Farrow came to stay with us in Beverly Hills. They had left the principal platoon of their adoptive family in England for this brief visit, as the troop movements involved in them all travelling were roughly the same as those of the Gulf War. But they did bring with them their own new, spectacularly beautiful son, Fletcher. He was 18 months old, blonder than Marilyn Monroe, bluer-eyed than a spring sky, with the face of a Kate Greenaway angel. And Mia, the day after they arrived, accorded me the singular and undeserved distinction of making me his godfather.

André was there to conduct a series of concerts with the LA Philharmonic. More music was forthcoming in our evenings at home, when improvised recitals materialised among the group of friends present. The best of these was the night when André was playing four-handed jazz with Dudley Moore, and Mel Tormé and Liza Minnelli were singing the closest of Kay Thompson harmonies. I managed to get a tape recorder on part of it, the hilarious segment where André and Duddles did piano impressions of great jazz pianists from Erroll Garner to Oscar Peterson, complete with irreverent commentary.

It was at this time that André and I finally wrote our first song together, entitled 'Jenny', the title of a powerful TV mini-series about the life of Winston Churchill's mother, that André was scoring for the BBC.

Mia's godfather, George Cukor, invited us to Saturday-night dinner at his elegant Georgian-style house on Cordell Drive. 'Uncle George' was possessed of the same old-world charm as his house and, as always, he provided not only the most delicious of dinners, but the most delicious of guests. The undoubted star of the evening was Laurence Olivier, recently recovered from a life-threatening illness in England, but now back in Hollywood playing the Nazi villain, Der Weisse Engel, opposite Dustin Hoffman in John Schlesinger's *Marathon Man* at Paramount, for which he would receive yet another Oscar nomination. Among the other distinguished guests were Maggie Smith and her writer husband, Beverly Cross.

It was a sparkling evening and, shortly before midnight, everyone drifted away, except Uncle George, Larry, Maggie, André, Mia and myself. We moved into Uncle George's cosy study for a nightcap and sat around telling stories, Larry with his leg up on a chair, a souvenir of his brush with death. The conversation got around to the English National Theatre Company's production of *Othello*, in which Larry had played the Moor of Venice opposite Maggie's Desdemona. That started the two of them on reminiscences about the beginnings of the National Theatre that, had anyone noted them down, would now be required reading for every student of theatre. It was nostalgic, and it was hilarious. Both, with their extraordinary and much-mimicked voices, were master raconteurs, and had the rest of us in a state of hysteria for an enchanted period of suspended time.

At the end of what seemed like ten magical minutes, it was in fact 5.00am when we finally stumbled out of Uncle George's den into early dawn light, aching with laughter. We had heard a hundred fabulous, never-before-and-never-again theatre stories. At breakfast later that morning, I asked André, who has the most retentive memory I know, how much of last night he could recall for posterity. Between us, we came up with maybe six or seven stories, which we attributed to the elliptical way both Larry and Maggie recounted their anecdotes, jogging one another's memories. They were uproarious tales, but I can't say unforgettable, because we had already forgotten them. The art had been more in the manner of their telling by brilliant actors than in the actual substance of the stories. It was an evening of magical butterfly wings from Mr and Mrs Prospero.

Uncle George had the nearest thing to a salon in Hollywood. He knew everyone from the great era, of which he was himself a major component. The house had an 18th-century aura about it. In the garden was the little guesthouse that for years had provided the secret romantic meeting-place for Katherine Hepburn and Spencer Tracy. Years later, after Uncle George had died, I regretted that I had never asked him for an inscribed photograph for my collection.

One day, I was browsing around George Houlé's bookshop and photo gallery on Beverly Boulevard when I came upon a large framed photograph of the mighty Mr Cukor, inscribed thus: 'To Leslie, with all my fondest wishes. Love, George.' I bought it on the spot, naturally, and wanted to know the story behind the inscription.

It was a good one. It emerged that the photograph had been given by George in 1938 to the English actor, Leslie Howard, whom George thought he was about to direct in *Gone with the Wind*, in which Howard played the noble Ashley Wilkes. Subsequently, there were various directorial upheavals during pre-production, and the history books now tell us that that monumental motion picture was ultimately directed by Victor Fleming, who scored the greatest double in MGM's history by directing *The Wizard of Oz* in the same year. However complicated the back-story, I am happy to have what I now proudly regard as *my* 'To Leslie'-inscribed photograph from the late, great Uncle George.

The doorbell rang shortly after midnight. Evie was in bed and asleep. It was Jack Haley Jr and Liza Minnelli. Liza was in a high state of excitement as she burst into the house. 'Les, darling, wait 'til you hear this! Wait 'til you hear this!' were her first words, as opposed to the usual 'Sorry to disturb you at midnight!' you might get from normally adjusted human beings. 'Jack, bring in the stuff!' was the next line, and Jack obediently lugged into my living room enough loudspeakers, cables, microphones and assorted tape-playing equipment to record the Berlin Philharmonic. While he was setting it all up near the bar, and I was thinking about saying, 'Hello, why don't you both come in?' Liza poured us both a large drink and told me the story.

She was currently making a film called *New York, New York* with Robert de Niro over at MGM, directed by Martin Scorsese, and this evening she had just finished recording the title song written for her and the film by John Kander and Fred Ebb, and she wanted me to be the first person to hear it, a privilege our long and close friendship had earned me over the years.

By now, Jack was all set up and ready with the reel-to-reel tape, and they played it. The huge MGM studio orchestra playing that kick-ass opening riff on these speakers in a domestic living room was a wake-up call to the dead. They had brought just the backing-track, and Liza, mike in hand, strutted up and down my living room performing her fabulous vocal live. And, naturally, it did to me, an audience of one, what it has done to packed houses in theatres, clubs and concert halls around the globe every time she has sung it from that day to this. It knocked me sideways. Wow! She threw her arms round my neck and screamed, 'Isn't it great? Isn't it *great*?'

I immediately thought, and still do, that I had just heard the best song of the entire decade of the 1970s. Thrilled, Liza ran the tape back and did the whole thing again, giving her performance the usual 110 per cent. 'There goes the Best Song Oscar!' I said with absolute conviction.

'You betcha!' she said, and sang it again. And that was just the beginning. She was on the greatest natural musical high I ever saw, atop that rare, once-in-a-lifetime mountain when a great star performer realises that God and Kander and Ebb have just given her a great star song that will be the cornerstone of her act for the rest of her life.

'New York, New York' did not win the Best Song Oscar that year. It was not even nominated. I could not tell you the titles of the five songs that were, except the Marvin Hamlisch–Carol Bayer Sager James Bond song, 'Nobody Does It Better', which I admired. The winning song was 'You Light Up My Life', which certainly didn't light up mine. The rest are long forgotten, deep in well-merited oblivion, while 'New York, New York' marches on, firmly established as one of the greatest standards ever written.

In his autobiography, cunningly entitled *Rex*, Rex Harrison ended the book in fulsome praise of his fifth wife, Elizabeth Harris Harrison, and dedicated it to her shortly before she divorced him. We learned this sad news in a phone call from 'Beauchamp', his house on Cap Ferrat. Rex was decidedly blue, and asked whether he could come up the hill and spend the weekend with us. He stayed six weeks, during which Evie and I got to know better than ever before the genuinely nice fellow that dwelled deep below the surface of the abrasive, cantankerous old misery-guts that we believed we knew so well.

Rex was so content in our rural environment that he had no desire to leave. For the first few days, he walked around the house with a morose, hangdog expression that made him look more than ever like Homer, his late lamented basset-hound. He followed Evie around like a huge basset-hound himself, deriving great comfort from her warm and sympathetic sweetness. And gradually, gradually he started to cheer up. He would spend hours chatting with us both, but especially with Evie in the kitchen when she was cooking, which he found particularly soothing. I never thought I would live to see Rex Harrison peeling potatoes, but he became quite proficient at it and quickly rose to number one in that capacity in Evie's kitchen in the ensuing weeks.

David Hemmings, newly divorced from Gayle – oh dear, oh dear – also came to stay, and with his irresistible energy and charm initiated Rex into all sorts of unlikely pastimes. One overcast morning I walked out into the garden to find Rex tugging at a long piece of string which went straight up into the air and disappeared into the clouds above his head.

'What are you *doing*?' I asked.

'Flying a kite!' he replied triumphantly. 'Hemmings taught me, and I'm rather good at it.'

Rex's conversion to Provencal life culminated in his buying the property next door. Predictably, Peter Sellers had done nothing with it, and readily accepted Rex's offer to take it off his hands. And so Rex it was who built the villa next door.

The road behind Rex's house-to-be was a dead end, firmly indicated by a great big red and white sign which read 'Route Barrée'. Rex's French being no better than his Italian, he misconstrued the meaning of the sign to be the name of the street and announced grandly to all and sundry that he was 'building a villa in the Route de Barrée'! Evie asked him exactly how, with his limited French, he influenced the architect and the builders on the site. 'I point a lot!' he explained. 'I'm extremely good at pointing. My kind of pointing gets results!'

And indeed it did. He pointed his way to a most attractive new home. But, sadly, he never lived in it. He was the happiest I ever saw him during those six weeks up on our hill, but when it eventually dawned on him that we only visited France for a limited amount of time each summer, he rethought his plans, kept the villa in Cap Ferrat and sold the house next door to another English family called George. And, given the great pleasure that he derived from his new friendship with Hemmings, it was bizarre that Rex's next romantic involvement was with Gayle.

Evie was born on her mother Adelaide's 17th birthday, on February 17, and Adelaide was staying with us in California for this particular birthday. Joining us for dinner was Glenys Hayward, the then wife of everyone's favourite tailor, Doug Hayward, and it happened that Glenys shared their birth date. There were three other guests, the beautiful actress and former Miss World Mary-Ann Mobley, and another chum and his new girlfriend, whom we had never met before. Being the kind of sentimental bore who likes to acknowledge such special occasions, I stood up at the end and said, 'It's not often that you get three people with the same birthday at the same table *on* the birthday, but Evie, Adelaide and Glenys *all* have their birthday tonight!'

Mary-Ann Mobley gasped, smiled her lovely smile and piped up, 'It's *my* birthday today, too!'

Before we could catch our breath, the girlfriend we had never met added, 'And it's *my* birthday, too!'

Five ladies out of five. I never tried to work out the odds, but a hundred bucks on that one would undoubtedly have bought most of Southern California.

Evie and I took our English actor friend Patrick MacNee to dinner at The Aware Inn on Sunset Boulevard. Patrick and Evie had worked together on a couple of TV and film projects in London, and he was best known to the TV world as the bowler-hatted gent called Steed in his celebrated TV series *The Avengers*. Halfway through dinner, our old singing chums Steve Lawrence and Eydie Gorme came into the restaurant to take the table opposite us. They came smiling over to our table to say hello. An inveterate punster, I took the golden opportunity that I knew would never occur again in this lifetime. I stood up and introduced them. 'Steve and Eydie,' I said. 'Steed and Evie.'

Burt Bacharach and I talked again, as we did every two or three years, about writing together, and he invited us down to La Costa Club in Carlsbad for the weekend. He lived in nearby Del Mar, where he kept and ran and trained the racehorses that vied with his music and various ladies to be the love of his life. Evie and I took Adam with us and, sailing down the San Diego Freeway on a glorious August afternoon, we had the radio playing. Suddenly, a voice broke into the regular programming to announce the unexpected death of Elvis Presley at the early age of 42, adding that there would be a full TV report on Channel Two at 5.00pm. Evie, having worked with Elvis, was particularly upset, and I said I was sure we would be at La Costa in time to watch the TV report.

We arrived shortly before 5.00pm, dashed up to our suite and turned on the TV just as the news began. The anchorman said, 'Elvis Presley died at his home, Graceland, in Memphis, earlier this afternoon.' The camera cut to a full close shot of Evie, with Elvis singing a voice-over, then slowly pulled back to reveal him serenading her in a scene from their film *Double Trouble*. It sent shivers down Evie's spine. Mine, too. Of all the thousands of film and TV moments they could have chosen, they showed this, a moment of memory and coincidence to stay forever in the mind.

Roman Polanski came over to our California house for drinks. We hadn't seen him for some time, so we had much to catch up on. Evie was cooking one of her irresistible Italian dinners, so we didn't exactly have to twist Roman's arm out of its socket to persuade him to stay and eat with us. His one-hour visit stretched happily to four or five. Around 11.00pm, he finally said he had to go. 'I promised to meet up with Jack,' he said – Nicholson, up on Mulholland Drive, whom he had so memorably directed in *Chinatown* four or five years before. And off he went into the night.

It had been a happy if brief reunion, but it was the unfortunate prelude to the disastrous news to which we awoke the following morning, that Roman had been arrested at Jack's house on serious charges involving a 13-year-old girl. The consequences of that ill-fated evening more than 25 years ago echo still today. We still see the now European-based Roman, with his wife Emanuelle and daughter Morgan when we visit Gstaad, or in Paris at a favourite restaurant on the Quai Voltaire. The world of film can only regret the consequential quarter-century gap in the creative life of the massive talent that had given us such classic films noirs as *Rosemary's Baby* and *Chinatown* while Roman was still in his thirties, and destined without doubt, in my view, to become the dark heir to Hitchcock's kingdom. In 2003, a quarter-of-a-century later, the Motion Picture Academy Members awarded him the Best Director Oscar for his superb film *The Pianist*.

If the imagination could stretch far enough to envision the Italian theatre having its own Rodgers and Hammerstein, we would be talking about Garinei and Giovannini. G and G, in the 1960s and 1970s, wrote and produced a string of enormously successful Italian musicals which seemingly ran for ever in Rome, usually at the Teatro Sistina. They were to the musical theatre what Sergio Leone's 'spaghetti Westerns' were to the cinema.

And so it came to pass that a pleasant-sounding Hollywood agent-turned-producer named Harry Bernsen telephoned me from Rome, with the news that G and G had decided to aim their biggest success, which had been playing to total capacity in Rome for three solid years, at the wider and more lucrative horizons offered by the West End and Broadway. Would I therefore please fly down to Rome for a few days as their guest to see the show and discuss adapting the song score into English?

To answer the question, Evie and I flew to Rome, happy to revisit our beloved Hassler Hotel, perched at the top of the Spanish Steps. The hotel, apart from being within fatally close striking distance of the terrible shopping street twins, the Vias Frattini and Condotti, is on the Via Sistina, a short stroll down the street from the Teatro Sistina.

We saw the show on our first evening there. Its title, *Aggiungi un Posto a Tavola*, which translates as *Add Another Place to the Table*, was *not*, it crossed my mind, as snappy a title as *Kiss Me, Kate* or *Hello, Dolly*, but then who was I to argue with a three-year sell-out, whatever it was called? The show was a smash, and its star, Johnny Dorelli, playing a young priest selected by God to deal, Noah-like, with a second deluge in the modern world, nearly drowned on stage eight times a week in the massive waves of audience approval that came crashing over the footlights at the end of every performance. It was amazing to witness. As the curtain fell, the entire packed house rose to its feet as one with a mighty roar, as though Italy had just scored the winning goal in the World Cup Final. It all looked and sounded highly impressive, but seemed to me to be something of an over-reaction, although, since the show was not unreasonably in Italian, I was perhaps not the best person to judge. But I was concerned that what drove an Italian audience to such heights of passionate acclaim in Rome might not be so easily achieved with the cooler customers of London's West End.

The show was a noisy, jolly romp, no threat in my view to the best of Broadway, but with spectacular production values. It was also pleasantly tuneful and, judging from the gales of merriment around me, hilarious – at least in Italian! Since the original book on which the show was based was English, I was easily able to confirm, by reading it, that the modern-day Noah story was indeed charming, if not fall-down funny. It also occurred to me that the endless stream of 'God jokes' were probably funnier for the massed Catholics in Rome, a stone's throw from the Vatican, than they would be for the assorted irreligious rabble who would later see it in London, a stone's throw from the nearest pub.

I was quite taken with the show's score, composed by Armando Trovailoi, whose main claim to fame in Italy was his marriage to the beautiful movie star, Pier Angeli. But Armando, a delightful and *'simpatico'* gentleman, was also one of Italy's most distinguished film composers, frequently described as the Italian Henry Mancini, though not by Henry Mancini. Henry always insisted that *he* was the Italian Henry Mancini. Anyway, Armando and his score were my principal reasons for agreeing to take on the project.

We had a pleasant series of meetings, overflowing with Italian charm, with the creative team. The task was not unattractive and reasonably straightforward, to create English versions rather than translations of some 20 lyrics. It would also involve the even more tolerable task of making maybe half-a-dozen trips to Rome and the Hassler as their guests, a hardship I was prepared to bear for the good of the cause. I suspect this last element was as much a deciding factor as anything, certainly as far as Evie was concerned.

Pietro Garinei took me for lunch to his favourite little bistro, 'Il Moro', hidden in an alleyway near the Trevi Fountains, where we consumed two bottles of his favourite Ligurian white wine, a Gavi dei Gavi called La Scolca, and the deal was done.

With the show's huge success, and the book, music and lyrics already written and raved about, adapting the songs into English was not overly challenging. I breezed through a first draft at some speed and returned to Rome to meet with 'the boys'.

The lyrics were well received, and Harry Bernsen's plans for the London production now swung into high gear. As diplomatically as I could, I suggested to him that a literal translation of the show's somewhat cumbersome title should be avoided in favour of something shorter and snappier.

We returned to LA, whereupon Sammy Davis called and said he was coming round to see me. Five minutes later, there he was on my Beverly Hills doorstep. By chance, I was sitting there with Tony Newley. Sammy was doubly delighted to find the pair of us together. He fixed us both with the Big One-Eyed Stare and announced in an extravagant British BBC accent, 'Well, chaps, I'm doing it!'

'Oh!' we said in unison. '*What?*'

He grinned a huge, evil grin and went into an unmistakable mime pose that neither of us could misinterpret. 'I'm playing Littlechap in *Stop the World* next year. It's all set. I told you I'd do it one day, and one day is *here*, baby!'

Newberg and I were on our feet in a second, hugging Sam in genuine delight. There was no littler Littlechap than Sammy at 5-foot-2, and no bigger or more perfect star on earth to play that role. He asked us to Americanise it for him, and to give him one big new song. I had always felt we could use one more song in the score, to end Act One, and we agreed that was where it should go. The show was going to be presented by the Nederlander Organisation, and Sammy wanted Hilly Elkins to produce it.

Hillard Elkins had produced Sammy in the musical *Golden Boy* in the early 1960s, around the time of *Pickwick*, when he had asked Wolf Mankowitz, Tony Newley and myself to write the musical *The Rothschilds*. Hilly had started out as a young William

Morris agent, representing Steve McQueen among others, and had been at different times in his colourful life an agent, a personal manager, a Broadway theatre producer and a Hollywood film producer, to name but four of his deftly interwoven careers. He was a passionate collector of Napoleana, drove like a maniac, ate frozen Afrika chocolate biscuits in the dead of night and married interesting women, especially Clare Bloom. He had a great line for sweeping aside any and all potential production problems. Whenever I would say to him, 'What if this or that goes wrong?' he would smile his inscrutable smile and say, 'We'll double-cross that bridge when we come to it!'

If troubles come in threes, here were mine. Firstly, Michael McAloney was an Irish drunk. And, like most Irish drunks, he had more than his share of blarney and charm. How else could this shabby, unkempt figure have contrived in his youth to woo and wed the wondrous Julie Wilson, the spectacular pride of Omaha, Nebraska, and Broadway and West End singing star of both *Kiss Me, Kate* and *South Pacific*, who had befriended and enthralled me in my early student days at Cambridge, and produce as handsome, well-mannered and perfect a son as young Holt McAloney? And how, above all, did he persuade Mary Chase, the venerable author of one of the greatest and longest-running Broadway comedies of all time, *Harvey*, who had turned down Rodgers and Hammerstein and Lerner and Loewe and Leland Hayward and Leonard Bernstein, to entrust to him the musical rights of her little masterpiece? The only possible answer to that last question, which she later gave me herself, is that Mary Chase was once an Irish drunk herself, which is how she came to write the play in the first place. But Mary Chase had cleaned up her act and become sober, whereas Michael McAloney never did.

But he had the rights to *Harvey*. And he brought the project to me. I weighed the plus of the play against the minus of McAloney, wondering whether the good that might come from the former at its best could overcome the harm that might come from the latter at his worst. It was a photo-finish, but I reasoned that, while there were a lot of Irish drunks in the world, there was only one *Harvey*. I told him I could not begin work on the piece for a year. No problem... he would wait. And wait he did, patiently and without complaint.

Second, Alan Jay Friedman is a walking encyclopaedia on the life and times of John Fitzgerald Kennedy. Alan had been involved in the Emmy-winning TV documentary about JFK, entitled *Young Man from Boston*. After Kennedy's death, he had worked for Bobby Kennedy until his assassination in 1968. Alan then focused his talents on trying to create a semi-documentary musical play built around his hero. He had written himself into a stupor with endless variations on the theme. But, imaginative as many of his ideas were, none of them quite held together for the piece as a whole.

In the same month that Michael McAloney came to me with *Harvey*, Alan Jay Friedman came to me with *One Shining Moment*. I saw the potential power of the story, and the huge possibilities of the score. I told Alan that I would figure out a way to become involved, provided I could first create a ten-day week.

Third, Blake Edwards and Julie Andrews wanted to pursue the idea of a stage musical version of *Major Barbara* as a return-to-Broadway vehicle for her. Blake then threw his curve ball. Much as they both loved André and Mia, and much as André and I wanted to write the score together, his long-term commitment to the London Symphony Orchestra was going to keep him 6,000 miles away from Beverly Hills for the next three years. Hank Mancini, on the other hand, lived six blocks away. Would it not make better sense for me to write the *Barbara* score with him, especially since Hank was constantly working with Blake anyway, and everybody knew that Hank and The Great Leslie also wanted to write together. (I was known as 'The Great Leslie' by Hank and Ginny and Blake and Julie, after the character played by Tony Curtis in Blake's movie *The Great Race*.)

There was no denying the logic of this argument. I said I would need to talk to André about it. They said they already had. Further, Blake and Julie were halfway through writing a screen adaptation of Julie's bestselling children's book *The Last of the Really Great Whangdoodles*, for Blake to direct, and for which they would also like Henry and myself to write the song score in the almost immediate future. I put my hands to my spinning head, and decided that the only sensible thing for me to do was to go with the flow, and leave it to the Department of Fate to sort it all out if it threatened to become a train-wreck, which, from where I was standing, was beginning to look like a distinct possibility.

Well, the Department of Fate had other plans entirely. Hank Mancini called from London to ask me whether I would like to write the song for the new *Pink Panther* movie with him. Of course I would. There was no need for me to move, because he and Ginny would love to come down and spend a few days with Evie and myself in France.

I knew that Henry liked to work at a piano. There wasn't one in our villa, as I worked from portable keyboards on my desk when I was writing music and lyrics together. So I called the nearby Fondation Maeght, the glorious contemporary art gallery and museum in the hills above Saint-Paul de Vence, and asked Jean-Louis Prat, the curator, whom I had recently met, whether there was a piano at the Fondation that Hank and I could use for two or three days. Jean-Louis was most accommodating. 'Yes, of course. There's a Steinway concert grand in the artist's villa. You can use that. I'll leave the keys to the villa for you at the reception office. But you can't have it 'til the day after tomorrow, as Miró is staying there. He's hanging his new exhibition.'

So exit The Great Miró and enter Mancini and The Great Leslie. The artist's villa was set cosily in a quiet corner of the Fondation's extensive grounds, and it had one unique feature — it contained hundreds of millions of dollars' worth of art. The walls were festooned with Picassos, Mirós and Chagalls. I found a further half-dozen large, unframed Chagall oils stacked against the wall behind a sofa. There were Kandinskys and Klees in the kitchen, and above the full Steinway concert grand in the middle of the living room, where Henry was about to compose his latest *Pink Panther* melody, hung a great red-and-black Calder mobile, on which the maestro clunked his head every time he stood up at the piano. We worked on the song for a couple of hours, then Henry got up from the piano and looked around the room at the staggering array of art works. He quietly closed the piano lid. 'Screw the song,' he said. 'Let's get some of this stuff into the car!'

Newberg and I were honoured with a tribute by the Beverly Hills Hadassah at the Hollywood Palace Theater on Sunset Boulevard, an all-star charity concert gala of our music. And 'all-star' was, in this instance, in no way an overstatement. With the ever-reliable Ian Fraser conducting a terrific orchestra of his choosing, out there singing and speaking our praises was as stellar a line-up of big-name performers and actors as I had ever seen. Among them were Burt Bacharach, Tony Bennett, Richard Chamberlain, Sammy, Steve Lawrence and Eydie Gorme, Robert Goulet, David Hemmings, Florence Henderson, Gene Kelly, Hank Mancini, Roger Moore, David Niven, Juliet Prowse, Lou Rawls, Peter Sellers, Paul Williams and a host more.

The producer of the concert, Franklin Levy, began the evening by announcing, 'Ladies and gentlemen, Mr Bricusse and Mr Newley!' and out on to the stage, wearing black tie and to wild applause, marched Adam Bricusse, aged 12, and Sacha Newley, aged ten. It was a touching moment, and the prelude to a knockout concert, by which Newberg and I were immensely flattered.

As though I didn't have enough on my mind, Sammy and Liza came up with a great idea for Christmas and New Year. We would all spend Christmas together in Florida, and Sammy and Liza would do a New Year's Eve gig at the Hollywood Florida Diplomat Hotel, the benign domain of Irv and Marge Cowan, the amiable innkeepers and good friends of all concerned. The show was to be 45 minutes of Sammy followed by 45 minutes of Liza followed by 30 minutes of the two of them together, doing medleys, parodies of one another's songs and special material, all of which I would write for them. And so it came to pass.

It was a memorable ten days of boats and parties and restaurants and friends, especially because it was one of those rare times when neither Sammy nor Liza was working, except for our rehearsals, which you could hardly call work. We spent most of the time on the floor, helpless with laughter.

The big night was all you would expect it to be. Sammy and Liza were both predictably sensational, at the top of their game, and around 3.30am we wound up in Sammy's suite, Sam, his delicious wife Altovise, Liza, photographer Milton Greene and his wife Amy, musical director Ian Fraser, Evie and myself. Sleep was the furthest thing from anybody's mind, so what to do? Sammy solved the problem. 'I got it!' he shouted. 'We'll do the show again!'

And do it they did – in the middle of Sammy's living room. Every last note, all two hours of it, with Fraser playing the piano and an audience of four, with all the verve and magic that had wiped out 1,500 people just a couple of hours before. And, if I had to take an oath, I'd swear the second show was marginally better than the first.

When it was all over, and the others went off to bed, Sammy, Liza, Evie and I stood out on the penthouse terrace, our arms around each other, as hordes of hungry, mewing seagulls wheeled around our heads, watching the sun rise up out of the Atlantic Ocean to herald the start of the first day of another year, a perfect end to a never-to-be-forgotten night.

Sammy's terrific revival of *Stop the World* began rehearsals. He revelled in the role of Littlechap, was word perfect on the book on day one and, of course, knew all the songs, since he'd been singing most of them for the past 17 years. The discipline and perfectionism that Sammy exuded infiltrated the entire cast, so that they were instilled with a sense of purpose, knowing they dare not let Sammy down. They all worked hard, but no one as hard as Sammy did. He treated every hour of every rehearsal as though it were the first night.

The main difference between Newley's original London and Broadway production and this one was that Newley's language of mime was replaced by Sammy's language, the language of tap. 'Gonna Build a Mountain' was about to become a dynamite, crash-bang show-stopper. The huge energy of the tap-dancing lifted the show to another level of impact. The piece lacked the poetry of Newley's version, but compensated for that with its higher horsepower. The set designs by Santo Loquasto were big, multi-coloured and sculptured standing pieces that looked as though they had been created by Arpel. Ian Fraser oversaw the musical side of the production, with sensational Billy Byers orchestrations, and the only questionable element in the entire production was Sammy's insistence that the orchestra be conducted by George Rhodes, his eternal nightclub conductor. Dear old George, a big, gentle, affable bear of a man, was fine when conducting 'The Birth of the Blues' or 'The Lady Is a Tramp', which he had done 45,000 times, but he had never been within a day's horse-ride of the intricate, high-tempoed, multi-rhythmed orchestral pieces being served up by Fraser and Byers, that ran like throbbing veins through the score of *Stop the World*. George was both ill at ease and out of his depth, and Fraser was the first to spot the potential danger this posed to the show. If there were to be a problem, we wouldn't confront it head-on until we started playing in the old Fox Theater down in San Diego.

It all went like a dream. We got to San Diego. Apart from George Rhodes fumbling around a bit in the pit, it was near perfect, and the musicians in the band were so good they didn't need a conductor, especially George. But Ian Fraser started growling a lot, like a lion with no supper. The opening night was a smash, and our week there was a sell-out.

And then we moved back up to LA for our official pre-Broadway opening at the Shubert Theater in Century City. And the big blow-up I knew was coming sooner or later came sooner, at the final dress rehearsal. Fearless Fraser fired George Rhodes on the spot. Hilly was aghast. 'You can't *do* that, Fraser,' he said firmly.

'I've *done* it, Hilly!' replied Fraser, equally firmly.

'What will Sammy say?' wailed Hilly.

Fraser was unfazed. 'I don't care. What he ought to say is "Thank you". My responsibility to this show is to make it Broadway standard. It can never be that with George Rhodes in the pit. Sammy knows that, but he hasn't got the guts to tell him. So *I* told him. George Rhodes couldn't conduct the Boy Scout Band, and Sammy has to face up to it.'

'Sammy will walk,' threatened Hilly.

'Let him walk,' said Ian. 'Better he walks now than he lets the show fall to pieces on Broadway with a conductor who can't even keep three-quarter time!'

'Let me handle this,' said Hilly. 'Let me handle this' was another gem from Hilly's collection of pet sayings, along with 'I hear you loud and clear', 'I'm ahead of you', 'I've got the picture' and 'That could've been me talking!' So we let Hilly handle this.

'Sammy will go ballistic,' I said to Hilly.

'Brickman, I'm ahead of you,' he replied.

'This is dangerous,' I added ominously.

'I hear you loud and clear,' said Hilly. 'I've got the picture. That could have been *me* talking!' (When he used two of them back to back, it meant he was concerned, and three in a row, that he was cornered.)

'But what if Sammy walks?'

Hilly smiled the inscrutable smile. 'We'll double-cross that bridge when we come to it!'

Sammy, predictably, went ballistic. George was his buddy and his big brother and all that stuff, but to no avail. Fraser won the fight, and put himself in the pit to conduct the first night. It was immediately a different show, and opened to a roaring standing ovation and rave reviews. Sammy knew he couldn't argue with that. The *Los Angeles Times* critic, Dan Sullivan, praised everything in sight, including the new book for the show, where, he shrewdly observed, 'American hands have clearly been at work', where, of course, none had. Newberg and I accepted this unintended compliment gratefully, as proof of our bilingualism.

We were scheduled to play the Shubert for three weeks. The theatre manager came to see us in Sammy's dressing room the next evening, and said that the box office was such that we could stay there for a year, and Sammy for the first and perhaps only time in his life could have lived at home, less than ten minutes away. But the schedule was set, and it was on to Chicago and New York. But the show was a smash, bigger than the original. It was a stunning personal triumph for Sammy, albeit a short-lived one. After another sell-out run in Chicago, *Sammy Stops the World* played a big box-office summer season at the State Theater of New York's Lincoln Center, and Sammy then left the show, only because his eternally precarious finances caused his managers, agents, staff and hangers-on to gang up on their genius talent and advise him to get his ass back to Las Vegas, where the *really* big bucks were. Playing to sell-out audiences on Broadway was a luxury Sammy Davis Jr couldn't afford. If he could, he could have stayed on Broadway another year.

John Williams called from Pinewood Studios in London. He had a problem. He was scoring Dick Donner's big-budget film of *Superman*, and it was sensational, he said. He had written a major love theme for the picture, and was embarrassed to tell me that two or three people had tried to put a lyric to it, but nothing seemed to work. They were running out of time. The film was due to open in a month. Could I fly in and meet with him and Donner, see the film and try to help?

Not overly flattered to be what turned out to be the fourth choice for this little chore, it did have the upside of giving me the chance to write an 'I'll show 'em' lyric. I duly flew up to London the next morning, and John and Donner showed me the film, which was indeed stunning. And there, all through the fabulous flying sequence where Superman carries Lois Lane up and over

Metropolis and flies her around the Statue of Liberty, was this most glorious melody, one of the greatest John has ever composed. As the music was already scored and immovably married to the finished picture, I asked Dick if I could have a videotape of that sequence, to go away and work with on my own, so that, whatever the voice-over lyric was going to be, I could make it relate to their exchanged glances, like unspoken dialogue. The lyric, which would eventually, i.e. the next week, be recorded by an as yet unnamed star female vocalist, clearly had to be about whatever was going on in Lois's understandably confused mind during this unusual moment in her life.

I must have watched that five-minute film clip for longer than all the cherished MGM musicals of my childhood put together. I was besotted by John's beautiful melody and, over the next two or three days, the lyric gradually started to come together. It was called 'Can You Read My Mind?' and, although I say it myself, it married both John's music and Dick Donner's amazing visuals most effectively, and was received by all and sundry, meaning Donner and Williams, with ecstasy and acclaim. It was immediately whisked across to America and, before I could blink, I was informed that the delightful and talented Miss Toni Tennille, of the Captain and Tennille, had made a fantastic recording of it, and that John and I had at the very least an Oscar nomination locked up. I smiled knowingly and said nothing, casting my mind back to Liza and 'New York, New York'.

I prepared to return to France. An hour before I left, John called again and said, 'Brickman, we're all taking the second Concorde to New York today, and you can come with us if you want to, except that I don't want to put you to all that trouble for nothing. It's just that Dick has this crazy idea that he wants to try out. It won't work, but I've agreed to spend Sunday morning in a studio with him and Margot Kidder, with *her* trying to do the voice-over. She can't sing a note, and the whole thing is a complete waste of time, but there it is.'

I said I was more than willing to go with them, if I could be of any help, but John, the eternal gent, said to trust him and leave it to him to ensure that Donner's crazy idea did not prevail, which would become self-evident as soon as they tried it. So off they all went, the weekend passed peacefully, with no alarms and excursions, and I went back to the South of France and got on with my life, and thought no more about it.

A month or so later, back in Los Angeles, Evie and I were invited to the world première of *Superman*. Jack Haley Jr, one of Donner's oldest chums, came to collect us with another old chum, Debbie Reynolds, Jack and Liza having by now gone their separate ways, alas. I was quite excited about the première, since I was reasonably optimistic that 'Can You Read My Mind?', because of its powerful visual support, could achieve the same sort of impact that Shirley Bassey had achieved 15 years before with 'Goldfinger', especially given that the *Superman* song was by no means as eccentric in content as the *Bond* song.

The magic moment arrived when Superman lifted Lois Lane up off the large, floral terrace of her Metropolis apartment. I remember wondering what kind of salaries the *Daily Planet* paid its lady newspaper reporters, that Lois should have such sumptuous uptown digs. Superman then swirled her up and away across the city for their enchanted aerial circuit of the Statue of Liberty. John's great theme established itself ever more strongly and kept them aloft until they arrived there and at the start of the vocal simultaneously. I knew it frame by frame. I waited for Toni Tennille's golden vocal chords to hit the opening title line of the song... and nothing happened. I sat bolt upright in my seat and glared along the row at John Williams, who was four or five places away. About a bar-and-a-half late, to my total horror, I heard the whining, toneless, flat *speaking* voice of Margot Kidder declaim the line 'Can you read my mind?' as though she were lodging a complaint. I sat transfixed as her far-from-dulcet Canadian tones, as far removed from lyricism as Vancouver is from Prince Edward Island, droned endlessly on through what now seemed the interminable song, slowly annihilating it as she went, never once in time with the music, always dragging behind it, and therefore never once synching my lyric to the visuals, which I had gone to such painstaking lengths to achieve.

I watched the rest of the movie in abject misery. At the end, I silently confronted John. He was beyond embarrassed, flustered for the only time in all the years I have known him, and he mumbled some asinine remark about there still being time to change things. I shook my head. 'Mistake, John. You should have let me come to New York with you and Dick. You know as well as I do that Donner is about as musical as John Wayne.' Shattered, I didn't stay for the rest of the celebrations.

Two or three months after the film opened to great worldwide success, Maureen McGovern gave us the consolation prize of a Top Twenty recording of 'Can You Read My Mind?' but it was unfortunately far too little far too late. I love Dick Donner and I love John Williams, but on that nightmare occasion they both came perilously close to losing a significant percentage of my high regard.

I surveyed the bleak landscape of what was left of my career. Not a pretty sight, until the phone rang the next morning and Hank Mancini asked me to collaborate with him on the song score of Blake Edwards's next picture, an MGM musical called *Victor/Victoria*, starring Julie Andrews.

5th Key Change

6th Key: F Augmented

Leo Fuchs called me. We had never met, although I knew he was a film producer, because his name had remained indelibly printed on my brain since that long-ago spring day in Rome when Evie and I were strolling through the centre of the city and I saw a giant movie poster, several storeys high, which announced Shirley MacLaine and Michael Caine in *Gambit*, directed by Ronald Neame and produced by Leo 'Fucks', in huge and embarrassing black letters, for all the world to see and snigger at.

Leo had a neat little idea for a film, made up of four one-Act comedies – one English, one French, one Italian and one American – each about 30 minutes in length, about illicit weekends, with the overall title of *Sunday Lovers*. Four screenplays, four stars, four directors, and so on. I was invited to write the English one and, to Leo's delight, persuaded Bryan Forbes and Roger Moore to come on board with me as director and star. We tried to recruit Mike Caine, too, but Mike was in Hungary shooting a John Huston picture called *Escape to Victory*, much to Leo's relief, as I suspect his budget was too fragile in any case to support both Roger and Mike. We ended up in style with

Denholm Elliott and Lynn Redgrave as Roger's elegant co-stars.

Leo was based in Paris at the time, so the project happily involved our spending lots of time at the Georges Cinq Hotel, especially as Leo also wanted me to adapt the French screenplay into English. My screenplay was called *An Englishman's Home*, in which Roger played a wealthy tycoon's chauffeur who takes turns with the butler playing lord of the manor at the boss's country castle whenever the boss Concordes away to New York for the weekend. This weekend is Roger's turn, and he ends up playing increasingly complicated musical beds with the American air stewardess he picks up at Heathrow and the tycoon's lady neighbour, who fancies him. The film was shot in England and France.

Also in Paris while we were there was a fairly frantic Peter Sellers, shooting the last – and worst – film of his career, some lunatic comedy about Dr Fu Manchu, which was in deep trouble. He called us every day with his latest bulletin of dramas. Peter had also, of course, got married yet again, this time to an exceptionally young and pretty English would-be actress called Lynn Frederick, who was not a lot more than one-third of Peter's age.

Peter called early one evening, sounding totally demented. I don't know what the production set-up on his film was, but he was obviously in a position of total power, because he had just fired the producer, and clearly the lunatics were about to take over the asylum. Twenty-four hours later, they had. Peter called the next evening in an ebullient mood, announcing that all their problems were solved, and he had never been happier, because he had just had a blinding stroke of genius and made *Lynn* the producer at three o'clock that afternoon. It was now 6.30pm. In a confidential whisper, he added (verbatim quote), 'And I tell you, Brickman, she's the best fucking producer I've ever worked with!'

I don't know what happened to that film, whether indeed it ever saw the light of day, and I don't much care, because I was more concerned about what was happening to Peter. I only ever saw him once more in his life, when Evie and I had lunch with him and Lynn at Eden Roc at the Hotel du Cap in Antibes during the next Cannes Film Festival. He looked to be, and in fact was, at death's door. His face was elephant grey. His ravaged heart, that had suffered and survived so much, was finally packing up on him. Cruelly, and ironically, he was enjoying one of the greatest successes of his career at the time, for his brilliant performance as Chance the Gardener in Hal Ashby's stunning movie of Jerzy Kosinski's *Being There*, for which he received an Oscar nomination for Best Actor. He was hoping, in vain, alas, to win the Best Actor Award either in Cannes or in Hollywood, as the crowning achievement of his life's work, but both were to be denied him. As we were leaving the restaurant, he walked with me, put his arm round my shoulder and said, 'I just hope Lynn will be all right. Keep an eye on her for me, Brickman.' We embraced and parted company, we both knew for the last time.

Peter died a few weeks later, visiting London for a last reunion with the comedic pals of his youth – Spike Milligan, Harry Secombe and Michael Bentine, the immortal Goons. I saw Spike at dinner at Scott's Restaurant a few nights after the funeral, and he said to me, mournfully and memorably, 'And if *we* don't start seeing each other more often, we're only going to meet a couple of times more before it's one of *us*!' Ironically, that was the last thing he ever said to me. In the last 20 years of his life, by some quirk of fate, we never saw each another again.

Lynn, the widow Sellers, phoned me and asked me to advise her on a financial problem. Peter had left her $9 million, and she read in the newspapers that Peter's three children, Michael and Sarah with Ann Howe, and Victoria with Britt Ekland, didn't have any money. Crazy Peter had left them nothing. What should she do? My answer was simple and straightforward. 'I'm sure he meant to, but you know what he was like. Look, you're in your early twenties, and so are Michael and Sarah. Victoria's in her mid-teens. If you want to sleep at night and be a heroine, give them a million each, and keep six.'

She thanked me profusely for my words of wisdom, and never

gave any of them a penny. Instead, she enacted an even greater tragedy. This once exquisite girl moved into a major house in Beverly Hills and swiftly found her way on to an exclusive diet of booze, pills and drugs, ballooned into a grotesque caricature of herself, and squandered Sellers's inheritance, precipitating her own self-destruction and early death while still in her thirties. An unworthy memorial to Britain's second ever comedic screen genius, a great flawed diamond, whom I always have and always will rank right alongside the first one – Chaplin.

Evie and I had lunch with Rex Harrison and Alan Jay Lerner at Les Ambassadeurs. It was rare for either one of them to be in London nowadays, and almost unique for them to be in town at the same time. They had remained close friends over the years, and Alan was one of the few people that Rex truly liked and admired, including his (Rex's) wives.

Rex continued to be totally impossible. After his little dalliance with Gayle Hunnicutt, he had taken up with our backgammon-playing Princess Boop, alias Princess Mary Obolensky. 'Mary O', as she was also affectionately known by her many friends, was a tall, attractive, blonde puppy-dog of a girl, sweet and friendly and full of fun, and Rex treated her appallingly. When they travelled together, he would buy himself a first-class ticket and put Mary in economy. After tolerating a few months of this, Mary gave Rex an ultimatum. Either she sat up front with him, or he came back and sat with her. In the latter case, she would bring on board a picnic superior to anything served in first class. Rex took the bait and the cheaper option, and flew from London to Nice with her in economy one day. True to her word, Mary went to Fortnum and Mason's and bought a stunning picnic and two bottles of fine Burgundy that cost about the same as five first-class round trips. She served the picnic in high style on the flight, only to have Rex complain that the Puligny-Montrachet was corked, something that would never have happened if he'd been flying first class. He never flew economy again.

Another famous wine-and-air-related incident occurred when Rex was living in a house on Wilton Crescent in Belgravia, and gave a lunch for a small group of senior British Airways executives who had offered him a fantastic financial package to do a series of high-profile television network commercials for them, both in America and in Britain, in which he would be presented as the symbolic stylish traveller-cum-spokesman for the airline. The lunch and the wine were served, and Rex again complained about the wine, sending it back in his own house. He wasn't happy with the second bottle either, by which time he was in a towering rage, an easy transition for Rex, but a terrifying experience for the onlooking BA execs.

Over coffee, they presented him with the scripts of the first half-dozen commercials, for his approval. He glanced through them, then fixed the quaking executives with his best withering gaze and tore into them with the following tirade. 'How *dare* you! Do you think I'm going to speak this *shit*, just so that you can sell tickets for your fucking awful airline!?' Whereupon he threw them and the deal out of his house, and didn't realise 'til some time later that this wasn't a script conference, where he always gave everybody hell, and that thanks to his famous temper he had just tossed millions of dollars and free first-class travel for life out into the street, reinforcing the widely held view that he was his own worst enemy.

Alan Lerner had just emerged from his seventh divorce, but was already searching with some intensity for number eight, whom he would shortly find. Between them, he and Rex had 14 wives, and the pair of them, a drolly cynical double act, had Evie and me in near-hysterics as they wickedly reviewed their widely varied marital careers. The high point of this retrospective came when Alan could not remember the name of his Number Six. He had only been married to her for three weeks, so it was sort of understandable, since it transpired he knew almost everyone he'd ever met better than he knew Number Six.

When Alan died in the mid-1980s, he left behind him an unfinished musical of the old 1936 William Powell–Carole

Lombard movie *My Man Godfrey*. His producer and our mutual friend Alan Carr met with me to discuss whether I'd like to finish it. I declined for a perfectly straightforward and obvious reason. 'If it's a hit, Alan will get all the credit and, if it's a flop, I'll get all the blame.' Sadly, the show was never completed.

That summer, because Evie and I knew we would be constantly yo-yoing back and forth across the Atlantic between London, Los Angeles, Rome and New York, we arranged to rent our then villa to Paul and Linda McCartney and their three children, Mary, Stella and James. At the end of their happy stay, Paul left for me the stirring lyrics to his newly composed *Bricusse Marching Song*, which, if nothing else, finally made it clear how to pronounce my name – 'Brick-us'. We once had a live-in Spanish couple who, in four months of 'Brickhouse' and 'Barkus' and 'Brisseus' and 'Briscussi' and 'Bacchus', never pronounced our name the same way twice. The best one of all was when Carlos the houseman said to me one evening when I arrived home, 'Mr Breakfast, will you please call Mrs Biscuits!' I wanted to slap him like John Cleese slapped Manuel in *Fawlty Towers*, saying, 'He's from Barcelona, you know.'

A brief excerpt from the deathless McCartney masterpiece:

We are Bricusse –
What more do we need?
What more do we need?
What more do we need?
If you prick us,
We will bleed.
Occasionally
Someone may trick us,
But no one's managed
Yet to lick us –
For... (loud with feeling)
We are Bricusse –
What more do we need?
(etc. etc. etc.)

The film of *Victor/Victoria* was a joyous experience, one of those all-too-rare projects where everything feels right from day one. In my obviously biased view, it ranks as one of Blake Edwards's best films. Its overall stylistic togetherness was highly impressive, mainly because Blake directed his own flawless screenplay with such élan, in addition to eliciting a quartet of fine comedic performances from his wife, Julie Andrews, and Robert Preston, James Garner and Lesley Ann Warren. Thanks to Blake and Julie, the making of the film had one other huge, built-in advantage, that all too rare 'family feeling'. Hank, Blake, Julie and I had all been good friends with one another for close to 20 years, Blake and Hank for 30. They had a fabulous director–composer relationship. Henry had scored almost all of Blake's movies, an almost unique collaboration, matched only in my experience by that of John Williams and Steven Spielberg.

Henry's brilliant talents and dazzling musical accomplishments are well chronicled, and need no further embellishment from me. Less well chronicled, perhaps, are his prodigious sense of humour, his kindness and his gentleness. Blake Edwards rated him about as funny as Peter Sellers, and Blake is a world authority on Sellers, Mancini *and* humour. In fact, it was Blake's black sense of humour – he is not nicknamed 'Blackie' for nothing – that always caricatured Henry as a sort of Jack Benny 'meanest man in the world' type. Once, on Henry's 60th birthday, to make fun of him, Blake took full-page adverts in *Variety* and the *Hollywood Reporter*, in which he thanked Henry for the music to *Peter Gunn*, *Mister Lucky*, *Breakfast at Tiffany's*, *The Days of Wine and Roses*, *The Great Race*, *Darling Lili*, half a dozen *Pink Panthers*, *10*, *Victoria/Victoria* and 'lunch in the commissary at Universal on 23 February 1958'.

The writing of the songs was a pleasant and painless process. With a screenplay and a storyline that good, they just fell into place, because the characters were so beautifully drawn. And, of course, it did the songs no harm to have such a dazzling trio of performers as Julie Andrews, Robert Preston and Lesley Ann Warren to deliver them. It wasn't 'til about halfway through shooting that Blake remembered what a formidable song-and-dance talent Lesley Ann was. He immediately found an ingenious way to incorporate a major musical moment for her in the cinematic equivalent of the middle of Act Two. At the time, Hank and I were hundreds of miles apart. He got a call from Blake in England at dawn one morning, urgently requesting a big new song for Leslie Ann by that evening. Hank called me in Lake Tahoe and, over the phone, we got the title for the song, 'Chicago, Illinois', which is where Lesley Ann's character, Norma, would sing it in the story. Two hours later, Hank called me back with the melody. Two hours later, I called *him* back with the lyric. Blake woke up to the new song at dawn the next day. It was rehearsed, staged, scored and shot the same day.

The film opened brilliantly the following spring. The notices were among the best everyone concerned had ever received, with the acknowledged exception of Julie Andrews in *My Fair Lady*, *Mary Poppins* and *The Sound of Music*, which I have always called The Three That Don't Count. For the rest of us mere mortals, the enthusiastic-to-ecstatic reactions to the film were an injection of the Elixir of Life. I still recall the dream review by Vincent Canby in the *New York Times*. When notices are that good, the critics become intelligent, discerning pundits imbued with the wisdom and insight of the ages, as opposed to the crass, biased, ignorant, frustrated-writer cretins that they more usually are when they pan us.

Victor/Victoria won seven Oscar nominations in that vintage year of *Gandhi* and *ET*. For that one year, the Academy inexplicably changed the Music Branch rules, allowing Henry and myself to elect to be eligible *either* for Best Song *or* Best Score, but not both, as I had been in previous years for both *Doctor Dolittle* and *Scrooge*, when I was nominated in both categories. It was a tricky decision, as we felt we had two likely song nominations in 'Le Jazz Hot' and 'Crazy World'. We chose to go for Best Score, since it contained both those songs and other stuff we liked a lot. No one ever satisfactorily explained this eccentric

Academy ruling to us, though the charming then President of the Academy, Richard Kahn, did attempt to when Hank and I bumped into him at a friend's dinner party one night. We listened politely, and decided that neither he nor the Academy quite understood the new ruling themselves. The following year, they changed it all back again to the way it was before, enabling Michael Legrand and Marilyn and Alan Bergman to receive *three* nominations for their lovely score of *Yentl*, one for Best Score, which they won, and two for Best Song, which they didn't. Hank and I reckoned all that back-and-forthing probably cost us a Best Song nomination. But the rules are the rules, even when they don't make too much sense.

Alarmingly, it was *15* years since I had won for *Doctor Dolittle* and 20 since Hank had last won for *The Days of Wine and Roses*. Like all nominees, we coolly tried to pretend it didn't really matter, that it was honour enough to be nominated, and all that other hypocritical horseshit. Of course it mattered. There is no win, place or show at the Oscars, no gold, silver or bronze, no coming in second. You win or you lose, and four out of five of you lose, as we all well knew from experience. It is pretty merciless, but that's the way it is.

On Awards night, Evie and I travelled with Hank and Ginny Mancini to the large and elegant Dorothy Chandler Pavilion at the LA Music Center downtown. And, with the red carpets and the cheering crowds and the TV crews and the 1,000 flashing cameras, and Hollywood movie stars as thick on the ground as autumn chestnuts, and all the other hoopla and razzamatazz, it really is the greatest show in Tinseltown, as good a definition of glamour as lunch at 21 with Joan Crawford. The good news was that we knew we would be put out of our misery early, because the music score awards were the second or third event of the evening. The two presenters were both friends of ours, Cher and Placido Domingo, which we chose to interpret as a good omen. They were probably equally good friends with all the other nominees, too. The agonising moment came when Placido took about ten minutes to open the envelope and, in the best tenor voice in the world, he sang out the seven most beautiful words of his career – '*Victor/Victoria...* Henry Mancini and Leslie Bricusse.'

I kissed and hugged Evie, and Hank and I pranced up on to the stage like a pair of spring lambs to hug Cher and Placido, who had just that moment became our two best friends in the whole wide world. The gold statuettes are surprisingly heavy and, in addition to their undisputed prestige value, would make an extremely handy weapon in times of war. For instance OSAMA BIN LADEN KILLED BY BEST SUPPORTING ACTRESS OSCAR would make a very tasty headline.

Hank spoke first, then me. I remember calling him 'Henry/Henrietta' and getting an unexpectedly big laugh, and ending on 'Evie, for *you!*' with my Oscar thrust skywards. That moment is everything they say it is and, having missed being there for my first one, when Sammy Davis received my statuette from La Streisand and went off around the world with it, I was overwhelmingly grateful for this opportunity finally to experience standing up there myself with the great Mancini and marching off with the little golden man.

It turned into an ever more enchanted evening for me and my friends as the ceremony progressed. It was like a private party for people I loved. The show's hosts were Liza Minnelli and Dudley Moore. Two minutes after Hank and I won, John Williams won for *ET*, and the three of us – Hank, John and I – embraced and war-danced in a moment of unbecoming frivolity amid the staggeringly large and impressive world press set-up backstage. That done, Hank and I repaired to the bar and allowed the show to continue without us as we consumed two of the biggest restorative cocktails in Oscar history.

Earlier, when Placido had called our names and I was heading for the stage, I heard a voice cry out 'Brickman!' I looked round and there on the front row was Dickie Attenborough. 'Bunter!' I cried back. He gave me a quick hug and a 'Well done!' As I ran to catch up with Hank, I called back to him, '*Two* for you!' And two it was.

He twice made the special walk up on to that great stage, to win Best Director and Best Picture for his epic work on *Gandhi*.

All the winners had to assemble on stage at the end of the show, so we were ushered back there early in readiness. I spent the last 20 minutes watching the stage manager's TV monitor with Mickey Rooney, who had just received an honorary Lifetime Achievement Oscar for his long and celebrated career. Watching Liza on the TV screen, he started reminiscing about how he had known Liza since she was a tiny baby, and his golden days at MGM with Liza's mother, Judy Garland. And suddenly it struck me. The Oscar I had just won and was holding in my hand was for an *MGM* musical! And time would prove it to be the last one ever to be made. My mind flashed back to when I was 14 years old, going to the Empire Theatre, Leicester Square, in London, on my first escapist MGM ecstasies. The last MGM musical... I felt I had just caught the last bus home.

My Italian is by no means good enough to determine whether *Aggiungi un Posto a Tavola* is a catchy title in its native tongue. My personal view is that it's a bit of a mouthful in any language and, although I managed to write an English lyric entitled 'Come Join Us at the Table' to fit Armando Trovaioli's opening title music, it certainly didn't feel like a West End show title. After much passionate discussion, we settled on *Beyond the Rainbow* as the London title.

A bigger problem lay ahead. Johnny Dorelli, the show's star, while loved and adored in Rome, was totally unknown in England and, if all the London-based Johnny Dorelli fans each bought two tickets, we would probably sell four tickets. Additionally, Johnny spoke limited English, by which I mean not a hell of a lot better than my Italian. These two factors combined to create the problem, because the rest of the show was totally recast with British actors, singers and dancers, leaving Johnny marooned, *ET*-like, on a different planet. Natural, easy charm in one's own native tongue is more difficult than words to translate into a strange new language. Listening to Johnny read the script in English instantly set the alarm bells ringing in my head. If he had been Maurice Chevalier, he might have got away with it, but he had never performed in England or in English before, and nobody knew who he was.

Amazingly, nobody but myself seemed worried about it. Pietro Garinei and Harry Bernsen, the respective Italian and American producers, somehow believed that Johnny was going to take London by storm. The English producers, Harold Fielding and Bernard Delfont, raised no red flags. They were all prepared to believe that what had happened in Rome in Italian was going to happen again in London in English, with a man who barely *spoke* English.

I pointed out that to take London by storm you needed to be Frank Sinatra or Sammy Davis or Danny Kaye or Liza Minnelli. Johnny, for all his charm, was certainly none of those. Then I had a brainwave – Tommy Steele. Not only had Tommy been an enduring top-of-the-line song-and-dance star in England for close to a quarter-of-a-century, he had also starred in Broadway and Hollywood musicals and, most of all, he was perfect casting for the role. *And* he was box office. Furthermore, our lead London producer, Harold Fielding, had produced most of Tommy's hit shows.

I talked to Tommy. He was interested. Now it all made sense. Big hit Rome musical comes to London. Big London star plays lead and makes big hit London musical. Simple. Logical. You would think. But no. It transpired that the object of the whole exercise in bringing the show to London in the first place was as much to make Johnny Dorelli a star as to make the show a hit. Nobody ever told me that when I signed on. In my view, it was never on the cards that it could happen. And it didn't.

The show opened at the Adelphi Theatre in the Strand. It was an amiable production that received amiable notices, and the critics agreed that Johnny Dorelli was amiable. It ran for eight or nine amiable months. The audiences who saw the show liked it, but not enough to command their friends and families to beat a path to the Adelphi to buy tickets. One or two people asked me why the priest in the story was Italian. I said I had always wondered that myself. Had Tommy Steele played it, the show might yet be running.

Standing at the back of the stalls one evening with Pietro Garinei and Harry Bernsen, I cynically observed that after this it might be a shrewd move to put Gina Lollobrigida into *Evita*. They both thought that was a great idea, too. I headed for the bar.

More than a decade later, I was in Rome for a couple of days, and I passed the Teatro Sistina. What was playing? A revival of Johnny Dorelli in *Aggiungi un Posto a Tavola*. And you couldn't get a ticket. It was a total sell-out.

It is splendidly philosophical, when disaster smites your beloved musical project into the dust, to pretend to shrug it off and smile bravely through your tears and say, 'Well, I'll never make *that* mistake again!' The simple truth is that you don't have to. There are plenty more brand-new mistakes, lined up and waiting for you, that you haven't yet made, but are surely going to. It is in-bred in the nature of the musical. There have never been as many musicals produced in the history of the world, and there never will be, as there have been and will be mistakes, big, fat, daft, obvious mistakes made in putting them on.

Let's start out with the oft-quoted and depressing statistic that only one musical out of every hundred that are written ever sees the light of a production day and, of those that do, only one in eight achieves any kind of success. That's an 800–1 shot going in, odds you would absolutely shun at the racetrack, yes? And while it only takes two or three minutes to run a horserace, it takes two or three *years*, and then only if you are *lucky*, to put on a musical. So multiply 800 by the number of minutes in a year (60 by 24 by 365) and you will conclude that writing and putting on a musical is hard-pressed to qualify under the category of 'a sure thing'. Simply put, the above analysis means that the average writer of a musical, in good health, if he keeps going and doesn't start slacking off, is looking at having a hit show somewhere between every 1,600 and 2,400 years. Hardly enough, you might say, to have you come leaping out of bed every morning, like Roy Scheider in *All That Jazz*, yelling 'It's showtime, folks!'

To tell the full horror story of *Harvey – The Musical* would require a volume all its own. Suffice to say that my association with Michael McAloney, the drunken Irishman who had the rights, surpassed Mary Shelley and Bram Stoker's worst nightmares. Henry Mancini read my book and lyrics, agreed to write the score with me, then met McAloney for 30 minutes and walked. Robert Preston read my book and lyrics, agreed to play the starring role of Elwood P Down, then met McAloney for *20* minutes and walked. This should have sent some kind of signal to me, but did it? Yes, it did, but I chose to ignore it, and soldiered on alone, brave but stupid, convinced that the piece was bigger than its problems. Wrong.

Behind my back, against the contract, the dire McAloney now signed a *third* Irish drunk, the once-wonderful but now recovering alcoholic Donald O'Connor, to play Elwood. O'Connor would, in time, regain some of his long-lost *Singin' in the Rain* brilliance, but not here, not now. This was his lowest ebb. He had no energy, no spark. He would rehearse reluctantly, minimally each day. He announced that he would create his own choreography, which turned out to be one 15-second, half-assed soft shoe shuffle midway through Act One, better left out, since it only served to underline the tragedy of his decline.

Once the show opened, he would not rehearse at all. If asked to, he would not be available for that evening's performance. McAloney, safely installed at all times behind a protective haze of alcohol, contributed nothing. The only talent on display was the formidable English musical star Patricia Routledge, playing Elwood's equally formidable sister Veta, stealing and stopping the show at every turn.

A word on the show's design. The sets were built to last. Had a nuclear device been detonated in the Toronto area, where we were playing, they would have been the one thing left standing when the radioactive dust cleared. When Pat Routledge made her Act Two entrance in a hideous green dress with vivid orange flowers, she was required to sit on a sofa covered in the same fabric.

Despite all this, the show played to capacity business throughout its season at the Royal Alexandra Theatre in Toronto, and the Nederlander Organisation, in the person of Arthur Rubin, came up there to discuss a national tour which, if successful, would lead on to Broadway. One condition – get rid of the drunken Irishman. Unfortunately, unlike Harvey, the drunken Irishman was neither invisible nor a rabbit. He refused to disappear, which meant that the show had to.

Mary Chase's Pulitzer Prize-winning little masterpiece remains to this day the fifth longest-running play in Broadway history. Mary Chase is dead. Michael McAloney is dead. I still believe *Harvey* would make a terrific musical.

When we were in California at the same time, we and the Michael Caines took turns to give alternate Sunday lunches for displaced Brits, actors, directors, producers, performers and pals who were working out there, but didn't know the territory. Anything up to 20, 30 and occasionally more refugees who heard about these impromptu events would turn out for them. This generated an unlikely mix of people, especially one Sunday, when it was Evie's and my turn to entertain, and about a dozen people turned up. They were all men. Evie was the only female present. And I realised as I looked around the room that virtually the entire quota of leading men in the British film industry was sitting around the place – Sean Connery, Albert Finney, Richard Harris, Peter O'Toole, Michael Caine, David Warner, Malcolm MacDowall, Roger Moore, Timothy Dalton, Oliver Reed, David Hemmings and Dudley Moore. Had a bomb gone off in that room, Benny

Hill would have become England's biggest movie star. Only when it was all over and they had gone away did it occur to us that we had omitted to record this historical event with a camera. To Evie's subsequent horror and fury, not one single photograph of her and 'The Boys' exists from that famous day.

Virtually the same thing had happened in reverse a few years before. We had a party for about 40 people at that glamorous time in Hollywood. Looking around the room, I realised that every girl present, about 20 of them, was a '10' – Joan Collins, Natalie Wood, Stella Stevens, Evie, Sharon Tate, Mia Farrow, Raquel Welch, Yvette Mimieux, Gayle Hunnicutt, Alana Hamilton, Tina Louise, Jill St John, Stefanie Powers, Samantha Eggar, and on and on, each more gorgeous than the next. Again, insanely, we took no photographs. It had to be a pretty upmarket gathering when Raquel Welch was possibly the plainest gal in the room.

Jackie Collins, Joan's spectacular baby sister, has known Evie even longer than Joan has known Evie, since they were teenagers together. And having grown up and lived in Joan's impossibly glamorous shadow when they were both young actresses, it was an enthralling process for us to observe Jackie eventually emerge from her chrysalis and become a full-blown literary butterfly. I remember the moment at dinner one night in London in the late 1960s when she whispered confidentially in my ear, 'I'm writing a book.'

That's not an easy line to react to. What made it easy was her next line. 'It's going to be called *The World Is Full Of Married Men*.' I knew right then and there she was already on her way. With a title like that, how could she fail? It was an anagram of Success. And so it came to pass. From that day forward, she pumped out the bestsellers at the rate of about one every 18 months for the next decade, when a couple of Jackie-written, big-hit, pot-boiler movies indelicately titled *The Bitch* and *The Stud* helped salvage Sister Dearest's career from a slump shortly before her finest hour as Alexis Carrington in her worldwide hit TV series *Dynasty*.

Today, Jackie has over 20 blockbuster novels to her credit and has sold more than 400 million books worldwide.

The sisters Collins are a phenomenon. Evie and I have always loved them both equally. Evie is the best friend of both, a high-wire act of consummate skill, requiring considerable diplomatic capabilities with which Evie is happily endowed to a lavish degree, which comes in very handy during those times when the sibling rivalry gets a little overheated, which it has been known to do from time to time over the years.

Jackie is the more sane and sensible of the two sisters, down-to-earth and grounded, a trusty Libra versus Joan's flamboyant Gemini. Both air signs, both ambitious high achievers and unspoken rivals, yet different as chalk and cheese, and happily highly compatible with Evie and myself, who both carry the friendly banner of Aquarius, the third air sign. Both sisters are also as competitive as gladiators. Both are born winners, huge personalities, bright as buttons, loyal to their friends and laden with a bounteous assortment of charms which attract people to each of them in droves, including the great and the near-great. And a highly attractive aura of challenge and daring perennially and provocatively surrounds the pair of them, on both a professional and personal level, at all times.

Jackie introduced the comparatively rare Hollywood pursuit of board games. Chez Joan, it would be poker or Scrabble. I have been playing cut-throat Scrabble with that lady on and off for four full decades. As in life, she is tough to beat. She made a serious study of every obscure two- and three-letter word in the English language and she can suddenly knock you sideways with 50 or 60 totally unexpected points, when you think you are winning comfortably, by completing fiendishly complex little paved blocks of two- and three-letter words that you didn't know existed and are totally enraged to discover actually do, and that Joan is the first person to have found any use for them for probably 200 years.

Chez Jackie, it was Trivial Pursuit. High-powered, take-it-seriously Trivial Pursuit, with hardened, seasoned players like Sean Connery, Michael Caine, Tony Danza and David Niven Jr locked in mortal combat, ego and pride on the line in every bitterly fought game. The most diabolical example of gamesmanship it has ever been my shame to witness occurred when Mike Caine returned from London and gifted the inner circle of the JCBHTPP (Jackie Collins Beverly Hills Trivial Pursuit Players) with smart-looking, new Trivial Pursuit sets that he had brought over specially for them all the way from Harrods.

The evil motive behind the apparently generous gesture quickly became clear to me. All the games previously played at Jackie's were so knife-edge competitive that Mike had found a truly cunning way to negotiate a telling edge in his favour, along the well-established lines of a Las Vegas casino. The Harrods' Trivial Pursuit sets were of course English versions of the game, so that some of the sports questions were more English than their American counterpart sets, which tipped the odds that vital hair's breadth that is the difference between winning and losing in the diabolical Caine's favour. For what diamond-dripping Beverly Hills matron has a chance in hell of answering a question like 'Which team beat Huddersfield Town to win the FA Cup in 1920-such-and-such and by what score?'

For 15 magical years, Evie and I shared many an idyllic summer day with David Niven at Lo Scoglietto, the most exquisite spot in the entire South of France. I would steer *Evie* the Riva neatly into Lo Scoglietto's little port, where Niv and the trusty white-coated Franco would be waiting, with our first 'beaker' already poured. The wine and the conversation and the laughter would flow, and mutual old friends like Johnny and Mary Mills, and Greg and Véronique Peck, and James and April Clavell would make up the small lunch parties either at the far end of the peninsula garden by the pool or on the big main terrace of the house, looking across the bay to 'La Réserve' at Beaulieu and the entire glorious coast down past Eze, Cap d'Ail and Monaco to

Italy. Sometimes, Evie and I would be invited early, and Niv would read us the latest pages he had written for his books, *The Moon's a Balloon*, *Bring on the Empty Horses* and *Go Away Slowly, Come Back Quickly*. He modestly pooh-poohed his phenomenally successful writing career as 'a bit of luck, chum', but the same quixotic sense of humour that kept us in stitches over lunch translated smoothly, seamlessly and *très, très* profitably on to those golden pages. He was always amused and delighted whenever a book appeared in a foreign language. One day, he greeted our arrival at his house with the words, 'Guess what the German for *The Moon's a Balloon* is...' And he held up the advance copy of the German edition. The title filled the entire front cover, reading *Vielleicht Ist Der Mond Nur Ein Luftballon*, literally translated as *Perhaps Is the Moon Only an Air-Balloon*, a heavy-handed Teutonic indication that the contents were likely to be less than side-splitting.

Niven's adopted land of Switzerland never saw quite as much of him as did the South of France. He lived in the canton of Vaud. Swiss taxes are famously low, but they do not exist at all for English people in the canton of Vaud, since legend and the Swiss tax man have it that in the early 19th century the canton expressed its gratitude for the sterling medical and charitable work of a group of English nuns and nurses by proclaiming that, henceforth, any English folk choosing to live there could do so free of tax. The shrewd Scot Niven was not one to deny himself the patent advantages of such a felicitous arrangement, and he unfailingly answered the call of the Swiss Alps during the skiing season, and invariably spent his birthday there every first of March, St David's Day.

Evie and I memorably shared his 70th birthday lunch with him at the mile-high Eagle Club above Gstaad. Niv confided in me one day that he had once received a slightly disturbing letter from the French tax authorities concerning the considerable amount of time he seemed to be spending in Saint-Jean Cap Ferrat, as much as seven and eight months a year, and would he care to explain himself? Niven considered the problem, consulted with his Swiss advisers, and won the day with a brilliant ploy. He explained himself by having his Swiss tax advisers write an eight-page response to the French tax authorities in the impenetrable Schwitzer-Deutsch dialect. He never heard from the French tax authorities again.

Whenever we were in London at the same time, we would meet for lunch or dinner at Scott's, always at Table 26, or the Connaught Hotel, where Niv always stayed. And one fine Monday in late June, he came over to have a picnic lunch with us and watch the first day of Wimbledon on TV. He arrived early, and went to talk to Evie in the kitchen, where she was preparing lunch. Then they both came into the living room and broke the appalling news. Niv had just come from Harley Street, where his doctor and specialist had advised him that he had contracted the dreaded motor neurone disease, or Lou Gehrig's disease, as it is known in the United States, for which there is no cure. And, over the next three years, we shared the agony of witnessing this precious and courageous man's slow decline. His bravery throughout was exemplary. His humour never once deserted him, although it must have been devastating for him slowly to lose the use of that wonderful voice, and other faculties.

The last time we saw him, we went to Lo Scoglietto for what we knew would be our final visit. He gallantly struggled to be a vestige of his former debonair self. Though he could barely speak, and was difficult to understand, he slowly told this story against himself about his condition. He had just returned from his final visit to his London doctors. There was nothing more they could do. As he was leaving the Connaught, also for the last time, he heard a cheerful voice hailing him. 'David! David!' And up to him came a friend from the far distant past, whom he had not seen for decades. 'How are you, David?'

David slowly and painfully replied, 'Not well. Motor neurone.'

The friend slapped him on the back and said, 'Splendid! And *I've* got a new Mercedes!'

As we left, David accompanied us to the entrance of the house. As we drove away, he raised his arm in a final gallant wave of salute and farewell to a close and loving friendship that Evie and I will treasure 'til our dying day.

Evie and I spent that Christmas in Gstaad, staying with Blake Edwards and Julie Andrews at their magnificent Chalet Fleur de Lys. The day after Christmas, I took Evie on a sentimental journey to a famous fondue restaurant called Le Cerf in the nearby town of Rougemont, halfway between Gstaad and Château d'Oex, that we had frequented with Niv in good times gone by. After lunch, I simply said to Evie, 'Let's go and find Niv.' We drove to Château d'Oex, not sure where we were going, but sensing we were on track. We drove past the town as though being guided by an invisible hand. A mile further on, we found a long, narrow cemetery in a fantastically beautiful setting in the valley between the two mountain ridges. We walked in, past maybe 200 or 300 graves, straight to Niven's simple headstone, a giant Celtic cross carved from Scottish granite. It read simply 'David Niven, 1910–1983'. I had taken a thousand pictures of Evie and Niven over the years and I said, 'One last picture with him, Eve.' She stepped forward in her brightly coloured ski suit and gently embraced the headstone. I raised the camera and, as I did so, into the shot I was framing flew an even brighter-coloured hot-air balloon with 'Château d'Oex' emblazoned on it, flying down the valley towards Rougement. The timing and the coincidence completely took my breath away. I was looking at Evie, Niven, *The Moon's a Balloon* and *Around the World in Eighty Days* all rolled into one, the best of his life in one photograph. I said to Evie, 'Don't move!' took five quick pictures and said, 'He wanted to be in the picture with you. Look!' I pointed up into the sky, Evie saw the balloon and burst into tears. One of the greatest men we ever knew in our lives, who lived with the priceless gift of joy in his soul, had left us one last indelible memory.

Ms Liza May Minnelli had met and married a terrific young man called Mark Gero. Young, tall and unreasonably handsome, Mark looked like Robert De Niro's good-looking baby brother. Evie and I took to him instantly. They were staying with us in Beverly Hills.

Liza came to me one morning and said, 'Les, you've got to help me with something. Daddy's got all these old 8-by-10s of Mama that I want to borrow and get copied. I keep asking for them and nothing happens. So I thought we might go down to his house together this afternoon to sort it out.'

It sounded innocent enough, and I agreed to go. So around 4.00pm, we drove over together in Evie's car to Vincente's house facing the Beverly Hills Hotel across Sunset Boulevard on the corner of Crescent Drive. Vincente, wearing his customary uniform of bright-yellow blazer and black slacks, greeted us warmly, and we went into the living room. The strong physical resemblance between Vincente and Liza became even more startling when they were together. Vincente was his usual charming, highly nervous self, another physical trait he shared with his daughter. We chattered merrily for a few minutes, with Vincente punctuating the conversation with his trademark, seven-note nervous laugh – 'Ha, ha, ha, ha, ha, ha, ha!' – and then Liza asked him whether she could look through some of his old photo archives with him. Vincente happily acquiesced, and off the pair of them went.

I settled into an armchair with one of Vincente's big art books, not knowing how long they might be. After about ten minutes, Liza reappeared carrying a wad of 8-by-10 photos, which she thrust at me in conspiratorial fashion with a loud stage whisper. 'Quick. Hide them.'

'What?' I said. 'You're *stealing* them?'

'Borrowing,' she replied firmly. 'To make copies.'

'But he doesn't know?' I queried.

'Shut up and hide them,' she said. 'We can argue later.'

'Hide them *where*?'

'Down your socks,' she suggested, and left the room.

Weighing the potential criminal charge of stealing rare archival photographs of Judy Garland from Vincente Minnelli's private residence, I stuffed the 8-by-10s of Judy in *Meet Me in St Louis* down my socks, as commanded by their renegade offspring, and had just pulled them precariously back up over the photographs when Liza returned with a second even bigger batch.

'Put these up your sleeves or down your trousers,' she proposed, 'and there's more to come,' and disappeared again.

With Vincente sweetly and unconsciously aiding and abetting her in the next room, Liza continued to rob her father blind, making several more trips back and forth until I was so stuffed and stiffened with concealed wads of Judy Garland stills up my arms and down my legs and down my trousers and up my back that I looked like a cross between Frankenstein's monster and the Michelin man.

'OK, that's it!' she said triumphantly, arriving with the final batch and, realising I was stuffed to bursting point like a Thanksgiving turkey, stuffing them under her black sweater. 'I think we've done pretty well, don't you?'

'*We?*' I queried. 'Has he got any pictures *left*?'

'Thousands,' she said. 'He won't even miss them. And anyway, I'll have them back in a week.'

'How?' I asked.

'Simple,' she said. 'We'll do the same thing in reverse.'

'You and someone else,' I vowed.

Vincente came into the room, and we chatted some more. He asked when Evie and I were returning to London. I told him next month. He smiled. '*I'll* be in London next month,' he said, 'for the launch of my autobiography. You and Evie must come. It'll be in the River Room at the Savoy.'

I said that we would love to, and asked what the autobiography was called.

He hesitated. 'Er, it's called.... er... it's called... er... I did know... er... it's called... er...'

'Daddy,' prompted Liza, 'it's called *I Remember It Well*.'

'Ah, yes,' he smiled. 'That's what it's called. *I Remember It Well*. Ha, ha, ha, ha, ha, ha, ha!'

We headed towards the back of the house, where we had parked Evie's car, with myself moving slowly, like a deep-sea diver in full kit. Vincente led the way. Liza whispered urgently in my ear. 'One more thing, Les. As we leave, I want you to steal Daddy's car.'

'*What?*' I exploded. '*No!*'

'You've *got* to!' she pleaded. 'That terrible old Cadillac. He's the world's worst driver, and he's going to kill himself if he drives it again!' She turned to Vincente. 'It's OK, Daddy. We'll see ourselves out.' She kissed him.

Vincente smiled vaguely and laughed the seven laughs. 'Bye-bye, dear. Thank you for coming,' he said, and wandered back into the house as his daughter and her best friend made off with the booty from their raid, the Bonnie and Clyde of Beverly Hills. Outside, Liza jumped into Evie's red Mercedes, pointing at the clapped-out old Cadillac parked across the driveway. 'That's it. Key's inside,' she said, and drove away.

I had no choice but to add 'car thief' to my swiftly growing criminal résumé. I got into the Cadillac. It wouldn't start. Liza was right. It was a terrible old car. I finally got it going on about the fifth try and, as I was boldly driving his car out of his driveway, the kitchen door opened and Vincente reappeared. He waved me away with a big smile as I stole his sole means of transportation, without a glimmer of recognition. 'Bye-bye,' he said. '*I Remember It Well...* Ha, ha, ha, ha, ha, ha, ha!'

Vincente's vagueness was an endearing and confusing quality. Evie and I did attend his book launch at the Savoy in London. We had arranged to meet André Previn and Mia Farrow there and go on to dinner afterwards. Evie and I were early, so we chatted with Vincente for about ten minutes before wandering on into the party-to-be. A moment later, André arrived with Mia and chatted with Vincente, with whom he had frequently worked in

Hollywood. As they moved on, three minutes after us, he said to Vincente, 'By the way, is Leslie Bricusse here yet?'

'No,' said Vincente with certainty, 'But I know she's coming!'

Major Barbara – The Musical was destined never to be. Lerner and Loewe's success with *My Fair Lady* clearly went to the Shaw Estate's head. Suddenly they became the world's greatest authority on musicals. Hank and I wrote a highly satisfying first draft score, and Jerome and Lawrence and Robert E Lee – they of *Inherit the Wind* and *Mame* fame – a powerful first-draft book. I recorded the songs in London with a lovely young West End singer, Liz Robertson, a Julie Andrews look-alike and sound-alike who was about to land the role of Eliza Dolittle in *My Fair Lady*'s first West End revival, and its author, too! Liz won the Variety Club Silver Heart Award as Best Newcomer of the Year, and Alan Jay Lerner's heart into the bargain, after Alan saw the show and understandably fell head over heels in love with her, the elusive and lasting number eight he had been looking for all his life. In Liz, he finally found his true fair lady, their happy marriage lasting until Alan's premature death seven years later.

The *Major Barbara* demos were greeted with acclaim back in the United States. Producer Larry Kasha was thrilled, Julie Andrews ready to commit. But the suddenly musically aware Shaw Estate was not. They graded our work like schoolchildren. They didn't like that melody, and this lyric and that scene were not sufficiently Shavian. Long story short, Larry could not get the rights free and clear without the ongoing interference of the Shaw Estate, which was unacceptable to us. You either grant the rights to a musical or you don't; it can't be conditional. We were all too experienced to need Aunt Sarah to tell us how to write our show. The greatest loss was the public's in not seeing the divine Jools's return to Broadway in a role she was born to play. But, wouldn't you know, the Department of Fate had something to say about *that*!

After the great success of the movie *Victor/Victoria*, the thought of it becoming a stage musical was quickly in Blake Edwards's head, as well as Henry's and mine. We were not unaware that, in Julie, we had one of the truly great musical theatre stars. Whether she would contemplate venturing back on to the boards after so long away from the theatre was a highly debatable question. The film of *Victor/Victoria* took up maybe 12 to 15 weeks of her life. A stage musical version of the same piece would devour two years, and it was much harder work, eight shows a week, every week. Julie's equally impressive theatre, film, television, concert and recording careers had consumed the last 25 years so effortlessly and successfully that the arguments for and against her going back to Broadway were equally strong. The starring musical roles she had turned down during that time would have provided glittering careers for at least three other performers!

It was agreed by Blake and Julie and Hank and myself, over dinner at the Edwards house, that we would write the stage show anyway. The least that Julie deserved was the right to like or dislike what we set before her, a privilege due and accorded to any superstar. We set to work.

I was walking down Rodeo Drive in Beverly Hills. As I passed Gucci, I heard a voice shout out, 'Leslie Bricusse!' I turned. It was Steve McQueen, standing in the shop doorway. I tried to recall how many years it was since I had last seen him, when his life had turned upside down and inside out when he went south, literally and figuratively, to make the film *The Getaway* with Ali McGraw down in Mexico, causing divorces and disasters in every direction. It wasn't that our once close friendship had ever ended; he had just disappeared right out of our lives at that time, never to be seen again until now.

We chatted for a while in the street, recalling good times shared, regretting good times missed, like when he asked me up to San Francisco to watch him try to kill himself in what would become the classic car chase in *Bullitt*. We hugged and parted, making no plan to meet again.

Outside Gucci's on Rodeo Drive, a very un–Steve McQueen-like setting, was the last place and the last time I would ever see him. He died of asbestos-caused cancer a year later. He was 50.

Elton John and John Reid invited Evie and me to go and stay with them for a couple of weeks in Montserrat, where Elton was recording his new album at George Martin's exotic and popular AIR Studio. Paul McCartney, Phil Collins, Eric Clapton and the Police were among other top recording artists availing themselves of this tropical paradise to concentrate on their music far from the madding crowd. The trip was too good to miss, and we flew on the appointed date from London to Antigua, then on an island-hopper to the precarious water's edge airstrip of Montserrat. John and Elton had taken two villas close to one another, with dramatic, sweeping views of the coastline and out across the Caribbean to the neighbouring islands of Guadeloupe and Martinique. It was bizarre, when we later flew to those islands, maybe 20 minutes away by air, to hear the local inhabitants' near-cockney English accents as we left Montserrat, and half-an-hour later the fluent French of the identical-looking Guadeloupans or Martiniquais, a quaint by-product of colonialism.

We stayed with 'Reidy' or 'JR', as John Reid was variously known, and his long-time, nice-as-pie young blond boyfriend, Paul Northcott. On the day after our arrival, I went down to the studio with Elton in the morning, not knowing I was about to witness one of the more amazing hours I would ever spend in any recording studio. The first surprise was that there were still some songs to be included on the album that Elton had so far not written. He took an envelope from his pocket. From the envelope he removed several scruffy-looking scraps of paper. These were Bernie Taupin's new lyrics, as always scribbled as poems on bits of paper, for Elton to consider as songs. This was how they had always worked, since the teenage Bernie had sent his first poems to London more than a decade before, and John Reid had shrewdly teamed them up.

Elton propped up all the pieces of paper on the music stand of the Steinway grand piano at which he was seated, and read them. I sat right behind him, looking over his shoulder. After a couple of minutes, the ten pieces of paper became eight, then six, and finally five, as the others were cast aside. He addressed the first piece of paper, and immediately played the musical phrase that the opening lyric line suggested to him. Within minutes, he had the bones of a lovely melody. He did not change one word of the lyric, though he might repeat a line twice, or jump back and do a complete stanza a second time elsewhere in his melody. He remembered everything he had done. He wrote nothing down. He changed a few harmonies, refined one or two progressions, and finally played the delicious finished product. I looked at my watch. Eight minutes. The song was called 'Lovers Leap from Burning Buildings'. He grinned, and moved on to the second piece of paper. The first song was memorised, locked in his head, ready to record for his next platinum album.

At the end of an hour, Elton had completed four of the five melodies for the album. He suddenly said, 'Oh, fuck it!' on the fifth song and got up from the piano. The second the natural flow stopped, so did he. What was riveting about watching him work was the confidence and certainty with which he approached his composing. There was never a glimmer of doubt about where he was heading musically. He read the lyric, he heard in his head what it ought to sound like, so he played and sang it, and that was that.

Away from the villas and the studios, our main food headquarters was a funky local restaurant called The Chicken Shack, a big, tacky-looking hut where delicious fried chicken was served fish 'n' chips style on old newspapers. We would travel back to the villas late at night in two cars. Whenever we had to stop for a red traffic light, Elton had a disconcerting habit of leaping from the passenger seat of his car, jumping up on to the front hood of our car, pulling down his trousers and mooning us through the windscreen. I suggested to him that *Moon over Montserrat* might be an appropriate title for the new album.

The working title for the album was *Restless*. The eventual title became *Breaking Hearts*. On the final night of our stay, Elton played the completed album at a celebration party at The Chicken Shack for everyone concerned in its making. Among the guests were Bernie Taupin and his tall, gorgeous brunette wife Toni, who had an equally tall, gorgeous, blonde actress sister called Rene Russo. Sitting next to Elton at our table was the quiet but sweet German girl who had served as tape operator during the making of the album. Her name was Renata Blauel, whose name we all pronounced in exaggerated cockney, omitting the 'T', as 'Rena-a!' A month later, at a white wedding on St Valentine's Day, in faraway Sydney, Australia, 'Rena-a' would become the one-and-only Mrs Elton John, a title Elton had previously reserved exclusively for himself.

The writing of the stage musical score for *Victor/Victoria* proceeded smoothly enough in the initial stages. The book of the show stayed close to a judiciously edited version of Blake Edwards's screenplay, which was, by nature, ideally suited to the theatre. But since you can't ask a Broadway audience to pay those astonishing ticket prices for a Julie Andrews's musical in which there are a mere six songs, of which she sings only three, there clearly needed to be more. Hank's and my basic game plan was to retain four of the film songs and add ten new ones.

But it was not the score that was to be the hold-up factor in our Broadway production process, so much as an endless succession of other problems and aggravations that would ultimately span close to a decade. First and worst, there was an interminable legal battle between Blake and MGM-UA about too much spending on Blake's part and too little promotion on MGM-UA's part on the post-Peter Sellers *Pink Panther* films on the one hand and *Victor/Victoria* on the other. This dispute dragged on unresolved for years, making several lawyers significantly wealthier.

Second, the accumulative pressures of writing, producing and directing a big-budget movie every year, which Blake had been doing for more than two decades, plus the additional burdens created by the pending lawsuits, eventually combined to drag Blake down with a serious onslaught of Epstein-Barr syndrome, which laid him lower than low for many months. These unwanted outside factors would ultimately cause the creative engine to grind to a halt, which it did. And getting it revved up again was no easy matter, because, as usual, we were all busy on other projects. Needless to say, the lawsuits were eventually settled for something like a dollar fifty.

I acquired the musical stage rights to *Goodbye, Mr Chips* from the James Hilton Estate and MGM. An English writer friend, Roland Starke, did a stage adaptation of the Terence Rattigan screenplay. The Chichester Festival in England said they would be happy to première it, and the title role went to our old chum, Johnny, now Sir John Mills, who all these years later was still irked that the role of the headmaster in our film had been given to Michael, now Sir Michael Redgrave, rather than to himself, especially since our Johnny had played a major role as a schoolboy in the 1939 Robert Donat version, and understandably wanted to claim that he had acted in all three. So from his point of view, here was compensation indeed. And because he was in such fantastic physical condition, having never gained one ounce of weight in half-a-century, he was able to play the young Chips as well as the old one. True, Robert Donat had done the same in the original movie, but he was in his thirties at the time, and Johnny was now well into his seventies, and could and did still wear the red velvet smoking jacket he had first worn in Noël Coward's *Cavalcade* at the start of the 1930s.

He gave a remarkable performance as Chips, carrying it off with a mixture of modesty, charm and élan. The audiences adored him, and the Chichester season was a sell-out, setting new box-office records for the festival. The show's director, Patrick Garland,

and I met with Bernard Delfont in London, and it was arranged that the show would move into Her Majesty's Theatre in the West End for Christmas.

A celebration dinner at Johnny and Mary Mills's lovely old Queen Anne house out at Denham for the Millses and the Bricusses and the Garlands followed in late November, to celebrate the West End transfer. As the dessert arrived around 10.00pm, the phone rang. It was Bernie (now Lord) Delfont to tell us that he had that afternoon assumed the chairmanship of a vast leisure conglomerate called First Leisure, and that his new duties expressly forbade him to have any association with theatre productions, so, sadly, he had to cancel *Goodbye, Mr Chips* in the West End.

We sat there stunned. We had no time to regroup, as this terminal body blow happened just days before the Chichester company were due to re-rehearse for London. As I said before, there are always more reasons for a show to go wrong than there are to put it on in the first place. We had just that week completed recording the cast album, so at least we had that as a pathetic souvenir. Other than that, it was, in every sense, 'Goodbye, Mr Chips'.

Johnny Mills doubted whether, at his age, he could wait another year for *Chips* to regroup and refinance, which is always a remote possibility once an existing, up-and-running production is disbanded. Johnny's main problems were his eyesight and his hearing, which were past their best. Mary, his wife, had the identical weaknesses. My mother was also named Mary Mills, Ann Mary Mills, and, when she died, I made Johnny's Mary my honorary mother, as she and Johnny had long been like an extra pair of parents to Evie and myself. Evie, remember, had met Johnny when they were filming *The Baby and the Battleship* when she was only 15!

The full impact of Johnny and Mary's hearing and sight problems was driven home to us a few months later when Evie and I went over to see them for a summer lunch in the glorious gardens of Hills House on the day of the Women's Singles Final at Wimbledon, which they were both keen to watch. We finished lunch early, to be in time for the 2.00pm start of the Final, and marched into Johnny's study to see the game. We had noticed during lunch that he and Mary were shouting at one another rather more loudly than usual, a natural recourse for the hard of hearing. The game was due to start. Johnny and Mary took two armchairs and pulled them so close to the television set that their noses were all but touching the screen, so that they could see. All Evie and I could see, sitting on the sofa across the room, was the back of their two heads. The game began, with the volume on the TV turned up to such a deafening level that the rackets hitting the ball sounded like the Duke of Wellington's cannons at the Battle of Waterloo. Evie and I sat on the sofa, helpless with laughter, until we could bear it no more, then slipped quietly out of the house, unheard and unseen by the preoccupied Johnny and Mary, and went home.

The dire prediction that she had made to me 13 years before – 'I have this terrible dream that I'm going to die in dark water' – came tragically true one dark December night when our beloved Natalie Wood drowned after falling from her and RJ Wagner's yacht *Splendour* off the island of Catalina, about 30 miles from the coast of California. The dreadful tragedy took Hollywood's breath away, and the massive media speculation that ensued about the circumstances of her death couldn't and didn't alter the one terrible truth, that the exquisite Natalie was gone. She was only 43. The gathering at Natalie and RJ's picture-perfect house on Canon Drive after the funeral was the most heartbreaking that Evie and I had ever attended. The sight of her two stunned young daughters, Natasha and Courteney – Natasha the image of her mother in *Miracle on 34th Street* – was unbearably haunting. Twenty years before, the film *The Misfits* had proved to be the last that its three stars – Clark Gable, Marilyn Monroe and Montgomery Clift – would make before their premature deaths.

Now again, with the untimely loss of Natalie, she completed a second trio of early deaths with her co-stars from her first starring movie role in *Rebel Without a Cause*, James Dean and Sal Mineo.

The wonderful week we spent with Roddy MacDowall in Gstaad at the last CineMusic Festival proved tragically to be the last time we would ever spend together. A few short months later, he, too, fell victim to cancer. Roddy was perhaps the most universally popular and best-loved human being who ever lived his life in Hollywood, certainly during our time there. Everyone adored him. He devoted huge quantities of time to his legion of friends, spanning several generations from his *How Green Was My Valley* childhood throughout his six decades as an actor. He was Elizabeth Taylor's best friend, and spoke to her almost every day of his life from her *National Velvet* and his *Lassie Come Home* days in the mid-1940s until his death more than half-a-century later. He was Julie Andrews's best friend. He was our best Hollywood friend. His range of acquaintances was quite staggering and embraced most of the history of motion pictures.

We invited him to dinner one evening, and he turned up with Myrna Loy. Myrna *Loy*! He refused another invitation because he had promised to fly to Florida to spend the weekend with Pola Negri. Pola *Negri*! Ye Gods! For years, I tried to persuade Roddy to write the definitive history of Hollywood, one volume per decade, starting with the 1930s. He was there for *seven* decades, and knew everyone in the community throughout that amazing period of time. His wit, his knowledge, his integrity and his intelligence would undoubtedly have combined to produce the standard work on Tinseltown, but he steadfastly refused to do it on the grounds that he knew *too much*, with the inevitable result that his honesty would corner him into compromising some of his friends. It was the greatest cop-out I ever heard, but he was right.

In the life of Roddy MacDowall, friendship came first and last, and there was no negotiating. He contented himself by leaving the world four volumes of his fantastic portrait photographs, called *Double Exposure*, with the brilliant concept that every celebrity whose image appeared was written about by someone equally famous. No departed Hollywood legend was ever more widely mourned or more sorely missed than the modest and phenomenal Roddy MacDowall.

Of all the lasting memories Gstaad brought into our lives, none compares with the amazing two weeks of the Sinatra Christmas. Roger and Luisa Moore had become good friends over the years with Frank and his spectacular fourth and final wife, Barbara. The friendship blossomed because of a nearly-but-not-quite romance between the Moores' daughter, Deborah, and Barbara's son, Bobby Marx, from her previous marriage to the 'good-looking one' of the Marx Brothers, Zeppo.

There was a famous Hollywood story that, at the height of their Hollywood fame in the 1930s, when their SJ Perelman-scripted movies like *A Day at the Races* and *A Night at the Opera* were all the rage, the Marx Brothers fired their agent and sent Groucho in to meet with the redoubtable Head of the Studio, Louis B Mayer, to renegotiate the deal for their next movie. Groucho fearlessly asked the mighty mogul for $500,000, an unheard-of sum of money in that era. Mayer was appropriately outraged. 'Five hundred thousand dollars!' he fumed. 'Well, for a start we don't even need Zeppo in the movie!'

Groucho pondered for a split-second, then countered, 'Without Zeppo, it's seven fifty!'

It was arranged that the Sinatras would take a nearby chalet for a couple of weeks over Christmas and New Year, while Evie and I would stay with Roger and Luisa at their cosy Chalet Fenil, just outside the village. The Sinatras brought their old friends and long-time drinking buddies George and Jolene Schlatter and Danny and Natalie Schwartz.

And what a two weeks it was! Apart from the whole town wanting to wine and dine the Sinatras, our best evenings were at home in one or other of the two chalets. Those evenings were perhaps more fun for me than for anyone else, because, when the rest of them were ready for bed, Frank was just getting started. He loved nothing more than to stay up, drinking Jack Daniels, of which Roger had thoughtfully commandeered the entire national Swiss supply, and reminiscing far into the night. Like most nightclub performers, Frank's favourite time was and always had been the wee small hours. All I had to do was turn on the switch and let him run. I learned more about MGM musicals during the night-times of those two intoxicating weeks than I ever could by reading every book ever written about them.

Christmas lunch and New Year's Eve both took place at Valentino's remarkably beautiful chalet, and it guaranteed my Happy New Year that my dinner partner, sitting between Frank and myself, was Audrey Hepburn.

I had long cherished the dream that my son Adam would follow my footsteps and reprise the three blissful years that I had enjoyed at Cambridge. But Adam, happily, is not inclined to follow in anyone's footsteps. He makes his own. Having inherited Evie's talent for painting, he studied Art and the History of Art for his A-levels at Cranleigh School in Surrey, where he boarded under the watchful eye of his ubiquitous godfather, Vivian Cox, himself an Old Cranleighan, who had returned there to teach. Despite a sceptical headmaster named Marc Van Hasselt, who predicted a life of decadence and debauchery in the seedy, smoke-filled bars and flesh-pots of the Left Bank and Hollywood for this wayward son of a showbusiness marriage, Adam produced shining 'A' results and a place for himself at Merton College, Oxford, where he would secure his Bachelor and Master of Arts degrees, confounding the cynical Van Hasselt's dire forecasts. I have always proudly regarded Adam's achievement as a shining example of filial one-upmanship.

The fact that he has gone on to a successful career as a professional artist, the only profession more perilous and precarious than my own, leaves me speechless with wonder every time I look at the latest of his many beautiful works.

Alan Jay Friedman and I had by now completed a fast-paced book and score to our John F Kennedy musical, *One Shining Moment*, which we workshopped successfully at the Eugene O'Neill Theater Center in northern Connecticut during an Arctic January. With the financial backing of two wealthy Beverly Hills friends, Leonard and Emesa Green, and the artistic input of Broadway director Dennis Rosa, we assembled a cast of teenage and early-twenties actors, to give the show a feeling of a young America college production, for a tryout production at the Drury Lane Theater in Chicago. Kevin Anderson as JFK, Alan Ruck as Lyndon B Johnson, and Megan Mullally as Jackie Kennedy, all three in their early twenties, were spectacularly good, and the show opened its intended six-week run to such rave reviews from the Chicago critics that the six weeks quickly became 12, then 20, then 30. The possibilities of an extended tour or even a Broadway transfer were explored, but quickly quashed, because of the extreme youthfulness of the cast, which made us wish that we had gone for older actors in the first place.

The Drury Lane was a theatre-in-the-round. To move to a New York proscenium theatre would require us to recast, rebuild, refinance and rehearse a totally new production with older actors. We explored the availability of smaller Broadway playhouses of around a thousand seats, but none of the numbers that Leonard and Em Green's money people came up with were sufficiently appealing for them to want to move any further forward. And so that one particular shining moment was over. As a gesture to the cultural advancement of our times, the Drury Lane Theater closed after our run, and was converted into a Cineplex.

John Williams asked me whether I would like to write the songs with him for an upcoming big-budget movie called *Santa Claus*, being prepared by Salkind *père et fils*, they of the *Superman* movies.

It crossed my mind that this could be a consolation prize for the fiasco of the *Superman* song. I loved John and I loved writing with him, so, of course, I said 'Yes'.

Nothing happened for six months, when I got exactly the same phone call about the same project from Hank Mancini. John had clearly become unavailable in the interim, with the *Indiana Jones* series and things that were going on in his life by then. And since there were no two better songwriting film composers on the planet than John and Hank, I happily said 'Yes' for a second time. This time it happened, but in a way that almost made us wish it hadn't.

Sooner or later, someone was bound to cast the diminutive Dudley Moore as the world's tallest elf. That moment came now. *Santa Claus* had a $50 million budget, huge for its day, and since they were giving young Duddles $5 million of that for his trouble, I doubt if he'd have minded playing Attila the Tiny Hun!

Musically, regardless of the merits or demerits of the film, a golden opportunity was wasted on this motion picture. Never before had there been a major musical film about Santa Claus. Henry and I campaigned incessantly to be allowed to take the rare chance the film offered to create a major song score.

The film was intended to breathe the very spirit of Christmas. It ended up as a less-than-hilarious comedy directed by a less-than-hilarious director, with a heavy-handed moral about the commercial greed of Christmas destroying the spirit of Christmas, leaving an unpleasant aftertaste of the meanness of mankind.

Hank and I nonetheless wrote six slightly smashing Christmas songs, which exist in print in the elegant *Santa Claus – The Movie* song folio. But try to find them in the movie and you'll be hard pressed. They are there, but they are background and incidental rather than foreground and focused.

The root cause of this musical mess was that the producers had made a deal beforehand with a major record label, allowing interpolation of their current commercial product into the final soundtrack, which, in our view, completely bastardised any artistic intention on our part. The way we saw it, the film was ironically ruined by the application of the same sordid values that it condemned in the story. It was a sorry experience, given its high potential and, for me, the abiding moral was 'If you mess with Santa, your toys won't work!'

The long wait for *Victor/Victoria*'s legal problems to be resolved continued, with no end in sight. In the interim, Hank and I mapped out and wrote a number of additional key songs we felt the stage production would need. Everyone liked the new songs, which only added even more to the frustration caused by the delay. The years were slipping by, and we seriously began to wonder whether the show would ever happen.

Temporary consolation was forthcoming in the unconventional shape of Blake Edwards's latest film, entitled *That's Life!*. This was the ultimate home movie. It was conceived, written and directed by Blake – no one but he could have thought up this one – and shot on location in and around his home in Trancas, north of Malibu on California's Pacific Coast. It starred his wife, Julie Andrews, *her* daughter Emma, *his* daughter Jenny, *his* son Jeff, Jack Lemmon, *his* son Chris, and Sally Kellerman, and the executive producer was *her* husband, Jonathan Krane. Also in the cast was Blake's doctor, Herb Tanney, and his co-screenwriter was his psychiatrist, which somehow made sense in the circumstances.

The script of *That's Life!* was maybe 20 pages long, and the dialogue almost entirely improvised during the shooting of the film. It was shot on a shoestring budget and a tight schedule. Everyone worked for scale or for nothing, and we were all recompensed after the film was completed and sold. Julie, playing Jack Lemmon's wife, would tell me hilarious and schizophrenic stories of how she would wake up at 6.00am with Blake, get up, go straight into make-up and get back into the *same* bed with Jack Lemmon one hour later! That's showbusiness, folks, and all in a leading lady's day's work.

John Uhler Lemmon III – 'Uhler' to his friends – was frenziedly funny in the role of a successful, happily married man suddenly panicking at the thought of reaching the age of 60, wondering what he had missed in life and trying to find out before it was too late. And it was Jack's attitude that gave me the idea for the film's theme song, 'Life in a Looking-Glass', as he gazed at himself in the mirror in morning, or do I mean mourning, despair? Tony Bennett sang the song beautifully over the titles, to earn another Oscar nomination for Hank and myself.

The English National Opera Company opened a revival of *Pickwick* at the Northcott Theatre on the campus of Exeter University. Evie and I drove down to see it, and were delighted to observe how well its Dickensian humour and dazzling characters, as well as the score, had retained their vitality and audience appeal close to a quarter-of-a-century after we had first done the show with Harry, now Sir Harry, Secombe. The theatre's artistic director, a Hungarian gentleman called George Roman, volunteered that, if there was ever any project I would like to workshop or try out prior to London, the Northcott Theatre and its resources were at my disposal.

Thanks to one of the Department of Fate's cunning coincidences, the following Sunday, Evie and I were having Sunday lunch at Mike and Shakira Caine's blissful Thames-side country house, and who were there with us but Harry and Myra Secombe. Evie it was, sitting next to Sir Harry, devouring Mike's finest roast lamb, who shrewdly told Harry of our happy experience in Exeter and that, in the interests of pleasure and profit, he should seriously consider blowing the non-existent dust off *Pickwick* and reprise the greatest stage success of his long and grand career, since he was now, in his mid-sixties, exactly the right age to play the revered President of the inestimable Pickwick Club.

Harry's eyes lit up as she spoke. The thought had registered. The penny had dropped.

Sean Connery's lifelong passion for the game of golf began when we were making *Goldfinger*, and he had to learn how to play the great game for his famous match against Auric Goldfinger, alias Gert Frobe, in the film. Little could I have guessed that this would benefit *me* a quarter-of-a-century later. We were having dinner with Sean one Monday evening at Wolfgang Puck's fabled Spago restaurant in West Hollywood. I mentioned to Sean that I had the previous day watched his fellow Scotsman Sandy Lyle win a PGA tournament in high style, and I fancied he would do well in this week's Masters Tournament in Augusta, Georgia.

'For how much?' snarled Sean, sniffing a bet.

We agreed $200, and he picked Greg Norman against my Sandy Lyle, the bet to be won by whoever finished higher. Sandy Lyle duly won the tournament. For the next few weeks, Sean was away filming. When he returned, he sent me a cheque for $210, which included 5 per cent interest for the delay in payment. In red ink at the bottom of the cheque was the sinister addendum: 'Golf bet – signed in blood!'

Elizabeth Taylor Hilton Wilding Todd Fisher Burton Burton Warner was Elizabeth Taylor's accumulative married name by the time she started her romantic year with our beloved George Hamilton. And an extremely handsome pair they made together. Pity they didn't think about it 20 years sooner. George called me in France to say that Elizabeth had been invited by the Cannes Festival to be the Guest of Honour at their upcoming 40th Festival, and would it be OK for the two of them to side-step the deadly Cannes Festival hotel life and come to stay with Evie and me at our summer villa for a couple of weeks in May?

My main concern was security, so we agreed to keep everything as low-key as possible. We arranged to have George and Elizabeth join us and Roger and Luisa Moore for dinner at the Colombe d'Or on the night of their arrival. As the four of us sat waiting for the low-key arrival, we heard the distant wail of police sirens, and screaming up to the gates of the Colombe d'Or, like Mussolini re-entering Rome, came four police motorcycle outriders escorting two huge, black stretch limos, filled mostly with luggage, with enough space left over for George and Elizabeth. The several thousand paparazzi following them fell for the first part of my plan, which was to have them assume that Elizabeth was staying at Roger's nearby house. When Roger departed after dinner, the paparazzi followed in droves, like news-seeking lemmings, (a) to see where Roger lived, and (b) to get pictures of Elizabeth as she arrived, which of course she didn't. The limos had gone to *our* villa to disgorge the luggage and had long since disappeared. Evie and I quietly smuggled George and Elizabeth up to the house the back way.

And that's how it continued. If we were going to lunch with the Moores, I would sit Elizabeth up front in the car beside me, in full view, smiling and waving like the Queen Mother and, when we left, she would lie on the floor at the back of the car with a blanket over her, to add credence to the idea that she was staying at Roger's. Unbelievably, we got away with this simple ploy for the whole two weeks, which doesn't say a hell of a lot for the intelligence quotient of paparazzi. This also had the built-in benefit of driving Luisa Moore insane, to my fiendish delight, with paparazzi hanging out of the trees and outside the gates of their nearby villa, La Torretta, for most of the next two weeks.

The biggest problems with Elizabeth were her luggage and her jewellery. She gave a new meaning to the phrase 'excess baggage'. Her 59 Louis Vuitton trunks and suitcases, for us a new houseguest, Olympic and world record, could comfortably have taken the Albanian Army on manoeuvres for a month. They flowed out of her and George's bedroom suite across most of the floor of the house that they occupied. I had taken the precaution of installing a sizeable new safe, just for Elizabeth, anticipating what I thought would be her needs, and using her birth date as the combination to open it. I went to see her while she was unpacking, which took up most of the fortnight. 'Elizabeth, where's the jewellery?' I asked.

She pointed to a steamer trunk. 'In there. Help yourself.'

'Where in there?'

'Everywhere in there. All of it. Just look. You'll find it.'

I looked, and I found it. Jewellery filled every drawer and crevice of the trunk. Jewellery cases from Harry Winston and Cartier and Van Cleef and Arpels and Boucheron, containing necklaces and bracelets and brooches and earrings and finger rings with stones the size of walnuts; emeralds, rubies, sapphires, diamonds and pearls. Their bedroom looked like a King Farouk garage sale, with enough baubles to fill 15 safes like the one I had prepared. Plus about 200 designer outfits to help her through their 12-day stay. Since we spent most of our time hanging out at the house or eating locally with friends, she maybe wore six outfits during her entire stay, preferring jeans and T-shirts the rest of the time. She could have made it with three suitcases, if she had left out the jewellery.

Elizabeth was looking fantastically beautiful at this time, thanks to the successful weight-loss regime George had imposed on her during the first six months of their relationship. She looked better than she had for two decades. Cannes was going to see her at her shining best.

The biggest problem of all was the Krupp diamond, the giant square-cut stone of God knows how many D flawless carats, the size of a square Frisbee, on which Richard Burton had unleashed God knows how many millions of dollars in a moment of advanced drunken romantic madness, even given the stratospheric film salaries they were both earning when he bought it. Elizabeth had a disconcerting habit of leaving this monster rock lying about the house. I was forever picking it up from unlikely places where she had left it, probably because her arm was tired. She was not unaware, as she slyly pointed out with her wicked sense of humour, what the insurance claim would be if the ring tragically disappeared. Mercifully, it didn't, though I added some distinguished-looking silver-grey hair to replace my erstwhile chestnut-brown during her and George's stay.

Elizabeth and Evie were a perfect pair, two glorious English beauties full of laughter, who got along like long-lost sisters. With George at his hilarious best, it was a fabled fortnight for everyone except Luisa Moore.

After the glamour of the Festival, Elizabeth invited us up to Paris, where President Mitterrand conferred upon her the Légion d'Honneur. We attended the ceremony with George and Elizabeth and Franco Zeffirelli and Doris Brynner, an unlikely couple, and in the evening George gave a small celebratory dinner party in a private salon at Lasserre, attended by Elton John and Adnan Khashoggi, an even more unlikely couple.

Elizabeth confided in me that she was hopeful she and George would marry by the end of the year. I asked George what he thought about this. He replied that he didn't want to be remembered for becoming the tenth initial, H, that Elizabeth added to the nine she already possessed. Nor would he be the first or only H, having been preceded seven husbands ago by Nick Hilton.

Our fun-filled days drew to a close without incident or a major jewel robbery, and we agreed to continue the dialogue in Acapulco during the coming winter. In the interim, George and Elizabeth attended a red-hot Hollywood birthday party for Evie thrown by our swashbuckling English entrepreneur pal, Peter de Savary, to celebrate the opening of his glittering Art Deco palazzo, the St James's Club on Sunset Boulevard, the former Sunset Towers, the most notorious apartment building in Los Angeles, where John Wayne had famously kept a cow on the penthouse terrace in the 1930s, to provide him with daily fresh milk. Peter had opened his Paris St James's Club the year before with a birthday party for me, when 70 of our friends had flown in from London and New York and LA for four days of sub-zero Paris winter weather and warm welcomes. He outshone himself with the LA party for Evie that was so hooray-for-Hollywood that I was seated between Elizabeth Taylor and Joan Collins, and Evie between two James Bonds, Sean Connery and Roger Moore.

True to their word, George and Elizabeth came to stay with us in Acapulco. At the airport, I was allowed to have the welcoming limo driven out on to the tarmac right up to the door of the arriving jet. Elizabeth gave me a kiss of greeting as she entered the limo while George was clearing Customs and Immigration for them. She got straight down to business. 'Leslie, why do you suppose it is,' she asked, 'that George doesn't want to marry me?'

I weakly ad-libbed that George probably had enough trouble sorting out his own life, let alone anyone else's, let alone Elizabeth Taylor's. George returned from his Customs and Immigration duties and joined us in the car. I confronted him directly with Elizabeth's question. 'George,' I said, 'Elizabeth and I want to know why you haven't got around to marrying her.'

George looked up from the confused pile of air tickets and passports and Customs and Immigration forms on his lap and grinned. 'It's because frankly I couldn't stand having those gold concierge cross-keys on all my suits,' he replied with a wicked grin.

They drifted amicably apart a few months later, George to remain a bachelor, Elizabeth to enter into her eighth marriage with Mr Larry Fortensky and thus acquire that elusive tenth initial, an F, which wouldn't even be the first or only F, having been preceded four husbands ago by Eddie Fisher.

Waiting for the screen musical to return was a bit like waiting for Godot to sing, so I redirected my aim at the theatre. I made one random skirmish into television musicals when the English film director Clive Donner, no relation to Dick, asked me to write a 12-song score for a new film version of Victor Herbert's *Babes in Toyland*, to be made in Germany, starring Drew Barrymore, Keanu Reeves and Richard Mulligan. The piece was shot at the same Bavarian Studios in Munich where we had filmed *Willy Wonka and the Chocolate Factory*. Germany's leading soap opera series at the time, entitled *Düsseldorf*, was being made there and, in 30-foot-high letters running the entire length of their biggest sound stage was the memorable slogan '*Düsseldorf* – das Deutsche Dallas'. Drew Barrymore was 11 at the time, four years after her eye-popping performance in *ET* and, during my few days there, I instantly and all too temporarily became the father figure she was desperately searching for. Drew was adorable and stunningly bright, her ever-present mother Jade a strangely contradictory figure, which would soon bring their complicated relationship to the boil.

Hillard Elkins delivered Frank Wildhorn to my door. He had called to say that he was representing someone he regarded as an unusually talented young composer, who was in desperate need of a collaborator, and could they drop round that evening to say hello. Evie and I were packing to leave for Mexico early the next morning, I was up to my furrowed brow in work, but I said 'OK' and round they came. Frank was still in his twenties, but pretty sure of himself, and explained that he had been working on 'this musical' since he was a student at USC, and asked would I give it a listen. I took the proffered audio-cassette with me to Acapulco, where I promptly forgot all about it for several days, until I saw it sitting forlornly on my dressing table one evening before dinner. Guiltily, I slipped it into my Walkman, sat on the terrace and opened the door to the next chapter of my life. Hilly was right. Frank was good.

'This musical' was *Jekyll and Hyde*, and the music was as good as the lyrics were bad. Put another way, the music was sensational and the lyrics diabolical. Apart from that, I also found it hard to believe that no one had ever had the brilliant thought of making *Jekyll and Hyde* into a musical before. But no one had. I called Hilly and arranged to meet with Frank as soon as I returned to LA.

The book of *Jekyll and Hyde* was even worse than the lyrics. No wonder Frank was desperate to escape. I said I would only get involved if Frank and I could start again from scratch, with only Robert Louis Stevenson as our guide. There was no other way to tackle it. Bruce Grakal, my brainbox Beatles lawyer, deployed his considerable skills to work out a settlement with Frank's previous collaborator, who was clearly a big Dylan Thomas fan, because he had no intention of going gentle into that good night. For a new composer who had yet to complete his first show, Frank had far too many people owning sizeable pieces of him. Bruce had to contend with lawyers and managers and agents and publishers coming out of the woodwork at every turn, to complicate and confuse what should have been a simple and straightforward matter. I felt sorry for Frank. The musical, like Hell, hath no fury like a no-talent collaborator scorned. A deal was painfully concluded, the no-talent collaborator generously disposed of, kicking and screaming, and the talented Frank was free to embark upon his *Jekyll and Hyde* journey. I was happy to be going with him.

Not since my halcyon days with Tony Newley was songwriting this much fun. I kept the music I liked best, and wove the resulting songs into my libretto. A strong storyline soon emerged from Dr Henry Jekyll's legendary exploration into the duality of man. Across that summer, aided by FedExes and faxes and phone calls and audio-cassettes flying back and forth across the Atlantic, the first-draft book and score fell swiftly into place. Frank fed me the new music wherever I needed it. His richly theatrical melodies, cushioned in his exciting contemporary style, soon made it clear that the score was going to contain more than its share of singable songs.

By summer's end, we had a first-draft book and score we were well pleased with. The reaction to our work was immediate and encouraging. Everyone realised what Frank and I had known from day one, that we could write good songs together. The enterprising Frank, God knows how, persuaded RCA Records in New York to release a concept album of the score, sung by Colm Wilkinson, the original Jean Valjean from *Les Misérables*, and a sensational and great-looking girl singer from Minnesota called Linda Eder, whom both Frank and I, before we met, had seen paralysing the competition week after week on an NBC-TV talent show called *Star Search*. No one came close to challenging her huge audience appeal and, in the end, the host of *Star Search*,

Ed McMahon, paid her $100,000 to go away. Where Linda Eder went away to was Frank Wildhorn, who displayed even more enterprise in bringing her permanently into his world as the voice of his music and the love of his life.

The greatest response to our songs, just as with Newley, came from singers. Frank came over to London to plan the album, which we were recording at George Martin's AIR Studios in Oxford Circus. Evie and I had lunch one day at Le Suquet, a favourite French fish restaurant, with Sammy Davis and Liza Minnelli, who happened to be in London simultaneously. Liza knew about *Jekyll and Hyde* and asked how it was going. I replied by asking them both if they'd like to hear a couple of the songs.

The expression on Frank Wildhorn's face when I drove by to collect him with Sammy and Liza sitting side by side in the back of my car was a photograph I wish I had taken. We went back to the Mayfair Hotel, where both Sam and Liza were staying. We played them just two songs. The first was 'This Is the Moment'. 'That's mine!' said Sam, promptly and proprietorially, without a second's hesitation. We played 'A New Life'. 'And that's mine!' yelled Liza. I grinned at Frank, who was near delirious with joy. We were on our way.

The Broadway ball started, if not exactly rolling, at least moving perceptibly forward. There was even talk, thanks to Frank's power-plant energy and enthusiasm, of a New York production as early as the following spring. Wiser heads prevailed, making it a year later. Wiser heads still proposed a regional try-out first, which is why and how we all found ourselves at the Alley Theatre in Houston 18 months later.

My telephone rang in early September. It was Ms Minnelli. She said, 'Where would you and Evie like to go for Christmas and New Year. Tokyo? Australia? Let me know and I'll see if I can get a gig there, and they can take care of the four of us.'

I half-jokingly said, 'Hawaii would be just fine,' and promptly forgot all about it.

My telephone rang again in early October. It was Liza, to tell me we were all set to fly to Hawaii for two weeks on such-and-such a date in December, to spend Christmas and New Year there. After cliff-hanging negotiations about whether the place would be completed in time, she had got herself the Hawaiian gig of all gigs, to open a staggering new hotel called the Waikaloa Beach Hotel on the big island of Hawaii. The deal went like this: four first-class, round-trip air tickets on Pan Am from London to Honolulu; the two-bedroom, four-bathroom Presidential Suite, with its 200-foot-long terrace overlooking the beach; our own helicopter (!); a plane for inter-island hopping; and free everything that the hotel had to offer. In exchange, Liza had to do one one-hour show, or longer if she wished, on New Year's Eve, for which she would receive the meagre sum of $750,000. Now *that's* a Merry Christmas!

We all agreed that the 10,000-square-foot Presidential Suite would have been a reasonable place to have spent the rest of our lives. On Christmas morning, Liza and I sat on the floor together having breakfast in front of the giant television screen, watching her father's ageless movie of *An American in Paris*. Humming Gershwin's main love theme during the 'American in Paris' ballet as Gene Kelly and Leslie Caron danced around the Place de la Concorde fountain, Liza said casually, 'I've always wanted to sing that,' to which I responded, equally casually, 'OK, I'll put a lyric on it,' which proved to be a fateful comment.

Liza's overwhelming generosity was, as always, a great joy, but it was by no means the greatest favour she did us that Christmas. She also saved our lives. Before she confirmed the Hawaii trip, Evie and I had been booked to fly to New York on the same Pan Am flight we always took. The tickets were on my desk for over a month. Liza's plans caused me to change that flight at the last minute in order to meet up with her and Mark instead. The air tickets I changed 48 hours beforehand were for Pan Am flight 803, now forever known to the world as the Lockerbie flight.

'Open the Door', the ravishing main theme from Bernardo Bertolucci's prodigiously beautiful film *The Last Emperor*, was the first of my two collaborations with the brilliant young Japanese composer Ryuichi Sakamoto.

Sakamoto and I sort of met under the most unlikely circumstances. It is worth telling. We did not need to meet for the songs. That was merely a matter of my finding appropriate lyrics for his haunting melodies. The executive producer of the film's soundtrack recording, Ray Williams, thought it would be a nice idea for Ryuichi and myself to meet while everyone was in LA for the Academy Awards, at which *The Last Emperor* won all nine Oscars for which it was nominated, including, naturally, Mr Sakamoto for Best Score.

Our meeting was to be at the Bel-Age Hotel the following afternoon at 5.00pm. I arrived at the appointed hour and went up to the suite. Mr Sakamoto's manager let me in, and we chatted courteously as he led me into the sitting room. There, laid out on the dining table, still in full evening dress and apparently dead, though with a hint of a smile on his face, was Mr Sakamoto. He reminded me of Peter O'Toole in exactly the same position playing the drunken actor Alan Swan in *My Favourite Year*. The manager went on chatting as though the circumstances were completely normal and nothing was the matter. And indeed nothing was. I stayed for an hour. The corpse never moved. We decided not to wake him. It had apparently been a kamikaze kind of party. Very few survivors. I felt happy for all of them. There are few feelings as great as winning an Oscar, and few feelings as bad as waking up to the hangover that inevitably greets the following day.

I left as quietly as I had come. I never met Mr Sakamoto, but I love his music and I will never lose that memorable image of him. I suppose I should call him my silent partner. A couple of years later, I wrote my second song with him, the title song for Bertolucci's *The Sheltering Sky*. I wonder if he knows.

At the opposite end of the cinematic scale was the embarrassing fate of a screenplay I wrote, entitled *Train of Events*, a sophisticated comedy thriller with an intricate plot and three though–I–say–so cleverly interwoven central roles for two men and one woman. I had written it speculatively, more for fun than profit, with Michael Caine, Roger Moore and Shirley MacLaine in mind as the leading trio. Much of the story unfolded during a journey on the Orient Express across Europe, hence the (I thought) witty title. I researched the piece in fanatical detail, one day calling Elton John at the Ritz Hotel in Paris to ask him a bizarre question. 'Would you do me a favour, my dear,' I said, 'and go downstairs into the Place Vendôme and tell me how many paces it is from the front door of the Ritz to the front door of Cartier's.'

'Eighty-six, Les,' he replied without a second's hesitation. 'I thought everyone knew that,' and hung up. He was right, by the way.

Roger and Mike both liked the script, but nothing happened until the day I got an urgent call from Dennis Selinger, Mike's much-loved agent at ICM. 'Menachem Golin is desperately looking for a vehicle to co-star Mike and Roger, and they both mentioned your *Orient Express* script,' he said.

Before you could say Menachem Golin, I was paid an obscenely high price for my screenplay, and 20 minutes later Evie and I were at the Cannes Film Festival with Mike, Roger and Joan Collins, whom I was lucky to recruit at short notice to replace Shirley MacLaine, who was far away making another film. The film and the stars were announced, with Michael Winner as director. I had known Michael since he was a 17-year-old undergraduate at Downing College, Cambridge, reading Law, and we had always been good friends, but sophisticated comedy thrillers had never, to my recollection, been the main thrust of his previous cinematic oeuvre.

I need not have worried. It did not remain a sophisticated comedy thriller for long. While I took the money and ran like a thief in the night, my old chum Michael took what I thought was my witty and clever screenplay, which all three leading actors had approved, and inexplicably proceeded to disembowel and 'improve' it by bringing in a bunch of TV comedy writers of his acquaintance, who, for reasons known only to themselves, God and Michael Winner, decided that this film should become a big belly-laugh knockabout farce, to which none of its three stars was by nature, style or temperament suited. Then Joan was dumped without ceremony from the picture in favour of some pneumatic American blonde whose name I have happily forgotten, because I was so appalled by everything that was going on that I never saw the disastrous finished product. Even the title was arbitrarily changed, to *Bullseye*, but the embarrassing mess of a movie they ended up with was anything but. Mercifully, it was never shown outside England, and it is a tribute to both Mike and Roger's high standing with the movie-going public that it didn't do them more damage than it did. It was no one's finest hour.

There are moments in life when the infinite perversity of both the film industry and the Department of Fate defy rational explanation. Take the instance above. I was paid a large sum of money for a good screenplay, which, in my view, I deserved, of which little or nothing was used, which, in my view, I didn't deserve. A bad screenplay was filmed instead, which it didn't deserve, and the press murdered it, which it did deserve. I still like to think that, if they had filmed the right screenplay in the first place, there would have been a different train of events, so to speak.

It is one of the classic ongoing inconsistencies of musicals and songwriting that you can work for weeks, months or even years on a project that comes to nothing and, conversely, receive huge rewards and lasting acclaim for work that has taken only days, sometimes even hours.

Happily for me, the songs for the *Home Alone* movies fall into the latter category. Late one October evening, my telephone rang in the South of France. It was John Williams, calling from California. Having started out as Johnny Williams in the 1950s and 60s, he elevated himself to the more dignified John Williams as his career blossomed in the early 1970s. By now, at the beginning of the 1990s, his career had become so distinguished and Oscar-ridden that I elevated him still higher and renamed him the more appropriately classical Giovanni, which I have called him ever since. I remain to him what I have always been, simply Brickman.

'Brickman,' he said, 'I've just finished scoring this enchanting little film called *Home Alone*, and there's this theme I think would make a charming song. But we don't have a lot of time. The film opens worldwide in about five weeks. It's a Christmas movie.'

He explained the story of Kevin being left at home alone by his vacationing family, which was to bring instant fame to young Macaulay Culkin, and the context of the song. He FedExed me the music. By the following Wednesday, we had completed the song 'Somewhere in My Memory' and, by Thursday night, we had two songs, since Giovanni had also composed a hauntingly beautiful Christmas carol, to which I added a lyric entitled 'Star of Bethlehem'.

The film opened shortly afterwards, becoming not only a massive box-office Christmas hit, but the most successful screen comedy of all time. A few weeks later, *Home Alone* was nominated for two Academy Awards – Best Score and Best Song – two for John and one for me, a wondrous extra reward for my long weekend's work. *Home Alone 2 – Lost in New York*, which rolled around, as sequels tend to do, exactly two years later, enabled John and myself to add three further Christmas songs from the two movies into an enchanting Christmas medley, which he still performs regularly each Christmas with the Boston Pops.

But a bigger bonus was forthcoming from the first *Home Alone* songs. When he received the final drafts of the two lyrics, John called me from Amblin Entertainment to say how pleased he was with the finished product. He suddenly said, 'Hold on a minute, Brickman.' After a few seconds, he came back on the line and added, 'That was Steven...' – he meant Spielberg. 'I told him how pleased I was with the songs, and he asked if you'd like to do *Hook*!'

Only in Hollywood. If John had called me five minutes sooner or later, the chances are that I would not have been aboard Pan Am Flight 121 from London to Los Angeles the following week, reading a brand-new, big, fat screenplay, on my way to a series of meetings with the best film composer and the best film director in the world.

It is fair to assume that a motion picture involving the awesome collective abilities of Steven Spielberg, Dustin Hoffman, Robin Williams, Julia Roberts, Bob Hoskins, Maggie Smith and John Williams would be an interesting project. The assumption would be correct, and the project would be *Hook*.

From that December morning when I attended my first *Hook* production meeting in producer Kathleen Kennedy's sumptuous suite of offices at Amblin Entertainment's Santa Fe ranch-style spread at the Universal Studios lot, I found it hard to believe that, 12 months hence, this staggeringly complex motion picture would be showing in thousands of movie theatres across America.

I had been around a few pretty fancy film projects, from *Doctor Dolittle* to *Superman* to *Victor/Victoria* to *Santa Claus*, and worked with a few daunting talents, from Rex Harrison to Peter O'Toole to Julie Andrews to Albert Finney to Sammy Davis to Alec Guinness to Blake Edwards, but never quite so many heavyweights at once. And everyone in the room was so cool about the unfathomable complications that lay ahead. But looking at who was talking, I realised that, given what this extraordinary group of people had achieved together in the preceding 15 years, from *Jaws* to *Close Encounters* to *ET* and the *Indiana Jones* trilogy, they had a great deal to be cool about.

Some five years before this, Steven Spielberg had tried to make a film of *Peter Pan*, starring Michael Jackson as The Boy Who Refused to Grow Up. John had written some memorable main themes for it. But it didn't happen and, if something Steven Spielberg wants to do doesn't happen, it can't be done. I remembered being in New York around that time, and spending Dickie Attenborough's first day of filming *A Chorus Line* with him in the Mark Hellinger Theater, when he was shooting the vast opening audition sequence. When he saw me arrive, he pressed a blue envelope into my hand and said, 'Brickman, darling, I was asked to give you this.'

This was a handwritten letter from Michael Jackson, whom I hadn't seen since he was a kid with The Jackson Five, performing with Sammy Davis in Reno, Nevada, telling me how much he loved the *Peter Pan* songs I had written with Newley, and how they had 'greatly affected my life'.

Finally, at last, it was about to happen. Not *Peter Pan* exactly, but a fascinating variation on the theme – Peter as a man who has finally grown up, and now is forced by circumstance, the kidnapping of his children by Captain Hook, to travel back to the world of his once endless childhood. Clever stuff, a brilliant twist in the tale, with a highly imaginative screenplay by Phil V. Hart.

Spielberg's enthusiasm for the project was infectious and overwhelming. John Napier, the English theatre designer, had already built Hook's amazing pirate ship, the *Jolly Roger*. It was gigantic, and Steven took me all over it with schoolboy relish, clambering way up into the dizzy heights of Hook's lavish cabin, overflowing with the baubles of his ill-gotten booty, far above the studio floor below. John Williams, who had no head for heights other than musical ones, did not accompany us. But we were both caught up in the swirl of Steven's vision and, in a blur of activity, we went to work, pouring out a stream of pirate songs and Hook songs and Wendy songs and Lost Boy songs and Tinkerbell and Peter songs, the audio-cassettes flying back and forth between us, John in LA and me in Mexico. I flew up for meetings whenever needed, which was frequently.

In the story, which was contemporary, Wendy, played by Maggie Smith, is now 90 years old. About six weeks into the shoot, John and I wrote a highly reflective and, we thought, slightly wonderful song for her character, entitled 'Childhood', which I regarded as the root song of the score, since it represented the very heart of what the movie was about. Steven thought so, too. He loved it, called it a home run, and wanted to shoot it the next day, which was Maggie's last on the picture. Maggie is not, alas, a singer, and so we somehow needed to create an instant overnight demo for a 90-year-old Wendy. I called Julie Andrews, who was just starting a picture of her own. Trouper that she is, and a good pal of Maggie's, she learned the song on the telephone with John and myself, drove over to the big recording stage at MGM on her lunch break next day, stood on the exact spot where Judy Garland had recorded 'Over the Rainbow' 50 years before, and sang 'Childhood' in the deliciously wavering voice of a 90-year-old Wendy. It was perfection on the first take. She was with us maybe seven minutes. Steven shot Maggie doing the song at four o'clock that same afternoon.

Dustin Hoffman as Hook was not keen to sing, even though he is musical and a good pianist. He reluctantly rehearsed a comedy song called 'Stick with Me', Hook's recruiting song for the children to become trainee pirates. Robin Williams, on the other hand, as Peter the man, was dying to sing in the film and, at a meeting in Steven's office, as a personal propaganda tactic, he improvised wildly funny imaginary dialogues he claimed to have overheard between John Lennon in heaven and Paul McCartney on earth, John urging mankind to 'give this man songs'.

Hook was an awesomely complex undertaking, given the time restrictions and the dazzling demands of the original screenplay. I noticed that Steven was now working with a lady screenwriter, changing things as they went. Even given the almost unlimited imagination and financing at his disposal, I was awestruck by Steven's ability to stay always focused on the ultimate objective and, at the same time, pay attention to the most minute detail of every day-to-day aspect of the infinitely complex creation in hand, while keeping an open mind to the ever-present probability of change, long after the 11th hour had been and gone, a unique and irresistible combination of talents, especially since he was additionally all the time bringing to the whole enterprise a constant and sustained burst of creative energy. And by 'sustained', I mean a *year*. No wonder John Williams called him The Young Prince.

But unhappily for Giovanni and myself, it became increasingly clear that the final film was going to be considerably overlong, an undeniable hazard for the always-vulnerable-because-they-are-so-easily-cuttable songs. We were philosophical about it, because we had to be. Had the film been envisioned as a musical a year sooner, rather than at the last minute, it could have been a prettier story to tell. As it was, a sprinkling of songs found their way into the picture, and the best ones sadly didn't. We were particularly heartbroken to lose 'Childhood' but, in the end, it had to go, because there was simply no time or place for it. But working on this film was always exciting and always challenging, as any Spielberg movie is bound to be, so remarkable is this filmmaker. And, at the end of the day, there was an unexpected consolation prize when the little lullaby for the film, 'When You're Alone', excruciatingly sung by Peter Pan's kidnapped daughter aboard the *Jolly Roger*, was nominated for an Academy Award. She reprised it, equally excruciatingly, at the Oscar ceremony. All of which made Giovanni and myself reflect still more on the loss of our beloved 'Childhood'.

Tom and Jerry have been in my life since I was a teenager. So when Hank Mancini called me one fine spring morning to ask me if I'd like to write half-a-dozen songs with him for *Tom and Jerry – the Movie*, my instantaneous reaction was to find myself back in the Ritz and Empire Theatres in Leicester Square, in London, in the mid-1940s, marvelling that these happy childhood memories should have come to seek me out nearly half-a-century later and allow me to become a part of them.

Hank and I had enormous fun writing those songs, which, of course, for lip-synching purposes, we had to do *before* the film was animated. It was the fulfilment of another lifelong ambition of mine, to work on an animated film for the first time. The entire production team, led by Roger Mayer of Turner Entertainment and Phil Roman, the film's producer, he who also delivers *The Simpsons* to our television screens, made it a delicious experience for Hank and myself, which I guess is the way one would like to imagine such a project would be.

The film made two irreparable mistakes, which worried me from the outset, but on which it was not our job to comment, although I did, and do again now. In all the years of all the *Tom and Jerry* cartoons, they never once spoke. They merely concentrated their energies on trying constantly to kill one another in the most outlandish and ingenious ways imaginable. In this film, they not only speak, they become inseparable pals with a common quest, to find the missing little girl. They even sing a duet together, called 'Friends to the End'. It's charming, and there's plenty of humour in the piece, but the constant death-defying conflict that was the lifeblood of Tom and Jerry's murderous head-to-head relationship is sadly missing.

Which brings us back to the great Joe Barbera, who, with his lifelong collaborator and business partner, Bill Hanna, created Tom and Jerry, and brought us more laughs than we could ever count. The man is a phenomenon, and an object lesson for us all. Some seven or eight frisky decades into his career – he looks 25 years younger than his considerable age – he remains as creatively inventive as he ever was, and is living proof and a constant reminder to everyone who meets him that, if the child lives on within the man, he will truly never grow old. Peter Pan please note.

6th Key Change

7th Key: G Undiminished

I guess I could claim it was all Liza's fault. 'OK, I'll put a lyric on it,' I had blithely said that Christmas morning in Hawaii when Ms Minnelli and I were sitting on the floor watching *An American in Paris* and she had commented on how much she had always wanted to sing the main romantic theme. A few weeks later, down in Mexico, I actually *did* put a lyric on it. It was a fascinating exercise, suddenly to be able to sing a great Gershwin melody that you had known all your life and no one had ever sung before. I called it 'Paris in the Spring', and I thought it was pretty damn good. The music was still in copyright, of course, and that should have been that, but I knew it wasn't.

Having adored Gershwin's glorious gifts all my life, I now became increasingly intrigued by the fact that nothing had ever been done, no attempt even made, to lyricise his instrumental works. I played my André Previn recording of *An American in Paris* over and over again, 20, 30, 50 times, and it dawned on me like springtime that the whole thing could and maybe should be allowed to sing, so evocative was the music. The title proposed the storyline. It was a perfect little 15-minute, one-Act musical playlet. Was it too sacrilegious even to contemplate? Probably. But hadn't Oscar Hammerstein in principle done exactly the same thing with Bizet's *Carmen* when he created *Carmen Jones*? Yes, but that was public domain. And no, it was already an opera with a storyline and a libretto to adapt and translate. Ah, but Forrest and Wright had most certainly done it and done it *three times*, no less, first with the music of Grieg in *Song of Norway*, then Borodin in *Kismet*, and finally Dvorak in *Summer Song*. So *there* was my justification... wasn't it? Yes, but that was public domain.

I argued back and forth with myself thus, but I already knew I was hooked, and slowly, in whatever spare time I could muster in the months ahead, like a jigsaw junkie licking his lips at the prospect of a million-piece, 40-foot-square puzzle of a snowstorm, I began to fool around with verbalising the ultimate musical intricacies of this dazzling little masterpiece sample of Gershwin's virtuosity.

And, of course, it goes without saying that, once you pass the point of no return on *An American in Paris*, your nose is starting to twitch at the possibilities of the rest of Gershwin's instrumental oeuvre, from *Rhapsody in Blue* to *The Cuban Overture* to the *Concerto in F*, and even to the preludes. If it works with one of them, you say to yourself, then it can work with *all* of them. And thus it was that for the next two-and-a-half years, I would devote an insane number of hours to tackling what, in effect, would become the world's biggest musical crossword puzzle, in an Olympian effort to create a concert-length theatrical evening made up of Gershwin's sung instrumental pieces.

Liza was everywhere else in our lives, too. She presented me with an Ivor Novello Award at that annual songwriting achievements event at the Grosvenor House Hotel in London. A month later, Tony Newley and I were inducted into the Songwriters' Hall of Fame at Radio City Music Hall in New York, only the fourth and fifth Englishmen, we proudly noted, to be so honoured, after Noël Coward, John Lennon and Paul McCartney. Once again, it was Ms Liza May who handed out our honours, and she and Linda Eder sang our songs for us. That summer, she was in London again with Frank Sinatra and Sammy Davis Jr with the modestly titled 'The Ultimate Event', where these three Titans of their trade brought the cheering capacity audience at the Royal Albert Hall to their feet time and again with an endless parade of the great songs they had made indelible in all our minds.

After the opening night, Evie and I went to the mercifully small private dinner, Frank's idea, three tables for 12 overlooking the Thames from the Savoy hotel, one table apiece for each of the three stars. As I looked around that glamorous gathering and thought of those glittering careers, it crossed my mind that I might possibly be witnessing the beginning of the twilight of the gods. I was, and far, far sooner than I could ever have imagined.

A few weeks later, we saw Liza and Sammy performing together again, this time at the Red Cross Gala at the Sporting Club in Monaco. Frank did not join them this time, as he rightly felt he had done more than his share of these events, and he said to me, 'If I do another one of these, they're gonna walk out as I walk in!' Sammy and Liza were both in fantastic voice, spurring each other on to even greater heights. They were sensational. Sammy returned to California the following day.

Little did we know we had just seen him perform for the last time. The day after he arrived home, he visited his dentist in LA. An X-ray revealed a shadow in his throat, and he was promptly diagnosed with throat cancer.

I'm wrong. We did see Sammy perform one last time after that, at a phenomenal evening our great producer friend George Schlatter had the inspired insight to put together at the Shrine Auditorium in Los Angeles two or three months later, just after Sammy had completed what at that time was wrongly perceived to be his successful chemotherapy treatment.

It wasn't by chance that Frank Sinatra, Dean Martin, Bob Hope, Shirley MacLaine, Eddie Murphy, Whitney Houston, Stevie Wonder, Michael Jackson, Bill Cosby, Richard Pryor, Goldie

Hawn, Gregory Peck, Clint Eastwood, Quincy Jones, Mike Tyson, Gregory Hines, Ella Fitzgerald, Jesse Jackson, Dionne Warwick, Diahann Carroll, Magic Johnson and hosts of others, the most staggering array of assembled talent I have ever seen, were gathered together in one place that evening to honour one man. All of them, picking up on George Schlatter's instinct, somehow *knew* they had to be there that night. All of us close to Sammy had to be there. And all of us were. Deep down, although we didn't want to admit it, we all harboured the nagging fear that we were going to lose him.

And the most hard-bitten, sophisticated 'Triple-A' group of Hollywood's 'we've-seen-it-all' cognoscenti who were present there on that never-to-be-forgotten night knew as they watched that, until that moment, they *hadn't* seen it all. That night they did. For maybe the first time in his life, certainly for the first time in *50* years, Frank Sinatra *opened* the show rather than closed it.

That night, before our eyes, we saw Sammy become the full-fledged legend that we had always known he was destined to be. That night, his immortality in our profession was indelibly constructed out of the words and songs and tributes that poured out from the hearts and the love of his friends and peers. They collectively built an indestructible monument of honour to him as we watched. He was publicly thanked for his pioneering achievements and his endless humanitarian generosity towards a thousand charitable causes.

The given reason for the evening was the celebration of his unbelievable 60 years in showbusiness at the age of 63. The real reason, thanks to the ever-perceptive George Schlatter, was that we were suddenly seeing what he was in full perspective, more than the performer, the man.

Sammy had done it all. Throughout his life, he had broken down every barrier, triumphed over every obstacle and injustice. He had travelled through and overcome the endless labyrinths of prejudice during his incredible 60-year journey. His limitless talents and his indomitable spirit combined to say more about the world he had lived in than any political spokesman of our time could articulate. For more than half-a-century he had been a front-line soldier, a true eyewitness to the painfully emerging history of the African-American struggle for equality and justice.

It all came together that night. And we all feared, but didn't want to face it quite yet, that he was going to be taken from us. God bless George Schlatter for giving us cause to be there.

One moment above all stood out from among a hundred outstanding moments that this remarkable evening provided. Gregory Hines, after trying, as he put it, 'to dance out' his love for Sammy, gently persuaded Sam to get into his tap shoes, which George had sneakily purloined from Sam's house and placed under his chair. The audience went crazy. 'What do you want to do?' ventured Greg cautiously. Sammy grinned his lavish evil grin, and replied, 'Whatever's easy for you!' breaking himself up. And then the two of them danced together. Sammy enthralled us all one last time, matching his *Taps* movie partner Greg lick for lick for a couple of magic minutes, until Sam ended it, like the line from 'Mr Bojangles', when, with a final graceful leap, he 'clicked his heels'. Greg kneeled and kissed Sammy's tapshoes.

Michael Jackson provided a meaningful coda to the evening with a little song he had written with Buz Kohan especially for the occasion. Entitled 'You Were There', it was a recognition of what Sammy had battled all his life to achieve to clear the way for the generations of talented young black performers who were to follow him. The last line of the lyric said it all in the compact, concisely crafted way that only a good lyric can: 'I am here, because you were there!'

While the magic of that famous evening was still upon me, I wrote Sammy a letter the following morning, telling him what the evening had meant to his friends, the musical expression and fulfilment of so much love from all of us to him, for all he meant to us. What I wrote in that letter obviously reached the inner place in him that I hoped it would, because a few days later he called to tell me that the letter was now framed and hanging between his only other two framed letters, one from Jack Benny and one from Fred Astaire. I said that was perfectly acceptable company to be in.

My last indelible memory of Sam took place at his house, 1151, Summit Drive, Beverly Hills, former home of Tony Newley and Joan Collins and, before them, Tony Curtis and Janet Leigh, on his 64th and last birthday, 8 December 1989, when we were still hoping and praying that what we were being told was true, that the throat cancer treatments had been successful and that Sammy would be resuming work in February.

Sammy was in the vast living room, sitting at the PacMan table, underneath the Leroy Nieman portrait of him in *Golden Boy*, with his arms raised in Rocky-style triumph above his head, when Greg Hines came in the room. Maybe four or five of the people present saw what happened. Evie and I were two of them. Sammy got up to welcome Greg. It maybe lasted 15 seconds. They greeted one another with a smooth exchange of hand movements and wondrous improvised dance steps, which incorporated greetings, love, humour, style, tradition and mutual respect and admiration, all expressed in the untranslatable but unmistakable silent language of great dancers. It was better than the best ten pages of dialogue ever written, and a beautiful sight to see, a final delicious, carefree moment to illustrate the last evening we would ever spend with our beloved Sam.

He died the following May, when we were in Houston preparing to open *Jekyll and Hyde*. Evie and I flew into LA for the funeral, which we attended with George and Jolene Schlatter. Sam was buried at Forest Lawn, beside Sam Sr, his father, and his 'uncle', Will Mastin, reuniting The Will Mastin Trio for eternity.

Afterwards, the four of us repaired to Le Dome restaurant on Sunset Boulevard for a late lunch and two hours of reminiscence about the thousands of glittering moments that we had shared with Sam over three decades, and the Schlatters four. There was no explaining the exquisite timing of life that had brought Sammy and me together at the beginning of those magical 1960s, and with no game plan ever even contemplated, caused him to sing so many of my songs over the ensuing 30 years; 60 songs, one for each of his 60 phenomenal years as a performer, starting with 'What Kind of Fool Am I?' in London in 1961, and ending with 'This Is the Moment' in Hawaii in 1989. No songwriter can ever have been more blessed than I was by Sammy. To the last, he carried the name of Talent before him like a banner. He is an enduring symbol to all people, black and white, of what is possible. His life was not exemplary, but his gifts were. He was the total and vibrant embodiment of the adage 'The secret of life is knowing when you're happy'. Oh, Sam, how wonderful it all was, the party that was your life!

Jekyll and Hyde was an instant success when it opened at the Alley Theater in Houston in the early spring of 1990, stylishly directed by the Alley's artistic director, Gregory Boyd, and starring Chuck Wagner, a Frank Wildhorn contemporary from the University of Southern California, as both the gentle Dr Jekyll and the evil Mr Hyde, and the golden-voiced and gorgeous Linda Eder, by now the purposeful Frank Wildhorn's fiancée, ending his own personal star search, as the tragic heroine, Lucy. The theatre-going public lapped it up, faults and all, packing the place to the rafters, and standing, stomping and cheering at the end of every performance. People saw it 10, 20 and 30 times, and its run was extended three or four times across the summer, creating an immediate cult following, a die-hard fan club that proudly named themselves 'The Jekkies', who were madly in love with both the show and its shining new star, Linda Eder. From the first performance to the last, the lovely Linda stopped the show with every song she sang, so her star search, too, was over.

Paradoxically, the biggest, most unlikely and almost insurmountable problem that *Jekyll and Hyde* faced, from the beginning of its extraordinary life, was that it smelled of success. It was, in fact, full of flaws, as most first-draft shows are, but what *did* work worked so well that it dragged people back into the theatre time and again. We were immediately pounced on by a dubious bevy of chequebook-waving wannabe entrepreneurs, most of whose 'Broadway' producing experience was, at best, a nodding acquaintance with the box-office grosses in the legit section of weekly *Variety*.

The problem was accentuated by the fact that the RCA concept album that Frank had so shrewdly parlayed was also an instant success. It sold amazingly well for an unknown show, and the songs started to be performed constantly on radio and television, especially Jekyll's musical call to action, 'This Is the Moment', which overnight seemed to become the anthem for every form of televised competition from The Miss America Beauty Pageant to the Winter Olympics to the Superbowl to the World Series. Its notoriety became almost embarrassing, with theatre critics relishing the cheap-shot opportunity to pick it off as 'ice-rink music'.

While Frank and I continued to work constantly with director Greg Boyd on improving the show, tightening the book and writing new and better songs, other darker forces were at work. Frank's desperate desire to move things forward into the fast lane led him instead into a ghastly misjudgement, a horrendous business alliance that the rest of us didn't find out about until it was too late. A flashy businessman promised and persuaded the innocent Frank that he would finance not only *Jekyll and Hyde*, but everything else Frank would ever write, in a cockamamie partnership deal that would make Frank the king of Broadway and rich beyond his wildest dreams. Frank, apparently, had never heard that one before, and proceeded to get himself and the show inextricably caught up in an entanglement from which it would cost him two or three frustrating years and a big bundle of bucks to cut himself loose.

All of these factors somehow combined to send *Jekyll and Hyde* sideways on to a bizarre and seemingly endless Yellow Brick Road, presided over by too many chieftains, when all we really needed was a few more Indians. After a mind-numbing, two-year legal deadlock, finally free of the businessman, the show embarked on a money-making but still far from perfect national tour.

The highlight of this otherwise desultory half-decade came when the irrepressible Frank convinced Atlantic Records – again, God knows how – that this was the perfect time to make the *second* recording of the by now two-and-a-half-hour score of our still unproduced Broadway show, this time a *double* CD concept album, which he, Frank, would produce and they, Atlantic, would release on the to-be-created Atlantic Theater label, which they, Atlantic, would form and finance, and he, Frank, would run for them. Amazingly, and at vast expense, all of this came to pass, and the resultant recording went on to become an even bigger success than its RCA predecessor.

The Yellow Brick Road finally went full circle and, in January 1995, there we were back again in our by now beloved Houston, this time at the 3,000-seat Music Hall. Once again, as in a recurring dream, Houston audiences went mad for *Jekyll and Hyde*, to the show-stopping tune of millions of box-office dollars. Finally, in the finest tradition of Yellow Brick Roads, ours led us to the Emerald City of Broadway. Thanks to the unflagging support of the ever-growing army of Jekkies, we crossed over at long, long last from the Yellow Brick Road to the Great White Way, and I am happy to report that we stayed there for four incredible years, gaining membership in the process of that most exclusive club, 'The Fifty Longest-Running Shows in Broadway History'.

The New York reaction to *Jekyll and Hyde* was predictably strange. Received comparatively coolly by the critics and ecstatically by the audiences, playing to eight standing ovations a week, every week of its long life, it was almost totally ignored by the Tony Awards committee. Our New York Jekyll, Robert Cuccioli, who gave a stunning tour de force acting and singing performance, was nominated, and was the odds-on favourite to win, but lost to the small and static performance of the lawyer in

Chicago. I was nominated for the book, but lost to *Titanic,* which maintained the proud tradition of its name and quickly sank. All it did that the original didn't was make it to New York.

The show's greatest strength, its score, and its greatest voice, Linda Eder, were completely ignored. In my view, the too-small, clubby and, I think, New York-biased Tony committee would do well to open its voting out in a more dependable and democratic fashion, in the manner of the Academy of Motion Picture Arts and Sciences, to allow *all* creative people in every craft the right to vote for their peers in each category, thus achieving the fairest selection of nominations, from which *everybody* professionally involved full-time in the Broadway theatre would pick the winners, just like they do in the movies. Six thousand votes speak a much louder and more acceptable truth than a mere handful in what strikes me as being almost a secret society.

Frank Wildhorn dealt swiftly with his disappointment by producing his *third* recording of *Jekyll and Hyde,* that most coveted of all recordings for every composer and lyricist, the original Broadway cast album, to which several more have since been added from the growing number of international productions around the world.

Evie and I had not seen Stephen Sondheim for a long time, but we bumped into him having dinner with a mutual friend at Orso's restaurant on West 46th Street in New York. We joined up and, at the end of the meal, we offered to drop Steve off at his house on East 49th Street on the way back to our hotel.

As our car crossed Times Square and Broadway, we saw three young men in the red berets of the Guardian Angels. Evie had never seen any of them before. 'Who are those people?' she asked Steve.

'They're Guardian Angels,' he replied.

'And what do they do?'

Steve couldn't resist the opportunity. 'They stop people going to see *Phantom of the Opera,*' he said.

For more than two years, I had written and rewritten and refined and perfected my lyricised versions of George Gershwin's instrumental pieces. During that time, I must have played the greatest recordings of each of these pieces 200, 300 and 400 times, maybe more, in an effort to perfect the sound of every syllable in the marriage of the words to the music. I had completed *An American in Paris*, *Rhapsody In Blue*, *The Cuban Overture* and the *Concerto in F*, plus the *Second Prelude*, which carried the title of the work overall, *In Search of Gershwin*. They finally reached the point where we could attempt demo recordings. All the pieces together ran somewhere between a total of 75 to 80 minutes. Not one note of music was changed, but the tempi of a few of the faster sections needed to be slowed slightly to accommodate the human voice. My greatest discovery was that buried in all this treasure were five 'new' beautiful Gershwin songs. Those reprised at the end would give me a natural concert-length 90 minutes.

Ian Fraser, as always, masterminded the demos, with John Williams acting as benevolent overseer to our efforts. The results were more successful than we dared hope. They proved the first and most important point that these pieces would and did sing, easily and naturally. I sent the completed recordings to some Gershwin experts of my acquaintance – Hal Prince, John Williams and André Previn among them. Hal and John wrote me glowing letters of approval. André liked what I had done but, as a purist, questioned the concept of lyricising instrumental works.

I had a series of meetings over the ensuing months with the heirs of George Gershwin's Estate, two nephews called Marc Gershwin and Leopold Godowski III. They were torn. On the one hand, they called themselves the Keepers of the Flame, yet the word was that they sold Gershwin melodies for TV commercials to companies like Dove Soap. They called *Rhapsody in Blue* the Jewel in the Crown, yet consigned it to a similar fate, advertising United Airlines. It seemed to me that they couldn't quite make up their minds whether it was about art or whether it was about money. On the one hand, they liked the idea that these new works, to which I now owned the intellectual copyright, would extend the Gershwin copyright by the length of my lifetime plus 70 years. On the other hand, they did not like the idea that I would co-own the works with them in that format.

The final New York meeting in the Gershwin World Series was a dinner at Delmonico's on Park Avenue. Evie was not with me for this flying visit, but Joan Collins was in town, and allowed me to recruit her for the day to apply her formidable feminine wiles to the cause of softening up the rock-hard hearts of the heirs to the Gershwin Estate.

The Delmonico dinner was a qualified success. The Gershwin boys and I by now pretty well understood one another's position, and Joannie did a stalwart job, playing it halfway between Mata Hari and Dorothy Parker, encouraging and cajoling them to get with the times and proceed with this dazzling project. Overall, I rated the evening a success in the same way that a French aristocrat would have considered an evening in 1789 a success if he were still alive at the end of it.

After a great deal of further legal back and forthing, Marc and Leopold said that I could go ahead with the *Concerto in F*, which I had retitled *Concerto for the Twentieth Century*. I pointed out that there was really nothing I could do with a concert or a recording that was only 30 minutes long, although I did take advantage of the offer sufficiently to arrange for opera singer Barbara Hendricks to sing the main theme from the first movement of the concerto, entitled *The World That I See*, at President Clinton's inaugural gala concert. The President himself led the standing ovation that the song received, though whether it was because of the song, or the fact that Barbara Hendricks, like himself, hailed from Little Rock, Arkansas, I have never been quite sure.

Beyond that, it was an impasse. Word got out that I had done what I had done, and I received a number of enquiries from major recording stars like Aretha Franklin. My ultimate wish is still for

In Search of Gershwin to become, first, a full-scale concert evening, and then a fully staged, choreographed, song and dance evening in the theatre but, for the time being, it's out of my hands.

He said his name was Graham Mulvein. I had never heard of him. He was a young, would-be producer, and he had an interesting idea to propose to me. He was convinced that an annual seasonal theatrical production of my movie *Scrooge* was commercially viable. He wanted to present the show in three or four major UK cities and towns each season for something like 15 weeks between, say, November and February and, in about the third year, when it had built its reputation, bring it into the West End. I liked the concept in principle, so I set Bruce the lawyer on him to work out a deal. With the co-operation of Cinema Center Films, who had made the motion picture, we went ahead.

Graham Mulvein was on friendly terms with the manager of the Alexandra Theatre in Birmingham, and a ten-week run was arranged for our opening season. We engaged a red-hot, redheaded young director called Bob Tomson, and drew up a list of possible actors to play the title role of the miserly old Scrooge. I called Richard Harris, who had been the first choice for the movie 20 years before, and who now, with his long white straggly hair, looked so much like Scrooge that he could have gone on stage without make-up. Richard modestly demanded a deal tantamount to about one-third of the gross theatre box-office potential, so that was the end of that.

I possessed a list of a dozen or so other Scrooges that had been drawn up, but not one single name on it got me enthused. The Department of Fate chose that moment to step into the picture. Tony Newley, my beloved old Newberg, after more than 25 years based in the United States, had decided to move back to England with his 90-year-old mother, Grace. The marriage to Dareth was over, Newberg was disillusioned with the United States, and he was returning to he knew not what. I called him. One phone conversation, and we had our Scrooge.

I wrote half-a-dozen new songs for the stage version, enjoying the fascinating experience of revisiting a successful project years later and actually finding ways to improve it.

Skilfully directed by Bob Tomson, and with an appealing cross-section of TV, film and theatre names in the other principal roles, the show opened in Birmingham on 9 November 1992. About a hundred London 'celebrities' travelled up for the opening on a specially chartered train, and the show received enormous publicity and glowing reviews. Newley got across-the-board raves, and was instantly back in business in England after his long absence. And so, in a variation on a former theme, were Bricusse and Newley.

Newley found the role of his life as Scrooge, matched only by his performance as Littlechap in *Stop the World*. He was merely sensational and, for me, it was the most satisfying and rewarding of professional reunions. I guess it was for him, too, because he went on to play it for six years, the last season triumphantly at the Dominion Theatre in London's West End.

Overseas offers for *Scrooge* started to come in, and the first productions were set for Australia, Japan and the Benelux countries. Evie and I, who hadn't been to Australia since our honeymoon, flew to Melbourne for the Christmas première at the gorgeous Princess Theatre. I don't know whether it had occurred to the Australian producer, David Marriner, that Christmas in Oz is in midsummer, but the temperature was edging up around 100°F when Santa Claus led the Scrooge Christmas Parade through the streets of the city. Keith Michell was splendid in the title role, and the production was first-rate, but I think the Australian government is seriously going to have to consider moving its Christmas to June, their midwinter, if *Scrooge* is going to continue appearing there, so that the show won't have to continue competing unnaturally with the Australian Open Tennis Championships taking place just down the street in the sizzlingly hot, midsummer sunshine.

We also went over for the stunning Japanese première in Tokyo, presented by the Himawari (Sunflower) Theatre Group, in which the great Japanese actor Ichimura played the role of 'Scroogie-san' in spectacular fashion, which he has continued to do for several subsequent seasons. The show sounded fantastic in Japanese, even though the only four words we understood during the entire evening were the four words, inexplicably sung in English from the song entitled 'Sank You Velly Much'.

With many annual productions of *Scrooge*, both professional and amateur, now taking place in England, the United States and around the world, it all goes to show that Graham Mulvein was right to have called me. And we were treated to an unexpected Dickensian bonus when Sir Harry Secombe decided that this was the right moment for him to reprise his role of a lifetime as Pickwick. Opening at the Chichester Festival in the summer of 1993, he successfully toured the show around the United Kingdom for several seasons, including a return to the West End, equalling the triumph he had first scored in the show 30 years before.

Anthony Newley died on 16 April 1999. Later that same day, in a state of shocked disbelief, I wrote his obituary for the London *Daily Telegraph*, feeling as though I had died a little bit myself. The cancer that had invaded him a decade before, causing the loss of a kidney, returned with a vengeance in 1997. His dearest wish, to play Scrooge for one more season, was to be denied him.

Evie and I had been in New York, on our way to visit him and his last love, Gina Frattini, in Florida. The end was sudden and, without changing our air tickets or our schedule, we went to a funeral instead of a reunion. His son Sacha and I spoke the eulogies. Dareth, his ex-wife, organised the funeral with loving care. Tony's devoted mother Grace, by then in her late nineties, was heartbreakingly present, and watching her that day was the saddest thing of all.

There was no one ever like Newberg. Sweet, lovable, generous, and fall-down funny. Writing together, we had been like two halves of one person. Our talents and our souls were in perfect synch. It was the ideal collaboration, because every day was pure joy. Evie, who was there at the beginning and there at the end of the 40-year friendship, always knew when Tony and I were talking on the telephone or working together, because of the constant peals of uncontrollable laughter that punctuated everything we said and did. Evie was the third corner of the Bricusse–Newley triangle. She understood everything about us both, she was our mascot and our inspiration, and she and only she totally shared our sense of humour.

I think Evie and I were closer to Newley than any other two people alive, because we knew every aspect of his life and were *involved* in every aspect of his life, the stage shows, the films, the TV shows, the recordings, the cabarets, the writing, the composing, the singing, the acting, the directing, the ups, the downs, the smiles, the frowns (sorry, Alan), the successes, the flops, the marriages, the children, the myriad women, the divorces, the houses, the settlements, the alimony... everything.

First and last, Newley was a man of the theatre who could have become a giant of the theatre. The best of the best of him was only seen on a theatre stage, playing a starring musical and acting role that he himself had helped to create as a writer and a director. Our collaboration consisted of just five shows, plus a handful of movie songs, far less than either of us wanted it to be.

One evening in his West End star dressing room, before a performance of *Scrooge* at the Dominion Theatre, with his name up in huge, bright, above-the-title neon lights on the front of house, where it belonged, he said to me quietly, 'Brickman, do you know what the greatest regret of my life is?'

'No, Newberg. What?'

He smiled his sad clown smile. 'That we didn't go on writing together.'

Mine, too, Newberg... mine, too. It was so easy for us, wasn't it? And we did it pretty well, didn't we? The songs just fell on to the page, didn't they? One a day, regular as clockwork. Imagine how much more we might have done. Of course it's a shame.

You were a shining light in my life, and in Evie's life, and in the life of any audience lucky enough to have seen you in one of your great theatre performances. You were a total joy, a talent supreme, a friend beyond compare, and a total bloody idiot in the way you handled your life and your career. And you were the brother I never had. No, that's wrong. You *were* my brother.

The story behind the delays that took *Victor/Victoria* more than a decade to make the less usual 'wrong way' journey from screen to stage would itself make a pretty interesting musical. Everybody's overloaded work schedules, the storm-in-a-teacup lawsuits that eventually got settled for peanuts but wasted three or four years in the process, the unscheduled illnesses and, above all, the endless search for a replacement for the irreplaceable Robert Preston... add it all up and you're suddenly halfway through the 1990s.

Hank Mancini and I anticipated there would be about 14 songs in our new and fuller stage score. In his heart of hearts, Blake Edwards really only wanted to put the film on the stage, which is a defensible argument if you have written, produced and directed a damn near perfect film.

But, painfully slow as the progress was, it *was* progress, so imperceptible at times that I hardly recognised it as such. My working attitude all my life has been to plunge whole-heartedly into the deep end of one project at a time, to be totally immersed in the story and the characters and the time and the place. I found the stop-and-start method, a song here, two songs there, extremely hard to cope with, especially when months became years.

But, miraculously, we persevered, and the final phase of the writing was set for the month of February 1994, at Julie and Blake's magical home in the mountains above Gstaad. From Feb First 'til finished, we all agreed. It was a wonderful idea, and a great family atmosphere pervaded the house. Julie Andrews really *is* Mary Poppins, the greatest looker-after on the planet, and she nannied us all within an inch of our lives, while Blake and his black sense of humour – he is not nicknamed 'Blackie' for nothing – presided over the proceedings with brooding benevolence.

During two inspired weeks of all-out work, the final breakthrough we had so long needed was finally realised. Living and working together under one roof achieved its purpose. It gave the project the *concentration* it had never had. Ideas were discussed and developed in the music room, the living room, the dining room, the kitchen, even in restaurants up in the mountains. One of my best lyric ideas came to me in the ski-lift carrying us up the Eggli Mountain to lunch. There was certainly no better, and maybe no *other*, way to finish that show.

We were only a song-and-a-half away from home when Henry had to fly back to Los Angeles to conduct a couple of concerts. He was scheduled to return three days later. He never came back. The unthinkable had happened.

The diagnosing of the terminal illness that was to take his life was an unimaginable blow to all of us. If I had to pick three people who were shoo-ins to live to a great age, the laid-back Henry would have been first among them. I always envisaged Henry sort of carved in stone, a Mount Rushmore figure, forever calm and unruffled, a monument to cool, the Clint Eastwood of music.

Blake had said at dinner a few nights before that Hank was having so much fun writing the show that he, Blake, was prepared to bet Hank would gradually move across from movies to Broadway from now onwards. We even talked about 'the next project'.

Throughout the final four months of his life, Henry battled as he had lived, quietly, modestly, philosophically, and with good humour, taking everything as it came. The only comment he ever made to me about his condition typified his preference for understatement – 'I guess that's how this thing works.' He never once complained. His courage and his integrity during this incredibly hard time were remarkable, as was his ongoing commitment to complete the score of *Victor/ Victoria*, which, against all the odds, he did four days before he died.

The night before, I spoke to him on the phone for over an hour from London, going ever so slowly over the final part of the final song in the score. It was a very complex piece entitled *King's Dilemma*, to which I had written the lyrics first. He was determined to nail it. There would be no second draft, no rewrites. I thought his chances of succeeding were, like his own, slim to none.

But nail it he somehow did, with the cleverest and wittiest piece of music in the whole score. Henry's extraordinary composure and determination during this time will forever serve me as a definition of 'grace under pressure'. There was an almost Norman Rockwellian quality to Henry, a quintessentially American characteristic. Like his favourite film actors, Jimmy Stewart, Hank Fonda and Gary Cooper, Henry Mancini was a quiet hero.

'*We opened in Venice,*' goes the glamorous opening lyric line of *Kiss Me, Kate*. *Victor/Victoria* was not quite so lucky. We opened in Minneapolis, and the show worked its way through the usual teething troubles. It was too long... this had to go... that could use a bit of a rewrite. Blake wrung every last drop of laughter out of the comedy scenes, and Rob Marshall staged the musical numbers with impressive Broadway know-how. And, above all, there was Julie, spectacular, vibrant, shining star Julie, professionally perfect in every way, whether singing up a storm, or dancing her brains out in *Le Jazz Hot*, or being a glamour girl one minute and a gay guy the next, or selling every ticket the box office had to offer, no matter how huge the theatre. A Broadway producer's dream. Standing ovations? Of course. How many would you like? Julie had it all, and Julie gave it all.

The show moved on to Chicago prior to Broadway. It was the hottest summer in many years; 105°F the day we opened, but still the crowds came to see Julie. Evie and I welcomed the fact that we had to join the *Jekyll and Hyde* national tour in Dallas for a few days, and leave the sizzling heat behind us. We arrived in Dallas. It was 108°F.

After we lost the great Mancini, it was agreed that we had to have an available composer on *Victor/Victoria*, for whatever changes to the score might still be needed. I opted for Frank Wildhorn, for obvious reasons. We were already working together anyway, Frank was prolific, and I knew that we could work both well and fast. We ended up writing more than a dozen new songs together, of which three ended up in the show, including Julie's eventual eleven o'clock song, 'Living in the Shadows'.

Julie Andrews returning to Broadway after an absence of 35 years was big news. And 35 and radiant was how she looked as she took her first-night standing-ovation curtain calls. Anyone in that audience of 1,600 would have told you you were crazy if you had pointed out to them that, three weeks before, she had celebrated her 60th birthday. The lady is a true phenomenon. A few hours before, in the car taking us to the theatre, our pop-music-loving London jeweller chum Theo Fennell had said in passing, 'One of the Andrews Sisters died today,' and I found myself saying, 'Let's hope it wasn't Julie.'

Though not as glorious as the movie's rave reviews, and nothing could have been, the notices for *Victor/Victoria – The Musical* were good enough to have us quickly become the biggest-grossing show on Broadway. Julie was back where she belonged, and it seemed the whole world wanted to see her. Which was just as well, because the break-even figure on this huge, glitzy production was higher than the gross of most other theatres. But Jools was packing 'em in, and everyone was smiling... until, for the first time in her career, Julie missed a performance. And, shortly afterwards, another one. And then another one. Just minor vocal irritations and throat infections, the doctors said. Nothing to worry about, but something that could not be risked or allowed to develop into anything worse. But she'll be fine in a couple of days, they assured the world.

But that was not the problem. If you are going to see a Broadway show starring Julie Andrews, you want to see Julie Andrews, and so, if she's off, nine people out of ten take the offered option of either a refund or rebooking for a later performance. A missed performance cost the production heavily. Two missed out of eight in one week, and the show's profit margin was gone. And that was the tantalising cat-and-mouse game our beloved Jools now had to play.

She would recover from her minor ailment and resume work, two or three weeks would go by and, just as we were all starting to breathe a collective sigh of relief, the dreaded lurgi would strike again. The strain on Julie was tremendous. The show was physically draining – singing, dancing and running around, with endless quick changes from her male to female wigs and costumes and back again. She was never still for a second from the moment she entered the theatre two hours before curtain up, to prepare her intricately detailed double-layered make-up, until she left the stage door some six hours later to greet her fans, be photographed and sign a zillion autographs. Endless press, radio and TV interviews, plus trying to organise and run her day-to-day family life as normally as possible, filled every day.

The year came and went, but the nagging, aggravating problems persisted. Jools battled gamely on, and extended her run into a second year. She took a month's vacation and fled to her beloved Gstaad for a rest that was more a collapse. She was close to burn-out. Liza Minnelli replaced Julie and filled the theatre for the four weeks she was gone, and then back again came Jools, like Rocky in the 15th round, to try to win the big fight. Finally, the doctors said enough, no more, and she withdrew from the show, handing over to Raquel Welch for the remainder of the run.

Worse was to come. A few weeks later, I had lunch with Julie in London when she was passing through on her way from Switzerland back to New York, where she told me she had arranged to have a simple 'procedure' to remove the 'intra-cordal cyst' that had caused her throat problem once and for all, which she couldn't do during the run of the show because it would have kept her out for too long. Tragically, Julie Andrews's golden voice was not to return. As the world now nows, the 'procedure' was unsuccessful. All her future plans for world concert tours, recording a series of albums of all her favourite composers, and a multiplicity of other musical projects that were always under discussion or in play in her highly active existence were not to be.

I wish I could say there was a happy ending to this story and, in a way, there is. Thanks to Julie's endless versatility and stoic resilience, there are, in fact, several happy endings. She now has more new strings to her bow than Robin Hood and his Merry Men. In the past five years, she has starred in big box-office movies like *The Princess Diaries* and its sequel. She has written a series of bestselling children's books with her daughter Emma. She is hugely in demand on the lecture circuit. She travels the world as a global goodwill ambassador for Disney. The Queen made her a Dame of the British Empire in the Millennium Honours List. And, above all, we shall have the musical likes of *Mary Poppins*, *The Sound of Music*, *Thoroughly Modern Millie* and *Victor/Victoria*, Julie's lasting legacy, with us forever, thank God.

In the late 1970s, at the height of the fame of *The Muppet Show*, and the height of his glittering era as James Bond, Roger Moore called me to see if I would accompany him to Elstree Studios, where he gave a delightful rendition of 'Talk to the Animals' to the assembled Muppets, watched adoringly by Miss Piggy and with jealous loathing by Kermit the Frog. We had lunch with Jim Henson and Frank Oz, the show's brilliant creators, and Jim mooted the idea of *Doctor Dolittle* in the theatre. I said that, charming and funny as I thought it would be, children needed to believe that the animals were real, and not puppets.

Little could I have imagined then the dramatic and awe-inspiring advances that were about to be made in the brave new world of animatronics. But by the early 1990s, I most surely did, and so I promptly set about the multiple tasks of acquiring the stage rights to *Doctor Dolittle* from Twentieth Century Fox and the estate of the author, Hugh Lofting, and approaching the Jim Henson Creature Shop in London. Jim had died far too young in

1990, on the same day as Sammy Davis Jr, delivering a devastating double blow to the world of entertainment. The London Creature Shop was now run by a brilliant young designer-director named John Stephenson, and John responded with immediate enthusiasm to the original idea of animatronic animals being used in the theatre for the first time.

Now all I had to do was write the show. Predictably, it took years rather than months for Bruce the lawyer to clear the complex rights, by which time I had not only written and rewritten the show several times, I had also found the way to produce it. Thanks to the by then five-year success of *Scrooge*, I had established a solid, friendly relationship with the big guns of the Apollo Theatre Group. We met to discuss *Doctor Dolittle*. The chairman of the group, Paul Gregg, came up with the inspired idea of casting Phillip Schofield in the title role. Phillip, though only in his early thirties, had been a major TV star in the UK for some years, and had also scored a long-running success starring in *Joseph and the Amazing Technicolour Dreamcoat*. That was the good news. The bad news was that Paul Gregg was so bowled over by the brilliance of his first idea that he promptly followed up with a second one, which was probably the worst idea since Hitler thought it was a good idea to invade Russia. He announced that the show would open the following summer at the Apollo Theatre, Hammersmith.

Let me tell you about the Apollo Theatre, Hammersmith. This is not your average bijou theatre. With standing room, it accommodates just shy of 4,000 people. It is so big it could not unreasonably put in a bid to become London's fifth airport. You could land 747s in there. It could house all the elephants in India. It is as architecturally appealing as the Kremlin, which it closely resembles, and every bit as cosy. It is also located directly on the M4 motorway leading out of London. The only people you see within a mile of it are driving cars. Drive-by trade is one thing, driving by without stopping another.

The theatre that Steven Pimlott, the director, and I desperately wanted, and constantly begged Apollo to let us have, was the recently refurbished Lyceum, which they owned and had just spent £57 million and several years restoring. With 2,000 seats, and perfectly located in the heart of West End theatreland at the far end of the Strand and the beginning of Aldwych, a stone's throw from Drury Lane, it was not only ideal for all our needs, it was empty and available. Apollo's somewhat shaky fiscal thinking, however, did not take such mundane matters as location, location and location into account.

On paper, the logic went like this. A 4,000-seat theatre would recoup the investment twice as fast as a 2,000-seat theatre. Ho, hum. With subtle overconfidence, they ploughed ahead and, apart from that one incalculable error, they were right. Prince Charles brought Prince Harry to the Charity Gala Preview, making three generations of the Royal Family to have attended *Dolittle* openings on stage and screen.

The production was lavish. Huge. Designer Mark Thompson covered the largest proscenium opening in Europe with a massive skyscape that wrapped around into the sides of the auditorium. Walkways were constructed up the inside walls of the theatre, and across the front of the 2,500-seat circle, to help bring the cast within shouting distance of the people at the back. The sets and the costumes were stunning. Among other things, the show had a seaport, a full-scale circus, a courtroom, a typhoon, a major shipwreck and a South Sea island. As a finale, Doctor Dolittle flew back home to England aboard a 20-foot-wingspan Giant Lunar Moth, which actually flew around the auditorium. (I told you the place should be an airport.) Phillip Schofield was spectacularly good as Dolittle, bringing a youthful freshness, charm and humour to the role that was so appealing I didn't even miss Rex Harrison. A generation on, it was like seeing 'Son of Doctor Dolittle'. The entire cast was first-rate but, of course, as we always knew, it would be the animals that stole the show.

The casting of the Voice of Polynesia, the second most important co-starring role in the show, was my personal crowning achievement in this production. I persuaded the divine Jools that it would be an uplifting and heartwarming thing for her to do. After all, if Angela Lansbury could play a teapot in *Beauty and the Beast*, there was nothing to stop Julie Andrews playing a parrot in *Doctor Dolittle*.

Always a good sport, Jools decided it would, above all, be fun, and she entered into the spirit of the piece as though playing Polynesia would be the making of her career. It was more than fun. It was hilarious. And it was more than hilarious. It was brilliant. The wonderful, side-splitting hours Jools and I spent together evolving Polynesia in a series of recording sessions were, for me, the highlight of the entire rehearsal period. Her inventiveness astounded me. She even sang a pirate sea shanty. Bless her heart, as a parrot, Julie *could* sing, because she skilfully and imperceptibly turned notes into squawks whenever and wherever she needed to. And, from the sea shanty, it was an easy step to get her to duet 'Talk to the Animals' with Phillip Schofield as the show's opening number, in which the mentor and the pupil celebrate the doctor's historic decision to learn to speak the languages of his animal friends. It brought the house down.

Doctor Dolittle received the best and most joyous notices of any stage musical I have ever been associated with, 90 per cent-plus favourable. The box office went crazy, the family audiences poured in, and, like Doctor Dolittle in the story, we were off to the moon... until the summer holidays ended in September and the kids went back to school. Then, and only then, did the full horror of the oversize and the location of the Apollo Theatre, Hammersmith, strike home. At half-capacity, we were playing to more people than capacity in all the other London theatres but two, but we appeared to be and we *were* half-empty, because the place was so insanely big. Half-term, Christmas and Easter school holidays, capacity again. Then half-empty again. And the word gets around that the show isn't doing too well, because there are lots of empty seats, like there would have been lots of empty seats if we had opened at Yankee Stadium.

Dolittle played for three years in the UK, and various pundits gifted with 20-20 hindsight told me later that, had we started out in the West End rather than in the Kingdom of the Castaways, we would still be running. Our consolatory comfort cushion is that the show is now preparing to embark on its American, Japanese and other journeys.

But for me, the *comble de malheurs* came at the last production meeting with the Apollo Bigwigerie, when Paul Gregg took me aside with a look of mingled guilt and wisdom and said, 'You know what we should've done, Leslie... we should've opened at the Lyceum.'

Andrew Lloyd Webber's 50th birthday party at Sydmonton Court, his and Madeleine's palatial house in Wiltshire, was probably the biggest bash of the last decade in rural England. Five hundred privileged guests were spoiled rotten for a weekend that will live in the memory. The amazing Madeleine, who produced the whole thing, had a massive movie sound stage-sized marquee erected alongside the house, dwarfing the formidable main premises. Lavish wines from the fabled Lloyd Webber cellar accompanied every meal. At the main birthday dinner on the Saturday night, Evie and I arrived with Joan Collins, the three of us houseguesting at Theo and Louise Fennell's Watership House on Andrew's estate.

As we entered, the first friends we saw were Alan Whicker, the celebrated and much-travelled TV journalist, and his diminutive girlfriend Valerie. They were talking to Madeleine Lloyd Webber and John Major, until recently England's Prime Minister. Madeleine introduced us and, to my considerable surprise, John Major knew far more about my songs and films and shows than one imagined Prime Ministers were required to know. He chatted with us enthusiastically for a while and we moved on.

Valerie, who is barely five feet tall, tugged my sleeve and said, 'I didn't want to spoil your lovely chat with the Prime Minister, but I was the only one at the correct altitude to notice that your fly was open.' And sure enough, the southern extremity of a Turnbull and Asser dress shirt the size of a three-masted schooner's mainsail was flapping around down there in the Wiltshire breeze. As I adjusted my dress and my thinking, I philosophised that if such things were destined to happen, it was more meaningful and memorable that they should happen while the country's elected leader was himself in full sail, praising my life's work.

You reach an age where you suddenly start looking back at some of the things you haven't done with your life, as well as the things that you have and, in my case, that sparked a powerful desire to fill in some of the gaps. I considered some of the larger and more important gaps. *Cyrano de Bergerac*, at the top of the list, was one of them. To write a tour-de-force star vehicle called *Sammy*, about guess who, was another. *Noah's Ark*, at number three, was another. I had never finally bitten the bullet and got to grips with them. Why not? This book was another, but this book could wait and, if I ever got around to it, fine, and, if I didn't, fine. There are far too many volumes of these self-indulgent, name-dropping ramblings cluttering up the shelves of the world's bookshops, anyway, so one set more or less of stultifying reminiscences one way or the other didn't much matter. You tell two or three amusing stories at dinner, and half the people present will chorus, 'Oh, you should write a book!' But, given the choice between creating a new musical play and trotting out your memoirs, of course the new musical wins every time. And so the memoirs must remain where they rightly belong, at or near the bottom of the list.

But back up at the top of the list, I realised increasingly that *Cyrano de Bergerac* and *Noah's Ark* were important. They had both travelled with me through the greater part of my adult life, and they still didn't exist, as I wanted them to exist, even though they had probably taken up more of my thoughts and my time than half-a-dozen shows that did. It was more than high time for me to do something about it. It was approaching now or never, so I finally decided it had better be now.

The desire to get to grips with *Noah's Ark* was given an enormous boost by the fantastic success of the Jim Henson animatronics in *Doctor Dolittle*. John Stephenson and I had started talking about *Noah's Ark* long before *Dolittle* even opened, as the ultimate showcase in which to display the state-of-the-art technical wizardry combining animatronics and filmed animation, of which the Creature Shop was now capable. While I completed the book and score, and recorded the songs, John started his designs and held 'animal workshops', supervised by his genius 'animal choreographer', Peter Elliott, experimenting, developing and perfecting the movement capabilities of all the creatures that would eventually inhabit our Ark.

As far as *Cyrano* was concerned, my cunning theory was to have Frank Wildhorn read the Rostand play, because I was certain that, with its overwhelming richness of language, poetry and humour, Cyrano could become a musical tour de force. Frank read it and fell completely in love with it. We had found our second collaboration.

Being one of the most lyrical plays ever written for the theatre, *Cyrano* is by its very nature as full of songs as a pomegranate is of seeds, and musicalising it was an orgiastic experience. I hardly knew where to start or stop. Music and lyrics started flying back and forth across the Atlantic in a blinding blizzard of creativity. For the big musical set-pieces, Frank went first, and I was given the rare opportunity to indulge myself in some truly lyrical lyrics, which this play, above all others, not only allows but demands, because Cyrano is himself a poet.

But always looming ahead of me was the spectre that had never gone away, the double-edged sword of the great three-hours-and-more length of the play, plus the fact that its translation was still, all these years later, in copyright.

And then one fine and sunny morning, sitting on my terrace in Mexico, eating my breakfast mangoes and watching the *QE2* steam slowly into Acapulco Bay right in front of me, I had one simple and obvious thought that was the solution to both of my problems. *Cyrano de Bergerac* itself, Edmond Rostand's one and only masterpiece, was long since in the public domain, free of any and all copyright problems. If, therefore, I were to do my *own* translation from the French, and edit the many talkier moments of the play as I went, as I had done with the recitatives I had already written, not only would my copyright problems disappear, but I could also exercise considerable if not complete control over the ultimate length of the show. The exhilaration that I experienced as I joyously ploughed my way through Rostand's glorious work, translating, adapting and editing at one and the same time, became an enviable triple play. I was living the musical author's equivalent of The Great Escape, and loving every second of it.

And so the game goes on. Every musical play or film allows its author and composer the luxury and the privilege of entering and inhabiting a completely new world, and living there for a while without having to travel anywhere except in his imagination. My adventures in the song trade have taken me from colourful Dickensian London to transvestite Art Deco Paris, from eccentric chocolate-factory owners to West Country doctors talking to animals, from cat and mouse cartoons to Neverland and to Santa Claus at the North Pole, and from dazzling 19th-century detectives and murderous schizophrenics to despotic 16th-century kings and 20th-century Irish drunks. I am currently dividing my time between the swashbuckling 17th-century Paris of Molière and Corneille and a Biblical ride on a big wooden boat full of animals. And everywhere I go, people are singing.

As George and Ira so aptly put it, who could ask for anything more?

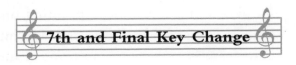

7th and Final Key Change

Coda

By the time anyone gets to read this, if anyone ever does, it will be a full half-century since the magical 'Auntie Bea' Lillie, my other-worldly yet real-life fairy godmother, wafted into my life to see the Cambridge Footlights Revue at the Phoenix Theatre in Charing Cross Road, and carted me off into the crazy world in which I have lived my much blessed existence thus far. The credit for the fact that I still love it all now as much as I did then can mainly be ascribed to the golden influence of my real-life guardian angel, my wondrous, gentle, beautiful, constant and unchanging, imperturbable and irreplaceable Evie, who married me exactly four years to the day after I began my professional career with Auntie Bea in *An Evening with Beatrice Lillie*, and who has held my hand through every major key change of my life, and who will as always be sitting beside me, still holding my hand, on the first nights of *Cyrano de Bergerac*, *Noah's Ark* and *Sammy* whenever and wherever they may open, assuming that they do.

06/06/06

Available November 2006

To order, contact www.musicdispatch.com